CHOCTAW TRADITIONS

CHOCTAW TRADITIONS

Stories of the Life and Customs of the Mississippi Choctaw

Tom Mould, Eddie Johnson, and Jay Wesley

University Press of Mississippi / Jackson

The University Press of Mississippi is the scholarly publishing agency of the Mississippi Institutions of Higher Learning: Alcorn State University, Delta State University, Jackson State University, Mississippi State University, Mississippi University for Women, Mississippi Valley State University, University of Mississippi, and University of Southern Mississippi.

www.upress.state.ms.us

The University Press of Mississippi is a member of the Association of University Presses.

Manufactured in the United States of America
∞

Publisher: University Press of Mississippi, Jackson, USA
Authorised GPSR Safety Representative: Easy Access System Europe - Mustamäe tee 50, 10621 Tallinn, Estonia, *gpsr.requests@easproject.com*

Library of Congress Control Number: 2025935029

Hardback ISBN 978-1-4968-5719-4 | Paperback ISBN 978-1-4968-5720-0
Epub single ISBN 978-1-4968-5721-7 | Epub institutional ISBN 978-1-4968-5722-4
PDF single ISBN 978-1-4968-5723-1 | PDF institutional ISBN 978-1-4968-5724-8

British Library Cataloging-in-Publication Data available

For Harold "Doc" Comby

CONTENTS

FOREWORD

In 1997, as I settled in for a summer of fieldwork in Mississippi recording the stories of Choctaw elders, I found myself spending all my spare time at the Tribal Archives, working with then-archivist Rae Nell Vaughn to find stories recorded in the past and tucked away in boxes, folders, and drawers. But I wasn't the only guest in the archives that summer. Four Youth Opportunity Program (YOP) students had been assigned to Rae to learn about cultural preservation. All were high school students at the time: Liasha Alex, Danielle Dan, Lionel Dan, and Curtis "Buck" Willis. One thing led to another, and soon, they started accompanying me to interview elders in the community. Before long, they were taking me to meet their own elders, and we interviewed them together. What began as a way to occupy the students during their long summer hours in the archives soon became a focused effort to train the students to conduct their own fieldwork. In 2018, as we began to develop the idea for *Choctaw Traditions*, training and working alongside YOP students became the heart of our work rather than a happy afterthought. A few days into the project, Makaylin Alex, one of the six students selected for the project, introduced me to her father. Or rather reintroduced me. She was the daughter of Liasha Alex, one of the original YOP student researchers from 1997. It wasn't long before we roped in Liasha's father, Bradley Alex, to share his stories for the book. When Eddie, Jay, and I approached Makaylin, Liasha, and Bradley Alex about writing the foreword for this book, they were excited about the opportunity, less so about the writing. "Isn't this a book about oral traditions?" they laughed. And so we agreed to meet and talk about their involvement in the project, the impact their participation has had, and their hope for where this work will lead, letting excerpts from that conversation serve as their foreword.

—TOM MOULD

Bradley Alex: In many ways, this book is kind of the same as what we did back in high school with the *Nanih Waiya* magazine. Jimmy Ben was the main photographer. I was an interviewer and did layout and also some photography. Austin Tubby was both also. We all had an assignment, and I had to get onto the other students because we had deadlines. And Linda [who would become Bradley's wife] and Trish Martin, used to be Trish Gibson, they used to be like, "Who do you think you are?" [*laughter*]

I said, "We need to finish this. Do your part." [*laughter*]

I used to wind up staying over and translate as such. And a lot of us proofread, along with Mr. Charles Plaisance; he was our counselor.

But it was interesting, very interesting. I learned a lot of stuff from the older ones. And there was a lady who told me to shout, really shout, war cry or whatever. So, me, Jimmy, we sort of did. She really put fire into us. I learned some things from her, and that even when the tape was off, she still talked. One time she told us to turn off the recorder and then told us personal things about growing up. Some areas, it was pretty sad, but it was interesting.

Liasha: In high school, I was in charge of photography too. They gave me a camera. I started because there was a darkroom. Remember? Behind the archives? And I learned how to do that. And when we got to your project, I was like, "Okay." I started learning how to document and record interviews. And a lot of it were stories that I've heard, and then I was like, "Oh, this is going to last. These stories are going to last through generations. It's going to be here," which I was glad that there was going to be actual written documentation and preservation.

Makaylin: I remember I signed up for YOP, but it was COVID, so we couldn't really be placed anywhere. And then they mentioned there was this project recording stories from our elders. They let us know that only a few of us were selected. And then I remember learning how to properly conduct an interview and looking in the archives. I thought that was interesting, looking at the old pictures that we were basically helping you select to put in the book.

And I thought that it was neat how the people that we interviewed my dad had also interviewed and were people he grew up with. And the same things that they were telling us during the interviews were the same things my dad told me. I just felt like it was all a learning experience, culturally and traditionally.

Liasha: When she mentioned she was working with you, I was like, "Listen, just listen when you go. It's going to be very interesting to hear all the stories the elders have to say."

Makaylin: But that was good though. I thought, like my dad said, to be prepared, but then at the same time it was easy to just sit there and listen and learn because it was easy for the elders to lure you in because you were always learning something. I heard some pieces from them, and then some pieces from my grandpa, and then my dad. And then to actually sit down and do these interviews, it was easy for me to put all the pieces together through the stories and the traditions.

Liasha: My kids were really interested in the book we worked on [*Choctaw Tales*] and also some of the storytellers that we interviewed. I was like, "Oh, that's your friend's great-grandpa or uncle."

And they were like, "Oh, really?"

And I think their friends probably would be interested in looking at that and trying to see what kind of impact their relatives had. So, when I saw the book, I was like, "It was pretty good." I felt pretty good about myself. It felt pretty good to actually see the book and hold it in my hands.

And then just the other day, I was on my phone looking for some stuff about the Choctaw, and it took me to the *Choctaw Tales* book. And this was digital, so it was kind of neat. It was on my phone, and I got my kids, and I was like, "Get in my account. You all can look it." They were reading it. It was weird and kind of a neat experience because we're so used to oral traditions. And it's actually on paper or in a digital format. It kind of sounds clichéd, but they saw and felt words in their hands. And I was like, "It's right there for them to look at it, anytime they want."

Bradley: We still need to ask the elders, or just to have a conversation. Let them tell us. That is our responsibility to write these down, so you take it up, continue and take it up. Memories come back, so we need to continue as much as we can and record it.

My grandma used to say if you're going to repeat something that you're supposed to repeat it word for word. That's how they used to keep the stories going, whatever happened from the elders. And I remember that she got onto my cousin, and she said, "That's not what I said!" She got onto her. There was my cousin, my sisters, they were older than I was. Everybody was older than I was. And I would just listen. And then my grandma turned around and asked my sister, "What did I say?" And she repeated everything word for word, and my grandma said, "That's exactly what you are supposed to say because I'm repeating from what I was told. And I'm repeating it word for word. And that's what I expect you to do."

And Doc [Harold Comby] and I, we talked about that one time. And that's how storytellers, that's how they were supposed to work, pass it on to the next generations. Doc was a storyteller.

Liasha: I hope we can just keep doing this. Archiving it. And putting it into a digital format where it's available. That would be neat because instead of actually handling the originals, you can just click, it will just pop up, audio and everything. Because I don't think a lot of people know that that exists. So much content is there. I didn't know. I didn't realize how important it was until I got a little older. But when you're young, you just don't realize how important your traditions are. But when you start to get older, start having kids, you start thinking about traditions.

I usually just tell the kids, every now and then something comes up, "Oh, man, this used to happen." Dad or Mom's or Grandma's stories or whatever. And I tell the kids that. And I was like, "There's another story that I heard." And some of my buddies that I grew up with in high school, we still exchange little stories, or something that was recent. They saw *na losa chito*,[1] or they heard somebody tell Bigfoot kind of stories.

A lot of it's not written, so we hear it through oral traditions. It's usually just casual talk coming up at family gatherings. We start cooking, and we start just reminiscing about stuff. "You remember this?" It goes into a lot of different topics and areas, and we hit a lot of the stories, even some of the stuff that's happened within the family that's kind of funny. And we just go along with it. It can go anywhere, just about.

Makaylin: I really believe this work is vital for our future generations to hear firsthand accounts of our elders and the knowledge that they hold of our traditional ways. This project gave us a chance to set time aside and to hear elders from each community and what their childhood was like on the reservation and even how traditions are properly carried out.

Not only will this project educate younger generations to come, but it will also be preserved for audiences that are not familiar with our tribe to teach them more about who we are. I feel that this project was much needed. Listening to each elder and their interviews, whether it was personal stories, traditional oral stories, or even just wise words, I treasured it all because I believe it is vital for my identity as a young individual and being Chahta. As a young woman trying to navigate her way for her future, listening to these traditions and stories was almost a reminder to never forget my roots because these very aspects are what makes us who we are. The older I get, the more I realize that it is my responsibility to hold and carry on these traditions onto the next generation.

PREFACE

She sat there unmoving, her head resting on her forearms, slumped over her desk. It had been a difficult morning. Her cancer was back, and she was in the middle of treatments that left her tired and in near constant pain. But Linda Willis was not one to be cowed. As I entered her office, I realized that she was talking to her assistant, working through her fatigue, getting the job done.

Twice during our conversation, she left the room, once to get water, the other time to be sick. I tried in vain to reschedule, but she wanted to talk. She had important things to share, and she refused to let her illness reshape her life. I began by asking her about the man who raised her, Chief Cameron Wesley. "I'm his granddaughter," she said. "My mother was Fannie Tubby. She was the baby of the family."

> I remember one time when I was a girl, I was a teenager by that time, and we were at his house. This student from Alabama came over to do some interviews like you're doing, and he [Cameron Wesley] wouldn't let us talk to that person. He says it's not our place to talk to him, that it was *his* place; he's the elder.
>
> So he talked to the person.
>
> After that interview, the man came out and started asking us questions, and then we got to playing tag with him. My grandfather didn't like that, so he got his shotgun and ran him off the place. [*laughter*]
>
> It was like that way when we were growing up. Any person that would come to see us or talk to us, he said it was *his* place to talk to the people.

And now it was hers. Her grandfather Cameron Wesley had died twenty-eight years earlier at the astonishing age of 106.[1] Her mother had passed away not quite two years previously. Sadly, Linda would only have two more years herself before the cancer finally won out. But on that chilly January day in 2000, Linda struggled through her nausea and headaches to share the stories she heard growing up, stories about sharecropping, traditional medicine, community ball games and picnics, holiday celebrations, and the prophecies that warned of future struggles, food scarcity, and war. She also shared the story that had captured that attention of the whole community and many throughout the state and nation of the trial of Cameron Wesley who was accused for killing a fellow Choctaw. Stories of the trial appear in the pages that follow, but for now, at the beginning of our conversation in 2000, Linda drew our attention to the history of scholars interviewing Choctaw men and women about their lives, their culture, their stories. I was hardly the first to come knocking, and I will certainly not be the last. I was not even the first to interview Linda. Almost thirty years earlier, Choctaw high school students writing for the student-run *Nanih Waiya* magazine interviewed Linda after she was crowned the 1973 Choctaw Indian Princess.[2] She spoke about the thrill of being selected, the hard work and constant travel involved, her plans for college when she finished, and her hobbies and interests.

She was not an elder then, but she was now. And with that role came the expectation that she would share what she learned with her children and grandchildren, who would then share what they learned with *their* children and grandchildren, and so on.

For some, like Linda Willis, that oral tradition included a university student or two. For Harold Comby, it included students, scholars, journalists, and local history buffs—too many to count. "You have to find out your purpose in life," Harold explained.

> And one of the things I didn't know until I came back from Minnesota, that my mom started inviting me to her house every Saturday saying, "Come on and eat."
>
> And I would tell her, "Oh, I ate already."
>
> But she used to say, "I know you didn't eat right. So come on over."
>
> And when I go over, she would start telling me stories about something that she had told me like four days ago. And I used to think, "She just told me this four days ago!" But then later on, it kind of came to me that what she was doing was that I was going to carry that tradition in our family, that she was instilling these stories to me.

This book is dedicated to Harold Comby—"Doc" to most who knew him—because he embraced this obligation like few others. One of the origin stories of how he got his nickname—and there are many—was that when all the other kids went outside to play, Harold hung back with the elders, sitting by their feet and listening intently, committing to memory all that they said.[3] Harold passed away suddenly in 2022, but his legacy as a firekeeper—one who is entrusted to preserve, and pass on, the knowledge of the tribe—lives on.

So does the work of cultural maintenance and preservation, both formally through the work organized within the Department of Chahta Immi and in tribal school curricula, as well as informally through the daily lives of tribal members.

Occasionally, that work is recorded and captured in video, audio, or on the page to be shared more widely both within and outside the Choctaw community. This book can best be understood as one small part of this larger enterprise, emerging as a collaboration between community and academic interests. It is intended as a resource for the Choctaw community as well as place of exploration for non-Choctaw audiences, those who know the Choctaw through literature, as neighbors, or not at all. Even in Mississippi, that last group is surprisingly large.

One might imagine that being the only federally recognized tribe in the state might make the Choctaw a household name in Mississippi. Or the fact that at the start of the twenty-first century, the tribe was one of the largest employers in the state.[4] Or that being represented by a gold star on the newly designed state flag in 2021 might help raise awareness.

However, distinction between institutional levels of federal and state recognition are often lost on non-Indians; the tribe's economic success has been overshadowed by the influx of large, multinational corporations to the state; and the state flag is regularly explained with boilerplate language that describes "a gold five-point star to reflect Mississippi's indigenous Native American tribes." By recognizing *five* tribes, the flag evokes connection to the historical "five tribes" of the Southeast rather than the one contemporary tribe federally recognized within the state today.[5] In doing so, the flag risks evoking the past rather than the present, to Indigenous peoples who *were* here rather than a people who *are* here. Couple all this with more than two centuries of efforts to remove and erase the Choctaw from Mississippi and half a century of sustained immigration from Mexico and Central America, and the result is continued invisibility or misidentification. "Even in this state, people still don't really know us," Melford Farve explains from his desk in the facility building at Pearl River. Melford is the communications writer at the *Choctaw Community News*, where he has worked off and on, mostly on, for close to three decades. "We're almost an oddity when it comes to different counties because they rarely see a Choctaw," he explained.

> Just last week I was at the tire company getting my oil changed, and this Black gentleman sat . . . we sat together, and we started talking. They live in Kemper County, which is not too far away, maybe a good forty-five minutes away. They came down here to do something, a flea market or something, but they came down. So he and his son came, and while they were here, they saw some Choctaws around. I guess when they went back home, he said, "You know, Philadelphia has a lot of Mexicans."
>
> And his father laughed, "Those weren't Mexicans; they were Indians." [*laughter*] (June 1, 2021)

"People just don't know about us sometimes," he concludes, no longer laughing. "We were here first and lived here, all our ancestors, through here. But you go down further south or even further up north where we're just not as known. There are probably people that are out of state that probably know us better than the people here do."

Jay Wesley tells a similar story of being mistaken as Latino in a parade where he was wearing his traditional Choctaw clothing. The confusion is all the greater when people are *not* dressed in their traditional clothes. "There's one thing I've always heard: 'I went to this place, and I didn't see one Indian!'" says Rae Nell Vaughn, speaking to a group of university students. "Well, it's not like I'm going to walk around in my dress, you know? I'm probably sitting right by you at McDonald's, and you didn't know!" Again, we laugh, but for Rae Nell, Jay, Melford, and their fellow Choctaw, it is a laugh that masks a deep history of being ignored, dismissed, pushed aside, or driven out and removed from their land. "There's a lot that needs to be shared, and it can be shared through these outlets," Rae Nell adds, outlets that she explains include museums, cultural centers, and not least of all, books.

In fact, it was Rae Nell Vaughn who sparked the idea for this book. Ever since *Choctaw Tales* was first published in 2004, we had been talking off and on about another book on Choctaw storytelling and oral traditions, but what that book might look like never quite coalesced until a conversation in 2018. Rae wanted to see this material make its way into the K–12 curriculum in the tribal schools. *Choctaw Tales* was being used in many of the classes, but she felt more information about the customs of the tribe was needed. I was not an expert in K–12 curriculum, but I had spent a few decades conducting ethnographic research, studying oral traditions, and writing books, a skill set that we figured we could put to some use for such a goal. We began to imagine a book that might capture both the oral tradition and tribal customs in a way that educators would find easy to bring into the classroom. But we knew that the success of any project—both practically and ethically—would require collaboration with the people who were engaged in this work on a day-to-day basis. So before moving any further, we paused and planned a visit. I would come to Mississippi, meet with old colleagues and new, explore what was currently being done, and discuss the kinds of work they wanted to see done in the future that might intersect with skills I could bring to the table. I wrote to Chief Phyllis Anderson to introduce myself and then began to make plans.

In December of that year, I made my way to Mississippi. My first stop was historian, educator, storyteller, and friend Terry Ben, who immediately introduced me to Eddie Johnson, coordinator of the Special Projects/Media Program, and Ty Isaac, multimedia production specialist, both of whom had been working on the Choctaw Cultural Legacy project, among many other relevant projects related to cultural preservation. Eddie then introduced me to Jay Wesley, director of the Department of Chahta Immi, which oversees all of these programs, including the Cultural Affairs Program and Tribal Languages, the next two stops on my visit. At the Cultural Affairs Program I talked with the head of the program, Phyllis McMillan, and met Wendy Thompson, Trudy Jimmie, and May McGeisy, as well as connected again with Lorena Alex. At the Tribal Language Program, I reconnected with DeLaura Saunders, Jason Lewis, and Pam Smith. I visited with Harold Comby at the tribal Justice Complex, Melford Farve at the *Choctaw Community News*, Louise Wilson at the Choctaw Elderly Center, and Sally Allen and Regina Shoemake at the Department of Social Services, all of whom had told stories for *Choctaw Tales*. I stopped at the Chahta Immi Cultural Center and museum and caught up with Martha Ferguson and Martha Spencer before touring the new building that also housed the archives where Eddie introduced me to Amanda Bell, the tribal archivist.

At each stop along the way, we talked about our families and the changes we had seen over the past few years before eventually turning to the possibilities of a new research project. Each stop helped clarify what people were and were not interested in doing. I left with all of us promising to keep in touch. And we did. We formed a small group committed to the work that included the director of Chahta Immi, Jay Wesley, as well as each of its program coordinators: Eddie Johnson, Phyllis McMillan, DeLaura Saunders, and Martha Spencer. It also included Amanda Bell, tribal archivist; Louise Wilson, director of the Elderly Nutrition and Social Program; Frederick Hickmon, principal of Choctaw Central High School; and Mallory Anderson, director of the Youth Opportunity Program (YOP). By the time we started the project, Tia Grisham had become YOP director and joined the group while Mallory and Louise stepped back. We shared plans and proposals for the book back and forth. Some of the committee members worked primarily as reviewers, ensuring the project aligned with their own program's goals and mission. Others worked as creators and developers, offering substantive suggestions throughout the process. As the project took shape, Eddie and Jay shifted from collaborators to coauthors, involved in every stage of the work except for the drafting of the words on the page. They were integral in establishing the goals for the project, identifying additional collaborators, navigating the process of getting Tribal Council approval to conduct the research, helping to set up interviews, talking through what to include in the book, and working to help ensure the accuracy of the material that follows.[6] Despite these efforts, publishing norms typically relegate this work to the acknowledgments page. This book joins a growing number of others, particularly in the study of Native peoples, that not only takes the mandate for collaboration seriously but also values and recognizes it appropriately. However, it is important to acknowledge that there are models that are more collaborative than the one we have developed. As the primary fieldworker and writer, I, Tom, have used first person throughout the book, offering both clarity in syntax as well as honesty in the limits of our collaboration.

METHODOLOGY

This book is based on interviews, primarily those I conducted between 1996 and 2000 and 2021 and 2023, but it also includes interviews conducted by others from the 1970s until 2022. The result is a collection of stories shared verbatim as they were told during an interview context. Although a powerful method for data collection, interviewing comes with its challenges. Establishing trust and rapport with someone is not easy, especially across cultural divides marred by deep physical, emotional, political, and economic trauma that continues today. It is not irrelevant that the Choctaw term for White people is *nahollo*, which Harold Comby explained is used to mean "stingy" and not necessarily "holy" as some definitions suggest.[7] It is one of the reasons why we decided early on in this project to mirror the methodology from *Choctaw Tales* by partnering with Choctaw students to conduct the interviews. Such a process offered tribal youth a chance to practice interviewing and learn from elders outside their own families, while helping put the elders at ease by recreating the most common context for storytelling: elders talking to groups of young people. Not all the interviews were done this way. The relationships I have built over the years resulted in many conversations between just me and the speaker. However, many were, and the process for doing so deserves some attention.

In the fall of 2020, we began working with YOP director Tia Grishman to develop application materials for high school and college-aged youth interested in participating in this project. By the spring, the application process was in place and underway. We initially received sixty-six applications for six spots, the number that programs within the Department of Chahta Immi could accommodate. Tia worked through the applications, winnowing out the ones who checked the interest box without adding any of the additional information requested and then balancing community representation with the strongest interest statements. She also identified one older student to serve as their monitor, who would oversee their work from the programmatic side of things. I received the list: Makaylin Alex, Lexi Flint, Lakylee Martin, Thomas Saunders, Jaeden Wesley, Meka Willis, and Taylor Ben as the monitor. Some last names jumped out at me. Alex, Ben, Martin, Saunders. These are common last names, but as many Choctaw will tell you, everyone is related to everyone, at least distantly. Lakylee Martin was not, as it turned out, directly related to Chief Phillip Martin, as I had initially wondered, but the rest of the names were appropriately familiar. I had worked with Liasha Alex on *Choctaw Tales* in 1997, when he was a YOP student. Sure enough, Makaylin Alex was his daughter. I had been working with Terry Ben since my very first visit to Mississippi back in 1996. Taylor Ben was his daughter. And while I had known her sister Pam Smith longer, DeLaura Saunders was head of the Tribal Language Program, and we had worked together off and on over the years. Thomas Saunders was her grandson.

We worked together from May 25 to July 16. We spent the first week in training, devoting most of our time on best practices in ethnographic interviewing since that is what would comprise the bulk of our work that summer, though we also spent time on systematic observation, photography, fieldnote taking, archival research, transcription, data management, and open coding. The students conducted mock interviews with one another that we then evaluated and critiqued. They practiced transcribing the interviews, identifying the stories, and annotating them. In the meantime, I worked with Eddie and Jay to identify elders to interview. By the following week, we began our interviews, with me as the lead and the students primarily as observers. By the second week, the students were consistently asking questions throughout the interviews. We had set a goal that by the end of the summer: each of them would have identified an elder to speak with, set up the interview, and then led the conversation with the rest of us present, a goal that to them had seemed impossible at the start but that felt imminently feasible by the end. All but one of the students met this goal, foiled by a common challenge of fieldwork, where people get busy with other things, cancel with no time left to reschedule, or change their minds.

By the end of the summer, we had recorded twenty interviews together, in addition to the twenty-one people I talked to on my own. Some students were more vocal in interviews than others, but all remained attentive throughout, never complaining when the one hour we had allotted for the conversation turned into one and half, two, and even one marathon conversation that lasted just over three hours. Nor did they complain when they had to don masks, even though most of the interviews we conducted were outside. They understood the risk that COVID-19 posed, even after vaccines became available. They all knew people who had died from the virus; they all understood that above all else, we had to keep the elders safe. The reservation had only opened back up to allow nonessential employees in buildings a few weeks before we started, and it locked back down a week after we finished our work together because of an outbreak during the Choctaw Indian Fair. The threat of contagion was never far away.

ACKNOWLEDGMENTS

The tribe lost many of its community members during the COVID-19 pandemic. Yet they persevered. Many of the elders, cooped up for far too long in their homes, were eager to meet with us, no doubt particularly because they would have a group of Choctaw youth as an audience. Those storytellers included are all listed in the "Storytellers" section with brief biographies to honor them and contextualize their stories. Their generosity and willingness to share what they learned from their relatives and from their own experiences represents the greatest gift an elder can bestow upon their community. This book is no less than a record of this generosity of spirit. Of course, they are not the only storytellers in this book. There are also the people who shared their stories with other researchers, recording them for posterity. All of these storytellers are listed in the "Storytellers" section as well, their work and generosity similarly appreciated.

The next most integral group of people in the production of this book is the collaborative team that helped develop the book from start to finish. They include DeLaura Saunders, Phyllis McMillan, Tia Grisham, Martha Spencer, and Amanda Bell, as well as Louise Wilson, Mallory Anderson, and Fred Hickmon, who helped develop the initial plan. Staff at the Special Projects/Media Program Sequita Phillips, Ty Isaac, and Jenisa Tubby were also incredibly helpful day in and day out during the summer of 2021 when we conducted the bulk of our fieldwork, whether providing equipment, helping track down contact information for an elder, or offering suggestions on how to approach a particular topic. Hillary Vaughn joined the staff in 2022 and provided integral help as well. Beyond those already mentioned, Jason Lewis and Pam Smith offered invaluable help with the language. Pam served as the primary translator on the project; Jason was always ready to help, promptly answering all of our questions about the new orthography and nuances in the meanings of many Choctaw words, old and new. Additionally, each of us has acknowledgments that speak to more personal gratitude.

FROM TOM MOULD

In Mississippi, I owe the deepest gratitude to all the storytellers who have taken the time to work with me, including those who offered not only their time, but their friendship, inviting me to join them at tribal events, at community celebrations and wakes, and for dinner, including old friends such as Carmen Denson, Melford Farve, and the late Harold Comby, and new ones such as Leonard Jimmie, Mark and Darlene Patrick, Dan and Ralph Isaac, and Susie Comby Alex. Particular thanks to Rae Nell Vaughn, the late Harley Vaughn, and their incredible daughters, Hillary, Mahlih, and Bree, who have been welcoming me into their home for almost thirty years and whose friendship has sustained both me and this work.

In addition, there are my Butler University colleagues who have welcomed me into a new institutional home; Elon University friends who continue to support me; our Wellington neighborhood group, whose friendship and support cannot be overestimated; and my folklore colleagues scattered across the globe who have offered support and insight over the years, helping me work through theoretical, methodological, intellectual, and practical issues in getting this work done. Those folklorists include Brandon Barker, Christopher and Christine Blythe, Ben Bridges, Ray Cashman, Michael Dylan Foster, Lisa Gilman, Henry Glassie, Di Goldstein, Elissa Henken, Greg Kelly, Megan Kenny, Andrea Kitta, Carl Lindahl, Lynne McNeill, Dorry Noyes, Aphrodite Nounanaki, Elliott Oring, the late Leonard Primiano, Pravina Shukla, and Jeannie Banks Thomas. Sincere thanks also to Alana Dunn at Butler University and the folks at University Press of Mississippi in getting this book into print, including Katie Keene, Shane Gong, Camille Hale, and Craig Gill. But most of all, thank you to Eddie Johnson and Jay Wesley for making our work together such a powerful learning experience. It continues to be an honor to know and work with them and to watch them devote themselves so fully to maintaining the traditions of their communities.

There is also my family: my mother, Lucille Mould; Rob, Laura, Caroline, and Charlie Mould; Diana and Dave Adams; Elizabeth, Erik, and Nathan Stein; Bill and Norma Barnett; Gentry, Chris, Payton, and Walker Byrnes; Erin Barnett and Mallin and Miller Barnett-Fiorenza; and Collins, Cadence, and Cora Barnett. Finally, there are my children Lily and Jack, whom I cherish and who carry on our own family traditions, and Brooke Barnett, who has created the best tradition of all for me with the family we have created together.

FROM EDDIE JOHNSON

I wish to acknowledge and express my sincere appreciation to all who contributed to the creation of *Choctaw Traditions*. First, I am thankful to my coauthors Tom Mould and Jay Wesley, for giving me the opportunity to participate in and contribute to the project. Their commitment to capturing Choctaw traditions and stories was vital in the development of this book.

I would also like to recognize Tribal Chief Cyrus Ben and the Tribal Council, Chahta Immi Cultural Center, Cultural Affairs Program, Choctaw Tribal Language Program, Tribal Archives, and the YOP for their support and for the resources they provided for our team. They allowed us to carry out the work of research, interviews, and access to vital resources for the development and completion of this book. My hat's off to the Special Projects/Media Program staff, including Sequita Phillips, Ty Isaac, Jenisa Tubby, and the YOP interns Lexi Flint, Lakylee Martin, and Taylor Ben. They played essential supporting roles during the initial stages of capturing the Choctaw oral traditions told in this book. I would like to express my gratitude and pay tribute to all Choctaw elders for their wisdom, guidance, and their commitment to seeing the culture thrive. They played a key role in making this work a reality.

I want to acknowledge and express my deepest appreciation for my late mother, Fannie Charlie Peoples. Her teachings of cultural knowledge, language, and the values instilled in me over the years have allowed me to contribute to the publication of *Choctaw Traditions*. For my cherished wife, Anita, and my son, Stonewall, I want to express my deep appreciation for all the encouragement and support in this endeavor. My wife, with her profound understanding of Choctaw culture and traditions, as well as her extensive network of contacts, greatly expanded the opportunities for our team to record stories that would have undoubtedly remained left untold without her help.

Finally, I thank God for granting me the privilege to work with Tom Mould and Jay Wesley and for all those who were involved in the making of this book. *Yakokih*!

FROM JAY WESLEY

I would like to acknowledge the staff at the Department of Chahta Immi for their contributions on keeping our traditions alive, chief and Tribal Council for constantly challenging our endeavors on staying true to who we are as Choctaws, my fellow colleagues within the MBCI tribal programs for providing guidance and resources, and the legacy of our tribal elders, past and present.

I would also like to acknowledge my family, who provide continuous support, encouragement, and assistance: my wife, Danielle, and my daughters, Kaylan, Leilani, Jocelyn, Jaeden, and Chloe.

CHOCTAW TRADITIONS

INTRODUCTION

Most collections of storytelling among Native peoples focus on narrative genres that can be roughly categorized as myth, legend, and folktale. The companion book to *Choctaw Traditions*, *Choctaw Tales*, follows this model by bringing together the stories that speak to a shared oral tradition—the stories of creation, encounters with the supernatural beings in the woods, animal stories, historical tales, and prophecies. For the most part, they are the stories that focus on a shared past and future. In putting together *Choctaw Tales* and revising it for a second edition, we knew we were leaving out a great many more stories in the oral tradition, stories that focus on more personal experience; stories that describe what used to happen all the time, not just what happened only once; stories that paint a picture of the customs and traditions that make life possible and meaningful; stories shared first- and secondhand situated in time, place, and circumstance, including the present. This book brings those stories to the page.[1]

By including these more personal stories, our work departs from the majority of books that present the oral traditions of Native peoples. It also departs from standard ethnographies that describe the customs and lived traditions of a people through summary and analysis by the academic author. *Choctaw Traditions* achieves these departures first by combining the two—narrative collection and ethnography into something I have called "storied ethnography"—and second by foregrounding the everyday stories that have been almost universally ignored in the literature of Native peoples.

The continued focus on sacred, ceremonial, and fictional narrative traditions may be both cause and effect of continued stereotypes of the "mystic Indian" that dominate mass-media portrayals and New Age religious practice. Careful reading of books that contextualize the stories in their social, cultural, performative, and historical contexts can help mitigate against these stereotypes, but greater attention to the everyday "kitchen-table" stories, as Keith Cunningham labeled them, is also needed.[2] Such stories do appear scattered piecemeal throughout some contemporary ethnographies, but they are typically treated as data embedded in the author's prose rather than as distinct narratives with attention to genre, form, art, and aesthetics.

Further, by presenting the stories as discrete performances, they are more easily shared with new audiences, whether in the classroom (one of the key goals of this project), in presentations to non-Native audiences (something Jay Wesley does regularly, glad to be able to use the exact words of the elders who initially told them), or with each other over coffee, a bowl of hominy, or a burger.

There is, of course, a trade-off in separating the stories from their performance context and grouping them according to topic and theme. The stories included in books such as Julie Cruikshank's *Life Lived like a Story* are contextualized within their conversational and biographic contexts in deep and powerful ways (1990). Such works should continue to be produced. Yet so, too, should the narrative-based model that foregrounds the oral tradition and puts stories more directly in dialogue with those of other tribal members.

This is not the first book to address the customs and traditions of the Mississippi Choctaw. The single most important work on the subject continues to be Bulletin 103 from the Bureau of American Ethnology *Source Material for the Social and Ceremonial Life of the Choctaw Indians* compiled by John R. Swanton. Combing through the historical documents from explorers, travelers, amateur scholars, and trained professionals, Swanton offers an impressive survey of what has been written about the Choctaw beginning in approximately 1755 with the unpublished writings of an unnamed "French Relation" until publication in 1931. The sources include major works by David I. Bushnell Jr., John F. H. Claiborne, Horatio B. Cushman, Henry Sale Halbert, and Gideon Lincecum. The book has been reprinted at least five times, including twice by the Mississippi Choctaw, once as a reprint in 1995 "Commemorating 50 years of progress," and again in 2021 with a newly formatted, large-print edition. All of these writings are from White men, though they also include in summary and translation the voices of Choctaw men such as Olman Comby, Israel Folsom, Isaac Pistonatubbee, Peter Pitchlynn, and Simpson Tubby. The voices of Choctaw women do appear in the book, but Swanton chose not to identify them by name or gender, referring only to material "collected by Mr. D. I. Bushnell." Bushnell worked extensively with at least three Choctaw from Bayou Lacomb, Louisiana: one man, Ahojeobe (Emil John), and two women, Heleema (Louise Celestine), and Pisatuntema (Emma), his primary informant. Swanton's title was an accurate one. The book is composed almost entirely of direct quotations from these manuscripts and historical writings, often including passages that run for multiple pages. Swanton moves among the passages adding commentary and critiques of the accuracy of the sources and information, as well as pointing out overlaps, patterns, and contradictions in an effort to contextualize the material and offer some preliminary interpretations.

Since then, there have been a handful of books that have taken up the task of documenting the customs and traditions of the Mississippi Choctaw, although far more have been devoted to the tribe's history.[3] In 1961, longtime Bureau of Indian Affairs (BIA) teacher in Choctaw schools Thelma V. Bounds published a small, aptly named book on Choctaw life, *Meet Our Choctaw Friends*, followed in 1964 with *Children of Nanih Waiya*, with the goal of introducing the tribe to their non-Native Mississippi neighbors, many of whom were either oblivious to the fact that Native peoples still lived in the state or harbored well-worn stereotypes about them. In 1986, Kendall Blanchard conducted extensive ethnographic and archival research for *The Mississippi Choctaws at Play* that includes data on sports, games, medicine, and supernatural belief systems, as well as direct-quoted passages from his interviews that include a number of personal experience narratives perfectly in line with those in this volume. In 1989 and 2013, popular press books were published that offered broad summaries of Choctaw culture for a general audience (see McKee and Akers, respectively). James Howard and Victoria Lindsay Levine focused as Blanchard had on one aspect of Choctaw cultural life, publishing *Choctaw Music and Dance* in 1990. My books *Choctaw Prophecy: A Legacy of the Future*, published in 2003, and *Choctaw Tales*, originally published in 2004, both include ethnographic research that sheds light on Choctaw life, particularly as related to their oral traditions, but including belief systems, medicine, recreation, politics, history, and day-to-day living. In his 2013 doctoral dissertation titled "Nanta Hosh Chahta Immi? (What Are Choctaw Lifeways?): Cultural Preservation in the Casino Era," Sean Gantt offers an analysis of many traditional cultural practices and the work being done by the tribe to preserve them. In that same year, Kennith H. York published *Choctaw Nationalism*, a wide-ranging book that provides York, the first member of the Mississippi Band of Choctaw Indians to earn a PhD, a chance to reflect on Choctaw history and customs from his own lived experiences, as well as those of family and friends.

All of these books and manuscripts offer important perspectives on the shifting cultural traditions of the Mississippi Choctaw. This book attempts the same, but in a distinctly different manner. By highlighting the stories people tell, the book grounds our understanding of Choctaw life in the oral tradition and centers it on the voices of Choctaw people, quoted directly. The most powerful and important source of information about Choctaw culture has always been the elders. This book privileges that legacy.

STRUCTURE OF THE BOOK

Choctaw Traditions focuses on the customs and traditions of the Mississippi Band of Choctaw Indians as understood through stories told by the people who participate in them. Each story offers the voice of an individual, sharing his or her own perspectives and points of view on traditions such as *iyyikowa*, marriages and wakes, ball games and picnics, work and play, holidays, and rituals. Accordingly, readers come to understand the diverse traditions of the Choctaw through the equally diverse experiences of individuals in different communities, in different families, at different points in time.

Those experiences do not always align, a fact that became quickly apparent in a conversation with a Choctaw woman I met during my return visit in 2018. She was at a table, beading with a few other women. As we exchanged first names, she quickly asked, "Tom who?"

"Tom Mould," I replied.

"I know you," she said. "You're the one who wrote that book. I don't agree with you." She went back to her beading.

I managed a small laugh and joked that she wouldn't be the first. Silence. I then tried to figure out what she disagreed with and why. We were about to start revising the book for a second edition; such feedback would be invaluable. We talked for twenty minutes. Some of the stories, she told me, were not how she had heard them from her elders. She shared no specifics and offered no errors in fact, but it was clear there were differences in opinion, practice, and interpretation. Her complaint highlights a tension that emerges from time to time about the "right" or "authentic" way to do something or what is, and is not, considered Choctaw.[4] It is a critique that is keenly felt by some in the community, discouraging them from sharing what they remember, even with their own children, for fear of "getting it wrong," despite the widespread recognition that customs vary from community to community, family to family.

This book will no doubt elicit some similar responses within the community. However, we have worked diligently to mitigate this risk. In addition to talking to people from all nine of the Choctaw communities and incorporating archival material to extend our reach through time, we have included multiple stories related to the same custom from people in different communities. There are not enough stories to draw definitive conclusions about how one community engaged with a particular tradition over another, but the variety is on full display rather than assumed or relegated to footnotes. Of course, not all the stories could be included, and some versions are, in fact, relegated to footnotes, but notes and brief, introductory essays help contextualize the stories historically and culturally and offer a sense of the dominant patters that appear again and again.

These introductions are not required reading, but they may help the reader situate the stories in a landscape that spans one hundred years or more. The notes at the end of most of the stories offer more specific context, often from the storytelling session when they were told. They also offer background specific to a particular story and note connections to similar stories shared by other Choctaw that, due to space, could not be included here.

The addition of these introductions and notes is not a sign of insufficient, incomplete, or incompetent storytelling, but rather the reverse. The storytellers in this book have constructed stories for their immediate audiences, building on shared understanding to create powerful stories that may reference the familiar while revealing something entirely new. When telling stories to the high school and college students participating in the YOP, many elders spoke directly to them, in Choctaw, referencing their family members, locating their stories in places on a shared Mississippi landscape, and constructing messages and morals for them as elders have been doing for the youth for as long as tribal memory and historical record exists. In other cases, they have shared their stories only with me, building on our relationship and referencing things we have talked about, experiences we have shared, events we have both witnessed. Sharing these stories with a broader audience, therefore, requires an act of translation. Some of that translation is linguistic, when storytellers shift into their native Choctaw language. But all the stories also require some degree of translation culturally, historically, or personally, to make visible the references already known to the storyteller and their initial audience.[5] The intended result is a book that places Choctaw stories and their storytellers front and center, speaking directly to audiences, with background information to situate the stories in time and cultural milieu.

PRESENTATION OF THE STORIES

To introduce each story, we have included the name of the storyteller, their birth year, their community, and when they shared it. The importance of authorship typically goes without saying, though in anthropological works where people are often anonymized, it is perhaps important to point out that oral traditions are valued both informationally as well as aesthetically and that knowledge is situated within lived experience, particularly in first- and secondhand stories. Accordingly, the stories are best understood after reading the brief biographies in the "Storytellers" section.

Community name is also included since just as dialect shifts from community to community, so too do customs and traditions. Before cars became ubiquitous, the geographic isolation of each community meant that intratribal gatherings were far less common, often confined to ball play and political negotiations. Intermarriage across communities helped ensure unity among the entire tribe, but distinctions remained. Bogue Chitto had a more extensive and long-lasting tradition of the Christmas *shilop*; the game of washers appears more widespread in Conehatta than in other communities today; and food-sale fundraisers are more common in Pearl River where location, centralization, and size make them more viable and profitable. As the stories suggest, however, there are far more subtle variations as well, some tied to community, others to family.

Most people identify with the community where they were born and raised. In a traditionally matrilocal society, the husband would have moved to his wife's community but retained his *iksa* or clan identity as well as community identity. Since the Choctaw were also historically matrilineal, children would take on the clan and community identity of their mother since they, too, would have been born and raised in the same area. However, as the clan system faded away, voting became formalized, and mobility across community became easier and more common, community identity has become looser and more inclusive. This is why some people will have more than one community listed, typically with their birth community listed first and their more recent community association listed second. While many of the storytellers have lived in multiple communities, only a few of the storytellers chose to list more than one.

The storyteller's birth year and the date they recorded their story is given to help locate the tradition temporally. Customs and traditions shift over time; storytellers regularly frame their stories with respect to these changes, but "then" and "now," "when I was growing up" and "a long time ago," are deeply situational and relative. Grounding each storyteller in their specific historical period both in terms of when they were born and when they shared their story allows readers to locate the tradition in time.

These dates are particularly important since the order of stories is based first and foremost around the customs they are describing. The benefit of such a structure is that readers can develop an understanding of the variety of ways traditions have been enacted across both family and community, as well as time. The drawback is that the reader may need to do some basic math in terms of birth years and dates told to be able to order them in a roughly linear chronology.

Although the book includes stories set as long ago as the creation of the Choctaw people, the time period described is mostly the twentieth century, when the storytellers were born and grew up. Their stories of personal experience track changes over the century that reveal both dynamism and stability. Secondhand stories from parents and grandparents, however, shift the picture further back in time to the nineteenth century, bringing these stories into conversation with material in John Swanton's *Source Material for the Social and Ceremonial Life of the Choctaw Indians*. In the introductory essays before each section, we have tried to offer historical context for the stories that follow, locating the reader temporally, not just culturally, in order to avoid the fallacy of an "ethnographic present," where change is ignored, and life is described as monolithic. However, when broad strokes of a tradition are offered, they are usually situated firmly in the twentieth century.[6]

One final note about the names and dates of the storytellers: One might think that these are fairly straightforward. They are not. Variable spellings for names were common in the first half of the nineteenth century, and government bureaucrats were notoriously careless when spelling names and recording birth dates. We have done our best to triangulate information, honoring the information given to us by individuals and their families. We relied on government records to fill in the gaps. While birth years are fairly consistent, birth dates occasionally vary. Ditto last and first names. Last names are typically spelled uniformly, but first names less so. Estelline Tubby, for example, had her name appear in print as

Esterline, Estelene, and Estaline, with people often pronouncing her name as the first, with a distinct *R* sound. I asked her about this back in 1999. She told me that people have always been doing that but that her mother was very specific that her name was with two *L*'s, and no *R*, just like her uncle's girlfriend for whom she was named. Similar discrepancies appear for Necey York (also appearing as Neicy, Necie, and Neesey), Emmett York (also Emmit), Laline Farve (also Lurline), Esbie Gibson (also Esbee), Betsey Solomon King (also Bettie and Betsy), and so on. We always deferred to family members (such as Kennith York for his mother, Necey, and his brother Emmett) but also checked as many sources as possible: photos of gravestones, draft cards, US Social Security records, US Public Records Index, online genealogical records, newspaper articles, and obituary notices.

TRANSCRIPTIONS AND TRANSLATIONS

The stories themselves are transcribed verbatim, capturing the oral tradition that continues to serve important educational, historical, personal, social, and artistic functions within the tribe. Ellipses, therefore, indicate when people trail off or shift gears, not omissions. However, different media require different approaches in order to ensure understanding. What is easily understandable when heard with varying intonations, pauses, emphasis, facial expressions, and hand gestures can be challenging to interpret when stripped of these performance qualities and displayed as only text on the page. Further, stories are shared in context, so pronouns may reference something said earlier outside the narrative text. Interruptions and asides are not uncommon, and verbal pauses, frequent. To address these issues, we have made some slight adjustments.

If a person said "she" in the opening sentence of their story referring to someone they had already identified, we added the name. For example, "She said . . ." might become "My grandmother said . . . " We did the same with topic so that "We used to play it," might become "We used to play stickball."

Aurally, we often don't register false starts—those moments when a person begins a sentence one way, then shifts gears to approach the idea another way. In conversation, we tend to follow the shift easily, dismissing the false start as quickly as the speaker does. On the page, however, these false starts can carry outsized weight, framing the sentence in ways difficult to shake. We have omitted these false starts except in cases where the initial statement contained some information that the following revision did not. We also removed asides that emerged because of an interruption—phone calls, someone entering the room, a burst of thunder. In a few cases, we also omitted asides when the person veered off into another topic, only to return to the story later, clearly indicating the aside was not intentional. However, in these cases, we explained the aside in the annotations at the end of the book.

In some of the interviews done in the 1970s and '80s, as well as ones we conducted ourselves, the interviewers interrupted with additional questions, unaware that the storyteller was not finished. In cases where the interruption reorients the narrator's story, we have left in these questions and comments. However, for interruptions that do not appear to disrupt the speaker's story, we have omitted them.[7] Finally, we omitted many of the verbal fillers, such as "you know," "and," and "well," that help move the story along orally but can have the opposite impact on the page.

We worked with living storytellers to ensure that they approved of the stories we included. All had given permission to record their stories and use them in the book when we first began talking, but we followed up once the stories were transcribed to make sure the stories were presented in a way they approved. In most cases, they were. In a few, storytellers corrected a name, clarified an event, or asked to fix the syntax of a story. In all of these cases, we noted these revisions in the annotations at the end of the book.

In terms of translation, the vast majority of the stories were shared in English. In some cases, speakers code-switched from English into Choctaw. In a few cases, this was because they were more familiar with the Choctaw term than the English one, but in virtually all the others, it was when they were quoting someone from the past who was speaking Choctaw. They repeated what they heard in the language they heard it. We worked with tribal language specialist Pam Smith to transcribe and then translate these passages. Tribal Language Director DeLaura Saunders, and Tribal Language Training and Evaluation Coordinator Jason Lewis were also incredibly helpful in this work, particularly in terms of working with the new dictionary and orthography, but also in terms of variations in dialect and shifts in meaning over time. In the stories, the Choctaw language as spoken is given first, followed by the English translation in brackets. In cases where storytellers offered their own translation, we have omitted an additional bracketed translation except in a few rare cases where the speaker only translated part of the Choctaw-language section. All of the translations we conducted follow the most recent orthography and spelling. However, for stories recorded in the past including material from historical sources that date back to the eighteenth century, we have retained their original translations.

Handling the spelling of community names has been a bit trickier. There have been three orthographies used in the past century, and all three continue to be used today. For example, one may see the community of Bogue Chitto, Bok Čito, or Bók Chito. The first is the oldest but most common today, dominating tribal and nontribal publications. The second emerged as a way of reclaiming tribal pride with a more distinctive orthography that used diacritical marks instead of borrowed English phonemes. This is the spelling used for the community's stickball team, for example. The third represents the newest orthography, used mostly in publications from the Tribal Language Program and increasingly in other tribal publications. We have tried to use the spellings most recognizable, common, and appropriate in each context. This has been more complicated when considering a community like Standing Pine, however, where some have shifted to using the Choctaw-language term Tiak Hikiya (*tiak* is "pine," *hikiya* is "to stand"). Since most people shared their stories in English, they said "Standing Pine." We have followed suit and used this English-language spelling for the community names that introduce each story. In all cases, however, the stories themselves are verbatim using the terms the speakers used.

BOOK SECTIONS

The stories are organized into six sections, each derived from the data itself. That is, we recorded the stories people told and then worked to group them in a manner consistent with Choctaw culture, the storyteller's performance, and the corpus itself.[8] We ended up with "The Land," "Recreation," "Community Events," "Life Cycle," "Health and Healing," and "Advice from the Elders." Within each section are categories to help structure the various customs and traditions related to each. The categories are not mutually exclusive, however. A story that describes weekend ball games may speak to the break from the chores of farm life, the recreation of the game, the dances held at night, the dating customs during intratribal events, and the medicine men working to ensure that their team wins. As much as possible, we have used the notes section to point readers to related stories that appear in other sections. Equally useful is the index, which will allow readers to find stories according to topic, theme, or character.

We begin with the land as both a practical and symbolic entry point, a category that aligns with the "Traditional Land Use" identified by the Cultural Affairs Program as a key area of traditional Choctaw culture. Practically, so many stories relate to the land that grounding the reader here first allows other traditions to come into focus. Sharecropping dominated the economic system for the Choctaw during the late nineteenth and throughout the first half of the twentieth centuries, scattering families across the Mississippi landscape. That dispersal helps explain the ball game and dance complex that structured so much of community life outside of work. Further, the land provided not only a means for entering the wage economy but also for survival. Hunting and fishing have offered critical means for feeding one's family, helping to provide a ready and steady source of protein throughout the year to accompany the vegetables they grew in their gardens and the fruits, nuts, and berries they gathered in the woods. Hunting and fishing also provided a chance to relax, socialize, and escape the farm for a day or two. Today, that balance has shifted, where hunting and fishing are typically valued more as recreation than as sustenance, but as the stories make clear, both remain important.

Symbolically, the land has always played a central role in Choctaw traditions. In their two creation stories—one of emergence from the Nanih Waiya Mound, the other of migration where a sacred pole signaled their territory—the land is a sacred gift from the Creator. In some versions, the Creator tells them they should never leave, a detail that makes the removals to Oklahoma beginning in 1830 and the work relocation programs of the 1950s, '60s, and '70s spiritually as well as economically, socially, and emotionally devastating.[9] Stories also tell of the Nanih Waiya Mound serving as a burial ground for the bones of their ancestors, situating the mound as a sacred place of both beginning and end.[10]

The book then moves to recreation as an act of balance with the labor associated with the economy of the land. The game of stickball serves as an orienting symbol around which Choctaw social life circulates, drawing together dance, music, entertainment, sport, dating, kin relations, foodways, medicine, religion, craft, and art. Where the land grounds the Choctaw in the economy of daily life, stickball grounds them in the customs that make life meaningful. Also included in this section are stories about other sports, such as baseball, softball, basketball, and volleyball; games known throughout the community, such as washers, rag ball, and cornhole; and some of the many games developed spontaneously in the face of boredom played among families and friends. Some of these games were and are played during community events, the next section of the book. The tradition of *iyyikowa* leads off. It, like stickball, serves as an orienting symbol for the tribe, one that expresses key values of generosity and mutual support. Where *iyyikowa* gathers people together to work, the ceremonies, holidays, and festivals that follow in the section gather people together to celebrate. It is not hard to connect the ceremonies and festivals of the past, such as the Green Corn Ceremony and Lowak Moshólichi with contemporary ones, such as the annual Choctaw Indian Fair and the festivals held at tribal schools in the fall and spring. As Christianity took hold, people developed ways to incorporate holidays such as Christmas and Easter into their cultural system, developing distinct ways of celebrating these days. Community-wide events blend into more localized family events as well, where visiting one's relatives was a critical way of maintaining kin relations and ensuring exogamy in marriage. During all but the small family gatherings, people found ways to offer goods for sale to facilitate the fun. Selling drinks at ball games, treats at house dances, and food at the fair helped families make ends meet or raise money for an upcoming expense—a vacation, a medical issue, fall school supplies.

The book then shifts from the daily calendar of working the land and the seasonal calendar of holidays and festivals to the life cycle, exploring the customs that help individuals move from birth, through childhood, to adulthood as they come of age, date, get married, have children, and then ultimately pass from this world to the next. Traditional Choctaw beliefs often coupled with

Christian religious rituals and practices underlie many of these customs, offering people a way to navigate the challenges of life in ways that align with personal, spiritual, religious, tribal, and communal values. Critical to navigating this path is maintaining balance, including in one's health and wellness. The next section on health and healing shifts to the many ways tribal members ensure protection from harm and healing from injury. This includes not only medicine but also the social customs that help govern daily interactions and the legal customs that help ensure peace and justice.

The final section is not one we intended to cover. It shifts gears from narrative to advice, from experience to aspiration. With so many of these narratives recorded between elder and youth, mirroring how these stories are often shared outside the interview context, elders shifted from historian to teacher and moral guide, just as they would have around fires, on front porches, and around the kitchen table. No doubt, this category would have been far longer had we actually asked people to share their advice to the next generation. Even so, it would have been triple the size if we had included all the examples. But the advice was extraordinarily consistent, particularly in terms of entreaties to maintain the language and not let the lure of money and mainstream media distract from what really matters in life. To avoid sounding too much like a broken record and risk alienating exactly those audiences the elders were trying to reach, we culled the list to ensure we were comprehensive but not repetitive. While the advice is specifically directed to Choctaw youth, the wisdom conveyed is powerful, and much of it is relevant for any audience.

These are the traditions the book includes. But anyone with even a passing knowledge of the Choctaw will recognize some glaring omissions. Missing are the stories about making baskets, stickball sticks, rabbit sticks, drums, traditional clothing, pottery, and beadwork. The same is true for stories about food: the hominy, *banaha*, *walakshi*, and fry bread. Although dancing figures prominently in many of the stories, this book does not tackle music and dance as specific art forms. These omissions are not because these subjects do not warrant attention. Quite the opposite. There has been excellent research on music and dance thanks to early work by Frances Densmore and subsequent work by James Howard and Victoria Lindsay Levine. Smaller but more numerous studies have been conducted on the swamp cane basket tradition, as well as work on sewing, woodworking, beading, and other material arts.[11] Foodways have received some attention, though all of these areas deserve book-length studies. Choosing to avoid being a jack-of-all-trades and master of none, this book focuses on customs. It nonetheless manages to encompass the vast majority of what Choctaw consider to be part of their traditional culture.[12]

THEMES AND PATTERNS

AT THE CENTER

Culture has often been described as a web. All beliefs, rituals, customs, artifacts, norms, traditions, and values are interconnected, some more directly than others but all part of a larger system. Tugging on one strand of the web necessarily impacts the rest. Despite these connections, webs have a center. For the Mississippi Choctaw, that center has been stickball. Take virtually any shared custom within the community, and it is or was either part of the stickball complex or related to it in less than one or two degrees of separation. For example, at the turn of the twentieth century, preparations for the ball game included the ball game dance with traditional chanters keeping the rhythm, part of a larger complex of social dances also performed during the multiday ball game. During those social dances, young men and women had an opportunity to get to know one another, a courtship that could lead to marriage thanks to the intratribal nature of the games that brought different clans or *iksa*s together. At least some descriptions of traditional marriages ended in a stickball game, bringing the process full circle. Along the way, traditional foods were cooked in the various encampments around the ball field. The work of skilled craftsmen was on display in the hickory stickball sticks that were shaved, bent, and tied to ensure lightweight but durable play and in the *toli*, the balls woven from thin strips of deer hide that required nimble, dexterous fingers. Swamp cane baskets were lashed to pots, beadwork to embroidered dresses, ribbon shirts to blowguns and rabbit sticks, or any of a number of household goods, farm implements, and farm animals as people gambled on the outcome of the game.

Historical records suggest stickball games were played to resolve political disputes such as land rights. Competition was fierce; games often resulted in broken bones and lost teeth. To ensure success, Choctaw prophets (*hopaii*) and doctors (*alikchi*) performed rituals before and during the games. Less esoteric spiritual beliefs could also be witnessed as taboos were maintained to ensure that the power of women, particularly related to menstruation, did not weaken the men's play. Women played stickball too, though early non-Indian observers paid far less attention to their games, offering them only the briefest attention.[13]

Politics, economics, spirituality, domestic life, arts and crafts, music and dance, foodways, and of course sports and recreation are all central parts of stickball. But stickball has changed dramatically over the past few hundred years, both as the result of and resulting in changes to the entire web of Choctaw culture. Stickball, therefore, can serve as a cultural canary in a coal mine, a custom that can be observed, tracked, and analyzed for larger cultural changes at work.

While stickball has been a useful and visible center of Mississippi Choctaw life, there is another center, one that exists as much as an ethos as an observable custom, though it is that too. It is relational, connecting family and neighbors in a web of social obligation. It is called *iyyikowa.*

"This would happen mostly in the springtime," Carter Williams explains from his office as facility manager out in the Standing Pine community back in 1997.

> It would happen if someone got behind in their work—planting or gathering wood. You didn't have to ask for help. They would hear that you were going to have an *iyyikowa,* and they came. Lots of men would get together for this. Sometimes they would do it at night. They would make a light out of a pine stump. Also, they poured kerosene into a Coke bottle or some other kind of bottle and put an oil cloth in there as a wick to make a light because they didn't have the money for lanterns. With no money, you make do. They were hard times, but it didn't seem like anything was wrong.

Translated into English, *iyyikowa* means "broken foot," an initially odd name for an ideology that ensures the health of the community. But the meaning is not difficult to decipher, particularly as it operates quite literally. When a person had a broken foot, her neighbors came to help. Of course, *iyyikowa* also operates metaphorically and metonymically: the broken foot could also be a broken arm, a barn fire, a flood, a death in the family.

Carter went on to explain the values underlying *iyyikowa* by contrasting the practice with a story he heard sitting around with other men after hunting and fishing all day.

> Two men decided to kill a hog and split it, each getting a half. But it was a custom to give a little bit of the meat to all the neighbors and the two men didn't want to do that. So one of them told the other to hang it up in the back of his barn, behind some crates, and tell the neighbors the pig had been stolen. So he did this.
>
> But the next day, the man who had hung the pig up in the barn went back out to get the meat, and it was missing. He told the other man what had happened.
>
> "Just keep telling people the pig has been stolen," he said, and went on.
>
> And all along, it was him who had stolen the pig and had kept it all to himself![14]

Carter burst out laughing. Such greed and stinginess could not be tolerated within the small Choctaw communities. Lack of job opportunities and resources required people to help each other. But of course, people do not always behave as they should. Stories remind us of that, but also of what we should do all the same.

These two symbols of Choctaw culture—stickball and *iyyikowa*—do not operate in isolation. They balance each other, the competitive with the collaborative.

Brian Billie notes an even more explicit connection. Speaking to the YOP students, he asks,

> Y'all ever seen a barn raising on TV, on YouTube, or any Amish? Well, if you understand that barn raising and how they come together to do that, *iyyikowa* is the same thing. We have it in our way. You could come from long, far away, and people used to spend a night in different communities to accomplish what they wanted to do. Kind of like when y'all played tribal ball in different communities. Sometimes y'all go to your cousin's house in different communities and eat over there and go back to play and then visit family. And it's the same, close to *iyyikowa.*

CONTINUITY AND CHANGE

Despite their contrasts, stickball and *iyyikowa* require the same commitment and provide the same opportunities for reconnecting with extended families and reestablishing communal ties. Or at least they did. Culture is dynamic, and traditions change. Overnight visits to play stickball are no longer necessary thanks to easy access to cars, and *iyyikowa* has faded, transformed from a community event to a family one. But that is the nature of tradition. Its stability helps us connect with the past to create a shared present; its dynamism helps ensure that it remains relevant and meaningful.[15]

The stories in this book track those continuities and changes, though often it is the change that is most recognizable. Elders reflect on the past, and the changes with today can be stark, with a sense of loss dominating perception and the stories they tell. Many people lament that *iyyikowa* has died out, that neighbors do not help each other like they used to, and that extended families do not gather like they once did. Yet observations of life today reveal that the generous impulse to help is not gone, and family remains a centralizing force.

People no longer call an *iyyikowa*, and community members no longer come out en masse to help a person or family in need, but help is still given either in small groups by family or institutionally by the tribe. When the Vaughn family needed wood to keep the fire going when Harley passed away suddenly in 2022, it was his son-in-law Terrence Comby who arrived with a pickup truck full of wood. When Lorena Alex needs something, anything, "I can depend on my brothers and sisters, so I could still call that [*iyyikowa*]. I would." Social get-togethers, cookouts, birthday parties, and holidays that were frequently celebrated with neighbors and friends have constricted to smaller circles of family. Family dinners, too, that once drew uncles, aunts, and cousins now typically draw only children and grandchildren, though such numbers can still fill a house.

But a sense of community that binds neighbors in reciprocal obligations and shared identity remains. Wakes and funerals continue to draw neighbors and coworkers from within the community and across the reservation as people pay their respects by tending to the fire, sitting inside with the body, or helping out around the home. Although team rosters are more expansive today, stickball teams remain tied to community, inspiring pride and social cohesion.[16] Community booths at the annual fair rely on people coming together to develop a theme, gathering objects, and constructing the display, all on a volunteer basis.

Increasingly, however, the tribal government has stepped formally into spaces once organized by communities. Wood for wakes is often provided by the tribe. Food and aid for the elderly is also provided through formal tribal programs. Much of the communal social life, too, has been taken over by the government. Community-wide "Christmas Tree" celebrations that were once hosted by one family or another have been replaced with a tribal Christmas tree lighting ceremony hosted by the tribal government. Thanksgiving feasts have been hosted in each community with tribal funds, although most recently, a single large feast is hosted by the tribal chief at one of the casinos at Pearl River.

One sees both centrifugal and centripetal forces at play. Centrifugal forces have pushed some social activities out to institutional control at the tribal level. Centripetal forces have drawn other social activities into smaller nuclear family circles. But in both, many traditions persist.

Another way to view these customs, then, is through the lens of continuity. People still find meaningful ways to get married, name their children, grieve for lost loved ones, and help each other in times of need. Food continues to anchor social, political, and tribal events. "If there's some kind of gathering involved, food is always there," Jay Wesley says, adding, "You have food, people will follow." And not just any food. "If there's no hominy there, you're not eating," says Eddie Gibson. "You're not having a feast if you don't have hominy. And there's usually chicken. And you can stop right there. As long as I have chicken, and hominy, and fry bread, I'm okay. I'm fine!"

Carmen Denson explains that food is more than instrumental. "That's the way we showed our love for each other." One summer evening in 2021, Carmen, Dan Isaac, Ralph Isaac, Donald Cotton, Williamson Isaac, and I gathered to talk in the back halls of Hope Baptist Church where Williamson is a deacon. Midway through our conversation, Ralph disappeared. Eventually, Carmen pointed to the church kitchen. "Ralph, he's doing it right now, he's setting up something for you. You're our visitor, so . . . " So he picked up fried chicken, mashed potatoes, green beans, biscuits, and drinks so we could eat together. It was a pattern I experienced again and again since I began visiting in the 1990s. I showed my thanks to people by taking them to dinner; they showed their generosity by doing the same. Those meals have changed, with restaurants often replacing kitchen tables and burritos and burgers as common as fried chicken.

With change comes innovation. For some, reflecting upon the past has provided inspiration for cultural revival and creation. The military-style snare drum has exploded in popularity in recent years, with young and old, male and female, picking up the instrument and integrating it beyond stickball games into most major public events. Stickball was once played throughout the year. By the 1980s, it was confined almost exclusively to the Choctaw Indian Fair. But in the past few decades, it, too, has expanded both in terms of when it is played—with demonstration games, all-star games, and interteam scrimmages—as well as who plays it—with the growth of children's leagues as well as women's teams, who draw as much of an audience as the men's teams.

Cultural borrowing and adaptation from mainstream media continue. Television and tablet games have replaced weekend campouts and rag dolls; volleyball and cornhole are more common than washers at family gatherings. But tribal members continue to find ways to adapt and integrate these borrowed customs into family and community life. Further, while Iron Warrior obstacle courses, 5K and 10K Rez Runs, and cornhole and volleyball tournaments have bumped washers, blowgun shooting, and rabbit stick throwing from competitions at the Fair, many of these traditions continue to be presented during cultural demonstrations, keeping them alive as both symbol and resource, visual reminders of a cultural heritage that remains accessible and relevant.

Further, cultural borrowing is not confined to mass-mediated society. Increased participation in intertribal customs such as the powwow and sweat lodge has brought a new source of inspiration from other Native communities across the country, encouraging tribal members to develop new customs and ceremonies to address emergent needs, such as dealing with the trauma and loss from the COVID-19 pandemic. Research is having a similar impact. Harold Comby explains: "At the present time, there's several people that are trying to raise up our culture. My mom calls it '*hayakachi okchalli*,' which means 'to show it' or 'to resurrect it.' I think the ceremonial pipe is one of the things that has been uncovered. And I tell those people, whenever we do things, it seems like it's easier to bring it up because we've always had it underneath; it was just being covered with something." Sometimes it is a faint memory that draws a custom back into the present, but Harold and others such as Dan Isaac and staff at the Department of Chahta Immi have found published sources a particularly fertile source, not least of them John Swanton's *Source Material for the Social and Ceremonial Life of the Choctaw Indians*. It is there that Harold found references to the use of steam and smoke for healing, making connections to sweat lodges and smudging so prevalent among other Native communities. Although members of the Choctaw Nation of Oklahoma have been coming to Mississippi to learn, revitalize, or strengthen their own traditions and customs for years, recently the flow of information has shifted, with Mississippi Choctaw going to Oklahoma to learn traditional pottery and firing techniques in order to resurrect the pottery tradition in Mississippi.

As old traditions fade, are transformed, or are revived, and as new traditions emerge, the work of cultural preservation continues. The Department of Chahta Immi is the face of the institutional efforts of this preservation with cultural affairs, tribal language, and the cultural center all falling under their umbrella. The Special Projects/Media Program produces videos, web resources, online materials, blog posts, and any of a number of resources that are used in curriculum and public programming.[17] Elders, however, are the face of noninstitutional efforts. As elders, they are expected to share the stories of the past, to ensure that the wisdom of past ancestors is passed down to new generations. Doyle Tubby pointed out that different families tell different stories, but they address the same key issues. "They're telling the same stories, but they're just telling it in their own way. When you go down, sit down to another family, listen to their stories, it's the same thing. It's just how they look at it differently, how they interpret it" (July 27, 1997). The work of the Department of Chahta Immi and research projects that led to this book focuses on these elders but shifts the intended audience beyond their families so that the tribe and the larger public can also hear what they have to say.

Communication is, of course, a two-way street. Without an audience, the words of the elders carry no weight. More than any other audience, it is the youth who are identified again and again as the most critical and important. Perhaps not surprisingly, then, they are also singled out as the biggest problem. "I wish they can learn what our elders know and do," said Lela Solomon, echoing many of her peers, "but my grandchildren don't even know what that means, and my daughter can't even make baskets. The small children don't even care to learn. Choctaw traditional ways are about gone. They don't even wear Choctaw dresses" (1982). Most elders also recognize themselves in these portrayals, however. They lament that they did not listen to their grandparents and parents as much as they should have. They mourn the loss of so much knowledge, so many stories, so much history. Their critique of the current generation is as much cautionary as reflective, warning today's youth against making the same mistakes they did, realizing only too late how much they could have learned from their elders if they had only listened.

Further, Alice Bell was not alone in 1985 when she remembered how difficult the past was and how much better life had gotten in many ways. "Oh, no. I wouldn't take nothing for today! There is everything just nice now. But they don't know! A lot of these young people, they don't know they're in heaven. They got a good school; they got a good house. They just living in heaven right here, but they don't know" (Weill, Williams, and Ferguson). She reminds us that the past is not always better than the present and that the positive new developments that have made life more comfortable should not be taken for granted. But as "soft" as the youth are accused of being today, reliant on their electronics and air conditioning, Terry Ben offers a powerful reminder of the resilience of the Choctaw, from removal efforts to segregation to today. "Just remember: Choctaws were hard workers and still are survivalists. They do a lot of things and persevere, just keep after it, keep after it, keep after it."

"They had to do what they had to do to survive. Each family was a little bit different, but they shared common problems, but they overcame." He adds, "We are survivalists. That's why we're here in spite of what was going on with segregation during that time period, in spite of all the assimilation attempts made by the federal government, we're still here. Choctaw people are strong survivalists. Hard workers." And then once more for emphasis, "Survivalists."

THE STORYTELLERS

Bradley Alex

BOGUE HOMA / PEARL RIVER. BORN 1955.

Bradley Alex was born in Paulding, Mississippi, in Jasper County but moved with his family to Bogue Homa when he was about five years old. He lived there until high school, when he moved to Pearl River in order to go to Choctaw Central High School. He grew up playing baseball and stickball, excelling at both. By high school, he had made a group of friends that included Hulon Willis and Leonard Jimmie, also storytellers in the community. He worked on the *Nanih Waiya* magazine in high school, where he met Linda, the woman he would later marry. They had four children, including Liasha Alex, one of the YOP students who worked on *Choctaw Tales* back in 1997. Bradley served in the navy after high school but soon returned to Mississippi, where he currently works as *itikana ikbi* or peacemaker for the tribe, helping to resolve disputes through reconciliation. His wife of forty-two years tragically died from COVID-19 in 2020. Bradley is one of the few elders we spoke to who still identifies with his *iksa* or clan: the Turtle Clan. Basket maker and storyteller Esbie Gibson is his aunt.[1]

Lorena Alex

HALLS, TENNESSEE / BOGUE CHITTO / PEARL RIVER. BORN 1952.

Following traditional customs of introduction and greeting, Lorena Alex introduced herself to the YOP students by naming her parents and community. "My name is Lorena Vaughn Alex. I'm sixty-eight years old. My parents are Clifton and Rene Bell Vaughn. They're both deceased. I live in Philadelphia, Mississippi, Neshoba County, Pearl River community. I lived here since, oh lord, probably '85." She added, "I have three children, one granddaughter, six brothers and seven sisters and there are just eight of us now. I finished high school in a public school out of state. I've had two years of college course." Like many tribal members, she has lived among many communities. Her parents initially moved to Tennessee to find sharecropping work. They moved back to Bogue Chitto when land and work became available when Lorena was a teenager. She works for the Cultural Affairs Program with her cousin Trudy Jimmie, both of whom conducted a series of Choctaw-language interviews with elders from 2003 to 2007 that are stored in the Tribal Archives awaiting translation. She has become expert at sewing and beading. Lorena and Harley Vaughn are siblings.

Susie Comby Alex

STANDING PINE / PEARL RIVER. BORN 1947.

One of nine children, Susie Comby Alex was born and grew up in Standing Pine before moving to Pearl River at age ten when her father took a new job. She graduated valedictorian of her class at Choctaw Central High School and attended East Central Community College, the University of Southern Mississippi, and the University of Arizona. Susie worked for fifty years as a librarian, retiring in May 2022. "I wasn't just a librarian," she says. "I was a grandmother, mother, storyteller." As a librarian for the tribal school system, she often brought her brother Harold Comby to speak to the seventh and eighth graders, who sat there spellbound by his stories.

Claude Yates Allen

PEARL RIVER. BORN 1948.

Claude Yates Allen was born on October 21, 1948, to William Allen and Sudie Mae John Allen. His father died when he was three, and he was raised primarily by his mother and grandmother, the latter of whom used to tell him "ghost stories" and warn him about wandering off. When he was twelve, he had to go to Memphis for eye surgery. His recovery required near-constant care, so he lived for a year with a White man there who helped take care of him. When he returned home, he attended Choctaw Central High School until the tenth grade but was anxious to start working. He joined the armed forces and married Rita Allen. He passed away on November 29, 2007.

Elizabeth Bell Allen

BOGUE CHITTO. BORN 1947.

Elizabeth Bell Allen was born on January 20, 1947, to John Levi Bell and Maggie Wallace Bell in the Bogue Chitto community. Her father farmed cotton and corn, and she worked with the rest of her family to tend to the garden that provided them much of their food growing up. She fondly remembered gathering with family and playing games with her cousins. She had two daughters, eight grandchildren, and twelve great-grandchildren when she passed away on January 10, 2018.

Sally Allen

CONEHATTA. BORN 1959.

Sally Allen was born in 1959. Her father was a sharecropper near Union in Newton County. She remembers being lucky in never having to use an outhouse since the owner of the land provided a bathroom with running water. She was raised to treat everyone with kindness, no matter their race or ethnicity, an ethos that she carries with her into her work at the Department of Social Services. When COVID-19 hit the tribe, she was interviewed for a national news story on the impact, noting that she lost her brother-in-law, son-in-law, and his grandmother all within an hour of each other. She is an active member of her church, pitching in at fundraisers to help support their mission.

Amanda Bell

PEARL RIVER. BORN 1969.

Amanda Bell grew up in Pearl River with her parents, Frank Bell Jr. and Rosaline (Anderson) Bell, surrounded by family, including her maternal grandparents, Thelma (Ben) Anderson and Irvin Anderson, and paternal grandparents, Ivenia (Lewis) Bell and Frank Bell Sr. Her grandparents taught her many of the traditional ways of living; her father taught her to enjoy running; and her mother taught her to sing the hymnal, read the Bible, and pray in Choctaw. Amanda was a Chahta Immi Cultural Center manager and tribal archivist and currently serves as an administrative coordinator in the Tribal Historic Preservation Office. She attended Choctaw Central High School, Haskell Indian Junior College, and Belhaven College, where she earned a bachelor of arts degree in history. She is a former Choctaw Indian Princess, stickball player, and stickball coach, with three young adult children, Shelbi, Wauseka, and Jordan. Judy Billie is Amanda's paternal aunt.

Cubert Bell

HENNING, TENNESSEE. BORN 1946.

Cubert Bell was born on December 1, 1946, to Willie Bell and Lillie Willis Bell in Philadelphia, Mississippi. Eventually, he moved to the Choctaw community of Henning, Tennessee. According to the Choctaw Cultural Legacy website, he is a veteran of the US Marine Corps and worked at Firestone Tires and Sears Automotive; as a community center director in Ripley, Tennessee; and as assistant director and tour guide at the C. H. Nash Museum at Chucalissa, in Memphis, Tennessee.

Hayward Bell

BOGUE CHITTO. BORN 1948.

Hayward Bell was born on January 16, 1948, and attended Choctaw Central High School. He served Bogue Chitto for years as a tribal councilperson, often fighting an uphill battle to develop greater economic opportunities for his community and tribe. COVID-19 hit his family particularly hard; he lost his wife and a son, daughter-in-law, and granddaughter within months of each other. Among his many efforts to maintain traditional Choctaw culture, Hayward gave his children Choctaw names, battling hospital administrators to accept non-English names on their birth certificates. An advocate for Choctaw civil rights, he fought against the discrimination he saw on a daily basis growing up in Mississippi, including racist housing practices.

Jesse Ben

PEARL RIVER. BORN 1955.

Jesse Brantley Ben was born on October 25, 1955, to Arthur Ben and Mary Briscoe Ben. Jesse grew up playing stickball with his brothers and cousins, getting his first pair of sticks from his uncle. When he grew older, he played for Konihata (Conehatta) and continued to be part of the sport even after he stopped playing by making stickballs for the World Series of Stickball tournament played during the annual fair. Early in his career, he worked in Chicago at the American Indian Center, but he soon moved back to Mississippi to work for the tribe, including as a language specialist for the Choctaw Language Program. Committed to ensuring that the language remained vibrant and relevant, Jesse worked to develop new Choctaw words for concepts that did not yet have their own term such as *hopáki im ikhána* for "historian," a particularly apt contribution considering his interest in Choctaw traditions. Jesse was a member of the Pearl River Mennonite Church. He passed away on June 21, 2013.

Terry Ben

STANDING PINE. BORN 1957.

Terry Ben was born on October 9, 1957. He was raised by his grandparents on a farm in Standing Pine with his brothers and sisters. With no running water until the late '60s, Terry has worked alongside his family since he was a child. He had aunts and uncles who had gone to college before him, paving a way for him to get his college degree and return to the tribe to serve in many educational roles, including history teacher and school superintendent. His deep knowledge of Choctaw history comes not only from his formal education, but also from what he learned from his grandparents. He explained, "My granddaddy was born 1895. His daddy was born in 1869. So that's how far back I can trace. Whatever was done in the past during the 1800s, transferred into the 1900s, and all that in terms of what I'm going to tell you, and what I know, and what I went through, and what I was taught. I learned a lot of things from my grandparents and also the elders in the community." Terry has followed suit with the many he has taught through the years, as well as with his own children, including Taylor Ben, who worked on this book through the YOP program.

Casey Bigpond

PEARL RIVER / MUSKOGEE CREEK / YUCHI LINEAGE. BORN 1983.

Casey Bigpond is both Mississippi Choctaw and Muskogee Creek/Yuchi lineage. He works for the Cultural Affairs Program helping to preserve Choctaw traditions, including making stickballs, stickball sticks, rabbit sticks, and drums, but his interests are regionally focused as well, drawing him to consider his Choctaw traditions in the context of other southeastern tribes, including Creek, where he learned stomp dancing. He held a naming ceremony for his oldest son a few years ago and plans to do the same for his other four children. An avid stickball player, Casey not only plays himself, but he has begun coaching youth and women's teams as well. Entrepreneurial in spirit, Casey makes and sells stickball sticks and rents large inflatables such as bouncy houses and obstacle courses for private and tribal events. He has constructed a large outdoor workshop, often inviting friends and neighbors over to learn to make stickball sticks or just enjoy some time sitting and talking. He is acutely aware of the negative influences colonization and missionary work have had on Native peoples and works diligently to maintain the distinct and unique aspects of his Native cultures.

Brian Billie

RED WATER. BORN 1973.

Brian Billie was one of the youngest people we spoke to, but he is an old soul, a traditionalist who prefers speaking in Choctaw and follows traditional customs such as how one should introduce oneself: "My name is Brian Billie," he begins. "I'm from Red Water. I'm the son of Herman and Doris Billie. My brothers are Herman, Herman Glen; my younger brother is Jeremy Kevin. My sister's name is Priscilla Gail. I have four daughters, Madison, Brianna, Kelsey, Matty. I have three grandchildren . . . I live in Red Water. I always wanted to move, but my parents never want to leave it, so I live down the road." Brian was raised Catholic and remembers going to church with non-Choctaw who were very curious about his skin and hair and language. Today, he is the manager for the tribal recycling center, but he has also worked for Choctaw Wildlife and Parks, using his knowledge of the land, waters, and environment to help create a sustainable life for himself and his community. Many of the stories he tells come from his parents and grandparents, but some come from friends and coworkers, including Estelline Tubby's son Robert Christopher Tubby or "Bullos," who tragically died from COVID-19 in 2020. Brian ruminates and reflects on how things have changed over the years, drawing connections between recent trends, news, and legal cases and old traditions, making sense of the world through a uniquely Choctaw lens.

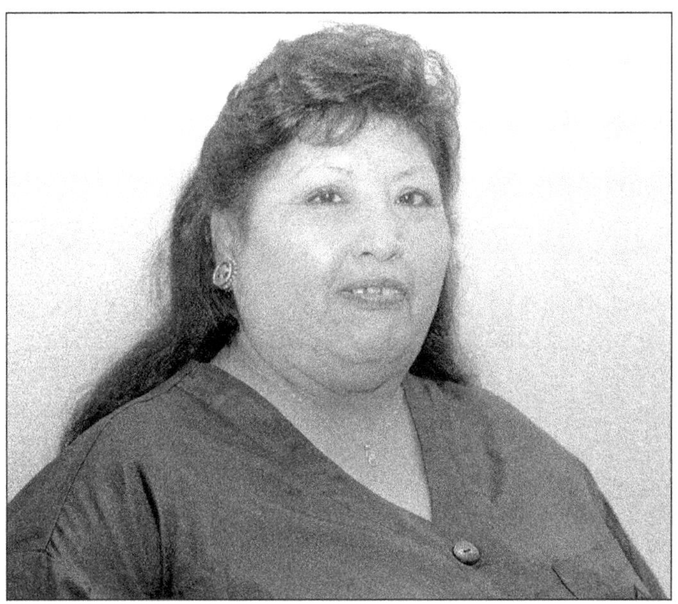

Judy Billie

PEARL RIVER. BORN 1946.

Judy Hickman Billie was born on November 8, 1946. She remembered growing up in an affectionate household where love for one's children was shown not through hugs and kisses but by holding them on your lap and talking to them, showing them attention. She created a career caring for tribal youth in her work at the Choctaw Health Department as an alcohol and drug counselor. Her knowledge of the traditions of the past helped her guide youth to reconnect with the values that would help them avoid addiction. Judy passed away on January 9, 2008.

Mahlih Bowden

PEARL RIVER. BORN 1991.

Mahlih Vaughn Bowden is the middle child of Rae Nell and Harley Vaughn and one of the very first Choctaw children I met when I first visited the tribe in late December 1995. Since then, she has become Choctaw Indian Princess, gotten married, and started a family. She works as a teacher's aide in the tribal school system, but she spends as much time or more volunteering for her community, whether serving on the Princess Pageant Committee, helping develop the community booth for the annual fair, organizing roadside cleanups, or helping run election campaigns for tribal office.

Billy Chickaway

CONEHATTA. BORN 1950.

Billy Gene Chickaway was born on January 8, 1950, to Henry and Annie Chickaway in Neshoba County, was raised in Tucker, but eventually moved to Conehatta. He attended Choctaw Central High School, where he played on the school basketball team and served as senior class president. He continued with his political aspirations after high school, eventually becoming a tribal councilperson for Conehatta for two consecutive terms. According to the Choctaw Cultural Legacy website, Billy has worked in management positions for a number of different organizations and has most recently served as a benefits director for Pearl River Resort. He is also a retired veteran of the Air National Guard, where he earned the rank of master sergeant.

Harold Comby

PEARL RIVER. BORN 1955.

Harold Comby was born on April 24, 1955, in Standing Pine but moved with his family to Pearl River when he was two. He was a master storyteller by all accounts, having learned by sitting at the feet of his elders and listening carefully to the stories they shared while many of his contemporaries were outside playing. One of the many stories of how he got his nickname, "Doc," derives from this early passion for learning everything about his culture. More than anyone else, Harold cited his mother, Rosia Isaac Comby, for much of what he knew, regularly asking her questions about Choctaw culture up until her death. Harold shared that information widely, with Choctaw youth and adults, as well as with dozens of non-Choctaw, including many anthropologists, historians, and folklorists.

Harold was an athlete in high school, playing football and basketball, and continued his love of sports first as a stickball player for Beaver Dam and then as a regular commentator for the World Series of Stickball tournament held every year at the Choctaw Indian Fair. His emcee skills were also on display on the powwow circuit; Harold was an avid fancy-dance and traditional powwow dancer who eventually hung up his mocassins and became a sought-after emcee for powwows throughout the region.

After graduating from Choctaw Central High School in 1974, he earned a degree in social work from Jackson State University and took additional courses in vocational counseling at the University of Southern Mississippi. He spent his career committed to protecting others, first as a youth counselor, then in law enforcement, serving as captain of the Choctaw Police Department and later as tribal coroner. He had four daughters and one granddaughter when he passed away suddenly on March 10, 2022, from congestive heart failure.

This book is dedicated to Harold in recognition of his work to preserve, share, and celebrate Choctaw traditions for future generations. It is impossible to overestimate the impact Harold had on maintaining Choctaw traditions for and with his community. He is deeply missed.

Evaline Davis

CONEHATTA / TUCKER. BORN 1945.

Evaline Davis was born in Philadelphia, Mississippi, and raised in Conehatta. Her parents were Willie and Venie Hickman. Years ago, her grandfather shared predictions and old prophecies with her. She said, "He said, 'One day, some day from here, everything is going to be changed up.' He said, 'Women are going to be the workers, and the men are going to be staying home babysitting,' or something like that. But that's what I heard from my grandpa, and it's true." Although her husband worked outside the home, she did too. She worked at a shirt factory in Decatur until she got married, moved to Tucker, and got work closer to home. Her jobs included factory work at the American Greetings factory, overseeing the money cart at the Silver Star Hotel & Casino, and digging ditches and hauling wood for tribal maintenance. Eventually, she settled into a job at the tribal museum and gift shop until she retired in 2023. Three of her four children are still living, but her husband passed away a year ago. Evaline creates beautiful, beaded jewelry such as medallions, collar necklaces, and earrings, many of which are sold in the museum store where she works.

Carmen Denson

STANDING PINE. BORN 1956.

Carmen Denson grew up in Standing Pine, attending Walnut Grove Elementary, the tribal school system for seventh through ninth grades, and then back to public school for the rest of high school, ultimately finding that he appreciated a more integrated classroom. Carmen was raised Christian, attending hymn sings with his father, Charlie Denson, well into adulthood. He sees the two traditions—Choctaw and Christianity—as compatible, although that is not always how preachers taught them, with many saying they had to give up their Choctaw traditions to follow Jesus. Carmen served as a councilperson for one term but recently took a job at the Choctaw Health Center, moving to Pearl River to be closer to work. Carmen remembers many of the old stories shared widely throughout the community, but he also shares stories this father told him about serving in World War II.

Charlie Denson

CONEHATTA / STANDING PINE. BORN 1923.

Charlie Denson was born on May 4, 1923, to John Denson and Lillie Solomon Denson in Conehatta but lived his adult life in Standing Pine. He worked most of his life as a sharecropper and day laborer except for a stint in the army during World War II and then later in life when he was able to buy and farm his own land and do maintenance work for the tribe. He went to school up until the third grade but had to board with another Choctaw family to be close to the school, which was more than thirty miles away by horse and wagon, a hardship on both him and his family that ultimately became untenable. Raised Baptist, Charlie grew up celebrating Christmas by hanging a sock for Santa Claus to fill and Thanksgiving with a big meal and a church service. He played rag ball and baseball as a child, often with the White kids who lived nearby. He got married at twenty-four to Mary Ann Williams and had six children, including his son Carmen. He remembers his grandfather telling him about the old funerary customs where "they had scaffolds just outside the door" where they put the body to decompose (1973). Charlie was a well-known figure in the community, particularly in Standing Pine, where he was a leader in his church, an avid hymn singer, and outspoken in politics. He passed away on January 5, 2004.

Theron "Duke" Denson

PEARL RIVER. BORN 1956.

Theron "Duke" Denson was born in 1956 and grew up in Dallas, Texas, before moving to Pearl River at the age of twelve. He received mixed signals about speaking Choctaw when he was growing up. On the one hand, his parents wanted him to learn English to be able to succeed in the schools he was attending. On the other, he was occasionally punished for not being able to speak Choctaw fluently. Duke attended college and played in the marching band, but he disagreed with some of the teachers and ultimately transferred to Haskell Indian Junior College where he says he got a good education. A guitar player and singer, he was a member of a number of bands. He was also an excellent artist, illustrating many of the storybooks for the Tribal Language Program with images that inspired the COVID-19 cutouts planted around the reservation warning people to mask up, stay at home, and stay safe. Duke was particularly interested in *na losa chito*, believing it might be the Choctaw version of Bigfoot, and appeared briefly in local media when Bigfoot hunter Tom Biscardi came to town in 2012. He was also a member of the Church of Jesus Christ of Latter-day Saints. He lost his cousin and one of his closest friends to COVID-19 and almost died from it himself, only partially recovering. He passed away on April 12, 2023.

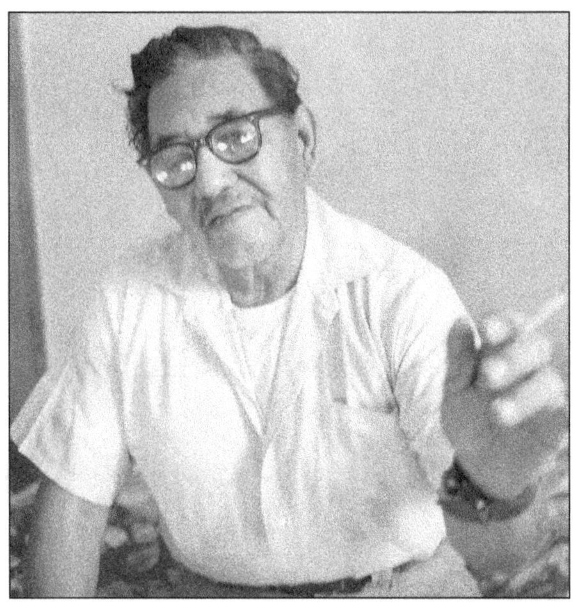

Pete Davis Dyer

OKLAHOMA / TUCKER. BORN 1912.

Peter Davis Dyer was one of the best-known herbalists and Chahta *alikchi* (Choctaw doctors) in the community in the second half of the twentieth century. He was born and raised in Eagletown, Oklahoma, on February 5, 1912, and served in the navy for sixteen years, the only time in his adult life that he wasn't practicing medicine. Hesitant to share specifics about the medicine he learned from the *kowi anukasha* (*bohpoli* or "little people"), he was happy to share home remedies that his neighbors could apply for themselves. He was skeptical of other doctors who practiced bloodletting but had learned the herbs the traditional way as he had. In 1975, he moved to Tucker and began practicing medicine in Mississippi, frequently sharing stories of the people he cured. He became something of a local celebrity when he got an office in the Choctaw Health Center so that tribal members could seek help from both Western and traditional medicines. Father of one son and two stepdaughters, he was a member of Holy Rosary Catholic Church in Tucker. He passed away on June 8, 1985.

Mary Lou Farmer

CONEHATTA. BORN 1917.

Mary Lou Farmer was born in Newton County on May 20, 1917, to John Farmer and Mandy Warner and lived in Conehatta throughout her life. She grew up with her father sharecropping for Floyd Loper. She remembered her childhood fondly despite the hard work of farming: getting up early, going to bed early, picking cotton, milking cows, and feeding hogs. She said, "It was hard work, but it was fun." Many of her recollections involved managing life around traveling the long distances among friends and family who were spread out across the area sharecropping for other people. She passed away in March 1986.

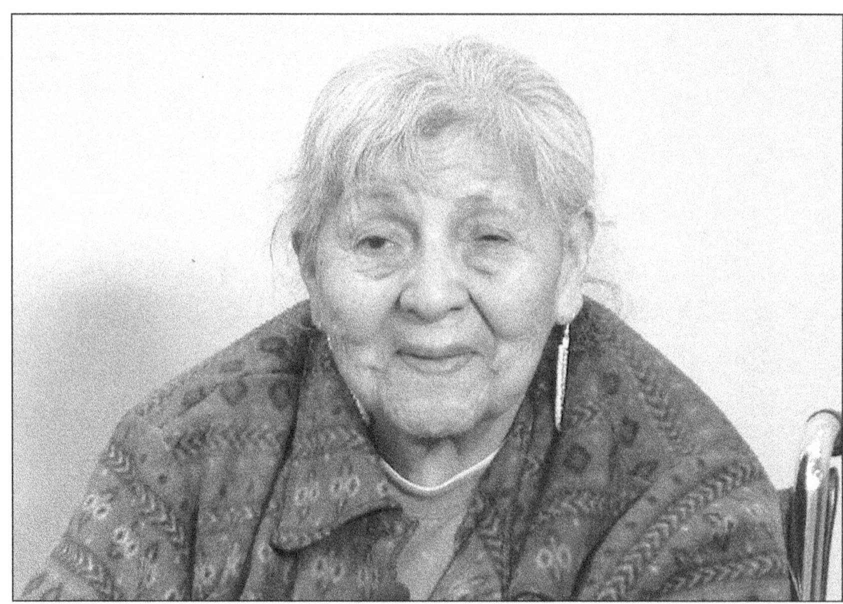

Laline Farve

STANDING PINE. BORN 1933.

Laline Williams Farve was born on September 9, 1933, to Lewis Williams and Mamie Smith Williams in Newton, Mississippi, and attended Conehatta Elementary School until the third grade. After she was married, she and her family moved to the Mississippi Delta, where they sharecropped for thirteen years before moving back home to the Standing Pine community. She worked as a custodian and cook, but is remembered best as a foster parent who cared for many Choctaw children as they transitioned to stable homes. She was also a skilled seamstress who made traditional Choctaw clothing. She had four daughters, three sons, and three stepchildren. Her brother was Carter Williams, a storyteller in Standing Pine and father of Linda Williams, also recorded in this book. She passed away on August 3, 2018.

Melford Farve

TUCKER. BORN 1961.

Melford Farve was born in Conehatta and lived a few years in Pearl River but moved to Tucker when he was still young and has lived there all his adult life. He is one of eight children. Both he and his father have served as Tribal Council representatives. Melford graduated high school from Choctaw Central in 1980 and went to work at American Greetings, one of the companies that set up shop on the Pearl River Reservation. He worked there for seven years, observing firsthand the transition many men and women made to hourly shifts and regular wage labor. The tribe offered a number of training programs and courses, including one on video production with East Central Community College that changed the trajectory of Melford's career, moving him into the field of communications, where he has spent the bulk of his working life. In addition to video production, Melford has worked for the *Choctaw Community News* for decades. In his younger days, he played some basketball and stickball but enjoyed video production more, at one point directing a short horror film based on a medicine man who terrorizes some local Choctaw youth.

Martha Ferguson

STANDING PINE. BORN 1949.

Martha Ferguson grew up in Standing Pine, where she remembers her childhood as fun and independent. There were rules, but she regularly broke them, fishing on her own, hunting with her uncle, or playing with snakes. In high school, she played basketball and participated in 4-H. After marrying songwriter, music producer, and historian Bob Ferguson, she took a job at the tribal museum, performing all the tasks from billing to mopping the floors. Soon, she began learning about the arts and crafts they sold—how to distinguish between and evaluate the different types of baskets, how to bead, and how to make stickball sticks. Before long, Martha was a permanent fixture at the museum, working there until her retirement in 2023. In addition to her long career in the arts at the museum, Martha was one of the extras in the film version of *Mississippi Burning*, shot on or near some of the spots where the historical events of the brutal murder of three civil rights workers occurred in 1964.

Jim Gardner

PEARL RIVER. BORN 1895.

Jim Gardner was born on March 10, 1895, according to government records and an interview published in a special edition of *Choctaw Today* in the summer of 1978, countering the obituary published in the *Clarion-Ledger* on Friday, March 18, 1994, which said he died five days after his 110th birthday, making his birth year 1884. Either way, Jim Gardner lived a long life. His day job was in maintenance at the tribal office building, but he spent much of his spare time focused on stickball. Growing up, he had been an avid stickball player, not stopping until he was in his fifties. He then turned to refereeing stickball games and making stickball sticks. He described early stickball games where a rain witch could bring rain by chanting and waving a black handkerchief in the sky. He was a member of Hope Baptist Church and passed away on March 15, 1994.

Calvin Gibson

CONEHATTA. BORN 1940.

Calvin Gibson was born on October 26, 1940, one of ten children born to Lillie Kate Farmer Gibson and Homer Gibson. He attended high school in Pearl River through the tenth grade, as far as one could go at the time. He finished his last two years of high school at Haskell Institute in Lawrence, Kansas, and then earned his bachelor of arts degree from the University of Southern Mississippi in Hattiesburg. By the time he sat down in 1973 for an oral history interview, he was working as a social worker for the Choctaw Indian Agency and caring for two foster children. Like his father, Calvin became a preacher and officiated hundreds of funerals for his fellow tribal members. He passed away on January 6, 2006.

Eddie Gibson

CONEHATTA. BORN 1953.

Eddie Gibson was born in 1953 to Lillie Kate Farmer Gibson and Homer Gibson. He grew up in Conehatta but has lived much of his life off the reservation in between Tucker and Pearl River. His community identity, however, is clear: "I think I'll always be Conehattian," he told us, laughing. Storyteller Lillie Gibson is Eddie's mom; Calvin Gibson is his brother; and Jaeden Wesley, who worked on this book through YOP, is his granddaughter. Eddie grew up speaking Choctaw in the home but going to a non-Choctaw Baptist church. His father became a preacher later in life. Their devout faith meant that he didn't participate in many Choctaw traditions as a child because they were told their culture was antithetical to Christianity. Eventually, he played stickball, often with Henry Williams, another storyteller from Conehatta. He also joined a dance troupe that his cousin started. He describes growing up as sharecroppers in a frame house without running water. Although neither of his parents was able to complete high school, Eddie graduated from Mississippi State University and has remained a diehard fan, greeting us with the popular rallying cry "Hail State!" Although he grew up with an "English" name, his wife has many nieces and nephews with Choctaw names, and his grandson is Tashka, or "Warrior," a name he says has grown in popularity in recent years.

Lillie Gibson

CONEHATTA. BORN 1919.

Lillie Kate Farmer Gibson was born in 1919. Her father was a sharecropper, and her stories reflect the transition she made from a rural farming life to one in an extended and more modern community. That transition in geography, as well as in time, involved newly available utilities, such as electricity and running water, amenities that appear in the humorous stories she told. Subtle and reserved, her wit imbued her stories of the past with self-effacing humility. She remembered watching her father doctor people who came to the house for help, often using steam to help purify and cleanse. It was her grandfather, however, who was the storyteller in their family. She said, "My grandpa would read that Bible. He would tell us to lie down and listen to what we had to say. And then after he read the Bible, he prayed, and he'd tell us to go to sleep, but I couldn't go to sleep. 'Tell us some more stories.' He'd think of some, but I went off to sleep before he could tell it all! While he would tell stories, my mama would sit there and make baskets." Lillie learned to tell stories and make baskets, as well as quilt and make Choctaw dresses. Calvin and Eddie Gibson, both of whom share stories in this book, remember her as a kind and generous person, always ready to bake a cake for a neighbor or help out in any way she could. Lillie passed away on November 11, 2007, at the age of eighty-eight.

Dolphus Henry

BOGUE CHITTO. BORN 1919.

Dolphus Henry was born on September 1, 1919, to Robert "Bob" Henry and Nellie Morris Henry in the Bogue Chitto community. He attended elementary school and then worked with his family full time farming. He served in the army during World War II. He became a Christian as an adult and eventually became a preacher, serving at a number of churches, including Bogue Chitto Baptist Church, where his nephew became pastor as well. Dolphus's father, Bob Henry, was a medicine man, and Dolphus remembered watching him doctor people in the community, including members of his family. Jasper Henry was his brother; Pam Smith, the translator for this book, is one of his daughters; DeLaura Henry Saunders, who shares stories in this book, is another. He passed away on March 1, 1988.

Frank Henry

BOGUE CHITTO / TUCKER. BORN 1927.

Frank Henry was born on May 10, 1927, to Jim Henry and Sallie Thompson Henry. At age eighteen, he joined the army to serve in World War II and was discharged on March 21, 1946. He did an internship with the Bureau of Indian Affairs before heading to the University of Southern Mississippi in Hattiesburg to finish his degree in elementary education. He worked for tribe as an educator first in the school system and then back with the BIA, this time as a health educator and then as a service unit director, working with the hospital. He passed away on February 12, 2004.

Jasper Henry

BOGUE CHITTO. BORN 1917.

Jasper Henry was born on August 20, 1917, to Robert Henry and Nellie Morris Henry in the Bogue Chitto community. He was attending Cherokee Indian School in North Carolina when he was drafted into the army to serve in World War II at age twenty-three. When he returned from war, he was trained to make watches but found that White people wouldn't hire him. Frustrated with the racial politics of the South, he moved to Cincinnati, where he worked for eleven years. He was later deployed to Korea for a short time and then worked in a military hospital in Colorado before moving back to Mississippi. He was a Baptist, like his brother Dolphus Henry. Jasper passed away on January 7, 1989.

Melvin Henry

BOGUE CHITTO. BORN 1911.

Melvin Henry was born on July 28, 1911, to Alvin and Martha Henry. He grew up sharecropping, which instilled a strong work ethic tied to the land. He initially critiqued the youth for not trying to learn the old Choctaw traditions but then admitted that he did the same when he was younger. As an adult, he became well known in the community for making large white oak baskets. In 1982, Bill Brescia and Carolyn Reeves interviewed him about his life and work. He passed away in April 1993.

Jackson Isaac

PEARL RIVER. BORN 1902.

Jackson Wilson Isaac was born on October 4, 1902, to Wilson Jim Isaac and Martha Waiter Isaac. He grew up in Pearl River and learned to make stickball sticks and rabbit sticks by watching his grandfather, uncle, and father. He went to Chilocco Indian School in Oklahoma but dropped out before finishing. At age thirty-nine, he was drafted into the army to serve in World War II. He passed away on March 21, 1992.

Judie Lene Isaac

PEARL RIVER. BORN 1942.

Judie Lene Isaac was born on July 11, 1942, to Wilburn Isaac and Mealie Isaac. She was interviewed for the Choctaw Cultural Legacy website, noting that she "attended Tucker Day School and Pearl River High School. She worked as 4-H coordinator for fifteen years, Choctaw Indian Fair Program assistant for twenty years, and activity coordinator for the Choctaw Elderly Center for six years. She was strong in her traditional beliefs and enjoyed expressing her knowledge of the past." She was also a member of Holy Rosary Catholic Church in the Tucker community. She passed away on November 18, 2017.

William "Dan" Isaac

PEARL RIVER. BORN 1968.

Dan Isaac was born in Pearl River, where the family of his father, Williamson Isaac, lived. While his father no longer knows their clan affiliation, his mother, Esterline Gibson Isaac, was from the Bear Clan in Standing Pine. Dan served in the US Air Force before returning to Mississippi, where he has worked many jobs in the community, including as a substance abuse counselor and marriage counselor. Like Harold Comby, Dan is an avid scholar of both Choctaw and intertribal traditions. Where Harold fell in love with powwow dancing, eventually becoming an emcee for powwows around the country, Dan fell in love with powwow drumming, forming the Southern Pine Drum Group with his brother Ralph and friends Donald Cotton and his son Jake Kirk, among others. Dan and his drum group travel the Southeast and beyond, playing at powwows, festivals, and local events, as well as for their fellow Choctaw at political rallies, community dinners, wakes, funerals, and celebrations. Dan is equally immersed in Choctaw music and dance traditions, forming the Mystic Wind Chahta Social Dancers, who perform Choctaw social dancing while Dan chants. Dan's insatiable quest to learn his history and culture has also made him a sought-after storyteller, participating in the Southern Storytellers of Mississippi event in 2022. Deeply spiritual, Dan is a firm believer in reviving and creating ceremonies to heal community members and the community from generational trauma as well as contemporary challenges.

Williamson Isaac

PEARL RIVER. BORN 1947.

Williamson Isaac was born on September 30, 1947, in Pearl River to Hugh Isaac and Celia Farmer Isaac. He attended Pearl River High School and has worked many jobs on the reservation including in ground maintenance at the Choctaw Health Department. He is a member of Hope Indian Baptist Church, just a couple of hundred yards down the road from his home. He serves as a deacon in the church, helping to run the church after their pastor died from COVID-19. Williamson not only leads church service until their visiting pastor Mark Patrick arrives, but he also regularly offers prayers at the funerals of his fellow congregants. People in the community also know Williamson as the person who can fix their lawn mower, tractor, or any other small vehicle. His yard bears evidence to this side business, with tires and engine parts stacked outside his open-air workshop.

Leonard Jimmie

PEARL RIVER. BORN 1957.

Leonard Jimmie was born on December 9, 1957. His father was Choctaw, his mother, Navajo. He has lived in Mississippi, New Mexico, and Arizona, but Mississippi has been his primary home. When Choctaw Central High School teacher Charles Plaisance introduced the idea for the *Nanih Waiya* magazine, Leonard and his friends Bradley Alex, Hulon Willis, Henry Bell, and Willard Keith Bacon jumped at the chance as a way to get out of class and out into the community. The magazine was based on the Foxfire project started by Dr. Wiggins in Georgia and has become an invaluable resource today, recording conversations with Choctaw artists, politicians, teachers, craftspeople, and elders throughout the various communities and documenting customs and traditions in much the same way this book does. After high school, he attended a year at Millsaps College in Jackson. When his father tragically died in a car accident, he returned home. Eventually, he followed the path of many of his peers by joining the armed forces. Back in Pearl River, he works in security at the Golden Moon Hotel & Casino. Although unable to complete his own undergraduate degree, Leonard made sure that his children have all been able to go to college.

Bobby Joe

BOGUE CHITTO. BORN 1953.

Robert "Bobby" Joe was born on January 1, 1953, in Kemper County, Mississippi, to Henry Joe and Effie Bell Joe. He grew up hunting small game, and as an adult, he raised and trained hunting dogs. He worked for seventeen years at US Motors but loved to chant and dance traditional Choctaw social dances. In his interview for the Choctaw Cultural Legacy website, he explained: "My daddy was a chanter. I learned to sing by listening to him. I remember when I was younger, he was asked to chant for a group at the Choctaw Fair. I got interested by watching him chant." He passed away on March 3, 2019.

Frank Bell Joe

BOGUE CHITTO. BORN 1951.

Frank Bell Joe was born on September 28, 1951, to Emily Bell Joe. He grew up in what he described as a strict family. They adhered to many of the old traditions, even after joining the Baptist church when he was eleven. His grandfather regularly shared with him prophecies that had been passed down for generations, some of which had been fulfilled, some of which were yet to come. He held great faith in traditional medicines after watching his father being cured by a medicine man, but he worried that there were fewer and fewer doctors. Frank held a number of jobs, including at the local hospital, the Bogue Chitto Elementary School, the police, and at the time of his interview in 1975, as a dormitory supervisor in Choctaw Central High School. He married Minnie Pearl Wilson from the Red Water community and fostered a number of Choctaw children. He passed away on May 3, 2004.

Berdie John

RED WATER / CONEHATTA / STANDING PINE. BORN 1965.

Berdie John was born on July 14, 1965, and raised in Red Water by her stepfather's parents, to whom she refers as her grandparents. She moved to Conehatta when she got married and then moved to Standing Pine when she got divorced. Growing up, she remembers her grandparents living off the land: fishing; hunting for meat such as squirrel, possum, raccoon, rabbit, and birds; and tending a large garden for vegetables. They also kept pigs and chickens, which offered an additional food source. She remembers always having plenty to eat. Basket making and caning chairs provided the income for the rest of their needs. Her grandfather was a minister at Calvary Baptist Church in Union, which meant that she was as likely to hear an impromptu sermon at home as stories from past elders. But she heard those too and particularly remembers the ones about *bohpoli* and the other beings in the woods. She has held a number of jobs at tribal offices, including working for Chief Martin and serving as the head of the Tribal Election Committee.

Grady John

HENNING, TENNESSEE. BORN 1934.

Grady John was born on February 8, 1934, to Otis John and Annie Mitch. He was best known in the community as one of the last traditional Choctaw potters, having learned the art from his uncle L. D. John. He loved country music and the old-time music played during house dances. He worked for years as an exhibit interpreter and local artisan at Chucalissa, a reconstructed fifteenth-century Indian village in Memphis, often giving pottery demonstrations to school groups and the general public. Despite losing both his legs to diabetes, Grady remained an active participant in the social and cultural life of the Choctaw community in Henning, Tennessee, where he lived most of his adult life. He passed away on December 16, 2001.

Eddie Johnson

STANDING PINE / TUCKER. BORN 1970.

Eddie Johnson was born on January 31, 1970, and was raised in Standing Pine, with four brothers and one sister. He grew up hearing stories, especially from his family and community elders. The stories were about growing up sharecropping, milking cows, and raising chickens, often including mishaps and rule breaking that elicited hearty laughter. At night, the stories shifted to scary encounters with various beings that lived in the woods just outside their back door. Eddie is a Baptist preacher with a church in Tucker. He has lived most of his adult life off the reservation, however, in and around Philadelphia, Mississippi. He has worked for the Department of Chahta Immi since its inception, currently serving as coordinator of the Special Projects/Media Program, where he helped create the Choctaw Cultural Legacy website, among dozens of other major projects. His job allows him to add to his already deep knowledge of Choctaw traditions with archival research, onsite training from pottery experts in Oklahoma, and ongoing documentation from the elders in all of the Choctaw communities in Mississippi. Eddie is an avid fisherman, a hobby that his son has embraced fully. He enjoys sharing traditional knowledge and the Choctaw language with others who are willing to listen, especially the younger generation.

Barcom King

CONEHATTA. BORN 1923.

Barcom King was born on August 6, 1923, to Jackson King and Betsie Solomon King and lived in Conehatta. He remembered watching stickball games before betting was outlawed. Games were rough and often ended in violence, perhaps partly because the bets were winner takes all. He joined the army at age eighteen and served in World War II. He had two daughters and four sons and was a member of Macedonia Baptist Church. When he passed away on August 4, 1998, he had twenty grandchildren and twenty-one great-grandchildren.

Richard McMillan

TUCKER. BORN 1961.

Richard Wyatt McMillan was born on December 24, 1961, to William McMillan and Arletta Gardner McMillan. He grew up playing stickball and remained involved in the sport even after he stopped playing, officiating games just like his grandfather used to do. He saw the sport become rougher once football became more popular in high school, with players bringing the same physicality to stickball but without the protection of pads. He passed away on June 1, 2021.

Sarah Jane Sampson McMillan

ARDMORE, OKLAHOMA / TUCKER. BORN 1951.

Sarah Jane Sampson McMillan was born on January 16, 1951, in Ardmore, Oklahoma, where she grew up, attending predominantly White schools. Her grandmother had moved to Oklahoma during the removal efforts at the turn of the century, but the family kept in touch with their Mississippi relatives. Growing up, Sarah visited family in Mississippi from time to time, including when she was fourteen and attended the Christmas tree event in Tucker that year. She fell in love with the cousin of her sister's husband, and in 1969, she went to Mississippi to get married, not knowing that they would end up moving to her husband's home community of Tucker. The transition to life on the reservation in Mississippi was not an easy one for her. The racial discrimination and relative poverty were an unwelcome shock, but she managed and raised her family in Tucker, where she lived until she passed away on November 10, 1995.

Jessica Miller

CRYSTAL RIDGE. BORN 1984.

Jessica Miller was born on November 7, 1984, in Mashulaville in the Crystal Ridge community to parents Jimmy Cotton and Sammie Wesley. She is the great-great-granddaughter of Cameron Wesley, well-known medicine man and leader. Her mother, Sammie, is the daughter of Benny Wesley, son of Sidney Wesley, who was the son of Cameron Wesley. As a child, she picked peas with her siblings and cousins in her uncle Clay Wesley's fields. She attended Choctaw Central High School, staying in the dorms during the week and traveling home on the weekends. As an adult, she took a job at the casino. She has four children and continues to share the stories she heard growing up.

John Mingo Jr.

STANDING PINE. BORN 1946.

John Mingo Jr. was born on April 3, 1946, in Leake County, Mississippi, to Arch Mingo and Annie Tubby Mingo. He was raised in the Nanih Waiya community near Crystal Ridge. According to the Choctaw Cultural Legacy website, "He attended Pearl River Day School and attended high school in Chilocco, Oklahoma. He is an electrical engineer by trade. Mr. Mingo is a rich source of Choctaw cultural knowledge and is skilled in making crafts like the blowgun, rabbit sticks, beading, stickball sticks, and wood carving." He passed away on August 13, 2020.

Caroline Morris

PEARL RIVER. BORN 1944.

Caroline Willis Morris was born on July 17, 1944, in Pearl River to Gladys Mae Willis and Claude Yates Willis, one of eleven children including brothers Travis Willis and Hulon Willis. She finished eighth grade and eventually went to Biloxi for work in the hotel industry. There she met her first husband, who was serving in the military at the time. She had two children, Rae Nell (Hockett) Vaughn and Bill Hockett. She divorced and remarried and had two more children, Tina Morris and Greg Morris. She passed away on July 16, 2010, just one day shy of her sixty-sixth birthday.

Mark Patrick

O̱TOKLO (CONEHATTA). BORN 1969.

Mark grew up in O̱toklo, what many White people at the time referred to as "Indian Town." Named for the Hontokalo Creek that runs through the area, O̱toklo is closest to the Conehatta community. Mark was raised by his grandmother, but his mother lived nearby on the same plot of land, allowing him to move easily back and forth between each home. He spent much of his childhood outdoors hunting, fishing, swimming, and occasionally pranking the nearby farmer with his brothers and cousins. Growing up Choctaw and Black made life difficult in the segregated South, often discriminated against by both Choctaw and non-Choctaw alike. Sports, however, offered him a place to earn respect on and off the field. A star football player at Sebastopol High School, Mark got a scholarship to play for Jackson State University but had to return home when his mother became ill and died when she was only forty years old, and he needed to help care for his younger siblings. Back in Mississippi, he finally accepted invitations to play stickball and became a standout player quickly, earning MVP of the World Series of Stickball tournament within five years of learning the game. He was still playing in the fifty-and-over men's league in 2021 and serving as a referee. Mark is also a devout Baptist, leading his own church and acting as interim pastor at two others (including Hope Baptist, where Williamson Isaac is a deacon), making Sunday mornings particularly busy. He and his wife, Darlene, are avid motorcyclists, often taking their bikes to Cherokee, North Carolina, to ride through the mountains while visiting their son and his family, including their new grandson.

Barbara Sam

STANDING PINE. BORN 1956.

Barbara Sam was born on December 31, 1956, to Dorothy Stephens and Golden Thomas in the Conehatta community. Her father passed away when she was young. She grew up helping around the house and working in the family garden. She married Gordon Sam and eventually moved to Standing Pine, where they raised their family. She learned to sew and bead from her mother, but it wasn't until after she was married and living in Standing Pine that she learned to find and cut swamp cane and make baskets from her aunt Phoebe York. She earned a secretarial degree from East Central Junior College. She eventually took a job at Standing Pine Elementary School, where she worked for more than thirty years.

Gordon Sam

STANDING PINE. BORN 1959.

Gordon Sam was born in Standing Pine, where he has lived all of his life. He married Barbara Sam. Like most of his peers, he grew up on a farm and was expected to do lots of hard manual labor. He also worked in a poultry processing plant before going to college. He feels lucky to have had good, steady work throughout his life. "Ever since I went to college, I've always had an office job. I always have been real fortunate to have jobs that, for example, the old Chahta Enterprise, where we built harnesses for Ford Motor Company and General Motors. A little old Choctaw man from Standing Pine was sitting in a desk. I was their personnel. I've only had two jobs. That one, and for the last thirty-one years I've been with the Department of Family Community Services. I'm the program manager there." Not one to sit around bored, Gordon took on a second job, at Pearl River Resort, once his kids were grown and out of the house. He worked in promotions for seven years before finally retiring. They were exciting years, however. He asked us, "You ever been to the casino where they announce and say, they're giving a car away or calling somebody's name to come up to the area, your names were drawn to get a prize, cash, boats, cars? I helped them do that. I helped give away millions and millions of dollars."

DeLaura Saunders

BOGUE CHITTO. BORN 1950.

DeLaura Henry Saunders was born in Bogue Chitto, where she lives today. Her parents, Dolphus and Inez Henry, converted to Christianity and initially accepted the prohibitions imposed by White missionaries to give up many of their Choctaw customs, first among them the house dances that had a reputation for drinking and fighting. Eventually, these restrictions were lifted as her parents established a balance between their new faith and their Choctaw culture. Since then, DeLaura has been deeply committed to understanding Choctaw history, culture, and language. She was already working in cultural preservation in 1974 when Choctaw Central High School students interviewed her for the *Nanih Waiya* magazine. She has been working for the tribal language programs for decades, a program she now directs. She also comes from a family of cultural translators who have been interviewed by non-Indians about Choctaw culture. Her grandfather Robert Henry worked with ethnomusicologist Frances Densmore; her uncle Bob Henry worked with anthropologist James Howard; her father, Dolphus Henry, worked with Sue Weill, Julia Williams, and Bob Ferguson; her mother, Inez Henry, worked with Geri Harm; and she is working on this book, as is her sister Pam Smith, who did the translation work, and her grandson Thomas Saunders, one of the YOP students for the summer.

Carrie Tubby

RED WATER. BORN 1914.

Carrie J. Tubby was born on May 3, 1914, in Carthage, Mississippi, to Ava Joshua. On November 1, 1973, Choctaw Central High School student staff members of the *Nanih Waiya* magazine interviewed her about home remedies, cooking *banaha* and hominy, making soap, and Christmas. She was a member of Mount Zion Baptist Church. She passed away on September 12, 1995.

Estelline Tubby

PEARL RIVER. BORN 1928.

Iona Estelline Tubby was born in 1928. Estelline was deeply interested in her culture and in medicine and wished she could have been a medicine woman like her grandmother. Despite the fact that her mother was not raised on the reservation and therefore did not always know what to teach her in terms of her heritage, her aunt and grandmother served as valuable sources of knowledge for her. She had a full career working in various roles at Choctaw Central High School and still managed to learn to quilt, make dolls, do beadwork, sew traditional shirts and dresses, and garden. Originally raised Baptist, she became a Mormon when one of her sons encouraged her to go to church with him and his family. She passed away on October 4, 2006.

Simpson Tubby

NESHOBA COUNTY. BORN 1867.

The Reverend Simpson Tubby was born in Neshoba County, Mississippi, on April 1, 1867, "a child of the forest," as he says in his pamphlet titled "Early Struggles," an account of his conversion to Christianity. In this autobiographical sketch, Tubby praises the White Methodist missionaries who introduced him to Christianity. He eventually became an avid missionary to his people in Mississippi, establishing the first Methodist church for the Choctaw. Baxter York remembers that "old man Simpson Tubby" was on the temporary Tribal Council with him in the 1930s and 1940s, when they drew up a constitution declaring self-government. Although she never heard stories directly from him, his daughter-in-law, Estelline Tubby—another of the storytellers in this book—carried on Simpson Tubby's storytelling legacy.

Harley Vaughn

HALLS, TENNESSEE / BOGUE CHITTO. BORN 1961.

Harley Vaughn grew up in Halls, Tennessee, where his family, including sister Lorena Alex, worked as sharecroppers. Harley worked hard growing up, often tasked with the most physical jobs on the farm. The family moved back to Mississippi when Harley was twelve. At age sixteen, he enrolled in Haskell Indian Junior College with a number of other Choctaw teens, including a few of his thirteen siblings, before transferring to East Central Community College, where he earned a degree in carpentry. He worked in construction and custodial services before becoming a bus driver for the tribal school system. When he and Rae Nell married, they moved to Bogue Chitto into a home owned by one of Harley's uncles before moving to Pearl River with Rae's family. Rae spoke to their three children primarily in English, while Harley spoke Choctaw. When one of his young daughters responded to his request to come to the dinner table by saying in a sugary, singsongy voice, "We don't speak Choctaw," he responded quickly and firmly, "*Binílih*!" the Choctaw word for "sit." All three obeyed immediately. Harley played the drum, made stickballs, and played stickball for the Bók Čito team, occasionally bringing his daughters with him to practice, leading two of the three to pick up the sport as well. Eventually, Harley and Rae Nell divorced, but they remained close friends, coparenting and cograndparenting until Harley passed away suddenly in 2022 from complications due to diabetes.

Hillary Meagan Vaughn

PEARL RIVER. BORN 1989.

Hillary Meagan Vaughn is the oldest of Harley and Rae Nell Vaughn's three daughters, with three children of her own. I met her when she was six. After years working as a dental assistant, she recently took a job in the Special Projects/Media Program in the Department of Chahta Immi, engaged in the same work of cultural preservation, education, and celebration that this book takes as its central task. Working with at-risk youth, Hillary offers workshops in various Choctaw traditions and history, often teaching as the elders did: through example. She sews traditional Choctaw clothing, does beadwork, and plays stickball and is teaching her children to do the same. In the summer of 2023, at the age of six, her son played his first stickball game. Her daughters are likely close behind.

Rae Nell Vaughn

PEARL RIVER. BORN 1964.

Rae Nell Vaughn was born on June 22, 1964, in Pearl River, but her father moved the family around the country for work. When her parents divorced, her mother moved the family back to Mississippi, where she grew up with a large extended family, including her grandmother, Gladys Willis. She and her siblings and cousins worked in the family garden, a chore she dreaded since it was brutally hot in the summer when they had to pick peas whose vines were so thick they stopped any air that might have cooled them off. The task was not without its occasional laughs, however. One day while picking peas, she was following along behind her grandmother when she fell over. "One minute she was there; the next minute she was gone!" swallowed up by all the vines and plants. After high school, Rae Nell earned a degree in criminal justice from Mississippi State University and worked as the tribal archivist. Eventually, she moved into the judicial system, serving a five-year term on the Choctaw Senior Youth Court before her appointment to the Choctaw Supreme Court in 2001 as the first female chief justice. Since then, she has worked a number of other jobs for the tribe, including serving as the chief of staff for Chief Phyllis Anderson. Rae Nell is related to many of the storytellers in both *Choctaw Tales* and this book, including her grandmother Gladys Willis; uncles Hulon and Travis Willis; mother, Caroline Morris; husband, Harley Vaughn; sister-in-law, Lorena Alex; and two of her three daughters, Mahlih Bowden and Hillary Vaughn.

Barney Wesley

MASHULAVILLE / BOGUE CHITTO. BORN 1927.

Barney "Bon" Wesley was born in 1927 to Cameron Wesley and Julia Bell Wesley, as one of five siblings, including Hubert Wesley. In a 1982 interview by Bill Brescia and Marian Isaac, Barney and his wife, Lena, described life in Mississippi during the twentieth century. White landowners made life unnecessarily hard, whether through sharecropping practices or not allowing Choctaw to hunt and fish on land that was once theirs. Barney became an expert craftsman, particularly in making drums and stickball sticks, skills he learned from his father-in-law. He regularly worried that important tribal knowledge was being forgotten. He passed away on October 23, 1992.

Hubert Wesley

MASHULAVILLE / BOGUE CHITTO. BORN 1933.

Robert Hubert Wesley was born on July 21, 1933, in Philadelphia, Mississippi, to Cameron Wesley and Julia Bell Wesley, as one of five siblings including Barney Wesley. He grew up in Mashulaville with his family. At age nineteen, he left for college. For thirty-five years, he lived outside Mississippi, mostly in Alabama, during which time he said his Choctaw language skills got rusty. In 1954, he won $500 on the *Strike It Rich* game show, the equivalent of approximately $5,700 in 2023. His wife, Gara, was present for a 1993 interview conducted by Jack D. Elliott Jr. and Ken Carleton. He passed away on February 11, 2006.

Jay Wesley

STANDING PINE. BORN 1975.

Jay Wesley was born and raised in Standing Pine by his mother. However, intergenerational childcare was common, and when Jay's mother was at work, his grandparents watched him and many of his cousins. Meeting the YOP students, he introduced himself the traditional way, first in Choctaw, then in English: "Hello, my name's Jay Wesley. I'm from the Standing Pine community. My mother is Rita Frazier; my father is the late Danny Wesley." He then explained, "The reason for doing that is so that way, it's our ancestry, people would know who is who and then where you belong and if you get in trouble who they can tell!" Chores around the house were divided along gender lines, so he ended up with most of the heavy, outdoor work like chopping wood. As director of the Department of Chahta Immi, Jay oversees the programs that help ensure that traditional customs, arts, and folkways are maintained, celebrated, and passed on to future generations. He does this not by sitting behind a desk, but by going out and participating in these traditions both at home and on the reservation, as well as by taking groups around the state to perform or present these traditions. He recognizes that culture is dynamic and embraces change, but he is also acutely aware of changes that he sees as an erosion of important community values that he works diligently to preserve. He and his wife have five daughters. One is a teaching assistant in Standing Pine; one recently graduated from Harvard; one recently graduated from Meridian Community College while caring for two young kids; one is a senior at the Mississippi School for Mathematics and Science (MSMS); and one, Jaeden, was one of the YOP students working on this project and a graduate of MSMS who is now attending UCLA.

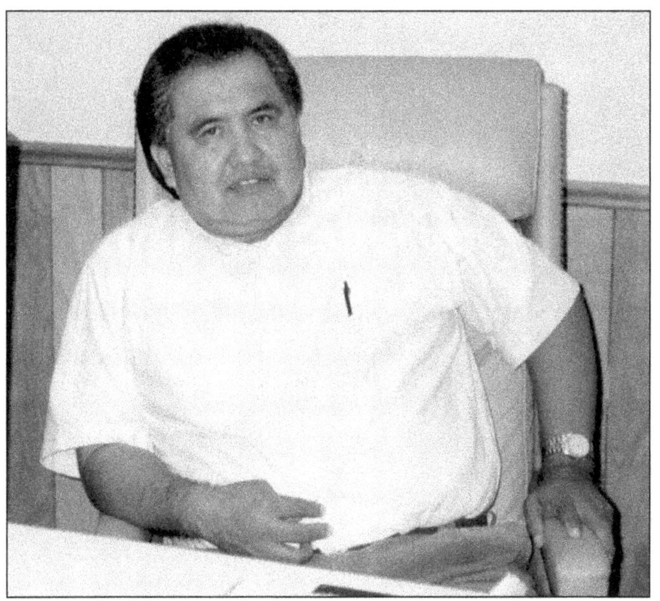

Henderson Williams

CONEHATTA. BORN 1947.

Henderson Williams was born in December 1947. In 1997, he was serving as the pastor of a church and had recently been appointed to be a judge for the Choctaw judicial system. Although he felt the old *shokhannǫpa* stories of Possum and Rabbit were important, he particularly valued historical stories, including ones from his own lifetime, such as the election of the first tribal chief, Calvin Isaac. A resident of Conehatta, he was also familiar with the stories people told of encountering spirits and creatures in the nearby woods.

Henry Williams

CONEHATTA. BORN 1945.

Henry Lee Williams was born in 1945 to Philmon Williams and Aline Steve Williams. He grew up one of sixteen children, playing stickball, hunting with rabbit sticks, and using pine knots as torches to see at night. He remembered sharecropping as hard work and having to walk to the mill to grind corn. His father told him farming was the only way to make a living, and Henry set out to prove him wrong. He joined the army and later served on the Tribal Council for four years. He worked at the Conehatta facility building as the tribe's recreation coordinator and served twenty-seven years as stickball commissioner, where he helped revise the stickball rules to help avoid serious injury. He built a sweat lodge in the backyard of his home, where he regularly hosted sweats. Always quick with a joke, Henry regularly teased acquaintances and colleagues as a sign of friendship. He passed away on September 25, 2011.

Linda Williams

STANDING PINE. BORN 1958.

Linda's father and his family are all from Conehatta, but her mother and her family are all from Standing Pine and Red Water. When her parents married, her father moved to Standing Pine, where they raised their family. Linda grew up surrounded by Choctaw medicine, music, sports, and stories. Her paternal grandmother was a midwife and knew herbal medicine; her father, Carter Williams, was a *chahta alikchi* who also worked at the Standing Pine facility building. Her father's mom's brother got a Purple Heart in World War II and often told her stories about Greenwood Leflore and Pushmataha and other famous Choctaw leaders. Linda grew up playing washers and softball and remembers attending the Choctaw Indian Fair years before they added the carnival rides, when people used to have to pack into buses like sardines to get a ride from the outlying communities to Pearl River to attend the fair and watch the stickball games. She grew up Baptist. Her father and her great-aunt Elsie regularly hosted Choctaw hymn singing in their home. Her grandmother was a storyteller, often entertaining them with *shokhannọpa* and scaring them with stories of *na losa chito*. Linda attended Standing Pine Elementary School, then moved into the dormitories at Choctaw Central High School for eighth grade and half of ninth until she moved back home to attend public school in Standing Pine, where she graduated. She went to college and then years later returned to get her master's degree in 2010. She has worked for the past four tribal chiefs and is currently the government services officer for the tribe and is also in charge of veterans' affairs.

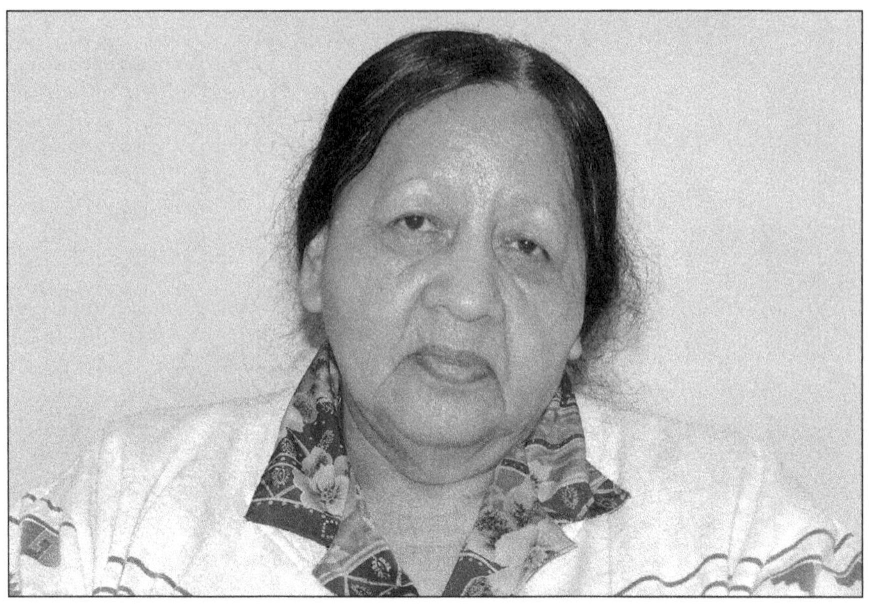

Ruth Williams

STANDING PINE. BORN 1936.

Ruth Sockey Williams was born on August 9, 1936, to Mike Sockey and Nephus Amos Sockey. She grew up in Standing Pine but moved to the Delta in 1961 for work. In the Delta, she often worked as a housekeeper for White families, where she learned English. Eventually, she met and married Carter Williams and had two daughters, Dinah and Linda Williams, the latter of whom is also featured in this book. She worked at Leake Memorial Hospital until she retired. Ruth passed away on January 29, 2023. Her obituary notes that "she was a member of Hopewell Baptist Church and enjoyed gardening, attending social gatherings, making friends, and talking to people."

Gladys Willis

PEARL RIVER. BORN 1926.

Gladys Mae Tubby Willis was born on June 5, 1926, in Pearl River, where she lived her entire life. She grew up without running water, working alongside her family in the fields picking cotton, hoeing the weeds, and picking peas. She attended Pearl River Day School, run by the Bureau of Indian Affairs, during the week and accompanied family and neighbors into the woods on weekends to go hunting and fishing. She learned to singe squirrel at an early age; squirrel would remain one of her favorite foods, even though it was harder and harder to come by as she got older, and squirrel and bird hunting became less common. She was justifiably afraid of snakes, something her grandchildren and great-grandchildren enjoyed exploiting, planting a rubber snake around the house for her to stumble across. "I think I had gone to get wood. I just went out there and noticed that thing, and I jumped again. I picked up the snake, rubber snake, tore it up and threw it into the trash. I'm not going to jump over it again!" she exclaimed, laughing. She and her husband, Claude Willis, had eleven children, including Hulon Willis, Caroline Morris, and Travis Willis, all featured in this book. She spent much of her adult life as a homemaker but became a cook for the Elderly Nutrition Program in 1980, where she worked for eight years before health issues forced her to retire. Gladys's home was always a busy one, with children, grandchildren, and great-grandchildren coming and going regularly, sometimes staying the afternoon, sometimes moving in for a year or more. Family dinners were common, with larger gatherings of thirty or forty people every few weeks. Gladys was never one to sit idle. As her eyesight failed, she moved from beadwork to crocheting blankets, something her hands could do on their own. She passed away far too soon on April 25, 1999, at the age of seventy-two and is buried in the family plot at Hope Baptist Church, where she attended throughout her life.

Linda Willis

CRYSTAL RIDGE. BORN 1953.

Linda Wesley Willis was born on August 8, 1953, the daughter of Fannie Wesley Tubby, the granddaughter of Chief Cameron Wesley. She grew up listening to the stories her grandfather told and shared them with her own grandchildren. In 1973, she was interviewed by *Nanih Waiya* magazine staff after she had been elected Choctaw Indian Princess (1973–1974). She remembers how nervous she was and how she couldn't believe she had won. In the late 1990s, she served as an associate judge, working in her community of Crystal Ridge. Chronic health problems eventually got the better of her, and she passed away at age forty-eight on July 20, 2002.

Russell James (R. J.) Willis

RED WATER / STANDING PINE. BORN 1940.

Russell James (R. J.) Willis was born on October 11, 1940, to Woodrow Wilson "L. E." Willis and Eather May Lewis Willis. His dad was a sharecropper who moved the family back and forth between Red Water and Standing Pine for work. He helped out in the fields, leaving little time for him to go to school. As he grew older, he wanted to learn English and worked with a teacher at Standing Pine Elementary School to enroll in the Sequoyah School, also known as Sequoyah-Tahlequah in Oklahoma. It was a lonely time, but R. J. eventually moved back home to Mississippi, where he married and got work in health education as both an advocate and translator. He passed away on November 28, 2002.

Travis Willis

PEARL RIVER. BORN 1958.

Travis Willis was born in Pearl River to Gladys Mae Willis and Claude Yates Willis, one of eleven children, including Caroline Morris and Hulon Willis. One of his main chores growing up was to feed the cows, which meant getting up at four o'clock in the morning and then heading off to school when he was done. On weekends, it was fishing and hunting. "Hunting, fishing, these things that people do for sports, we did that for food. There was a saying, 'What you kill is what you eat.'" Hunting and fishing trips included pitching washers and horseshoes. Back at home, it was basketball and stickball, though the latter caught up with him in 1982 when a player flipped him during a game, and five back surgeries later, he hung up his sticks for good. His home was a welcoming one. His son Kevin regularly brought two fellow classmates, Coushatta boys from out of state, home on weekends so they wouldn't have to stay in the dorms at Choctaw Central High School. Travis is a Baptist minister who has led a number of churches in the area and regularly offers prayers and eulogies for friends and community members. At a family wake, his brother Hulon Willis dropped him into a set joke, in classic *shokhannǫpa* style, of the preacher who asked who was ready to go home to the Lord. Everyone had their hand up except Travis. The preacher asked Travis whether he didn't want to go home to the Lord. "I do," he replied.

"Then why didn't you raise your hand?"

"Because my daddy said I needed to come home right after church, so I better go on and go."

Everyone laughed, Travis most of all. Travis's first wife was Navajo, and his children, grandchildren, and great-grandchildren are multiracial, spread out across the southern United States. He was the last family member to see his mother before she passed away, and he mourns the loss of the regular family dinners she hosted that kept his family so close.

Louise Wilson

BOGUE CHITTO. BORN 1950.

Louise Willis Wilson was born on September 10, 1950. Before Louise was born, her grandmother's husband passed away. As was sometimes the custom, his brother married his brother's widow, Louise's grandmother. That man was John Hunter Thompson, the grandfather Louise learned so much from growing up. In particular, he shared stories of the past and prophecies of the future, stories that have stayed with Louise and that she has shared with her own children and grandchildren. She also learned the many "no you don'ts"—customs and taboos guiding appropriate behavior.

Her family moved around when she was young as her father sought training and work, first to Ellisville, Mississippi, where her father was trained as a watchmaker, then to Cincinnati, Ohio, where he trained to make S&H Green Stamps. By the sixth grade, they had moved back to Bogue Chitto, where Louise returned to "Indian schools." She went to Haskell Indian Junior College and got married, but her husband died in a car accident, leaving her with two small children to raise. Growing up, she remembers her mother telling her to never look at a White man because if you do, they will come and catch you and take you away. She has served many roles for the tribe, including YOP director when research for *Choctaw Tales* and *Choctaw Prophecy* was being conducted and director of the Elderly Nutrition and Social Program when this book was first being conceived.

Baxter York

PEARL RIVER. BORN 1907.

Baxter York was born on May 24, 1907, to John York and Necey Phillips York. According to Bill Brescia, his mother ensured that he and his brother, Emmett, received an education. As children, they attended the first Choctaw school in Leake County, yet later, their mother would mourn their departure to the Chilocco Indian School run by the BIA in Oklahoma. Baxter was a member of the first temporary Tribal Council set up in Mississippi after removal along with Simpson Tubby, another storyteller in this collection. He helped develop the constitution and bylaws that were adopted in 1945, establishing the Mississippi Band of Choctaw Indians as a self-governing nation. His brother was eventually elected the first tribal chairman and trained Chief Phillip Martin for the position he held for twenty-eight years. He was interviewed twice for the *Nanih Waiya* magazine, once about politics, and the other about culture. Two of his children, Jake York and Kennith York, appear in this book. He passed away on October 27, 1975.

Jake York

PEARL RIVER / CONEHATTA. BORN 1950.

John Walter "Jake" York was born on February 22, 1950, to Baxter York and Grace Sam York. One of ten children, he grew up in a family where education, politics, civic engagement, and tradition were highly valued. Jake carried on Choctaw traditions first through stickball, becoming known throughout the community as one of the best players of his time. Later, he became well known for his stories and his efforts to preserve the Choctaw language. Jake worked at a bilingual-education summer camp to help children maintain the Choctaw language. During camp, he was able to share the other tradition in which he excelled: storytelling. Tall tales were his specialty, but he also shared the origin stories, the old legends, and the animal tales that had been passed down through the generations and that he adapted and created anew. He passed away on December 14, 2014.

CHAPTER 1

THE LAND

SHARECROPPING

"They planted cotton and corn for the Whites," remembers Esbie Gibson. "Whatever the cotton is worth, the White man and the Choctaw would both get half each. If it's corn, they get half each." But she adds that they had to also have their own garden in order to feed themselves. "They planted peas, potatoes, peanuts, and they have a garden, pig, and cow, and they don't have to buy milk, meat, and lard when they kill a pig" (1982). Gladys Willis describes winter as being particularly difficult in terms of food:

> We didn't have that much food except what was grown in the field. In the winter, we had dry peas, corn. They used to make hominy. They had a pasture of collard greens. So in the winter that was mainly the food.
>
> And they used to put up hogs for meat. And lard—that was where it came from. They used to kill two hogs. One early in the fall, and one about February, January; they'd kill another one so they could have lard. Not much. They don't buy much throughout the summer. They didn't have no refrigerator, so they didn't have ways of keeping meat. So they would hang it up. They used to have a place called a "smoke house"; they would hang their meats up there. (May 23, 1996)

As lands were taken from the Mississippi Choctaw during the nineteenth and twentieth centuries, the independence of family farming and hunting that served as the primary form of work for families shifted to the dependence on working for White landowners. Just as legislation that promised forty acres and a mule to newly freed Black men was reneged upon almost as soon as it was passed, so too were treaties that promised 460 acres acres to each male Choctaw head of household.[1] With no land of their own, Black and Choctaw families were forced to accept contract labor offered by White landowners that became collectively known as sharecropping, named for the common provision of paying landowners back with a share, typically 30 to 50 percent of their crops. While some families were able to find farms to work nearby, others had to move to the fertile soil of the Mississippi Delta either for the season or until they could move back home.

While some sharecroppers treated their workers fairly, stories abound of physical abuse, exploitation, unpaid wages, and unfair labor practices that resulted in de facto indentured servitude. The result was a push-and-pull tension with landowners trapping their tenants on their land for years of virtually free labor on the one hand, and on the other, forcing tenants out after stripping them of their crops in order to make way for new sharecroppers or to shift to mechanization.[2] Either way, the Choctaw found themselves as pawns with little recourse other than sneaking away in the middle of the night in search of better conditions.

Beginning in the 1920s but not widely available after the 1940s was the opportunity to move onto reservation land and once again gain some independence in their work. However, the poverty rate was high, and by the 1950s, the General Employment Assistance Program began relocating Choctaw families to one of eight major cities scattered across the United States for work.[3] The program was well intentioned from a wage-labor model but served once again to drive the Mississippi Choctaw from their homelands just as the removals to Oklahoma had done in the previous century and the boarding-school system was continuing to do during this period.[4] Many families moved back to Mississippi as soon as they could, finding the severing of cultural, social, and familial ties not worth the possible financial gains.

OLD ENOUGH TO PLOW

BOBBY JOE, B. 1953—BOGUE CHITTO
TOLD ON JANUARY 6, 2000

I remember when I was a little one. And my father, he did sharecropping and planted cotton and corn. And that's what I was, growing up. And when I got to about eleven years old, my father was still doing it the old-fashioned way; he was following with the mule by himself on fifteen acres of corn and cotton.

And my mother, she gave me an ice water jug. She told me, said, "I want you take to take this water to your father. He probably done got thirsty about now." It was about nine thirty, ten o'clock.

She wrapped it up with some kind of sheets for the jug so the water can be still cold. And I tote it over there. And when I left my father, I feel sorry for him, working all by himself that fifteen acres of corn. And I walked over there, and he stopped. He was taking a drink of ice water. And I looked around, and I told my dad, I said, "If you show me how to work," I said, "I'll help you."

And he said, "Well, you still too little yet."

And I said, "But look like you needed help. You all by yourself."

"Well, it is a big field." He said, "I'll think about it."

After next morning when he got up, my mother fixed breakfast. And he eat. And he woke me up, and he said, "Well, you want to eat?"

I said, "This, yeah."

So he said, "Go ahead and eat. I'm going to go out there to the barn, and I'm going to catch an extra mule."

He said, "You run out there when you finish eating and you start walking."

And just as soon as I got through eating, and I was ready, I run out to the barn, and he catched two mules, put the bridles on it, and he fixed a plow. And he said, "You go out there to the cotton field and start plowing. Just as soon as I get through with the corn, I'll come out there and join you."

And he took mules and plows, and I go with him. And we got out there. He said, "This is how you do it," you know, show me, just like you're driving a car. And he plowed for maybe about ten yards, and he stopped.

He told me, "Now grab this plow handle."

And I started. And he said, "This is how you do it. This plow is going this way. So you need to put this sideways, just a little bit like that. Don't push it too much, just ease it down like that and the plow is going to go for you. If you be doing this sideways too much you're going to cut too much and just go to the other side."

And I done it. I pushed it too much.

And he stopped it and said, "This is how you got to do it. I won't tell you again; you can't just push it down real quick. Just like that; just turn the other way it just cut the other row."

So you got to do it. You got to have a lot of patience to do that.

Once I got started, I mean I picked it up just like that. And when I started, and I just ease it along just like that, and the plow just goes straight. And I said, "Well, this is how to do it." And that was it.

After that, that's what we do. And just like I say, wasn't enough money. We get money at once a year.

NO REST FOR THE WEARY

LINDA WILLIS, B. 1953—CRYSTAL RIDGE
TOLD ON JANUARY 7, 2000

By the time I was nine years old, I had lived with my aunt with my grandfather, so we moved away from there. My aunt decided to get married again and moved to the reservation. So then, I knew who my mother was, so I decided to live with my mother.

That first year, I babysit my brothers and sisters. But the following year, I had to go to the fields.

My dad would get me up at four o'clock in the morning to cook breakfast since I was the oldest. I would cook breakfast and have it on the table by five thirty so we can eat breakfast and get out to the fields by six o'clock. And then by eleven o'clock, Mom would say, "Go cook a lunch." And then I had to run to the house, cook lunch, and had to have it on the table by twelve o'clock. They'd come in, wash up, and eat their lunch, and then we'd head back out to the fields.

By six o'clock, "Go on home. Cook supper." Have supper on the table by the time they get in the house. We have supper, and we clean the dishes and then head for bed. It was like that. Same thing over and over for six days. On the seventh day, we would do that wash. That was on Sunday. I would be washing while they would go fishing. And that was our meat for the day on Sunday, was fish. They had to go fishing. We were living close to Nanih Waiya, and they had to walk to the cave, Nanih Waiya Cave. I guess it was pretty far; we never did go with them, my brother, to fish. We never went with them, but I guess it was a pretty far walk.

FIFTY CENTS A DAY

DOLPHUS HENRY, B. 1919—BOGUE CHITTO
TOLD IN 1985

I grew up in a family that was a tenant sharecropper. We used to go out and pick cotton for fifty cents a hundred [pounds]. I used to go out and chop cotton for twenty-five cents or fifty cents a day. And I used to chase the cows about three hours for a dime.

So, that's how much the life has been changed as of this day that I'm proud of it, that I'm Choctaw.

EVERYBODY WORKED

GORDON SAM, B. 1959—STANDING PINE
TOLD ON JULY 6, 2021

Just starting out, I might've been about like seven, eight years old. I lived right at the end of the sharecropping years. At that time, everybody worked. When you have adults working in the field, us youngsters would take care of chores. We had chores. It was our contribution to the family.

Of course, summertime, like probably the main crops that my uncles would plant would be corn and cotton. In those days, once the cotton would start growing, then rest of the family like my aunts and some neighbors would come together, go out to the field, and what they called "chopping cotton." If there was too many in one area, you would clear and put more dirt on the roots of it so it would grow higher.

I remember seeing that. I must've been about maybe seven, eight years old at the time, but I remember. Of course, at the end of the day, everybody got paid.

Then once it blooms and it's ready to be harvested; then cotton picking came in.

My family was always around that area where we lived. The homeowners and the landowners provided jobs for them. Of course, at that time, we're a tight-knit family, and we would have houses close by to each other that we all worked.

That's the part I remember.

And us kids, I remember we actually had a lot of chores. One of our responsibilities was we planted gardens. That was another part that we contributed to our family. Of course, we got stuck with picking corn or peas or whatnot. And we had an oldest aunt that was kind of like the chef of the family. She stayed back and watched us, tell us what needs to be done, and cook for the family. It was a lot of work, but hard work never hurts anybody. I've always heard that hard work builds character.

A lot of guys my age that came from the farm; they know what work is. And a lot of us had an opportunity to . . . We still had schooling, and a lot of us are educated. A lot of us still do a lot of gardening here and there, but it's something that we never forgot where we came from.

In the wintertime, when the harvest season was over, my folks, of course we lived on a farm, so there was a dairy farm there that they went and worked. It was owned by the same people. They went and milked cows first before they actually went to the field, and after they get out of the field, they went and milked cows again. When the harvest season was over—and that was pretty much full time—they was milking Jersey cows.

Also remember that us kids, like I said, we had chores. And one thing I remember, it was kind of hard work for us, but we enjoyed it, especially when they say, "If you churn milk, when you all get through you can have ice cream." You still have to churn that one, too, a little, but churning milk, there's three parts to it. As you churn, I don't know how long it takes, I can't remember, it depends on how fast you do it, I guess, but I remember that as you churn there's this white stuff that would come up. It was called cottage cheese. And as you keep going, the milk would get a little thicker; then you would have buttermilk. As you keep going and it really gets thick, who can tell me what that is? The last one, what do you think that would be? [*directed to the YOP students*]

Taylor Ben: Butter.

Butter.

That was the life of the farm. But like I said, you had to wait.

ONE OF THE FAMILY

LORENA ALEX, B. 1952—HALLS, TN / BOGUE CHITTO / PEARL RIVER TOLD ON JUNE 10, 2021

When I was about twelve years old, we moved to Tennessee. My dad was a farmer. He drove a tractor, plowed the field, corn, cotton, soybeans. That's what he did for a living, and we lived in a frame house. We lived on this White man's land. His name was Beasley Robinson. I'll never forget him. He was a real tall man. He smoked cigars all the time. I never did like cigars. Anyway, he was nice to us. He was like one of the family, and he was real nice. We lived on his land and worked on his land, too, like chopped cotton, picked cotton, pulled cotton, pulled grass. We picked strawberries and tomatoes—that's to earn the money for us to eat, buy clothes, or whatever since daddy was just a farmer, and mama was just a housewife.

FRIDAY TREATS

LORENA ALEX, B. 1952—HALLS, TN / BOGUE CHITTO / PEARL RIVER TOLD ON JUNE 10, 2021

I remember one time, too, where Dad was working somewhere else, and there was me and my two sisters and Mom. We were out picking cotton, and every Friday, he'd never miss; we were always looking for Friday.

Friday afternoon, we had to walk from the house to the field where we had to pick cotton. It was about a mile, but this man would come in a truck. I remember it was a black truck, and there was oranges, apples, sweet potatoes, coconut, and some candies. We had to save money now in order to get what we want, so mom used to have some few monies so if he would drive all the way to the field where we were at, we'd get some of those.

And I thought that was something special. I remember that, and I'll never forget that.

ABUSIVE LANDOWNERS

LINDA WILLIS, B. 1953—CRYSTAL RIDGE
TOLD ON JANUARY 7, 2000

My grandfather Cameron Wesley used to work hard. I lived with him for several years. He worked hard 'til he was old.

I remember a White man just beat him to death, but he would get up and just go.

He was a sharecropper. This old White man would just beat him up. But he's got to keep working with him, so . . .

I guess the White man was just real mean.

MOVING IN THE MIDDLE OF THE NIGHT

HUBERT WESLEY, B. 1933—MASHULAVILLE / BOGUE CHITTO
TOLD ON DECEMBER 18, 1992

We were living towards Gholson [Texas], on the other side of Gholson somewhere back that way when I was born. And we lived there until, after so many years, we moved in this area.

But when we left from over there, back in that time, Choctaw people were sharecropping, and lot of landowners didn't like the Choctaw to move off and move on to somebody else's place. And lot of times they had to move at nighttime.

So, a group of families got together, and they moved, late in the afternoon when we left. I remember that it was late in the afternoon. And we travel from the other side of Gholson, all the way back in that swamp somewhere, at nighttime.

Late in the afternoon, we would camp out somewhere in the woods back there. The men would get out and hunt, and the women would get out and fish, and they all get game together. And we have supper and things like that. After, early in the morning, the men would go out and get us some more squirrel and rabbit, and we would eat breakfast, and we would move on until finally we got to [Mashulaville].

I was like maybe somewhere around seven years old, I guess, and we would camp out like that every night. And I don't know how long it took us. I don't remember all that much, but we did camp out several nights. And finally, we got close to Mashulaville. My dad was chief of the tribe, small tribe. He was the leader. Five men come with him over here, and they went 'round this area to find out the landowners, who they were, and find out if they wanted any sharecroppers. So they find some houses over here. We're first about eight-tenths of a mile here where we moved in, several of them right in this area. But altogether it amount up to twenty-five families.

CHEATED INTO DEBT

BARNEY WESLEY, B. 1927—MASHULAVILLE / BOGUE CHITTO
TOLD IN FEBRUARY 1982

Choctaws should have their garden. But long time ago, the Whites wanted them to work in their fields, and that is where they worked and weren't able to do their own gardening. A few had gardens. They used to plant something about two rows, and then they eat off that, and that is how they made their living.

That is how they made their living, but they got into a big debt. When they were farming, they [White landowners] did what they weren't supposed to do. They didn't do that to me. They used to charge the people [Choctaws]. Even the Choctaws moved and lived elsewhere, and then they moved them back to work for them.

When they did work in the fields for them, and then when they decided to move again, they [White landowners] charged them with so much interest. And the other person that they're going to move to their land to work for them, then the other party pays the bill. They stay there for about a year, and they don't like that place after the bill was paid, but bills were charged back and forth as the people moved. That wasn't supposed to happen, but it did since they were Choctaws.

They planted corn and cotton, and no matter how much they grew, they [White landowners] used to get all of it, put it into their barns and didn't let the Choctaws have some of the corn or cotton. They didn't want the Choctaws to come back and live there, so they took all the houses away where the Choctaws used to live.

CHEATED

MELVIN HENRY, B. 1911—BOGUE CHITTO
TOLD IN FEBRUARY 1982

An old man told us that when the Choctaws went to Oklahoma, the Whites from the East wanted to kill all the Choctaws and then send all of them to Oklahoma.

They went to Oklahoma, and the place was awful, and some of them came back, moved back here. And some of them stayed there.

Some of them started coming back, and the others went to meet them to help them move back. And they said, "It's a terrible place, so we are going back to where we lived before."

Grandfather used to stay close to Stallo [Mississippi], and he was going to move there to Oklahoma after he sold his land, but somebody, I think it was Mosley Morris, went to Oklahoma and came back, said the place was not a very good place to stay. And they didn't go.

Old man used to work for this White man, and my grandfather's daughter married him. He said it will be alright if you all don't go. You can buy the land here and stay here and help him. So they bought the land, and we didn't go to Oklahoma. Some of them already packed their stuff in the wagon, but he came and saw them and didn't want them to go, so they stayed.

One of them people in Oklahoma now living a better life now; everything turned out to be better for them. They went and agreed upon each other, and here they didn't. And somebody came back visiting their relatives, and when the Choctaws made good crop of corn or picking cotton, if they make a good crop, it was known that the White people would take their crop, accusing them they don't know how to plant or can't work and would take everything away from them by making them move by hitting them with something, lock the door, and let them stay out, knowing they will take the crop away from them.

When winter comes, some of them would cut shrubs, dig the riverside, and another White man would come by and said, "I won't treat you the way he did." And they would go work for them, and he would be the same person who takes the crop away from them. They didn't know how to speak English and count, so they didn't know that White man was cheating them.

CATCHING A CHEATER

BRADLEY ALEX, B. 1955—BOGUE HOMA / PEARL RIVER
TOLD ON JUNE 30, 2021

My father had a third-grade education. So did my mother. He was good with the mathematics too.

That's one thing: he caught this guy cheating while they were picking cotton. And the guy that was doing the weigh-in. He [my father] was looking at how much it cost, the weight, how much it's supposed to be that they're supposed to be paying. And the guy was cheating everybody.

He [my father] told the owner when he came, and he fired him [the cheater]. They put my father in that position during that harvest, and he worked for them for a little while.

LANDLORD'S SON

HAYWARD BELL, B. 1948—BOGUE CHITTO
TOLD ON JUNE 30, 2021

Going back to the sharecropping. They had family too, just like we had family, that worked in the field. And there was a boy, I think he might've been a little bit older than me, but he used to go out in the field just like I did. But of course, kids will be kids. We used to fight. He said some things to me I didn't like, and I would get back at him and not just in talking ways but other ways, you know? And we both got a whipping from our parents, but I didn't like that, probably, when he's saying things about Choctaws to me.

Tom Mould: Oh, he was a non-Choctaw kid.

Yeah. They were the landowner family that had the land that we lived on, tribal people lived on. But we both still had to work in the field, that sharecropper landowner and Choctaw.

He would say, "Choctaws are dumb," type of thing. "Drunkard."

And I didn't see that, you know? I didn't see that in my dad. And so it made me mad. But I also saw his older brother get drunk. I said, "Well, your brother's a drunk. Is he a Choctaw?" That type of thing, you know? But I don't know, it could be just me, but those type of things stood out in my life that I wanted to show the difference, and if we can do things the Choctaw way and prove to non-Choctaw that we're just as good, it could be nice.

THE ORIGIN OF CHOCTAW IN HENNING

CUBERT BELL, B. 1946—HENNING, TN
TOLD IN 2016

I was probably the only the Choctaw child here [in Henning] at that time. There is another family that was here, but the young man was a little older. They're Abel and Emma Anderson, and Leon Thomas was here first, probably. Came in 1951 is what I understood.

What had happened with that was that the landowner liked the work that Mr. Anderson and his family were doing and asked him if he had any relatives that would like to move here. And if they would, Mr. Abel and the landowner would take the truck there and bring them back over here. So that's how we wound up over here.

And consequently, as the farming season started, they made a trip to Mississippi quite a few times because when my grandmother and them moved here, she talked to her children to move here as well. So we had my grandmother's children's sons, particularly, moved here to do farm work, sharecropping, and all that stuff to go with it. So we had abundance of family almost together.

MOVED TO THE DELTA FOR WORK

TERRY BEN, B. 1957—STANDING PINE
TOLD ON JUNE 10, 2021

A lot of Choctaws during the nineteen hundreds moved away from here because there was no jobs, because of other social issues like segregation, all that. There were no jobs here—Leake County or Neshoba County. So they moved to the Delta, where the land is fertile around Greenwood, Mississippi, Greenville area. There are lots of Choctaws grew up there.

DANGEROUS WALK TO WORK

SUSIE COMBY ALEX, B. 1947—STANDING PINE / PEARL RIVER
TOLD ON JUNE 9, 2021

When we were growing up, my parents were what they call "sharecroppers." So we had to go even to the Delta to pick cotton, or they would hoe the cotton or whatever.

My brother was walking too close to the road, and my mom kept telling him, says, "You need to get off the road."

We were on the side, a little bit farther from the highway, but he said, "Well, there's room for me to walk."

Eighteen-wheeler hit him and took his leg.

So he's a paralytic, and he has problems with that. And his wife used to do a lot for him, but she passed away with this COVID.

MOVING TO RESERVATION LAND

FRANK HENRY, B. 1927—BOGUE CHITTO / TUCKER
TOLD ON JULY 23, 1997

I recall just a little bit the hard times that we had. My parents, my grandpa and my daddy, they were sharecroppers at one time. And as soon as the government allotted forty acres of land and a house on it, they moved into Bogue Chitto community.

A BRICK HOUSE

FRANK BELL JOE, B. 1951—BOGUE CHITTO
TOLD ON APRIL 16, 1975

We picked cotton with our own hands. And so we'd plant some corn, harvest it. We raised some hogs; we had two cows, and I guess the time we were living there, we thought we had it made.

So, I guess living in a brick house and living on the reservation is something I'm very proud of.

Right then when we were living on the landlord's [land], we used to get up early in the morning, being called up in the house to go after some cows, and this was about four or five in the morning. That's the thing that I didn't like.

But now whenever you want to do something other than getting ready to go out and work, you don't have to; you can take your time going out.

GETTING OUT OF THE COTTON FIELDS

HENRY WILLIAMS, B. 1945—CONEHATTA
TOLD ON JUNE 24, 1997

Before, people go to work in cotton field. Usually, cotton field, everybody goes. And they stay over there all day. Come home. But they had a good time. Even that, they tell stories when they get a chance.

People working, hard times. But they still enjoy it. It don't seem hard to them, back then. It was earning to buy groceries. It didn't seem to be hard work for them. They laugh about it. Even hot, sunny day. They didn't cry about it. They enjoyed it.

When I look back, my feet still burning. [*laughter*] I used to be in cotton fields barefooted.

I don't know if this guy [referring to YOP student Lionel "J. J." Dan sitting with me] ever pick cotton, but cotton stalk sometimes about this tall [*indicates about three feet*]. Sometimes little higher, but shorter ones used to be a problem for me. You have to bend low, and your back becomes pained. And I used to get on my knees to pick them cottons and put them in my sack behind me.

I used to think about if I was ever going to get out of that cotton field. Because my daddy trained me how to grow cotton, how to plow cotton, how farm works, how to put gear on the horses and mules. Keep me out of school. He didn't have no vision. He tells me that's my lifetime's work. I'm never going to get out of cotton field as long as I live. So he teached me how to do farm work. but I got smart. I joined the army. [*laughter*]

CHICKEN CATCHING, SHARECROPPING, OR THE ARMY

BRIAN BILLIE, B. 1973—RED WATER
TOLD ON JUNE 30, 2021

My father said back then either it was chicken catching or sharecropping, and he did the sharecropping. He didn't want to be doing the sharecropping, and he had got tired of catching chickens. But he had to save money because they weren't hardly money around. But when he came back from the military, he said he had enough money to buy a car, send money back home to help family, his mom.

He would have dreams, and he would talk about his dreams. It bothered him, but talking about it helped him out too, though. He told me some people had it worse, that they can't shut off the dream.

LIMITED OPTIONS

HAROLD COMBY, B. 1955—PEARL RIVER
TOLD ON JUNE 1, 2021

We did sharecropping. Back then there was social services available, but it wasn't like a lot of handouts. We didn't have distribution, and most of the time jobs were not available. Probably the only jobs available, good jobs, were with the federal government and schools. So that's where my dad worked.

One other thing was that a lot of Choctaws hauled pulpwood or short logs. And then later on, when the chicken houses started coming into play, a lot of Choctaws cut chicken. I tried it one summer, and it's hard work. Your hands get so large and so numb that you can barely move it after work. So I learned my lesson, and I went to college!

REMEMBERING OUR PAST

RAE NELL VAUGHN, B. 1964—PEARL RIVER
TOLD ON APRIL 22, 2020

I can remember being with my grandmother out in the cotton fields. Not very long—not as long as my mom and my other aunts—but I remember those things. I can remember being at my grandmother's house and no running water. I remember when she got a TV. I remember when she got a phone, a TV, little black TV with bunny ears and aluminum foil on the antenna. I remember lining up to go to the outhouse. I remember pumping water from a well. I remember her living on a dirt road. I can remember also her getting her first brick home, FHA [Federal Housing Administration] home.

As people, we want our next generation to do better, but as a tribe we also want to make sure that we remember who we are. Remember our language. Remember our customs and our culture. Those are the most important things.

FARMING AND GARDENING

Money was hard to come by and ran out quickly, but small-scale farming and home gardening helped ensure there was always food to eat. The work was hard and shared by all, male and female, young and old. The big fields were for cash crops; the small plots were for the family table. Although the work was for the benefit of the group, people tell stories of getting to keep the small sums they made as children to spend on candy and other small treats.

All farmers and gardeners know that rain makes or breaks a crop. Too little rain, and the crops wither; too much rain, and they rot. Either one spells disaster, which explains the many taboos and rituals both for predicting and bringing rain, as well as avoiding it. Before weather forecasters and monthly calendars, people also paid close attention to nature to know when to plant and when to harvest.

Keeping chickens, hogs, and cows was also an important part of feeding one's family. Kids grew up learning to milk a cow and snap the neck of a chicken with just a quick twist of the wrist for those special fried chicken dinners. Cold weather signaled hog killing time, when it was cold enough to cure a hog for later use.[5] The size of the hog and the amount of work needed to butcher one typically meant it was a communal affair, with families and neighbors gathering to help each other with the process. "The fall time of the year, when it was pig killing time, a neighbor might invite him to come on over," explained Terry Ben in 1996. "'Hey, help me out.' Kill a couple hogs and all that. Go up there, and after that, the neighbor would give him a big slice of ham or whatever. So that's the way it was primarily as far as getting along with everybody and as far as trying to get a little extra food on the table."

Home gardens continue to be maintained by some, but they are becoming rarer. The wage economy has replaced self-sufficiency and bartering, and canned vegetables are easily available and affordable. But Rosalee Steve offers yet another explanation. In the past, "it was easy for us because we can go out in our backyard, dig a hole and plant a seed, and then we have some to give us to eat. But now it seems that the ground is getting old. Our vegetables and things won't hardly grow like it used to be" (Weill, Williams, and Ferguson 1985). Prophecies support her diagnosis. Bobby Joe remembers his father and grandfather warning him that when the end of time is close, the plants will no longer grow.

> And they told me, said, "Even though you'll want to plant a little garden somewhere in the back of your house, somewhere, keep watching it." Said, "The things you planted, it's not hardly going to grow anymore. You ain't hardly going to make corn anymore. You ain't hardly going to get rain anymore and put that water in that plant. And, someday, you're going to learn some more. If you plant it, it maybe won't nothing won't come up anymore." They say then you be know when the time is getting close. (January 6, 2000)

Louise Wilson heard similar prophecies from her grandfather about the land getting old and crops no longer growing. Regina Shoemake heard prophecies that the farmland will disappear, and people will starve. Linda Willis heard prophecies that the forests will disappear, and there will be no more animals to hunt.[6] On the one hand, the worldview portrayed in these prophecies suggests that a land that cannot sustain its people cannot sustain itself, a dire view of the future. On the other hand, this worldview is built on the premise that the land typically *does* provide, not just from the earth through farming, but in the woods through hunting and gathering, and the rivers through fishing.

PREDICTING RAIN

JACKSON ISAAC, B. 1902—PEARL RIVER
TOLD IN FEBRUARY 1982

My daddy was a . . . My grandpa was a prophet, but Daddy was known. They live over yonder.

But time was a dry year and no rain. Two Whites come into my daddy's house, and he called Uncle Wilson and said, "When is it going to rain?"

And he hold his head down to the ground and said, "It is going to rain Saturday, Sunday. And it will rain about four or five days."

Then those two fellows said, "Alright." They reached down the pocket, both of them, and gave him ten dollars apiece.

And Saturday it started raining all day, Sunday all day, and five days now, it brings flood, covered all the ground.

And ever since then, all the White people ask, "When is it going to rain?"

RAINMAKERS

MARK PATRICK, B. 1969—O̱TOKLO (CONEHATTA)
TOLD ON JULY 7, 2021

Y'all know about the snapping turtle? It'll bring rain in the storms; snapping turtle would bring rain in the storm.

Of course, people eat snapping turtles, but if you see one, you just let him go because if you harass one or whatever, and you make them mad enough, it'll be a storm within minutes. Within minutes.

And one time we all got a whupping because we had whopped, not really whopped, but a big snapping turtle . . . We found one about this big [*indicates about a foot*], and we got some limbs or sticks or whatever, and we started beating the shell. Of course, we didn't hurt him.

And we came home, and we told my grandmother about it. Oh gosh, we got a whupping because she said, "Whenever you do that," she said, "man, there'll be a storm." She said, "One time it almost took the roof of our house off," is what she told me. She was dead serious when she told us that, too. She said, "You don't ever mess with a turtle like that."

That's why I was telling somebody on Facebook, I said, "I think somebody flipped a turtle over." It was the reason we're getting all this rain. So that was another belief. You flip a turtle over, or you harass a turtle, the rain and the storm.

Or if you take a dead snake, and you hang it on the fence post, it'll rain.

If you take a cow skull that you find out in the pasture, and you extend it straight up towards the sky, it'll bring rain.

I tried it one time. I think I stood it up, boom, just to see if it was going to rain. I can't remember if it rained or not. So that's why when older people tell us something, they would just tell us with such a straight face. And a lot of it is true, but a lot of it, you're just like, "Is that really going to bring rain?" Because first they teach you about God and tell you that God is responsible for everything. He's the one that brings rain. Not because you do a rain dance or because you flipped over a turtle or whatever. And then on the other hand, the same ones that tells you all about God and how He's responsible for the rain and stuff, then they tell you stuff like this. You're like, "Okay, you're really confusing me now."

And so a lot of the things that they would say, you would be like, "Hmm, I wonder if they're telling the truth." Just like they say, "Oh, it's fixing to rain. Man, my knee is aching, or my back is aching. It's fixing to storm." And we would just laugh because it's like, "Okay, you told me about this, and you told me about that, and now you're saying your knee hurts because it's going to rain. What has rain got to do with your knee hurting now?"

They *were* telling the truth because I hurt! [*laugh*]

SIGNS OF RAIN

EDDIE JOHNSON, B. 1970—STANDING PINE / TUCKER
TOLD ON JUNE 11, 2021

You can tell it's going to rain when the dogs and cats prepare. Usually, they eat grass and regurgitate. Why? I don't know, but it does happen. You see a dog eating grass, *ombachi̱h* [it's going to rain]. It does happen.

GOOD FRIDAY

TERRY BEN, B. 1957—STANDING PINE
TOLD ON JUNE 10, 2021

Granddaddy used to make it a point to plant a lot of things on Good Friday because he said the crops would grow better and yield better fruit. He planted before Good Friday. He planted after Good Friday. But whatever he could, certain things, he tried to plant it *on* Good Friday. In particular, the morning or, if nothing else, sometime during the day. He made it a point to work hard that day.

I don't know the reason, but he always told me that, from his point of view, that the crops turned out better and more fruit. The corncobs were longer, peas longer, more peas, and that type of thing because it was Good Friday. Of course, there's a religious connotation to that Good Friday.

MAPLE TREES SIGNAL SPRING

EDDIE JOHNSON, B. 1970—STANDING PINE / TUCKER
TOLD ON JUNE 11, 2021

There's one thing I heard. This was an older lady that told me back in Standing Pine back when she was still alive. She used to say Choctaws used to watch the seasons closely. They don't as much anymore, [instead] depending on the weatherman.

The thing about the seasons, a lot of times it'd be observations of trees and plants and how they grow. One of the things they would say, I remember, was, "The maple tree will be the sign spring is here." And they'd say, "Chokcho bikoblit hikit iyah toffapit alah." "The maple tree is starting to shoot forth buds; spring is here." So you watch for the maple. The maple tree would be red at the tips when they bust out at springtime. That was one of the sayings.

GARDEN OR STARVE

MELVIN HENRY, B. 1911—BOGUE CHITTO
TOLD IN FEBRUARY 1982

"Someday you might be worth something, in the future," he told me. So they told us to work; that is what they used to tell us.

They told them [the women] to do the same.

Like one day, you will be all by yourself, and if no one can work for you, you will work for yourself. And they try to teach us everything they could teach us, like plowing the field. Where the food will come from, and in stores, it takes money. And when the money runs out, you will go hungry. And you will think where the money will come from for food.

But if you planted something in the field, the food will be there to eat.

Most people grew up from pure lard and planting potatoes, and he enjoys eating it.

Plant peanuts for a few rows, and when it's time to eat them, he boils the peanuts and eat. In stores, if you going to buy food from the store, and then there is no money, you will go hungry, he used to tell us. And that is what we learned; so we plant our food in the field.

THE VALUE OF MONEY

EDDIE GIBSON, B. 1953—CONEHATTA
TOLD ON JULY 1, 2021

In his early years, my father sharecropped. I think it was from all that hard work that they did, and they instilled it on us. There are times when I didn't quite agree with everything they did, but that's being young.

One thing he did for us three boys—me, Wayne, and Ronnie—was that he gave us like five or six rows of cucumbers each. And back then, the cucumbers was a big thing.

He said, "This is yours, yours, and yours. You take care of it. You hoe it, get the grass out, and take care of it. Pick it, and we're going to take it to Newton. Sell it, and you keep the money."

So that's how he taught us early in life to take care of things, to do things, to earn your money.

GROWING UP ON A FARM

LOUISE WILSON, B. 1950—BOGUE CHITTO
TOLD ON JUNE 10, 1997

Growing up on a farm with my grandparents, they were hard workers, so therefore they made us work hard because my grandfather believed that if you keep kids . . . Now I'll tell you, there was twelve grandkids living with them in a four-room house. So he believed if you were kept busy that you would stay out of trouble.

So he kept us busy on the farm. We had cows to milk. We had a little dairy thing where we sold the milk and stuff like that. Plus, we had a big garden because there was no monies to buy groceries, so we had to garden. So we would can or freeze the food and things like that. We also had hogs to help get meat to the home and things like that.

And we had cotton; we grew cotton and corn besides the vegetable garden. So we were all kept busy, one thing or another. We took turns cooking, cleaning, on the farm. So we stayed busy.

But when there were times when we was through with daily activities or the daily tasks that we had, and it was usually late in the afternoon, and he would take time to sit down after eating supper or something like that, we would be sitting down and just talking about the tasks and stuff. And there would be a time when he would start telling some things of long ago. Both he and my grandmother. And that was the time we had storytelling. I wish I could remember most of it, but I can't. But the ones that I do remember just kind of stuck in my mind.

GROWING ONE'S OWN FOOD

EVALINE DAVIS, B. 1945—CONEHATTA / TUCKER
TOLD JUNE 3, 2021

Well, as I was old enough to know, my grandpa and my mama, they was a farmer. Their last name was Farmer. But, they were farmers too! [*laugh*] Planting.

Well, my grandpa used to plant corn, peas, potato. He used to have a big patch. But Mama used to have a small garden there on the side of the house. And when they get everything grown, when it grows up, Mama used to can them. She used to put them in a jar. Tomatoes, peas, beans, or whatever.

And then when Grandpa had a big old patch of corn, they used to pull that corn and put them in . . . I call it a shack. Whenever we needed cornmeal, of course, we didn't have money to buy flour much because we didn't have no money back then, and mostly they do was that they have to farm. They have to grow some stuff. Vegetables and all of that.

But Mama and Grandpa, they raised chicken, hogs, and get the eggs from the chicken from the home. And that's all they did. And Mama used to just can those vegetables and put them in the room. And it used to be all just piled up over there. It looks like it sits full, but it didn't. I don't know how she used to do it. But I never did try it until I got older.

THE WORK OF AN ELDER

MELVIN HENRY, B. 1911—BOGUE CHITTO
TOLD IN FEBRUARY 1982

This spring, I'm always planting my pea patch, watermelon, corn, peanuts, and things like that. I got some hogs; got some horses, too, so I got to take care of these too. And I got to cut hay, shell corn, pick peas in the summertime, and well, I get through work in summertime about July, and I decided to make [white oak] baskets. Just sitting around the shade tree and kind of not do anything sometimes. When I feel like I want to go fishing, I just pick up my fishing pole and go fishing. When I come back, I work on my basket.

HOG KILLING

TERRY BEN, B. 1957—STANDING PINE
TOLD ON JUNE 10, 2021

Everything that we ate came from the farm. Granddaddy, Grandma raised pigs. Every day, the pig had to eat—in the morning, lunchtime, in the evening—what they called "slop." Or sometime, they ate cornbread or whatever that Grandma cooked extra. Anyway, it was one of my jobs to feed the pig, and then once the pig got to be about three, four hundred pounds—my granddaddy usually raised two pigs—and around in October, there would be a hog killing day. It was one of those traditions: hog killing.

Granddaddy would invite a certain family, a friend of his or whatever and his wife, the man and his wife, to come over to help out with the hog killing. Usually in the month of October, he killed two hogs. It's an all-day job. I'm not going to go into the process; it's too gory too soon after lunch. I'm not going to go that route. But these are things that had to be done. Put food, so that in the summertime, Grandma would go in the smokehouse, and if she wanted to cook maybe ham for Sunday lunch or whatever, she would go to the smokehouse—the meat would be hanging up there—she'd take a knife, put it inside the little tray, whatever, go back in, wash it real good, cut it up, fry it. You had ham. That's the way it was. Everything was raised on the farm.

SHARING THE MEAT

MARTHA FERGUSON, B. 1949—STANDING PINE
TOLD ON JUNE 4, 2021

Just the tame pigs, they raise to kill. And when they raised it, they usually have a bunch of families so they could split it, the meat. So they like to see all my cousin and kinfolks and get to eat together and then take the meat home and feed them since we didn't have refrigerator or anything. So it has to be eaten that day or next day, at least.

RAISING HOGS

MARK PATRICK, B. 1969—O̱TOKLO (CONEHATTA)
TOLD ON JULY 12, 2021

Since I was a young boy, I've always raised a pig. At least one pig every year, I would raise them.

And then when we got ready to kill the pig, kill the hog, I would just have to, like, "Okay, y'all do whatever y'all got to do. I'll be back." [*laugh*] I wouldn't come back until he's hung, and we had him dressed, just cut him up and all that.

But yeah, that was part.

And then, if we had more than one hog, they would dig out somehow, and they would find a way to get out. And then they would get in the woods, and we'd have to hunt him down and get him back home and put him back up and patch up the fences.

TAKING A PIG FOR A WALK

MARTHA FERGUSON, B. 1949—STANDING PINE
TOLD ON JUNE 4, 2021

One time when they bought a pig that's supposed to be fed to the butcher, they took it to the house and fenced it in.

And once in a while, I opened the gate and sit there and talk to the pig. And they got to know me. So whenever I opened, it followed me everywhere. I said, "Let's go to the water place."

In Standing Pine, there was spring water here, here, here, all over the place and down below there where I live.

So I took that pig over there, and he'd just lay in it. And then got mud all over it. And whenever I'd go, got up and follow me. We went to another spring. He lay there, and all I hear is, "Ooof." She was satisfied.

So went back, put her back in before time for them to show up. "I'll go ahead and take him to the cage and put him back so it won't go anywhere." [*laughter*]

I talked to the pig, and also make a sound, how the pig sound. I went ahead, and every time she does it, I do it. She does it; then I do it. Then, I'm going to learn pig talk. And mom always laughed.

Even there was a potbelly pig came over last year at the house. I don't know where it came from, but it wasn't ours. And my son was out there, "You got a visitor."

I said, "Really?"

"Yeah, there's a potbelly pig out there that doesn't belong to anyone, looks like."

And I went out there and looked. "Oh, I'm going to try to touch it." I don't really want to touch it just since it's a strange pig but, I can touch it.

"Show me."

And I went ahead, "Err err," and here it came, came over. And then it went ahead, "Err err." And I went, "Err err." And it came, and I touched him.

"Now you try it." And the pig took off. [*laughter*]

So I guess it's a friendly pig type. So it just came right straight to me. And I just pet it; it was strange.

"Mom, you could tame anything you want as it is."

I grew up by myself, and animals were my best friends. [*laughter*]

"NOT THE GRAY ONE!"

MARTHA FERGUSON, B. 1949—STANDING PINE
TOLD ON JUNE 4, 2021

That childhood, it was fun. Self-independent.

Every time my parents dropped me off to be at my grandfather's house, about four, six houses down, it was trees and road. It wasn't too far. I could go over there, turn around, and come back.

After they dropped me off, I went ahead and came back because that's where my animals were.

My father's sister went ahead and gave me six chickens. I raised them, and they got big. And from that, it's supposed to be food source since we don't have money.

My mom start killing them. I went, "Not the gray one! Not the gray one!"

"Why not the gray one? It's chicken." [*laughter*]

NOT DEAD YET

MARTHA FERGUSON, B. 1949—STANDING PINE
TOLD ON JUNE 4, 2021

The fun part is killing the chicken. Mom was the one that's the head leader.

She says, "Catch the chicken." So we caught a chicken.

"Catch all the roosters." So that's what we did.

We had about ten or eleven. So we need three roosters. So we got three roosters.

And this is how you killed chicken. You can wring them by the neck or get an ax and let somebody hold it, then you chopped the head off. After that, you hang it up and let the blood drain out. After it drain out, then when it stops, we'll go ahead and boil water.

So dip it in and start pulling the feathers out. Once you get it done, then get a paper, burn it, and get all the hair off and then from there, start cleaning the guts out. So, step by step, she taught us how they did.

But each time it's killing time, she wring the neck. This is how you do it the old way. [*She motions wringing the neck with a quick twist of the wrist.*]

She just threw it down. And I just stood there, watched it. I went, "Mom, I don't believe you killed the rooster."

"It's dead. I broke the neck."

"How come he's sitting down and getting ready to go?!" And she be like [*eyes open big in surprise*], "Catch the rooster!" [*laughter*]

I remember that. It never left my head; every time I think about it.

But my aunt was there with us. She did the same thing, but she killed hers. She said, "That's how you do it."

But she [my aunt] always says *I* did it. *I* wringed the neck, and that rooster got up. I said, "That was Mama, not me! I didn't touch none of those roosters that day!"

And she said, "No, you did it. I don't blame your mama, I blame you." [*laughter*]

MANY WAYS TO KILL A CHICKEN

TERRY BEN, B. 1957—STANDING PINE
TOLD ON JUNE 10, 2021

Everything was raised there [on the farm]. Like eggs. You had chicken eggs. Anytime you wanted fried chicken, Grandma said, "Go get me a chicken."

So I went up there, and I would get my little dog to chase it down, get that chicken. Or sometimes if I got tired, I'd get me a little rifle and shoot him in the head. Or sometimes I'd get a stick and hit the chicken in the head with the stick, kill him. And then I would have a little stump there—I would have a little hatchet—and I would take the head off, give the chicken to Grandma.

And Grandma would have a little bucket, about that high [*motions about a foot off the ground*], tin bucket, about a gallon or so, and she poured some hot water in it, put the headless chicken right there, and she would pluck it. Pluck, pluck, pluck, pluck.

Then afterwards, she'd cut up the legs and all that and clean it real good and then gut him and then cut him up in pieces and get some flour out, roll it real good, get some hot grease, put it on the stove, you had fried chicken. There was no Popeye's during that time period, and we cannot afford to go to Popeye's anyway; there was no money.

RESOURCEFUL

LORENA ALEX, B. 1952—HALLS, TN / BOGUE CHITTO / PEARL RIVER TOLD ON JUNE 10, 2021

Mom loved to cook outside, so she did that. The time we were growing up, cook outside like meat, vegetables, biscuit, or cornbread.

During those days, we used to get commodities, too. The commodities that we'd get were different from the ones we get now. They were good, but they were different. So that's what we lived on, too.

And Dad also fed some hogs every day. And we grew some roosters. I remember we had a lot of roosters. But that was part of our money to eat on. So, we used to grow roosters.

I couldn't believe it to this day. We were little, and we did a lot, I thought.

When we lived in the tribal frame house, Mama, she always cooked outside, always had something cooking for lunch or supper. When it gets cold, we had this chimney, they call it *áshobolli*. She would cook there, too, maybe beans or sweet potatoes or biscuit or cornbread. She just did that, too, so we save electricity.

NEVER THE STORE

LORENA ALEX, B. 1952—HALLS, TN / BOGUE CHITTO / PEARL RIVER TOLD ON JUNE 10, 2021

Mom was good at killing chickens. She used to say, "Y'all get out there and run and kill one of those chickens." And we went and grab something, try to hit it. We all would miss it. The chickens were just fast now. Because she was thinking about frying it and make a dumpling. When we finally did, we would take a turn. And she would just pick it up, grab the neck and just twist it two or three times and just throw it on the ground. And all of a sudden it just quits, and it dies. I couldn't do that to save my life. [*laughter*] I tried. To this day I couldn't do it.

But we had to learn how to do that, too. Clean it and fix it and everything. Cut it.

Dad did hunt a lot and fish, so as far as squirrel and rabbit, we had to fix them. So I could still do that. I can't stand it, but if I have to, I'll do it. But now with too much cholesterol we don't do that anymore.

We used to cook turtle, too. You have to boil it and skin it and everything. We used to do that, too. Either we'd eat it boiled or fried.

We hardly went to the store that I remember. We hardly did.

A LESSON FROM MORNING CHORES

BILLY CHICKAWAY, B. 1950—CONEHATTA
TOLD IN 2016

I remember as a youth that we had to hoe the garden before going off to school. We would go in the garden and do what the Choctaws call *okchali*. That's putting dirt in and around the plant and getting rid of the weeds.

One time I was hoeing the garden, and I accidently cut a plant. I looked around, checking if anybody saw me, and then I put the plant back into the ground and went on my merry way.

Later on, my grandmother was working in the garden and came across the plant I had cut and saw that it had wilted and died. After I came back home from school, she asked if I had cut a plant. I told her I did cut it, but I replanted it. She told me the plant had died. I went to see for myself. I told her I will try not to do it again.

It was a teaching moment where she talked to me and showed me that these things [vegetables] will keep you alive, so you need to take care of it. I learned my lesson.

KEEPING THE DEER AND BIRDS OUT

RAE NELL VAUGHN, B. 1964—PEARL RIVER
TOLD ON MARCH 14, 1996

I remember grandpa running string around the garden to keep the deer and the stuff out. They used to put the flying thing out—it's like a cloth, and it's white, like cloth on it. And that was to keep the animals out, primarily the deer out.

I know, too, they said something about a dead bird, hanging a dead bird. That was to keep the crows out. Dead bird. They'd hang a dead bird.

MIX-UP AT THE FARMER'S MARKET

SUSIE COMBY ALEX, B. 1947—STANDING PINE / PEARL RIVER
TOLD IN 2016

They [people at the farmers market] used to grow some stuff and make seedlings and then give it away. So Mom told one of my brothers to go get some for her. They used to give them fertilizer and some plants to grow. She said, "Be sure to get plenty of tomato plants."

Well, there he went. And when he brought it to the house, he said, "Momma said for me to leave this with you."

And I said, "What are they?"

He says, "Tomato plant."

And I looked at it. "Doesn't look like tomato plant to me."

Momma, when she looked at it, she said, "It's not tomato plant."

And he said, "Yeah, when I told them I want tomato plant, that's what [they gave to me]."

He bought a whole bunch. It was eggplant! [*laughter*]

We had a lot of eggplant. We gave it away. Even other non-Choctaws heard about it, so they came and got it. We just had to pick eggplant every day. There were long rows, so we had plenty of eggplant to give away!

HUNTING AND FISHING, CAMPING AND COOKING

Just as home gardens provided food for the table, so, too, did fishing and hunting. Hunting was a male activity; fishing was more inclusive. Both could be done as solo activities, but the narrative tradition is dominated by stories of families heading into the woods together for the weekend. Men hunted and fished while the women cooked. Children played in the woods and in the water when they weren't being tasked with cleaning the fish or helping prepare the food, learning the skills of their parents first through observation, then through participation.

People remember these weekends fondly. Although they were necessary to provide food, they were also fun, allowing people to relax outdoors, away from the endless tasks of farm and field. Storytelling around the campfire served as entertainment, functioning to educate, amuse, and scare, often simultaneously. It was particularly nice to be outside in spring and fall, though the constant threat of snakes runs through many of these stories, adding an element of both danger and humor as screams of "*Sinti*!" sent men and women of all ages scrambling.[7]

Warm weather was for fishing, cold weather, for hunting. "I remember when it was winter, and there were no stores to go to, families would gather to hunt and to eat together," explained Melba Jean Smith in 2016. "The men did the hunting, mostly rabbits and squirrels, and the women would gather at an appointed place and prepare to cook. Even if it was cold, we would gather together."

Throughout the twentieth century, blowguns, rabbit sticks, and snares were being replaced with shotguns, though these earlier technologies did not disappear. Instead, they shifted from instrumental to symbolic use, performed at the Choctaw Indian Fair as a display of traditional Choctaw culture and as part of an effort of cultural education and revitalization in the annual youth rabbit stick hunt sponsored by the Choctaw Wildlife and Parks Department.[8] The impact of these shifts in technologies, however, paled in comparison to the restrictions that increasingly limited people's ability to hunt. "We used to build fire and people get together, go hunting," explained Lela Solomon back in 1982. "Now it's the White man that is in the way where they can't go hunting in certain places. They can't be anywhere else hunting except maybe the tribe's land—that is probably about all." Barney Wesley concurred, noting that White people are stingy with their land, requiring permits and permissions (see "Permits and Permissions" in this collection). Even chopping wood is off limits. "Nowadays, the Whites own the land and are stingy with the trees," said John Hunter Thompson in an interview in 1979. The irony of being restricted from land that was taken from them through unscrupulous, unethical, and often illegal means is hardly lost on the people then and now.

This irony is particularly rich considering the ethos of conservation and sustainability that underlies Choctaw hunting practices: hunting only in cold months when female animals have already raised their young; eating all game, including racoons, possums, turtles, squirrels, birds, and "trash" fish such as *shopik* or grinnell, as well as deer and rabbit; and eating all *parts* of those animals, wasting as little as possible. "When you go fishing, don't waste anything," said Harold Comby in 2000. "If you catch a whole bunch of fish, eat what you can and give the rest away."

There are exceptions. A family with no food will hunt out of season; the entrails of possum are tossed rather than eaten. But with "No Trespassing" signs and fewer and fewer landowners willing to allow hunting on their land, Choctaw families find themselves forced to buy what they used to grow, hunt, fish, and gather.

HUNTING AND BONDING

TERRY BEN, B. 1957—STANDING PINE
TOLD ON MAY 30, 1996

My grandad, during that time period, he would get together with some of his friends around Standing Pine, not only Choctaw friends, you know, but White friends, and they would go into the woods, maybe the Pearl River swamp here or elsewhere for a whole weekend or a whole week at a time. One person might be designated as a cook. Tend to the fire, cook whatever was killed, maybe rabbit, deer, maybe squirrel, whatever was killed. They would enjoy hunting.

BLOWGUNS AND SLINGSHOTS

HENRY WILLIAMS, B. 1945—CONEHATTA
TOLD ON JUNE 24, 1997

We get together. My uncles and daddy and grandpa would get together and go out. We used to come back home about three, four, five in the morning. And we killed a bunch of birds too, with this blowgun. And we use this slingshot too. Sometimes, birds be up higher in tree that we can't reach with the blowgun. We used to use that slingshot and knock that bird down.

We don't have that rubber that we used to have. These tubes we got it from, the tires. Used to be strong and throw those rocks pretty fast. We don't have that type of tubes anymore. So, I've been looking for it, though, for slingshot, because when I go fishing, there's a lot of snakes that I need to kill while I'm fishing.

RABBIT STICKS AND BLOWGUNS

TERRY BEN, B. 1957—STANDING PINE
TOLD ON JUNE 10, 2021

My grandfather's younger days, they would have—maybe October, November, December—they would have get-togethers where the men in the certain community or a small club or whatever, friends would get together and say, "Let's go hunting rabbit. On this occasion, let's use rabbit sticks." And they would use rabbit sticks.

And on different occasions, they had guns, obviously, but there was old customary way of hunting anyway, so they used rabbit sticks in twentieth-century America a whole lot.

Also, whenever my grandfather said when times were really hard, it was hard to buy shells, but still they had to put food on the table. He would use a blowgun at nighttime. In daytime, it's hard to get close to a bird and kill a bird with a blowgun. That's why they hunted at night a whole lot. Birds are sleeping in the tree. You can use a blowgun to get close and shoot. Plus, save on ammo.

There were no laws at that time. Now, you can't hunt at night. You get a stiff fine and some jail time.

He would make his own blowgun. Go out down to the river. During that time period, there was a lot of cane, lot of swamp cane so they would just collect it. Of course, how to do it was passed down from grandfather to father, so he knew how to do it. It's easy to do. I've seen it made as far as blowgun and darts and all that.

Dart would be made out of two things, either wood, just carve out of wood, either that, or maybe get a small clothes hanger, clip it on the ends, make sharp points, get your thread and get some cotton for the tail.

Rae Nell Vaughn: Did you ever use that cattail . . . ?

Exactly. Whichever one was readily available.

NIGHT HUNTING

TERRY BEN, B. 1957—STANDING PINE
TOLD ON MAY 30, 1996

My granddad, he liked to hunt. During that time period, it was not illegal to hunt at nighttime, in the early twentieth-century time period. So he would go nighttime hunting. He'd have these old carbide headlights. Maybe even before the invention of that, they would get these old pine knots at nighttime and light it up. They would take their guns, and they would go and maybe hunting birds inside trees; they were sleeping at night.

And he told me sometimes at nighttime, he would see a glow of light, maybe a mile away, half mile away. And he knew what it was. It was these little people who turned themselves into a ball of light and just kind of bobbing in the fields and among the trees. And they, too, were looking for birds and something like that to hunt something to eat.

BLOWGUNS AT THE FAIR

DELAURA SAUNDERS, B. 1950—BOGUE CHITTO
TOLD ON JANUARY 31, 1974

The blowguns that we have are also supplied by several of the craftsmen in the different communities that we have. They're made from the swamp cane, and the inside is drilled out. There's usually two different kinds used—the smaller kind was used at night for short distance, and the larger one, the six to eight feet long, was used in the daytime for longer distances. The darts they have in there are sometimes made from two different kinds of material. One is from the cotton, and the other is from the cattail.

These weapons that we used to have, sometimes used as weapons for defense purposes, are not used anymore except maybe for a very few older people still do at times like during the fair when they used to have these contests. A long time ago, they used to use it for contests.

For some reason, they weren't used in last year at the fair, but they're just used for competitive sports purposes rather than what they were originally used for.

TRAPPING BIRDS

JOHN MINGO JR., B. 1946—STANDING PINE
TOLD IN 2016

You would take a small box and prop it up with various sizes of sticks and set it up like a small hill. Then you would take cornmeal and bait the birds. The birds would then come underneath it. I would go back inside my house and watch through the window. When a whole bunch of birds come together, you pull the string, and the trap would drop. And that's how we used to catch birds.

CATCHING BIRDS

HAROLD COMBY, B. 1955—PEARL RIVER
TOLD ON JUNE 4, 1997

My mom said when they build a house, it used to be near a stream, and they used to clear it on the side of the stream, the bank, and they would pile all the brushes together, and some kind of birds would come in. And she said they used to use the blowguns to kill them, and clean the birds, and eat them.

I remember I had a BB gun, and I killed one, and I'd bring it to her, and she'd pluck the feathers and cook it for me.

And then she told me how to make a . . . killing thing, I guess. Two-by-six, and put a little stake here, and throw cornmeal underneath it. All the birds would get underneath and eat, and I'd pull that stick out, tied to a string from a distance. When all the birds get under there and then I pull it and that two-by-twelve would fall on the birds and kill them. And then I would take the birds to her, and she would prepare them for me.

I still remember that. Once you throw cornmeal or flour out, you'll be amazed what comes, what sees you.

RABBIT HUNTING

MARTHA FERGUSON, B. 1949—STANDING PINE
TOLD ON JUNE 4, 2021

We [females] were not allowed [to go hunting]. My uncle got chewed up because I went with him to train his dog. And he did kill a rabbit in front of me. I went ahead and tagged along anyway, even though they said not to.

He had carried two rabbit sticks on the side, extra rabbit sticks there. "If I lose one, I've got two more to work with."

And he went ahead, and at some field, he turned the dog loose, and all he did was whistle. Seemed like he would just run over. He would run fast over that corner, then, "It's gone this way! Run that one. No talk."

I said, "Okay," and I sat down and just watched them. When finally, I said, "What you looking for?"

"That rabbit is going to come out. And this is one chance. He's going to come out, sit up, and I'm going to hit him. When I hit him, it's going to kind of knock the sense out for a few minutes. So once it's done like that, I'll go pick it up and hit him on the head and kill it that way, and take it home to eat."

So that was the month of February. And sure enough, that rabbit came out, sit up, and he went ahead and was running. But he went ahead and just throw it in, knocked that rabbit on the head. And from there, I thought it was dead, but it start wiggling. He picked it up and hit it with his rabbit stick. "Now it's dead. This is how you kill the rabbit, and this is how you hunt."

OUTSMARTING RABBITS

HENRY WILLIAMS, B. 1945—CONEHATTA
TOLD ON JUNE 24, 1997

Go fishing. That's what we do in the summertime. In the wintertime, we hunt rabbit.

We used to, but we don't anymore. Because people put up "Posted: No Trespassing." It's hard to fish, also, because there are places you can't go in. Couple of times, I got chased out. I didn't see that "No Trespassing" sign on the post somewhere. I overlooked. Couple of times I got chased out for fishing.

Same thing with hunting rabbit. You can't just go out there and hunt rabbit anymore. But we used to. When I was a kid, we don't have no weapon like shotgun or rifle. We don't have those type of weapon to kill rabbit, so we have rabbit stick. About that long [*indicates about eighteen inches*]. We used to bring in about ten rabbits. Because we have about twenty dogs. That way, rabbit's not going to get away.

About twenty of us hunting that rabbit.

Rabbit always goes in a circle. It's not like the deer. Buck deer just go on. But rabbit just circle around.

When you're hungry enough, you're going to get to know how to hunt. If rabbit goes this way [to the left], I go this way [to the right]. By the time the rabbit get to me, that rabbit is not going to be fast like it was. Tired out.

Bunch of us used to know that. If rabbit goes this way [left], we go this way [right].

But some dogs are faster than us. If they caught up with it, they eat it up before we get to it. [*laughter*] They don't do that like these duck birds and quail birds; they bring it to you. But our dogs never bring it to you. They're going to eat it. We don't train them that way. We train them to chase the rabbit, but we don't train them to bring it to us.

We had a good time. That time, there was no "Posteds." These White people surrounding us, they used to have a bunch of cows at that time. But today, that's what they say, to protect their animals in the pastures. That's what they say. But they used to have lots of that when we was hunting.

TRAINING HUNTING DOGS

MARTHA FERGUSON, B. 1949—STANDING PINE
TOLD ON JUNE 4, 2021

My uncle trained the one dog that came in that he bought. He went ahead and killed a rabbit, saved a skin, and then he started dragging him. "Hold that dog. I'm going to drag it. Come on. Let's go."

So I went over there at the field. We had the big field; it goes all the way around. At one place, he went over there and dragged that rabbit skin and just dragged it all over the place. And he said, "This is my masterwork. I'm going to teach that dog how to hunt. So, now let it go."

So I went ahead and let him go. And I went to the road, and all he did was start whistling, or making a sound, and, "'Go this way, go that way'; that's what I'm saying."

I said, "It don't sound like it. You're just doing the whistling and growling like a bear."

"Yeah, but this is how you train them."

And that's how he trained his dogs to hunt, even squirrel or raccoon. Whenever he was ready to go hunt raccoon, he had one dog that hunts raccoon, one rabbit, but one that spotted rabbit; rest of them follow. So that's why he trained each one of them. He said, "Now, I got hunting dogs."

THERE GOES THE RABBIT

EDDIE JOHNSON, B. 1970—STANDING PINE / TUCKER
TOLD ON JUNE 11, 2021

When you hunt rabbits, they probably tell you, "They don't run straight." They run zigzag, and the rabbits, they'll do some crazy stuff. I ain't lying. They'll swim across the creek just to escape. They'll hide.

If you jump a rabbit, if you've got dogs or even if you yourself, a rabbit has a tendency to run zigzag. But the thing about it is it has a path. It knows its area. It smells; it sees just like anything. It knows its area. It'll go about a mile or even less; it'll make up a circle. And if you've got dogs, you have to learn to listen, observing where it's going. It's going to make a circle and come back around to where it started.

I've seen that. I've killed rabbits because of staying put close by where the dogs jumped it. I stayed put, and I've had where rabbits were coming right in front of me, easy shot.

One incident . . . this is funny. My older brother was always bragging about hunting and all that.

We were out with Barney Wesley. Barney, he is a good hunter, I ain't going to lie. But he had this long-barrel shotgun. I don't know how long. It looked like a Kentucky rifle, one of them long ones, but to me, I was ten years old [so everything looked bigger]. [*laughter*]

We went up to his house, and it was rabbit season. Normally my family, what we were taught was we don't go hunting until the first hard frost. You remember the season, the science? That's part of it. They told it, so I always practiced it. I still do. I don't go hunting for rabbits, I don't eat rabbits in no summertime. During the hunting seasons, you have to wait to the first frost, and reason I say that, we had frost and everything.

We went down to Barney's house. He lived up here, Arlington, somewhere in this area. He was the drummer. I think he was even a medicine man. But we went up there, and my brother, he was driving down the road early in the morning. I mean, we got on the road by three thirty, something like that. And coming from Standing Pine all the way up here in the Arlington area and the road was twisty and turning going up big old hills; it looked like it was like a bluff.

But the thing about it, we were going down a dirt road getting close to Barney's house, and my brother ran over a rabbit. He picked it up. "Roadkill." [*laugh*] He goes, "Oh, we got a rabbit already." [*laugh*] He throws it behind the seat. I'm sitting in the back. And he throws it right at the feet. It was a big old rabbit, a swamp rabbit too. And we go on.

I think we got there around five something. Anyway, Barney's ready. I'm ten or something like that. My younger brother was nine. My older brother had a gun. I think he had a .22 rifle. Barney had that big old shotgun. And there we were. I remember being the mule, I guess you call it that. You carried the rabbit for the older people.

And that's what we were. So we were expecting the whole bunch of rabbits to haul. But that's what my uncles used me for when they would say, "Let's go hunting." They'd say, "Ed, let's go." [*laugh*] So we'd wear that vest, and they'd throw it in there.

And my younger brother, he's a year younger than me, he came along, and he was excited. We didn't have no gun. I was hoping I could get one of them to give me a gun, but, no, they didn't trust us. So they went out there. I felt like taking my BB gun at least, but I didn't. But we went out there, and daylight started running around six. It's kind of cool, but it wasn't too bad.

We didn't see nothing all morning long, and maybe about nine o'clock . . . From six o'clock to nine o'clock, nothing. We was just walking in circles, and it was getting hard to walk. Like, "Come on, let's go back."

The dogs finally jumped one [rabbit], and it made its circle. This is where it gets funny. [*laugh*] It made its circle. And we were all standing kind of few feet apart. And we were in the back so that we won't get in the way or get shot by them or something like that. And Barney was listening. He was standing and listening and listening, and he looked at us, and he went like that [*motioned to where the rabbits would be coming from*]. In other words, he was telling us they're coming. And he pointed that way, and going that way to the left, and then made its circle.

And you could hear the dogs chasing it. And it went further away, but they started turning our way. That's when he waves his hand and pointed. And he was standing there, and he stepped up to the area where they had jumped it. Here comes that rabbit out of nowhere. And he cocks his gun, and he stands there and follows that rabbit with his gun. Click . . . [*nothing happened*]

That rabbit stopped right in front of him. After that happened, it stopped right in front of him. I'm talking maybe fifteen feet away. There it sat, right beside a log. It's hiding. He's trying to camouflage himself. He's made his circle. He's hoping the dogs had maybe gone by. Dogs are still coming. He left the dogs way behind. They're beagles. They don't run fast, but they'll trail. And they stick their nose to the ground, there they go. But I think he had about five, six of them or something like that. And he had a good one trailing everything. And the rest of them were just yelpers. But my brother has come up. We were a few feet apart. He went up maybe about a good ten feet. And then when he [Barney] misfired . . . boy, he didn't have no bullets in there! [*laugh*] And he goes [*shakes his head, frustrated*].

And here comes my brother. He [Barney] motions to come shoot it. And then my brother goes over there; he's not that far away, there he goes, fired. And it's a .22 I guess it's semi-automatic. I'm not sure. I can't remember. I think it had a rod and you fill your bullets in at the front and you could fire one right after [the other], pow pow pow pow pow. Missed it all 'til he finished his bullets. And there goes the rabbit. And here comes the dogs. [*laughter*]

Tom Mould: They never got that rabbit?

They never got the rabbit. [*laughter*] There it went.

So we didn't kill anything that morning. And the thing about it, we went back to Barney's house, I think. But it started raining, and it was a little bit cool that morning. There goes my younger brother. He sounded like a coon dog. He goes, "Whoooooh, it's cold. I wish I didn't come . . . " We followed him all the way. It's like, "Shut up. You shouldn't have come if you were going to [complain and cry]." [*laugh*] We didn't bring extra clothes. We stayed overnight.

The next day, went hunting again. I think Barney killed one then.

So that's the hunting trip: two big swamp rabbits. One of them roadkill; one of them shot by Barney. Well, that's what we ate.

RABBIT AND CORNBREAD

LALINE FARVE, B. 1933—STANDING PINE
TOLD IN 2017

They would boil the rabbit in a large pot because they didn't cook just one. Several hunters would go out and bring back many rabbits.

The women would take them and boil them. When they finished cooking, they would prepare the cornmeal and bake the cornbread near the large pots on the fire. When they were finished, the hunters would gather, and we would eat. It used to be real good.

RABBIT FEAST

LILLIE GIBSON, B. 1919—CONEHATTA
TOLD ON AUGUST 5, 1997

The women stayed back home and cooked at their own place, and then bring all the food to this one house, and then they'll bring the rabbits in about this time [around two p.m.]. Then they'd go and skin them and get them all cleaned. They'd have big black pots, and they'd put the rabbits in. Rabbits, squirrels, anything except for snakes.

After that, about around five or six o'clock, they'd have big feast. Everybody that went hunting and their families would come to this house, and they'll have a big feast. We used to call it "rabbit supper."

After they finished eating, they probably would have dancing out there. They'd have a good time.

CAMPING AND HUNTING SQUIRREL

MARK PATRICK, B. 1969—O̱TOKLO (CONEHATTA)
TOLD ON JULY 7, 2021

There's just many stories about our camping trips. When I say camping trips, I'm talking about just in the backyard. We'd just go off into the woods. It's not like we had to pack up a camper or a set up tent or anything. When I say, "go camping," I'm talking about just getting a crocker sack [burlap sack often used to carry potatoes]; you put your machete in, a few items that you're going to need for fishing or hunting. You might take a gun, and basically, we go out there, and we'd gather wood, start a fire, and we'd just lay across the ground and sleep all night.

I said sleep but, most of the time, we didn't sleep. We would have somebody, an old uncle or a cousin or somebody that would come along, and he would be our storyteller. He would be our comedian for the night, just kind of kept everything going. When we were camping, we tried to stay as quiet as possible, but you could hear laughter just echoing through the woods because, this is how funny some of us were.

My oldest brother, Robert, and I, sort of last minute, we planned and, "Let's go camping tonight." It's a Friday or whatever it was, and we didn't have school the next day, so, "Let's go camping."

We gathered our things, and we went way off into the woods. We both had guns. This was our plan: we was going to catch fish by night and kill squirrels in the morning. It was during the wintertime.

So we bundled up; we took our ax where we could chop some firewood. It was probably about three of us, four of us, and we stayed up as late as we could. I said, "Early in the morning, we're going to set up." I said, "There's going to be . . . We're going to kill a few squirrels."

I remember us waking up late because we stayed up as late as we could, and we overslept. I remember laying there, and when I opened my eyes, you saw probably fifteen, twenty squirrels, just right above us. As soon as I woke him up, I said, "Faniyat lawah hoke" [There are a lot of squirrels]. Soon as I said, "The squirrels," he jumped up.

By the time he got his gun, all the squirrels just disappeared. [*laughter*]

I thought that was one of the funniest things.

HUNTING SQUIRREL

MELFORD FARVE, B. 1961—TUCKER
TOLD ON JUNE 1, 2021

I only went hunting once. And that was for squirrel. My brother-in-law said, "I want to take you hunting." So we went.

He had one of those flashlights where you can wear it up here [*points to forehead*]. He'd be looking up in the trees, and I could see all—I never really noticed it in my life, but squirrels up in the trees. It was, to me, it was kind of, hmm. I never even noticed them up there because they would jump from one tree to the other.

That was a good experience, but I just never could get into hunting. I wish I did now, thinking about it.

FISHING AND HUNTING TOGETHER

HAROLD COMBY, B. 1955—PEARL RIVER
TOLD ON JUNE 1, 2021

We did the old theory of sustenance fishing, sustenance hunting.

We used to go to the swamps and take out nets, throw it in there. There'd be like four or five families come together. Then we'd fish, and the woman would come in like maybe eight o'clock, nine o'clock, and then clean, cook. Then we'd eat, and we'd divide the fish equally among the people, families. Then go home.

Then during the winter times, deer, rabbits, squirrel.

FISHING TRIPS

BARBARA SAM, B. 1956—STANDING PINE
TOLD IN 2017

A long time ago, when I was still small, my dad's nephews, they used to do that one day [out of the year]. I think it used to be the Fourth of July. Everyone used to gather. The wagon . . . we'd put all our stuff in there and go all the way into the woods, where the creek ran across. They'd be there fishing and cooking.

We were there in the morning. We went early, just before daybreak. And so, it would be several of us. Once they finished cooking breakfast, when they finished eating, they went fishing. We would gather up the leftovers we brought. Then at lunch, they cooked the fish they caught. They cleaned and fried. Yeah, we would be there all day. That's how we used to do it.

FISHING WEEKENDS

CAROLINE MORRIS, B. 1944—PEARL RIVER
TOLD ON MAY 31, 1996

We used to go camping at night. When we were growing up, when I was like six years old or something like that, we used to go and get our stuff and our gear in the wagon, and here we go. It takes forever for us to get to the river. And then Friday night, they get the hooks out, and Saturday morning, we go get the fish. Spent the whole day Saturday and Sunday morning, lunchtime, pack up and get back so we can get back to school. That used to be our pastime, something interesting. Go to the woods.

Harley Vaughn: That's when they all start telling those scary ghost stories. Sitting out there. [*laughter*]

My grandmother, Sweeny Willis, she used to tell stories, but I guess I can't remember any of them. You'd be just listening to what she was saying, and all of a sudden, the owl would make a sound, and everybody would squeal. [*laughter*]

FEAR OF SNAKES

SUSIE COMBY ALEX, B. 1947—STANDING PINE / PEARL RIVER
TOLD ON JUNE 9, 2021

Both my mom and dad liked to fish.

I don't know how old I was, but I learned too. We had community ponds in each community. She said, "Don't go out where there's a lot of grass; there might be snakes."

I said, "Don't tell me 'snakes.' I'm not going to fish!" I said, "I'm just scared of any kind of snake."

She said, "Well, they're just out in the open."

All I can say is, my husband liked to go to Beaver Dam to fish, and there were a lot of snakes.

If he catches one, the fish is moving around and all, slapping the water. Here comes the snakes! [*laughter*]

FISHING ALONE

MARTHA FERGUSON, B. 1949—STANDING PINE
TOLD ON JUNE 4, 2021

I went fishing. And I got spanking out of it, too, since I go by myself as usual. And there's a creek there in Standing Pine that you can go fish. And sometimes they wouldn't have enough money. Salt meat is the one, or just lard that you cook and make biscuit and rice and eat that one. That's how we lived. But to have fish, you have to go fishing.

So I went in and dug up a worm, and once in a while find crickets, and from there, I just put it in a bottle and make a bag and just put it around my waist and got a string, and I could find sticks out there to fish with since it's a creek.

So whenever I go there, there's a tree laying there. I'll go ahead and just sit there, find the fish. And I got a stick that you could . . . it's kind of like, stick's about this [three feet] long, but yet it has an arm. And once you stick it in the water, when you catch fish, you just throw it in, and so fish would still be alive and soft and not hard.

So that's what I did. And I caught about six fish and brought it back, clean it, and fix it up.

And I was cooking one day when Mom came from work, and she said, "Oh, I smell fish. You went fishing again, way over there? I told you not to."

And I said, "Don't bother me. I'll eat by myself, all the fish. And you're not going to get nothing."

Then she hushed up. Grandma was fussing and fussing, "She needs whipping. She don't need to go there, all by herself."

I said, "Yeah."

"A snake could kill you."

I said, "Yeah, so far I've seen a cottonmouth and also seen a copperhead."

"You have? They're big."

And he [my uncle] said, "Well, how did you see it?"

"I took one of your dogs with me, and I was just standing there, and that snake went through between my leg, and that's how I saw a good look at that. That's cottonmouth." I mean, it was long, going by, between my leg. And copperhead, it just went ahead and went around, crawled by, then went to the water.

So I said, "I seen it all." I said, "They touch me. Their soft skin, and . . . " And Mama go, "Eeeee." [*laughter*]

MESSING WITH SNAKES

MARTHA FERGUSON, B. 1949—STANDING PINE
TOLD JUNE 4, 2021

After I finish fishing by myself and just walking along, there was a big sand there. Once in a while I'd run into a black runner. It start running. Once it hit that sand, it can't move that fast. So I used to run over there, got a stick, run over there, and jump on the back of the black runner. And it tried to bite me. I said, "Stop that," pop! [*mimes smacking snake with stick*]. Hit him on the head and it just goes [*uses hands to indicate the snake was stuck, trying to slither away but unable*]. And I get off and it started to go. I jumped on the back, hit him. That was fun.

It was long. That's why it was easy to get to. From here to there, for me as a kid, it was a long snake. It was fun.

MAKING STRING

MARTHA FERGUSON, B. 1949—STANDING PINE
TOLD ON JUNE 14, 2021

When Grandfather and I went fishing, several of us went to Ross Barnett Reservoir, I think it was. I was at age twelve, but I was following my grandfather around with lights, and that's where we got a cane to fish with. Threw the hooks in where the water's flowing. And over that side was a tree.

When it was time to go, he said, "We're going to take the cane with us. So come on, we're going to go and get a string."

"There's no string here. Where are you going to buy a string at?"

"I'm not buying it." He went to the tree, and he just knock out two things and got his knife and then start peeling. Then it just got smaller and smaller, but he went ahead and pull about four of them. And then from there he got the bark off and then he said, "Hold it with me." And we went ahead and start tying like a ponytail, and the string made. And it was real strong. We went ahead, and he went ahead and got another four.

We did that one, and it hold one side of the car, that fishing cane, and another one holding. And when we got home, it was still strong. I couldn't believe that that could turn to a string and hold that. I asked him, "What type of tree it is?"

He told me, but it was said in Choctaw, not in English. So I don't remember.

But I remember the string, and I told my late husband about that. He said, "What kind of tree was it?"

I said, "I don't know."

I was just twelve years old. And all I did was help him and then help braid that tree bark or whatever string that was made. And it was nice and soft too. When you finish making it, it's real strong. And he tied that cane with it. And we brought it home.

ACCIDENTAL SWIM

RUTH WILLIAMS, B. 1936—STANDING PINE
TOLD IN 2017

I did go fishing, but as for me, when I was back here, somewhere across Standing Pine, we would go, women alone. When they went to church, we went. It maybe was Mary Comby. "Don't fall in the water," her mom kept saying. But as she was walking around, she fell in the water, the creek [*laughter*], the Standing Pine Creek.

Still, Kelly Chitto, our sister-in-law, was like, "Oh no! How are we going to get her out?"

She fell into the water, going up and down like this [*bounces both hands up at down at the wrist*].

She went and got a long tree branch and threw it in there. "Catch the tip of the branch," she said.

When she finally grabbed on, we kept pulling and got her out [*motions with both hands as if pulling her in with a pole*]. [*laughter*] So we just quit going fishing.

POLE THAT DON'T CATCH FISH

GLADYS WILLIS, B. 1926—PEARL RIVER
TOLD ON MAY 19, 1997

I never did fish. When they used to go camping, I never did fish. After I got older, if I was going to learn how to fish, I could have fished, but when we first married, without kids, he used to want to go fishing. So we'd go. He'd give me a cane, and he said, "You do this, and you do that, so when the fish bite, you pull them up." I would just sit and play with the cane. I never did care about it. And he'd catch lots of fish, and he said, "How come your fishing pole don't catch fish?"

"I don't know." [*laughter*]

That's when probably he got tired of me. So when he'd want to go fishing, he'd say, "I'm going fishing," and I'd say, "alright," and I'd stay. [*laughter*]

TRAPPING AND PARALYZING FISH

EDDIE JOHNSON, B. 1970—STANDING PINE / TUCKER
TOLD ON JUNE 11, 2021

Nowadays, you can't go fishing without a rod and reel. But what I remember was that you could actually get in the water and trap fish, lure them into an area, and you can catch them.

Or even using certain kind of nuts—I want to say black walnuts. One of those nuts would paralyze a fish. You could pick it up with your hands.

Those were old methods.

DISAPPEARING GAME

RUSSELL JAMES (R. J.) WILLIS, B. 1940—RED WATER / STANDING PINE
TOLD ON NOVEMBER 4, 1973

I believe this was before the White men come over this land, and when Indians lived on this land, they had a lot of things to eat. But whenever the White man come over here, the buffalo is gone, the deer is gone, and the rabbit is just faded away now. Now, they can't hardly find a rabbit now.

About that time before White man come, they need to eat, they need wild meat or something like that, they usually just go on out in the woods and kill them and eat them. But these times they have to buy a license to kill that wild meat.

NATURE'S GUARDIANS

BAXTER YORK, B. 1907—PEARL RIVER
TOLD ON JUNE 21, 1974

The old way of the Choctaw was to believe in what they called a "Great Spirit." They don't say God, or they don't say Christ or anything, but they believe that was Creator. They called it Great Spirit, and that belief is they don't believe in cutting up the land.

They say it belongs to the Creator. They don't believe in putting up a poster, "You can't go fishing here." Putting up poster, "You can't come in here," "Can't trespass," and so on. Why? Because it belongs to the Creator.

They claim that they placed the Choctaws over here in this country, this particular area here, to watch all the natural things that the Creator's got here. And that's the reason why the Choctaw is as close to the nature than any Indian race we got in this country here.

PERMITS AND PERMISSIONS

BARNEY WESLEY, B. 1927—MASHULAVILLE / BOGUE CHITTO
TOLD IN FEBRUARY 1982

They are stopping things for us and a place to live as well. If we are to step on a White man's yard or woods, we have to have some kind of paper or permit. It's their land now. One day, we want to have a place to stay. It's their place. In order to walk on it, we have to have permission. It's not us, it's them. They are stingy with their land. If we ask and are given permission for us to enter, we can, but today that is hard to do. Their land is not so big, but if we go, we will come back out with nothing. We won't even have a place to hunt.

HUNTING RESTRICTIONS

BRIAN BILLIE, B. 1973—RED WATER
TOLD ON JUNE 30, 2021

I thought our reservation was never ending as far as we can see until I went hunting for my uncle. When I went hunting for my uncle, I found out we had tribal lands to a point, and we can't go to other lands without permission.

CHOCTAW KNOW BEST

BRIAN BILLIE, B. 1973—RED WATER
TOLD ON JUNE 30, 2021

Working with the Wildlife [Mississippi Wildlife, Fisheries, and Parks], I also noticed that they were doing fish studies and what the Choctaw eat. What they thought, primarily, was brims, perch, catfish, and bass. One thing they didn't know was what we call *shopik.*

And the older ones [Choctaw elders], they eat everything. That was one of the things that was on their list.

I remember that guy. After we collect them, we put them all in the bucket. After timing was over, we had to record what kind of fish, what it weighed. And he told me, identify the fish: red ear, long ear, pumpkin, white perch or black perch, bass, brims, catfish.

I remember I couldn't hurry up and think of what *shopik*'s real name was; it was grinnel. And I remember I was giving them all the fish, and I got to the *shopik*, and I know not to put your finger in the *shopik*'s mouth, because it has . . . feels like teeth, but it'll have enough pressure to bite you. So you grab them on the side.

I'd given it to him, the guy recording it, and he put his hand out. And I said, "*Shopik*." And he put his thumb inside the *shopik*'s mouth, and it clamped on and hold him. I remember him jumping up and down on the boat, and I laughed at him. And he slapped it around for a while. And he was so mad, he threw it into the woods. I said, "Why are you throwing it in the woods?"

He goes, "That's trash fish."

I said, "No, it's not. People eat them."

He said, "No, y'all don't."

I said, "Yes, I do. They do."

And he goes, "Show me."

So I collected five of those. After we came back, put everything up, we had to . . .

I remember the ladies down here, the older ladies would say, "Bring it." So we'd go to them and say, "Nani hachinnaho̱?" [Do y'all want fish?]

Natah? [What is it?]

"*Shopik*."

They're like, "Okay. How many?"

I say, "We got five."

She goes, "I only need one or two." So they bring a bag, and you put it in there.

He was like, "So they do eat it."

I said, "Yeah."

So we gave away the five. He said he had to put that on the study because that's what the people are eating too.

And he showed me that we can eat gar too. And he said, "You can have gar balls [patties] from the tenderloin of the gar." How to clean them. But he said, "Don't eat the eggs. Sometimes they're poisonous."

So things like that. Then you go and teach your kids and teach your friends that you fish with what you learned. Makes good fishing stories.

USE IT ALL

HAROLD COMBY, B. 1955—PEARL RIVER
TOLD ON JUNE 4, 1997

My mom has told me is that they used to eat possum and raccoon and stuff like that. I think that that was part of when they didn't go on the removal. She says they hid in swamps, so the people had to do something to survive. That's the only sustenance they got, I guess, whatever they could eat.

This was as early as a couple years ago she was eating stuff like that. She had us eat turtles, big turtles. Didn't taste too bad. My mom loves it.

And you've heard people that say Indians never waste anything? Like a pig. Some people still butcher their own hogs, and they use almost every bit of it, except maybe the hooves. Like my mom, when she cooks, she just split the head in half and just put it in water, cook everything: eyes, brains, and everything. Pigs' feet, pig knuckles. Even the pig intestine. And make crackling from the skin.

HUNTING POSSUM

HAROLD COMBY, B. 1955—PEARL RIVER
TOLD ON JUNE 4, 1997

Another thing that she had mentioned was that they used to go out and hunt possums at night. What they used to do was throw dirt at the possum so they would roll over and play dead, and then one of the ladies would carry a big stick, and they will put the tail on there and let them hang there. But she said what they used to do was put the shovel handle or some kind of stick handle on the head and let somebody pull the tail so that they would break the neck of the possum.

KILL TO EAT

LOUISE WILSON, B. 1950—BOGUE CHITTO
TOLD ON JUNE 10, 1997

My grandfather told me of a time when the whole family got up early in the morning. They left, and they walked and walked and walked. And I couldn't tell you where it was they went, but it had been in that area in Bogue Chitto. They walked for like two days, maybe way out in the woods. And if they needed something to eat, they'd be by a creek, so they fished or whatever. But they're looking for a deer and anything like that to bring in a lot of meat.

He said that it was more or less like a picnic, kind of like you go on vacation or something like that. It would be hot, but they would still be going out to hunt like that. And he said that they'd get several deer.

They had—just like you see in pictures—they had these sticks lined up, and when they cut the deer, they do dry the meat just like they did in these books that I've seen. And he said they dry the meat, hang them up. And he said that people, our people believe that you don't waste anything. When you kill, you kill to eat it.

GO GET ME *SHOKATTA*

TERRY BEN, B. 1957—STANDING PINE
TOLD ON JUNE 10, 2021

Let me tell you another story, a little different side dish. Sometimes, especially in the nighttime, you're going down the road, do you ever see a possum? How many of you seen a possum? [*All the students raise their hands.*] Okay, you know what a possum is. What's the Choctaw name for possum? *Shokatta*, okay? In the fall time, we had persimmon trees. "Persimmon," what they call *ǫkof*. And when the frost came, it made the persimmon taste better.

So, there were two groups that liked the persimmon. One was the *shokatta*, and of course my grandma. She loved to eat the persimmons too. But on top of that, every now and then she would say, "Go get me *shokatta*."

And so the best time to get the *shokatta* is nighttime. He would come around at nighttime, climb the tree, and he'd be eating. And so at nighttime, I'd take the flashlight on that tree, I'd see the shining eyes, and I'd get a rifle and knock him down, take it to Granddaddy.

Granddaddy would take that *shokatta*, and we had a chimney with the fire going, and he would put that *shokatta* on top of the fire and roll him around, roll him around, roll him around, and get all that hair out. And then after that, he'd turn to Grandma, said, "Your turn."

And so Grandma would take that *shokatta* and get one of those pails, gallon, large pails, metal pails. She would put water inside it, and she would clean it. She would get a knife, get all that hair and things like that off that *shokatta*. And then she would cut off the tail, head, feet, and all that, throw it out, gut it up, cut up in small pieces and then, afterwards, put some salt, pepper, whatever, and put it on the stove and boil it. Boil it for about three, four hours. And then she'd put it on the dinner table. If you did not know what it was, it tasted just like pork, but if somebody told you *shokatta*, you would turn and walk away. But Grandma was a good cook.

COOKING POSSUM

MARTHA FERGUSON, B. 1949—STANDING PINE
TOLD JUNE 4, 2021

From seven years old, they start training me to wash dishes, cook rice and not meat yet. They always say, "You might burn stuff. So we'll wait 'til you get to be a little higher." So as soon as I reached twelve, they taught me how to cook meat and when it's ready or not ready. And that's what I didn't know. So they taught me a lot on that one.

Way back, there was no refrigerator, anything. Mostly Thanksgiving was my uncle's favorite day to hunt and bring the animal in. So we can go ahead and skin it and then cook it. Sometimes we eat about ten o'clock at night, but they brought it in, squirrel, rabbit. Once in a while, raccoon, if they find it. Possum, they found it, but you have to feed them at least a month to two of your own food, then kill it.

What's fun about that possum, my grandfather showed me, you don't have to chase those possum. Once they come around, get you a stick.

"Am I going to shoot it with the stick?"

"No, you don't shoot it. You just go over there and hit him hard on the head. When it growls, just hit him hard, several times. It'll drop dead."

Like he was dead, and you could pick it up by the tail. And that's what I used to do.

Whenever I saw possum, I said, "You guys want possum?" Went back, and they were still out there. So all I did was hit him with a hard stick, just dropped dead, pick it up, brought it home, throw it in a tub or whatever. And they just feed it for a couple months. That's during the month of October to February, though. You don't kill any type of animal after those days because they tend to have babies. And once they have their babies, there'll be plenty of food to be supplied for during the season that we tend to kill the animals.

Grandmother. Every time somebody says, "You want this one, this one?" "No, this is the day I'm getting it. November 2 to February 2. Go ahead and you can kill animal. We can eat it. But after that, don't bring anything. If you kill it, you eat it. You fix it. But the family can't eat that one."

And I finally asked her why since they're available. "Well, if you overkill the animals, you won't have any animals to eat again for the season that's coming up. And we don't have money. Make sure the stock is always there. The animals, they have their babies. They have to raise it. Give them time; let them raise it."

That's what I was told growing up. That's why when somebody says, "I'm going to kill this one, this one." Sound like, what do you call it? Elimination? Or kind of getting rid of all the animals at once. If you just keep at it. "We can kill and then freeze them." That's not right, I always thought. But I never did tell them why. But it's their parents; they ought to taught them right from wrong on that one. The season of any animals.

ROADKILL

MARTHA FERGUSON, B. 1949—STANDING PINE
TOLD JUNE 4, 2021

My uncle, I used to tease him. He's the one that likes to hunt. He has two dogs or three dogs, and then he calls them all "Red." Red One, Red Two, Red Three. And all three dogs look like twins.

"Uncle, you got three dogs to feed?"

"Yeah. We're going to go hunt. This time we're going to go hunt for rabbit."

And I start laughing. He said, "What?"

"Why all this time when you've been hunting rabbit here and there by yourself?"

"Yeah."

"I bet you picking up a roadkill and bring it home." [*laughter*] "And then everybody suffers from eating that." [*laughter*]

"Don't tell me that I'm doing that!"

I said, "I think you do because you don't take your dog. That's when I know when you're bringing the rabbit." [*laughter*]

I said, "That's a roadkill. It's used." [*laughter*]

"If you were not my kinfolks, I'll punch you out."

PICKING HUCKLEBERRIES

EDDIE JOHNSON, B. 1970—STANDING PINE / TUCKER
TOLD ON JUNE 11, 2021

I had Esbie Gibson come stay at my house for a few days. She used to live in Standing Pine; she knew that area. That was years ago. She stayed with me because she wanted to pick blackberries. No luck because in the past it would grow wild and all that. But we found out that the places that she knew of and the little creeks and all that, people began to spray weed killer, herbicides, and stuff like that. That kills them off. Roadsides, even the dirt roads, they spray stuff so that they can maintain them.

So they call that "huckleberry." They will pick that.

We used to do that. Sometimes we'd ask somebody who owned a pasture. They grow around the creeks and those areas. And that's where the snakes would come out. Be a green snake hanging onto it, and you'd grab it and then all of a sudden "*Sinti*!" Start running. [*laugh*]

But that's what she was wanting to do. But the areas that she knew about, and she asked me, and I thought, "Yeah, I know some places." Then I found that they weren't there no more.

PICKING WILD PLUMS AND WALNUTS

MARTHA FERGUSON, B. 1949—STANDING PINE
TOLD JUNE 4, 2021

Where I live, there was plums, wild plums growing. Red one, yellow one.

And I had a black walnut [tree]. You have to hit a brick with it and then pull those nuts out. And I had food, ready-made food right there. So it was good.

And the plums in the spring, I mean it was down this way [*points toward the east*], but it was full of them, and I just go picking. And then go to the back porch and just sit there and eat.

Tom Mould: Do they have wild plums out there still?

I haven't seen it. Ever since they started spraying poison, I haven't seen that type. But the plums were great. It was really good. Nice and ripe.

FETCHING WATER

AMANDA BELL, B. 1969—PEARL RIVER
WRITTEN ON MARCH 11, 2024

My grandparents, Irvin and Thelma Anderson, from the Conehatta Community taught me the good life.

As we spoke in Choctaw, Grandfather asked me if I would like to go fetch some water with him. I said, "Yes." He had two pails in his hands, and we began our journey. We walked through the gravel road, up the hill, and into the woods. It felt like we walked forever, and it was hot. Finally, we came to the spring site. I was amazed because I've never seen anything like it: water coming out from the ground. Grandfather gave me some water to drink, and it was cold and delicious. He filled up his two pails of spring water, and we journeyed back home. Grandfather taught me to enjoy the great outdoors, and to this day, I enjoy the great outdoors.

RECREATION

STICKBALL

The common moniker of stickball as "the granddaddy of all field sports" is an ambitious one, and yet it still does not seem to do justice to the role it plays in Choctaw culture.[1] More than any other, stickball stands as the most recognizable symbol of traditional culture for the Mississippi Choctaw and the most recognizable design element after the ubiquitous diamond design. The tribal seal is dominated by a pair of stickball sticks in its center. Just below the sticks is a drum and drumsticks. They, too, represent stickball.[2] Chatting after dinner back in 1996, Harley Vaughn and his mother-in-law, Caroline Morris, discussed the connection. "Each ball team has a drummer," explained Harley. "The drum is giving them the effort to give it their all. The drum is the heartbeat of the game."[3]

The drumbeat is the heartbeat of the game, metaphorically but also practically. "When everything is going good then the sound is not going to be that loud," explained Caroline Morris. But if it's getting rough . . . " she trails off in laughter. Harley picks up the thread: "It does. It follows the game, how it's played. The louder it gets, the drum always follows it. When they're playing, that's what you [the players] hear. You really don't hear anything else but the drum. You know all these spectators can scream and holler at you, but you won't hear that; you'll just hear the drum."

The drumbeat that is so important today barely gets a mention in the historical record beyond its use during the social dances that preceded play. Such a change is perfectly in keeping with shifts in the game over the years. Virtually every aspect of stickball has changed since the first written records of it appeared in the middle of the eighteenth century, including the construction of the ball, the size of the field, the form and size of the goal, the number of players, the score needed to win, the clothing worn, and the role of prophets, medicine men, and local leaders. For example, scoring appears to have shifted regularly over time: Bossu, observing between 1751 and 1762, indicated 16 as the score to reach; Romans, observing in the 1770s, recorded that the score was variable, with teams deciding the number needed to win before each game; Catlin, observing in the 1830s, said it was 100; Cushman, observing in the 1830s as a child but writing from other sources as well in the 1880s, noted a range from 10 to 20, and Halbert, observing between 1884 and 1899, said it was 12.[4] Similarly, the ball field is described as having goals 150 feet apart, 200 to 225 yards apart, 250 to 300 yards apart, and half a mile apart; the number of players as 20, 30, 40, 75 to 100, and 600 to 1000; and the goal first as an opening created with 2 poles with a top beam lashed across it spaced 60 paces apart, then as a goal spaced 6 feet apart with posts 20 feet high, followed by a goal 1 foot or more apart and 15 feet high, until it becomes a single pole 20 feet high, or a split-log goal that offered a 12-inch face, height unknown. The clothing also shifted, from breechcloths, to uniforms with hats, to today's T-shirt and shorts. The only constant seems to have been 2 teams, 1 ball, 2 sticks, and an open field.[5]

Although the game is often referred to as "the little brother of war" to describe its role in settling disputes to help avert war, only Henry Halbert mentions this use, offering two examples, both between the Choctaw and the Creek: one in 1790 to decide ownership over a beaver pond, the other over land ownership between the Tombigbee and Black Warrior Rivers. Unfortunately, despite his description of *intra*tribal play, where "the vanquished always cheerfully accepted their defeat," the *inter*tribal games with the Creek ended in battle. Further, even intratribal games could exacerbate rather than mitigate violence: "In some cases, the fights that began at the stickball match were so serious that they carried over into future relations between the communities or families involved" (Blanchard 1981:39). Rather than precluding war, stickball seems to have been a prelude to it. Like war in the past, however, stickball today is viewed by many as a rite of passage for young men in the tribe. Bradley Alex muses: "Stickball, that's the only thing I think we have to prove yourself that you're worthy."[6]

Competition was not confined to the field. Scaffolds were erected where people wagered their goods against those of the opposing teams. Objects being wagered were tied together and placed on the scaffold. At the end of the game, the victors simply claimed their bundled wagers. Stories of people literally losing the shirt off their back are rife throughout the historical record (Swanton 1931:140–53). Coupled with the increased rowdiness and violence spurred on by excessive drinking, stickball was soon targeted not only by missionaries but also by state legislators as a vice that had to be outlawed. Estelline Tubby remembers stories of the missionaries rounding up and burning people's stickball sticks in Bogue Chitto (Mould 2004:157–58). In 1898, the Mississippi legislature added "Choctaw ball games" to the list of unlawful gambling, stripping the sport of its important entertainment and economic functions and driving it underground (see Blanchard 1981:41–42).

The response to stickball and its ultimate revival under the regulated auspices of the tribe is a pattern seen also in house dancing. Drinking and fighting became endemic of house parties, where a fiddle and a guitar guided mostly young men and women in dancing until the early hours of the morning. Crackdowns by tribal police drove house dancing virtually out of existence until tribal schools revived the dances in a school setting, transforming the music and dance form into a symbol of ethnic pride taught to children as part of their cultural heritage.

The stickball of today avoids both the gambling and the fighting. No scaffolds of wagered goods; no fights after the games. But vestiges of both remain. People bet on brackets for the tournament, as many across the country do for the NCAA Final Four college basketball tournament. And while fights are rare, competition remains fierce, with backroom maneuvers to try to lure the best players to one's team, trash talk on and off the field, and occasional accusations of cheating when games do not go as expected or desired.

The sport will no doubt continue to evolve, but for now, its basic rules and parameters are well established. Field size is relatively stable at 100 yards in length with end zones included so that it can be played on the football field at Choctaw Central High School during the fair. The goals are made from 4 x 4 wooden posts at a height of 12 feet. The ball is made of a rock core wrapped in cloth strips and covered in woven strips of leather. The total number of players allowed on the field is 30 from each team. And the game ends after four 15-minute quarters for the men, and 10-minute quarters for the women, 35-and-over men, and youth, rather than when a particular score is reached. The widespread dictum that there are only one or two rules is no longer the case. Each year, a list of the rules is issued to each team and player. There are rules for who can play, how to line up, and how to start dead balls. The 2023 rule sheet included 13 infractions an individual must avoid, including intentionally touching the ball with anything other than sticks; inappropriate use of sticks such as swinging them at toss-ups; and a long list of inappropriate hits, including early and late hits, body slams, clothesline hits, and intentionally pulling hair.

Trends that have ebbed and flowed over the past century include wearing horse tails in the manner of stickball player Tul-lock-chísh-ko,[7] face and body painting, symbols burned or painted onto stickball sticks, and breechcloth aprons worn over shorts. Players no longer automatically play for their community team, instead assessing a number of factors, including (1) choosing a team that has been winning as well as choosing an underdog team; (2) joining friends as well as avoiding rivals; (3) making good on a bet; (4) playing in honor of someone, often a recently deceased relative; (5) finding a good fit in terms of coaching style and personality; and (6) "jumping for jerseys," where a player switches teams over the years to accumulate as many different jerseys as possible. The default, however, remains playing for one's community, an identity deeply embedded in the Choctaw who grew up in Mississippi.[8]

Exhibition games may be played occasionally, often away from the reservation, but the primary setting for stickball is the annual Choctaw Indian Fair where the boldly named World Series of Stickball is played over the course of two weeks, culminating in the finals on the last night of the fair. Practices begin months earlier as teams develop their roster and their strategies for winning. Players dust off their sticks that have been sitting idle in a closet or return to pawnshops to get their sticks out of hock.

Despite efforts by missionaries in the nineteenth and early twentieth centuries to outlaw stickball, the game has only grown. Youth teams have flourished, with participation in the State Games of Mississippi,[9] typically held in June, then culminating in the World Series at the Choctaw Indian Fair, with two age categories—Pushmataha for ages ten through thirteen and Tulli Okschi Iskhko for ages fourteen through seventeen. Women's teams have thrived as well. Given little attention in the historical record, women's stickball went dormant by the early twentieth century. When it remerged at the century's close, it was relegated to exhibition games. In a few short decades, however, women's teams exploded in numbers and popularity with their own bracket and avid fanbase. Videos of stickball games abound on the internet. Multiple documentary films have been made about Choctaw stickball, both amateur and professional. A casting call in the summer of 2022 for a Marvel TV series spinoff based on the Cheyenne superhero Echo prompted some Choctaw to drive to Georgia to play stickball for a scene in the show. The only commercial video game ever made about the Choctaw is a stickball game. And the only book-length study devoted to Choctaw sports is dominated by stickball.

The stories people tell about stickball mirror many sports stories: tales of come-from-behind wins, unscrupulous play, heroic sacrifices, incredible goals, superstar players, shocking defeats, and underdog victories. But above all else, there are stories of injuries. Stickball remains an incredibly rough sport. Two ambulances flank the field for every game, but the twisted ankles, dislocated shoulders, knocked-out teeth, and fractured toes and fingers rarely rise to the attention of the medics. Many older men say the sport has gotten too rough for them. "Nowadays it's all changed to where football has come into full roll. And when these younger guys started coming out, they still had the football skills," explained Richard McMillan in 2011. "They try to hit each other, and they try to knock you senseless. That's what made me decide, 'Hey, I'd rather make it to work next week before I'm laying in the hospital.'" Richard is not alone in naming football as the culprit of rough play, but all admit that stickball has always been a rough sport. Every stickball player has an injury story; most have many. And while these stories are shared predominately by men, the rise in women's stickball and the ferocity with which it is played ensures that women will have more and more stories to tell about first games, worst injuries, fierce rivalries, and triumphant wins.

THREE-DAY CELEBRATION

HAROLD COMBY, B. 1955—PEARL RIVER
TOLD ON JUNE 4, 1997

My mom has told me that there were certain times of the year they would pack up everything in their wagon and go to certain areas.

She recalls one time where they went to Union, the area surrounding Laird Hospital, that open area, where all the Choctaws would meet and camp and dance and sing and eat, play ball for three days and three nights. And she says that the woman of the family would take clothing and just make dresses and shirts and whatever, and the men would make stickball sticks. And some of the White farmers would give them two cows, so they would butcher and barbecue them and just have a big feast for three days.

Whenever they went on that trip, that three-day celebration, my mom said they used to pull the leaves from the cornstalk and put it on the wagon to make mattresses. Put a quilt on top of it. When they get there, in turn, they would use those corn leaves to feed the animals. That was a way of improvising.

LITTLE BROTHER OF WAR

RICHARD MCMILLAN, B. 1961—TUCKER
TOLD IN 2011

They call it little brother of war.

My grandfather used to tell me that it was just a symbol, that the people, the communities, a long time ago, they'll have a little gathering over in like Tucker or Standing Pine. And there used to be called runners that would go and tell the communities, "Hey, we got a festival that's going on two moons," or whatever, "suns," or whatever, and they'd all go and meet over there. And they'll start.

Communities would gather up and start playing.

And they would usually have, like Tucker was going to play against Conehatta. Conehatta's team would throw out their valuables, and Tucker would throw out their valuables, and they would play for the valuables there. And whoever won, they'd get all of it, then divide it among themselves.

STICKBALL GAMES

LOUISE WILSON, B. 1950—BOGUE CHITTO
TOLD ON JUNE 10, 1997

And another thing my grandfather talked about was stickball games. He said that nowadays they've got rules and regulations for the stickball, and it's only once a year. But years ago, in his day, when he was a young man, he said that they would have it just whenever they felt like it, whenever the elders got together and said, "Hey," you know, "why don't we have a stickball game this weekend?"

And they said, "OK." They would go all out to have these stickball games.

And he said that they chose to have a stickball game between Nanih Waiya and the Bogue Chitto Clan. And back then, they didn't have cars or anything like that. So the family, the women would bring the pots and pans, carry everything that they would need because he said now we want to do this for days.

He said back then it took about two, three days to get there by walking. And they would do that. And he said just before they get there, they would know it; they would start singing. And they would sing. I remember one song said something like, "Biscuit a̱nonachih, mayyalika" [Make the biscuits for me; I'm on the way]. And he kept saying it over and over like that. And, "Okli tolachi̱h" [We're going to play ball"], he would say. The songs, what it was is like, what they plan to do, is more or less all the words he was talking about. He said, "Make sure to have the biscuit done because I'm on my way, and we're going to play ball," or something like that. And everybody would be singing it on their way on this little trail that they had made.

The families and they all come out there. When they come out there, they will bring their pots and pans and things like that. But the one, the home team, as you would so call it, the one that invited this team to come over there, they would already have their pots out there. Their hominy. And he said that back then it really wasn't hog meat that they ate; it was cow meat that they had. It was beef. And they make those biscuits outside. So by the time they arrived, they would have something. They always had food to eat all the time.

Well, he said they would drink. They'd start drinking. They would have moonshine, or they would have the homebrew. It was called a homemade beer. I remember how that was made because I seen my aunt do that. But they would have either moonshine or homebrew, and all the men will be out there, and they would drink, and they laugh, and they carry on just having a big old party until the next morning. They know they were going to have a big fight because that's the time the ball games were going to start early the next day. And he said that once they have this dinner and all of this, that the next day the team was over here and other team was over here, they getting ready, getting prepared. And they whoop and holler, and they just get ready. And they have their outfits on and everything.

They have medicine men out there, he said. And so here they come. They had the game.

And he said they didn't have no time-outs. They had no resting time. It just went on and on and on. And it could go on for all day, through the evening because he said back then they didn't have limitations. They had somebody to come in after them, take their place; they get out, somebody else takes their place and things like that. That's the way it went.

And so he said lot of them get beat up, broken nose, and everything like that, but they had to stay like that because they didn't have cars to go to the hospital or anything like that. But the medicine men were there to help fix some of the problems that they had.

Then the next day they would play ball again. Same thing. And he said it could go on for three days, and he said you could just imagine how tired everybody was by the time it ended up like on the third day or whenever it finally ended. They didn't need to be mad at each other anything like that; they got to see that this was a great game. You won or lost, whatever happened.

And then they may make a date. "Since you invited us, you come to us at a certain time, and we'll play stickball over here." So that they would invite them.

And that's how he said they used to do it a long time ago, whereas now we have it during the fair as far as competition. He said, yeah, there were times when women did get in there and play. They got hurt just like the men did, but there were times when women did get in there. But he said that they prefer not to go in there. But if they didn't have enough because it went on all day long, that they didn't have enough to rest or anything like that, then maybe they would get thrown in there, not thrown in there [*laughter*], but let them go in there and let them, you know, play stickball too.

But he said in his memory, he remembers most times, they were good times. He said they worked and worked, but when it was time to play stickball, it was time for them to be like little boys again.

GAMBLING AND FIGHTING

BARCOM KING, B. 1923—CONEHATTA
TOLD ON JUNE 21, 1973

They used to set up a table on which they placed things. Like long time ago, there were many things that a person would like to have, like shirts, pants that were perfectly made, and beads of all kinds. And these were some of the things that were placed on the table. Winner take all.

They used to play against people they didn't know. Fighting would usually occur when one team played against players they didn't know. So in order to stop the fighting, they had to stop the game.

ROUGH GAMES

BOBBY JOE, B. 1953—BOGUE CHITTO
TOLD ON JULY 30, 1999

My momma was telling me, she told me that her daddy was playing stickball at that time, when he was young. Her dad was born and raised over here in Bogue Chitto. When he was young, he used to go out there. Well, he really didn't play; it was his dad was a full-grown man. He used to play stickball against the Imoklasha.

Anyway, he said the Bogue Chitto team come over, even though they was going to have to walk back then. When they come over, when they played that stickball game, they had a bet against one another for something. The Bogue Chitto team would bring some kind of things: make beautiful sash or some kind of things. They built it; then they bring it over. And those people, they had it the same way.

But he said, talking about a stickball game, they had rough games. They were mean ones.

They were called Imoklasha Choctaw. Their language is same as us.

Anyway, when they played that stickball game, they don't go by numbers. The Bogue Chitto team go out and have about a hundred of them. And they came the same way. No referee, no nothing. All they do is just get somebody to toss up that ball. That's when the game begin.

They said—talking about them fighting—they would start fighting one another. Rest of the team was trying to get them balls, trying to score in that goal. And they said that the Bogue Chitto women came out to the edge of the field, and those ladies, they met, and all they did was start fighting on the edge of the ball field because they're trying to get whatever they betted against that game. They try to keep it. And if they win, they're going to get this Bogue Chitto stuff that they bring. So they want to keep both of them. Bogue Chitto doing the same way. Try to keep what they got. That's the way the women would fight one another.

They said when the game was over all the Bogue Chitto team was nothing but bloodshed coming back home. Broken leg, broken arm, being cut up. Nothing but blood coming back home. The women do it the same way.

They say a lot of times Bogue Chitto was going to win that game. That's the way they used to play.

WHIPPING UP THE PLAYERS

THERON "DUKE" DENSON, B. 1956—PEARL RIVER
TOLD ON JUNE 15, 2021

My great-grandmother told my mother that during the stickball games, the women would have switches and whip the players in order to get them mad. They wanted to get the players mad, so the players would be mad enough to go out and kill somebody on the field.

NO BLOOD, NO GAME

HENRY WILLIAMS, B. 1945—CONEHATTA
TOLD IN 2011

Some White people would ask, "Hm? How come y'all play that? A lot of blood."

"There's no blood, there's no game," I say. "You got to hurt each other. You got to hurt somebody. You don't get hurt, it's not stickball." [*laughter*]

FAMILY SUCCESSION

HENRY WILLIAMS, B. 1945—CONEHATTA
TOLD IN 2011

I started playing around when I was twelve years old because at that time my grandpa was still playing, and the community decided that he just got too old. So, because of injury, they didn't want him playing, so I replaced him. My daddy looked at me, "Put it on" [referring to the team jersey]. I didn't volunteer; I didn't say I can play. My dad says, "Put it on." That's when I started playing stickball.

FOLLOWING FATHER'S FOOTSTEPS

HILLARY MEAGAN VAUGHN, B. 1989—PEARL RIVER
TOLD ON JUNE 7, 2023

I was introduced to stickball—it was my dad, going to all his practices. Sometimes it was, I *had* to go, but eventually it was just something that we did: we went to his practices; we went with him riding in his little green Ford Ranger, two seat . . . It was so small! [*laugh*]

To this day, I still remember the old field.

This year, me and Bree, my younger sister, are playing with Bók Chito to represent my dad [who passed away December 2022]. Because we're originally playing with Pearl River, that's who we've been playing with for a while.

So, I remember the old field, bumpy roads, mud, just hole in the wall somewhere, and it was just a pasture. No trees, no lights, it was just open pasture. It was hot. Hot July, June, Bogue Chitto day.

And stickball also isn't just a team; it's a family. And so everybody there, they just welcomed everybody. It was fun. Of course, when I was little and I was there, we played with the other kids. But while playing, we would have our sticks or have something and act like we're playing stickball.

So that's where I got introduced, was him.

EARNING A SPOT ON THE TEAM

MARK PATRICK, B. 1969—O̱TOKLO (CONEHATTA)
TOLD ON JULY 12, 2021

I had kind of played around with some sticks in earlier years because my great uncle was making stickball sticks, but I just couldn't get into it until it was after high school. I had graduated high school, and I got recruited for football at Jackson State University. From there, I think one of my cousins said, "Mark, as athletic as you are, why are you not playing stickball?" I said, "I don't know. I just hadn't got the interest."

So, we got in his backyard and started practicing just throwing. He said he would just underhand, just throw in. Within minutes, I was beginning to catch and scoop and throw, and I was just getting used to the sticks and everything. I mean, within minutes. And he said, "Man, I'm playing with Conehatta this year; you ought to sign up. I'll go ahead and tell the coach."

One thing led to another that summer, which I've never played in the youth. I was about nineteen years old at the time, and I went to Conehatta.

Conehatta had one big rivalry. There was one team that they could not, for years, could not beat. You know what team that was, at that time in the nineties, early nineties? Beaver Dam. Beaver Dam was pretty dominant at the time, and they had probably 150 players. Everybody wanted to play.

I remember my wife—who was my girlfriend at the time; we weren't married yet—she said, "You ought to play with Beaver Dam; they're the best."

And you know why I decided I'm not going to play with Beaver? It's just because she said that. My purpose is, "Okay, we're going out to beat the best." So I said, "What Conehatta has is about community anyway." So I signed up.

And because I've never played, these guys have been playing all these years, "How fair would it be for me to just come in and take a starting position? These guys are just not going to like me very well, I wouldn't think," I was thinking.

So I went to practice, did my very best. I was running full speed, and they were getting ready to pick the starters for the fair; fair is coming up. And, I remember this one guy, and I'm not going to call his name, but there was one guy in practice, he just kept scooping the ball, just running around people. He was just dominating practice.

One day I said, "Man, I'm going to hit this guy. I'm going to show him some of my football skills." So, just as he scooped the ball up, man, I just nailed him. But when I nailed him, I didn't know his sticks was going to come up right here [*points at his forehead*], and it leveled him right here and split him wide open. Blood just covered his face.

And they were like, "Whoa, man!" Of course, he was okay, just a lot of blood.

And the coach came up to me; he said, "Man, the way you hit, you're going to start on defense."

So I started. I was a starter first time that I've ever played.

Anyway, make a long story short, we played this game, this game, this game, this game, all the way to the championship—Beaver Dam. So we beat Beaver Dam in overtime.

Overtime lasted almost an hour. So we were dead tired. We had played the night before. Beaver Dam had played on Thursday night, so they had a day to rest. But we didn't. But we were determined, and we won.

JUST ONE BIG HIT

HILLARY MEAGAN VAUGHN, B. 1989—PEARL RIVER
TOLD ON JUNE 7, 2023

Now, my first time I played, I think I was fifteen, and I was so scared. I went to my dad's practices, but it's always different when you first get in. Now, when I played though, it was coed, so it was boys and girls at that age.

This was before they had the different divisions.

But I was so scared. But my dad always told me, and I still carry this with me . . . Because every year, it never fails, it's like, I just got to get hit one good time, and I'll be ready. But it's always, you're anticipating, you're like . . . But yeah, my first game, I just thought, "I got to get hit one good time, one good time." And I did, and then I'm like, "I'm ready. I'm ready."

I told myself, "I just got to get hit, and I'll be ready."

And so, that's where the story comes in, where I had my first big hit. Now, that wasn't a game, though; that was at practice. And it was an accident; it wasn't an intentional hit, but stuff like that happens.

And I remember it was me and another girl, and I can't remember her name; we were going after the ball, and I don't know what happened. I don't know if she fell, and then I tripped over her or something, and then that's how they just called it, out of bounds, and said, "Just get the ball. Throw it up."

In the middle of all that happening, she was laying this way on my side, her knees up facing towards my body. And I was getting up, I was on my hands and knees, and then another player who was coming full speed, could not stop. She hit me on my side, which caused the girl's knees to charley horse me, and my lungs just . . . [*mimes not being able to catch her breath*]. And I fell over, and they're like, "Calm down; calm down . . . " And I was freaking out. I'm over here thinking I'm going to die.

My first big hit was at practice, and it was on accident. I've gotten hit in the face, on the eye, on the arm, the legs, but that's the hit I always remember.

I thought, "Okay, if I can take that hit, I can take any hit."

TAKE IT OR QUIT

BRADLEY ALEX, B. 1955—BOGUE HOMA / PEARL RIVER
TOLD ON JUNE 30, 2021

Stickball, that's the only thing I think we have to prove yourself that you're worthy, it seems like.

It was like this also. If you know that a new player came up from on the opposite team, you went for him. Either he was going to take it or quit. Especially the new guys that came upon us. We used to tell them, "They're going to come after you, but be ready." You learn how to fall down and roll.

FIRST BLOOD

BRADLEY ALEX, B. 1955—BOGUE HOMA / PEARL RIVER
TOLD ON JUNE 30, 2021

I used to play stickball. I started playing when I was about thirteen. And that was the first kids' youth stickball exhibition we had, skin against shirt. They picked a team, boys, and my brother was on the other side, the other team. And he's the one who ever hit me the first time and draw blood, right on top of my head. He almost knocked me out. I heard "tok" [*laugh*].

I told my mom, and she said, "Well, you deserve it."

And he said, "You should have moved." [*laughter*]

SANDWICHED

BRADLEY ALEX, B. 1955—BOGUE HOMA / PEARL RIVER
TOLD ON JUNE 30, 2021

I had a lot of damage to my body because of stickball. I had messed up my knees.

Conehatta had two big guys. I saw the one on this side coming, and I knew what I was going to do. The ball came, and I ran over there. And as soon as I'm about to pick it up, I didn't see this big guy coming. And he hit me on my shoulder. At the same time, they pushed me toward this way, and they hit me. And they crunched me. Both of them fell, and I fell too. Anyway, they made a bread sandwich out of me.

I had dislocated my shoulder, and I didn't feel it at first. I went and tried to grab my stick and got it. And I went like this, and it was all the way over here. And I looked at it, I said . . . When I went like this, it was all the way over here. And I said, "What's going on?" I was standing there just by myself playing.

But it was sticking up, my shoulder, that part. It was sticking up way far up.

And I went to the EMT. I got somebody to come in. I went to see the EMT. They said, "It's broken."

I said, "Are you sure?"

They said, "Yeah."

So I didn't go in. And I went to the hospital, and they said, "Oh, we can know . . ." And when they took the X-rays, "You got to have surgery now."

And throughout that weekend, I was in pain. I was in pain, so they had to do a reconstructive one.

STRONG MEDICINE

HAROLD COMBY, B. 1955—PEARL RIVER
TOLD ON JUNE 4, 1997

Stickball was off-limits to the younger kids because back then there was a lot of medicine men, and they openly exhibited their powers. I've heard of even stories where they used to carry mirrors. I guess the medicine man or *hopaii*, whichever name they used, they just shined a light on the opponent. And I've even heard that one of them cracked the other one's mirror. I guess that's how powerful his medicine was.

PASSED DOWN

HARLEY VAUGHN, B. 1961—HALLS, TN / BOGUE CHITTO
TOLD ON MAY 31, 1996

I know one guy who has a horse tail. It's a big old belt, about four inches wide. And it looks real good. It means that he can run fast like a horse when he wears that tail. Nobody can catch him.

I think it was passed on from his father, father on down. From his grandfather. He said it's been in his family for quite a while. He still has it.

HORSE TAIL

JOHN MINGO JR., B. 1946—STANDING PINE
TOLD IN 2016

One time, I wore one with a horse tail. I played that way at one time. I used to play in the middle because I was fast. And when they did that, the tail of the players would go like this [*shows waving flowing motion with his arm*] as they went by.

GOALIE

HARLEY VAUGHN, B. 1961—HALLS, TN / BOGUE CHITTO
TOLD ON MAY 31, 1996

I know one guy that you could throw the ball at him, at the goal, he'll stand there, he'll catch it. In reverse, he can throw the stick, and he can tell you, he can hit that pole in front of him. That's how good he is.

He's old now. He retired. He was good. There was no way you could get a ball by him. Nowadays, players stand against the pole. He never did as far as I know. He would move up two yards and stand there. That ball was coming towards him, he was going to catch it either way.

The game has changed a lot, how you play and how you're going to win the game.

HULA DANCING

MELFORD FARVE, B. 1961—TUCKER
TOLD ON JULY 10, 1997

We had a local character in Tucker. And they put him at goalie for some reason. And I didn't see it, but my brother-in-law was laughing at him at halftime. "You're supposed to be standing there. You're supposed to stand straight up."

But every time the ball would come, he'd go this way, and he'd go the other way. Looked like hula dancing. [*laughter*] He was dodging!

SMACK TALKING

MARK PATRICK, B. 1969—Q̱TOKLO (CONEHATTA)
TOLD ON JULY 12, 2021

I don't know if they still do it or not, but every year there's a place called Chucalissa in Tennessee in Memphis. People always told me about Chucalissa. They said, "We go over there; it's a short field, it's a small pole or whatever. What they do is they demonstrate the game of stickball, and just a few people, they just mix and match. You ought to go."

And so, we decided to go that summer. We drove on up. Just as we were getting to the parking lot, this guy was standing at that front door on the outside, just as we pulled up in my truck.

In my toolbox, that's where I had my sticks. And they said, "You need to go ahead and sign up because after so many people sign up, it's going to be a limit." So several people from here, from various teams, was going to go. I know that I wanted to participate, so I got there.

Just as I was pulling my sticks out of my toolbox, there's this guy, I guess he was Choctaw. He was speaking in English to me, but he was standing there, and he was a real smart aleck. I mean, he was just a real smart aleck. He said, "Hey, I see you got your sticks. They're giving stickball lessons over here. You probably need to get some stickball lessons if you're going to play against me."

That's what he said. Darlene, who was my girlfriend at the time, before we got married, she says, "He has no idea who he's talking to, does he?"

I said, "Nope, he doesn't." So, I didn't say anything. I just kind of grinned and got my sticks, and I went on in. That afternoon, we were going to be demonstrating, and I made sure that I was on the opposite team that he was on. And boy, I was pumped because I was only twenty-four at the time. I was pumped, and I just, I could not wait to get him on that field.

I roughed him up pretty good during that demonstration game.

After that, he came and he said, "Hey, I'm thinking about taking a team to Georgia, maybe. Do you think you'd like to be on my team? I really want to take you and want you to be on my team."

I said, "Nah, I got to get some more lessons." So, I left it there. [*laughter*]

MISSISSIPPI VERSUS OKLAHOMA

MEAGAN VAUGHN, B. 1989—PEARL RIVER
TOLD ON JUNE 7, 2023

There was the little rivalry at the very beginning with Tvshka Homma [the first stickball team from Oklahoma to play in the World Series of Stickball tournament in Mississippi].

And the first game was with Bók Chito. You talk about stickball pride, not only just Bók Chito, but stickball pride in general. This was the first game that I had seen where the tribe came together, and we did a whiteout at the stadium to let Tvshka Homma know, hey, this is where it started; this is our game; you're just a visitor. Because there was that little issue of, they were saying, or what we were hearing was, "They're the champion of stickball," and it's like, "Oh no, wait until you get here; we're going to show you who's the champion." So there's that big rivalry.

But it was just neat how everybody as a tribe came together and wore white. Because Bók Chito is white and red. That stadium was white; and you saw where Tvshka Homma fans were; and you saw the whole stadium was white. And everybody was just like, "Get them, get them, get them . . . "

And I want to say it was a blowout game, like the first game. It was a blowout game. And that was a good game to watch, especially with the rivalry going on.

HANGING UP THE STICKS

TRAVIS WILLIS, B. 1958—PEARL RIVER
TOLD ON JUNE 14, 2021

I played it until 1983. And the reason why I quit playing is my back was hurting one day. I went to the hospital, and they referred me to a back surgeon in Meridian. This was 1982 or '83, after the fair.

This doctor, he was an old guy, probably retired by now. He saw my X-ray and all this stuff. He said, "I saw you fall."

And I was sitting there going, "What?"

And he said—I guess I had that look on my face—and he said, "I was there when y'all were playing." He said, "You fell on this side when that guy flipped you over."

It was a big guy. I tried to jump over him, too, and he flipped me.

And he said, "I saw you fall." He said, "I saw the way you fell." He said, "I'm going to give you a piece of advice." He said, "If you don't quit playing now, you'll be in a wheelchair because your back is that bad," he said.

And I had, in total, like five back surgeries.

OUTLAWED BUT UNDERGROUND

DAN ISAAC, B. 1968—PEARL RIVER
TOLD ON JUNE 27, 2021

We had stickball, and when missionaries came, it was violent to them. People would die, or there was a lot of gambling going on. And to them, with all the feasting, they thought it was a waste of food. They were like, "All this celebration, they're going to be starving later on; they're going to be hungry; we need to stop all these celebrations."

Because we're a people that love to have feasts and giveaways and gambling where it would be like for a game, we would maybe bet a horse.

He [*pointing at Carmen Denson*] would have a horse; I would have a horse. Or the women, there was always all the pots and the pans and the utensils, and there would be a designated place where they would cook, next to the where they fix their plate.

So, that's why we gambled a lot. We knew we could make more, but it was things that you made, you bet it.

So, when it was outlawed, we still wanted do things like sports. So when baseball came, and it was accepted by the missionaries and churches and everybody, it was our way of saying, "Let's keep it going; let's play baseball, let's play basketball; let's whatever, football."

But everyone here knows that stickball was still here; it was underground. We would play it deep in the woods and forests somewhere, and it actually never was totally outlawed for us. But for the public, we played baseball, and it evolved from that, I think.

That's my belief, just speaking to elders; different elders have told me these things.

PICNICS AND BALL GAMES

Choctaw "picnics" evolved out of the stickball game weekends common in the past. Instead of games that lasted one or two days, with people dancing late into the evening, these picnics were day-long affairs, begun as soon as people could gather and over by evening, so people could get back home. Instead of stickball, they played baseball and softball. Host teams provided the food, but sold drinks to help defray the cost, a practice common throughout Choctaw social life such as during house dances and community Christmas celebrations. During breaks in the ball games, or after they were finished, people might play washers, while the kids continued to play amongst themselves. In more recent years, volleyball and cornhole tournaments emerged.

"It was almost like a powwow," explains Carmen Denson, making the connection between the Choctaw picnic and the pervasive intertribal powwow circuit that crisscrosses the country today. "But Choctaw liked that because there was no such thing as casinos. There was no such thing as cell phones. We were poor, so we didn't have too much TV too. So every family usually goes to the games. It was a big thing in the community. And also the food was free!"

Transportation remained a challenge as it was with stickball. Although cars were more common, young players in particular typically needed to be picked up by their coaches in order to get to the games, something that continues to a lesser extent today. Throughout these stories, we see the commitment of adults in the community to put together teams, coach and encourage them, and raise funds to pay for jerseys and equipment. While many of those teams were community based, family was beginning to rise in importance as an organizing principle for social life. "We had a family baseball team that went for a lot of years," remembers Gordon Sam. "My aunts and then their friends, they would have a softball team, and my grandpa and my uncles used to have a baseball team. When they got old, and they couldn't play no more, the younger generation just picked it up." But the competitive spirit to win meant teams recruited from other families and other communities. Bradley Alex recalls playing for three different family teams, none his own family. "When I was a teenager, I played with the adult teams. I played with three different adult teams. I had my glove. When they pass by, if I wanted to go play with them, they honk the horn. I got my glove and chased the truck and got in it."

Although most games were intertribal, teams occasionally played White and Black teams as well, testing the waters of integration. Sometimes the games were collegial. Other times, there was friction, as deep biases, stereotypes, and assumptions surfaced on the field. But racial lines could be as blurry then as they are now, and it was not always easy to distinguish Choctaw from non-Choctaw, particularly in cases of intermarriage. The stories told with the most laughter involve

Choctaw teams assuming their competition cannot understand them when they speak in Choctaw, only to find the tables turned, to great humorous effect.

A more serious theme runs through many of the stories as well: using medicine to impact the outcome of the game. During stickball games of the past, this was an acknowledged role of the medicine man. However, over time, such practices were deemed unfair and unacceptable. While some believe they were stopped, others say they were just driven underground. Today, surprise wins and unexpected outcomes may still evoke accusations that a team used medicine to win.

Today, softball has pushed baseball to the sidelines, just as formally organized tournaments have replaced informal community games. In 2022, the tribe hosted the Chief's Fourth Annual Summer Slam Softball Tournament with four divisions: men's, women's, coed, and men's forty-plus, Youth leagues and school teams, however, keep baseball, basketball, and football as well as softball and stickball a central part of recreation and sport within the tribe.

PLAY ALL DAY, DANCE ALL NIGHT

EVALINE DAVIS, B. 1945—CONEHATTA / TUCKER
TOLD JUNE 3, 2021

Well, they used to call it "picnic."

And they used to gather up the team, and they used to all go around that ball field, and they used to have a picnic. And ladies be out there cooking, and they used to have a lunch out there. And they'd be playing all day long.

They used to do that as far as I can remember. But that was baseball. They gather up the communities. That's what they used to do. So that's why they have the games going all day long.

And then after the ball game, they used to have a dance. They used to have a dance, and then they'd be dancing all night 'til Sunday morning.

PICNIC

MELFORD FARVE, B. 1961—TUCKER
TOLD ON JUNE 1, 2021

One of the social gatherings is called a "picnic."

Most communities back then had baseball teams, and they would play each other during the summer. One team, like Tucker, was going to invite Conehatta.

The thing about it is you feed them. You're going to do the hominy.

I remember mornings, the women, either the ball players' wives or mothers, they'd be doing the hominy and frying the chicken and the *shoti* [kettle, typically large, black, cast iron]. I guess somebody set up a long table. We didn't have the tables we have now. You can go to Walmart and get these tables, but back then they had to build it.

So mornings, you'd see smoke from the fire and people getting the food prepared. And then once it was getting ready, they would . . . I can't remember if they ate first. I think they did. They would eat first, and then the baseball team would play and have a good crowd out there. Afterwards sometimes, the daughters of the men, the men's daughters would form a team, wives and the women would play each other.

Some of the community might call for a picnic, and we'd go over there, and they would feed us too. It was good interaction. Our communities didn't really see each other 'til either fair time, and here you can have them, and you can interact with each other, and there was no alcohol involved, so it was just good sportsmanship. It was always a good feeling getting together like that.

But no one's done the picnic in a long time. I wish somebody would, just to form a tradition that used to be a tradition.

It was also a time for the young people to meet or play. We'd have a pickup baseball game or something, use a rolled-up paper cup or something like that. It was just generally being together, I always felt.

Fair time was like that too. Fair time was people I've never seen, or they were relatives, but you didn't know them. Mom would point them out. "That's your cousin," or "They're this," or "They're that."

PUTTING A TEAM TOGETHER

LINDA WILLIAMS, B. 1958—STANDING PINE
TOLD ON JUNE 15, 2021

When I was growing up, I'd say I might've been like six, seven years old. Well, there was nothing to do during those days. There was nothing to do. And so I guess my dad's nephew, some of his nephews wanted to play ball, or they wanted to do something on Saturday evenings and Sunday evenings, afternoons. They don't have anything to do. So they wanted to start playing ball, which was baseball. So my dad said, "Well, if y'all going to really play," he says, "then play hard." He said, "I'll try to coach y'all and get y'all started."

And so that's how he did. He formed a team, went around the community and asked who wants to play. And he formed a team, organized it, and that's how they got started.

And he also told them then, because these are young boys, and so he also told him that "y'all going to have to help me too." Because a lot of times when we have games, he used to want to sell drinks to make a profit for the team. So he told them that they're going to have to help him.

And they did. They did. And that's how their social life was.

FROM PITCHING WASHERS TO PITCHING SOFTBALL

LINDA WILLIAMS, B. 1958—STANDING PINE
TOLD ON JUNE 15, 2021

When I first began, it was fastpitch [softball] because when my father was having picnics and going out to communities, they started having females' game too. So, I was little, but he said, "Play." So elders, I mean the people who were older than me, played. But I played along with them. And I started pitching fastpitch, and that's how I got to learn pitching.

And then, I think it was later on in my teenage years, that's when things changed, and they started playing slowpitch, and I started pitching slowpitch.

But I have to say I was a good pitcher because what my dad taught me and putting that washer in that hole: aim it, and throw it; aim it, and throw it. And I could do the same with the softball pitching, my strikes. That was hardly a time I threw balls. If you're going to stand there and watch me, I'll strike you out! [*laughter*]

It was just a game of fun, and we all used to enjoy it. We'd laugh if we fall down, slide or whatever. And those ladies used to love to say something and make themselves laugh and make others laugh. And so, it was just a game of joy and have fun.

CELEBRATING THE BEGINNING AND END OF SCHOOL

GLADYS WILLIS, B. 1926—PEARL RIVER
TOLD ON MAY 19, 1997

When they had the first day of school, they used to play baseball and softball in the afternoon. Then at night, in the evening, they used to have stickball, and then they used to dance at night. They used to do that a long time ago, when I was still going to school. The first day of school, and then the last day of school, they do the same.

IF YOU DON'T TRY .-.-.

EVALINE DAVIS, B. 1945—CONEHATTA / TUCKER
TOLD JUNE 3, 2021

My husband played baseball back then. All I knew was that he was playing baseball about every weekend. Sometimes Saturdays, sometimes Sunday, sometime both.

I never played myself, not no kind of game, so I never knew. But my cousin over at Standing Pine, he started a team, and he wanted me to play with him. I said, "I never played any ball, so I don't know."

"Well, get out there. You'll learn it. I'm going to teach you. You're going to learn it."

So my husband said, "If you don't try, you never learn it."

So those two guys got me out in the field. I just stood there looking.

One time a ball liked to pop me on the head! [*laughter*]

CLEATS UP

MELFORD FARVE, B. 1961—TUCKER
TOLD ON JULY 10, 1997

Sometimes they played White teams.

One game in particular, this guy, this White player, came roaring into third base, and he slid, but as he was sliding, he had his foot up, so you could tell he was trying to spike the guy, the third baseman. And he did. Created a large gash on his leg. Everyone knew he did it on purpose, and that caused a lot of friction right then.

I don't think they ever played them again. I don't think they did. It just caused a lot of animosity.

SURPRISE IN THE WELL

MELFORD FARVE, B. 1961—TUCKER
TOLD ON JULY 10, 1997

It was really laid back, back then. Nothing was hurried. Everything was done, just go, go, just go do it.

The older guys used to get us to go get the water.

There was a big house right near the baseball field.

The owner always let us. They had an old well back there. They used to tell some people or certain kids, "Go get the water." And we had to haul this big old Igloo and take it there.

One time in particular, the man who let us, his son lived there, and we knew him. He was about our age. Went to school with him. And me and two of my other buddies who were there, we're trying to get some water, and we didn't know how to run the well, really, I mean how to work the bucket down, because it kept getting caught. So he was watching us all this time. He said, "You don't how to do it."

We said, "We're trying."

He said, "Nah, y'all don't know to do it."

He kept saying how every time we tried it, we still couldn't get the bucket going. So finally, he said, "Let me show you how it's done."

He got off the porch and come over, and he starts doing it, and it goes down real smooth. "See? I told you y'all weren't doing it right." We could hear the bucket hit the water down there. And then he slowly started drawing it up and drawing it up. And he's still bragging about it. "I know how to do this," you know, "My daddy taught me."

And just as the bucket came up, he was about to grab the bucket, but some big old frog had gotten into the water, so as he was reaching for it, it jumped out, scared him, let go of the handle, "Whooosh." Hit the water. [*laughter*]

We just cracked up laughing.

He gets even more angry. "I'm going to show y'all." Walks back. We thought that was pretty funny. [*laughter*]

JOB WELL DONE

BRADLEY ALEX, B. 1955—BOGUE HOMA / PEARL RIVER
TOLD ON JUNE 30, 2021

We had a couple of baseball players that could have made it. Man, they were great. One was Jimmy Williams Sr. and one was Elton Shoemake. Man, they were great. They were great.

I played with them. I liked those groups that I play with.

Both of them back-to-back, they hit a home run. This was a Black team that we played against. They didn't have a fence, but they had some sort of a rope or something like that that no one has ever hit beyond. Those two hit way beyond, in front of a house, the yard. They said no one has ever hit that far. Both of them were left-handed hitters, and they could pull.

And they congratulated them. They even gave them money. [*laughter*] The game like that, if you did something they never did, they pick up and get money out of their pocket and they give it to you. So they congratulate you. They give you money or give you a soda or give you a beer or whatever. [*laughter*] It used to be fun.

COMING TOGETHER

BRIAN BILLIE, B. 1973—RED WATER
TOLD ON JUNE 30, 2021

The development club used to do one. My dad and them, they used to do trash pickup on the side of the road, and they pick it all up. And the people that had the tractor would cut the grass and pick up the trash. And afterwards, they come together to the softball field. They would have the elders, the women, would be cooking the food, and they would have volleyball.

What's that bottle? Whoever can finish the bottle of maybe Kool-Aid or whatever. Things like that. They played washers, softball, and everything around each other. And everybody laid back to watch. And some of the parents would have a chair out, but they would sit and watch where the kids are at all times or that family, they come together, so, they watched each other. My parents still have pictures of the bottle drinking or that old softball field. Back then it just had a backstop. Didn't have a fence around it.

MEDICINE ON THE MOUND

HAROLD COMBY, B. 1955—PEARL RIVER
TOLD ON JULY 23, 1999

In some instances, medicine man will tell you people are jealous, or people want to hurt you because you are a good ball player, or things like that. We have a bad habit of Choctaws hurting each other.

Not too long ago, my nephew used to work for recreation, and he told me that they were raking up the dirt around the pitcher's mound; they found a medicine pouch on there. He said some of the people from Bók Chito who are supposed to be the most traditional group, they didn't want to even get close to it. If you want to get rid of it, you could burn it, but you have to use gasoline or kerosene on it and burn it.

HELP FOR A HOME RUN

EDDIE JOHNSON, B. 1970—STANDING PINE / TUCKER
TOLD ON JUNE 11, 2021

My grandfather on my mom's side had teams over the years. He died before I was born; back in the sixties, he died. But he used to have teams, and a lot of people talk about the ones that used to play for him, and they'd tell me, "I used to play for your grandpa," and all that. Anyway, sometimes he'd get this particular man that practiced medicine to help him on the team. My family ain't innocent doing that. [*laughter*]

But my mother swore up and down that they were playing a team same way as what I was told, and the game was tied, and the medicine man took a bat. I guess it was a wooden bat; I don't think there was aluminum back then. He took a bat as he sat there, and they watched the game. There was no dugout; you're looking at a bench; there's no bleacher. It was a bench people sat around, and they brought lawn chairs if they had it. They would be wooden, homemade stumps, they dug it around and put wood on it and nailed it down. It'd be something like that, but he was sitting on the edge, and he took a bat, one of the bats, and he kept on rubbing it, rubbing it, rubbing it. And she noticed that. Like I said, it was a tight game, and it was getting close to the end.

So, I don't know what inning it was, but rubbed and rubbed and said, "Come here," to my mother. "Come here." It was going to be her turn to bat, and he said, "Take this, that's how you're going to hit. You're going to hit a home run."

The pitching was tough because the way the pitcher was pitching. She was saying it was hard to hit. Some of those ladies knew how to throw knuckleballs and stuff like that and keep you from hitting. She got out there, pow! Gone.

And they didn't have fences back then, and the ball rolled past, and she went around the bases, scored, and broke open the game. I don't know by how much, but she swore up and down it was that medicine man rubbing that bat that did the trick. [*laughter*]

I was wondering was it just psychological? Or was it real? Because sometimes you can put something in someone's mind and say, "This is magic. You will hit it."

PREPARING FOR GAMES

CARMEN DENSON, B. 1956—STANDING PINE
DAN ISAAC, B. 1968—PEARL RIVER
TOLD ON JUNE 27, 2021

Carmen Denson: Women are not supposed to touch your bat or your personal bat or your personal glove because they will weaken you. And that's the belief. If there was a very important game coming up, some people didn't even go to bed with their wives.

Dan Isaac: I think it was a form of purification, they call it. Where you're going to stay pure. And they also say conserving your energies. And the woman, because they have the extra gift that they bring forth life, they have that extra power. Just like with an eagle feather, you can't have an eagle feather near a woman, especially when she's on her, what we call "moon phase." So when a woman is near, even the [stickball] sticks, they would say, "Don't touch my sticks. Don't even get close to it."

Nowadays, people say, "Go get my sticks." And the women go get it or stuff. It wasn't like that.

SPEAKING CHOCTAW

LINDA WILLIAMS, B. 1958—STANDING PINE
TOLD ON JUNE 15, 2021

Way back in those days, we hardly had interracial marriage.

I remember one game. It was so funny. Our boys was playing against . . . There was a Black manager on the team, and they just assumed these people were all Blacks. My dad knew these people, and his wife was Black. *He* was a Choctaw, and his wife was Black, and those kids were half. So they were understanding because my dad knows who they are, and he talks to them. So they understand when you speak Choctaw, and they can speak it too. And my dad knew that. But the kids, the teammates, didn't know that.

And I remember the catcher was catching, and he said something in Choctaw because he was talking to the pitcher. "Just throw it over here. He can't hit it," or something like that. And then that batter, he turned around and said, "I know exactly what you're saying," in Choctaw. Everybody laughed. [*laughter*]

And even me, I was startled, too, because I said, "Oh, he can speak Choctaw!" Everybody, every one of us were like that. And I remember standing there listening, and he told him, "I understand what you're saying. I can speak Choctaw," in Choctaw. "I understand what you're saying. I can speak Choctaw." And he was shocked. Every one of them were shocked.

Today, I can laugh about it. It was funny.

But like I said, during those years, it was just a few or very seldom that was like that. So you never could tell.

So he got caught. And then that was the funniest moment that he had throwing them. And he didn't know what to say after that. He shut his mouth and then . . .

When they came home, he goes, "I didn't know he spoke Choctaw." And that's when my dad said, "Yeah, he's a half Choctaw."

And that's why he told me I need to be careful what you say no matter where; not only here, but no matter where you go, y'all need to be careful how you say things.

PICKUP BASKETBALL

HAROLD COMBY, B. 1955—PEARL RIVER
TOLD ON JUNE 4, 1997

My nephew was playing center for the Choctaw Central High School. He's half White. But he grew up with my mom, so he's pretty good speaking [Choctaw]. So, they went to play some basketball. He said, "Towa it a̱pilacho̱h takossapat saho̱kla hikiyo" [Throw the ball to me; this Black guy can't stop me]. "This guy can't hold me." He thought it was a Black guy guarding him. But that guy said, "Chimáwah kiyo̱." It means "That's what you think." [*laughter*]

CODE BREAKERS

MARK PATRICK, B. 1969—O̱TOKLO (CONEHATTA)
TOLD ON JULY 27, 2022

I got a couple of funny situations. We were talking about football. When we were in junior high school, my brother, who is a year older than I am, was playing for Sebastopol High School. A lot of Choctaws, they didn't know that we were on the team, much less that we were even part Choctaw. We could fluently understand and speak Choctaw. So they had this technique that they used. They would go to the line of scrimmage, and they would call their plays out in Choctaw, not realizing that we were on defense, and we could hear the whole conversation. We could understand their plays and where they're going to throw the ball or where they're going to run it. We were basically the code talkers of our team, and we were breaking the codes and telling our teammates what was going on.

Anyway, the quarterback got up there, and he said, "Well, pimma ish iyakma pit chi, pilalachi̱h [Well, if you go this way (*points to the left*), I will throw it to you].

My older brother, Robert, he turns over and says, "Otis, he's fixing to throw him the ball, the guy right there. You watch him." Sure enough, he stepped out in front of that ball, intercepted it, and ran it back for a touchdown. [*laughter*]

Of course, we won the game. [*laughter*] And then later they realized we knew exactly what they were saying, and so they never did that. I don't know if they ever did it against another team, other teams that didn't understand Choctaw, but they certainly didn't do it against Sebastopol because they realized that we were there, and we understood everything. [*laughter*]

GAMES AND PLAY

In addition to major sports, smaller, more informal games were common also, played during as well as apart from the ball game cycle. In the past, there was chunkey, a game played among two people at a time on a cleared narrow track by throwing long, slender poles at either the rolling chunkey stone or at the opponent's pole. Like stickball and handball, it was a sport that required dexterity and aim in throwing and inspired aggressive gambling over each game.[10] Chunkey is no longer played, though Jackson Isaac describes playing a similar game in the mid-1900s with rabbit sticks. Also no longer played is a version of jacks observed in the 1770s, or the corn game, though DeLaura Saunders played a version similar to both while growing up in the 1960s, using bottle caps or checkers in place of the corn (see "Bottle-Tops Game"). The bullet or moccasin game, where a bullet or stone is hidden beneath a row of hats, handkerchiefs, moccasins, or socks, and opposing players guess where it is hidden, has similarly died out, though many of these games are being demonstrated to the youth through the Department of Chahta Immi as part of their educational outreach programs.

Played in the past and still today is the game of washers or rings, where people pitch large metal washers into small holes dug into the ground.[11] Today, cornhole dominates backyard barbecues and local competitions, showing up for the first time as a competition at the Choctaw Indian Fair in 2021. But washers has hung on, played by old and young alike. At an election night political party hosted by one of the candidates for chief on June 6, 2023, washers was highlighted on flyers alongside house dance, bingo, Choctaw hymns, live music, including both a powwow drum group and a solo singer, and a cupcake walk. Players were mostly men from their late teens to middle age, but a few older players and a few women joined in as well.

When played by adults, these games often included some friendly betting, though nothing like the ambitious gambling of old stickball games. With far more free time and energy, children engage in a much broader range of games, where creativity, imagination, recycling cast-off goods, and resourceful use of the natural landscape provide the tools for play. Scraps of cloth and crumpled paper cups became balls; tree limbs and sticks from old mops and brooms became bats; corn husks became dolls; and tires, bottle caps, sticks, and cans all got repurposed for various forms of play. The primary goal was to have fun. But staying cool was another. "Summer times it was hot," says Billy Chickaway.

> We were always barefoot, and you go walk on the grass, you *couldn't* walk on the grass because it was so hot . . . We didn't have any toys. We made our own toys and that's how we got along. Sometimes friends would come over and then because the house set on piers, you play underneath the house. We just had a lot of good times playing, imagining, using your imagination, and running through the woods. The woods was a lot cooler than the outside. You'd be looking for this or that or thinking about other things and playing and running and so forth. And that's how you built up your wind, build up your stamina, and made you a lot stronger. ("The Games We Played" 2017)

As in any community where smartphones and TVs are ubiquitous, many elders bemoan the shift from creative, physical, outdoor play to more passive, indoor viewing entertainment. But the old games are not gone, new games continue to be added and developed, and imaginative play and roughhousing continue to evoke cries of "Go outside!" from parents, grandparents, aunts, and uncles. And like generations in the past, mass media offers fodder for creation, not just passive entertainment, as kids act out their favorite TV characters, though not always in ways one might expect or hope.[12]

RABBIT STICK THROWING GAME

JACKSON ISAAC, B. 1902—PEARL RIVER
TOLD IN FEBRUARY 1982

Sometimes you want to socialize with them [rabbit sticks]. Game. You can heave them because you got three sticks, and I have three sticks, and she got three sticks—that will be nine. We play a game of takeaway.

I throw my rabbit stick away over yonder about twenty feet, you chunk at it, and if you hit it, you take away from me. And I throw; I take away some of them. You take all of them, and it's a game; that's the end of the game.

But we used to play that way. So we win. Sometimes we bet twenty-five cents a game who gets all the clubs, and we win a dollar. Twenty-five cents a game but a dollar on part and twenty-five cents each.

RING TOSS

EVALINE DAVIS, B. 1945—CONEHATTA / TUCKER
TOLD JUNE 3, 2021

They call it a "ring toss." That's all I can remember that we used to do. And play marbles. Those are the only two games that I can pretty well remember.

Back in those days, the family used to get together in somebody's house. But they let each other know where they're going to be playing and all of that. So everybody knows where they're going to be playing. So they gather up at the house, and they play.

You just make a little hole there and one up front, and I don't know what the distance is, but you just have to toss it in, try to put the ring in the hole, and the score would be to twenty-five. And they got partners. They got two over here and two on the other end and then the one that's not exactly facing but facing the other way, the other person standing here, and they come across there, and it's just like an *X*. [*She motions with her hands that the players toss crisscross.*] That's how they used to play it. But they got to make sure, throwing, tossing those rings in the hole, they got to make twenty-five points.

When they make twenty-five, they get out of there, and there's another team that's coming up to play again, and that's all it is. So it's just once you make the twenty-five, you sit down, and you and your partner sit down, and then the other partners come in, and whoever wins that, they get to sit down, and then there will be someone coming in.

WASHERS ALL DAY

LALINE FARVE, B. 1933—STANDING PINE
TOLD IN 2017

They used to play washers all the time. Sometimes they used to play washer all night and into the morning. Sometimes they would quit just before the morning.

They would dig up two holes. There would be two players that made up a team. They were positioned opposite from each other, one behind each hole. If a washer was tossed into the hole, I think it would count as five points. That's how they used to play it. I think twenty-five would be the winning score. I think it was twenty-five, or maybe thirty.

They continuously played. And there would be a lot of players. They would play until almost morning, or even into the morning. Sunday, they played all day.

A RINGER IN WASHERS

JAY WESLEY, B. 1975—STANDING PINE
TOLD ON JULY 28, 2022

My grandma actually had a playing field, right in the front yard. It was all dirt, and we had grass on the side, and then she had a little hole. And they used to play washers into the night.

She used to be pretty good. She kind of threw it, and because she knew her land, she threw it maybe about three feet in front of everybody else, slide it into the hole. Throw it and slide it into the hole.

PITCHING WASHERS

LINDA WILLIAMS, B. 1958—STANDING PINE
TOLD ON JUNE 15, 2021

I remember the washer throw. They used to have it all the time.

That's how I started pitching [for softball] because my dad told me, "Start doing washer throw. One day you might be a pitcher."

And so, I used to start doing that washer throw when I was little. And I got good. I never missed a hole. Sometimes I put in three or four together, I mean right after another. And so, that got me to play pretty good.

And then, that's when my dad said that "you can be a pitcher now." And then, he started training me to be a pitcher when I was older.

RAG BALL

SUSIE COMBY ALEX, B. 1947—STANDING PINE / PEARL RIVER
TOLD ON JUNE 9, 2021

We had a rag ball, Momma used to make. Together we'll play rag ball and cut off a limb as a bat. We'll put a shoe or something as bases; we'll find something that wouldn't hurt our running. When we get to the base, we wouldn't get hurt or have our foot cut or something; we always had something there. We just had all kinds of makeshift bases, makeshift bats she used to make us; Momma was good at making stick balls.

"STICK" BALL, CORN DOLLS, AND MUSICAL LEAVES

DELAURA SAUNDERS, B. 1950—BOGUE CHITTO
TOLD ON JUNE 29, 2021

There weren't any kind of toys and stuff to play, but you made up games with sticks or branches or wrapped up some rags that you found and made a ball and used some kind of stick to play ball with.

I remember once, when they were picking cotton or working on the cornfield, how my other aunt used to try to teach us to make the corn doll, how you fold the corn husk leaves and tie it with another husk after wrapping it in the middle. And then we tried to make some corn dolls.

I remember cousins and my sister; we were playing out in the grass. You take the longest—and I don't remember at the particular grass they call, but it was a slim leaf that grew out of it. I used to take those. I'd hold it in a certain way. Then you could make sounds. So we would try to outdo each other to see who could make the weirdest sound. Then pretty soon we'd take turns going, "Pfft, pfft pfft." [*blowing sound*] So those things. [*laughter*]. Except you had to be real careful with those because it would tear if you blow on it too hard. So you'd have to get another one. [*laughter*]

SIMPLE FUN

ELIZABETH BELL ALLEN, B. 1947—BOGUE CHITTO
TOLD IN 2016

We didn't have toys because we couldn't afford them. So we would play with a tire. If there was an old tire laying around, we would put dirt in it and roll it. The dirt would start falling out. That is what we would play and have fun with since that would be our toy.

And we would also use a stick and a lard can since there was a top on it. We would put a nail through it, and since it could roll, we would use the stick to push it. We used to think that we were really playing. [*laugh*]

On every Friday night—the Wallace family was my mom's side of the family—my dad used to take us to go see them, or our other relatives. When we got there, our cousins would also be there, so we would play together. And like us, they didn't have much either. They had a long house. You could go all the way through from one end to the other end. We would all get together and go through the house. We would really think we were playing, going through the house with our cousins.

And that is how we used to play.

TIRE CASING

JOHN MINGO JR., B. 1946—STANDING PINE
TOLD IN 2016

They call it tire casing, with the casing. We would place the casing on a tall hill, then we would get inside it [tire casing] and race each other down the hill [*hand motions indicate rolling head over heels*]. That is what we used to do.

FLOATING AND DAYDREAMING

GORDON SAM, B. 1959—STANDING PINE
TOLD ON JULY 6, 2021

Sometimes you've got to have some leisure time away from work. These days, vehicles, they don't have what they call "tubes," but back in my day, inner tubes was a valuable commodity to us. It's something that you could patch up. You'd be driving your tractor across the field, going to the canal, blow it [inner tube] up, throw it in the water, and just lay there and daydream, you know? Just daydream about what you want to do in life.

HOMEMADE GAMES

HAROLD COMBY, B. 1955—PEARL RIVER
TOLD IN 2017

I know my parents used to use the Coke bottle caps for checkers: one side had the top up, and the other side had the top down. And then we would use cardboard. We would take a ruler and make out the squares and darkened some of the spots out, and we would use that as a checkerboard.

Another thing is we used to play what we call "rings" or *tali chanaha pila* [metal hoop]. We played that.

And if we went to a neighbor's house like on a weekend night, like a birthday party or something, we would do what we call can *halhlhi* [kick the can]. We would set a can, and somebody would guard it, and we would have people trying to come and kick the can. The last one, if you got caught, you would lose.

BOTTLE-TOPS GAME

DELAURA SAUNDERS, B. 1950—BOGUE CHITTO
TOLD ON JUNE 29, 2021

They had learned to play with bottle tops. Kind of like jacks, except we didn't have a rubber ball. But we would just throw them up in the air, however many pieces each person had. You just throw it up in the air. Then you establish what your points was going to be. So how many of those flipped up or how many of those flipped down, depending on what the points were to get the scores.

You just threw them up, then how it fell, because you decided your points how it was going to be, or else if you were able to hold out your hand and catch as many as you could, then you had greater points.

HIDE AND SEEK

TERRY BEN, B. 1957—STANDING PINE
TOLD ON JUNE 10, 2021

For any student, any school you go to, recess time is the most important time of the day. Recess, anywhere you go. Thirty minutes in the morning; thirty minutes in the afternoon. It was time to, maybe a short game of baseball or whatever. The girls' favorite game during that time period was jacks.

Do y'all know what jacks is?

You have a little ball and those different type metal things. The girls would gather around and I guess have competitions.

The boys played baseball and then just play tagged or hide and seek or whatever during that time period.

I'll tell you one thing that we did: we played hide and seek one time. And so, behind Standing Pine Elementary was an underground sewer line that has not been used for years. You had a little manhole on one side; you had a manhole, maybe about fifty yards down.

One time I said, "Nobody's going to find me." And so I took that manhole cover off. I looked inside, and I went because I knew where the other opening was anyway. I got to the other side, looked up and all that. They never found me.

I never told anybody; principal never knew it; teacher never saw me. It was not something to do. I would not do [it again], but I did do it during that time. I don't know, just a young person. [*laughter*]

KICK THE CAN

MARTHA FERGUSON, B. 1949—STANDING PINE
TOLD ON JUNE 4, 2021

We played kick the can. And one place they lived in, in Standing Pine, way off, close to the woods, was an older house, a long one. It's like a storage, middle bedroom, and living room, and the kitchen. And that's the way it looks.

I think they took Uncle Ray since he had polio, taken to hospital. So they left, and Uncle was there again. "Okay guys, we could play kick the can." It was just between darkness and not real dark. "If it gets real dark, we're going to quit."

So we played that one, about a whole hour of it, laughing and going on. And one of the kids looked and, "Hey, look at the window right there."

And somebody was standing there smoking a cigarette, and we didn't have cigarettes. It was a cigar or something. You could see the light. It's dark inside, but it was there. And every time it smokes, you know how the cigarette lights up, it was like that. We just sit there and watched.

And Uncle said, "I'm tired of it. Just let me go see what it is."

So he looked at it; he went in; he said, "There's nothing here, nobody in the house."

It was just kids and him, so. Nobody smokes, and we don't have cigarettes. And that's what we saw. We just sit there and watched it, see what they going to do, or what's going to happen. So that's strange.

My uncle said it's a ghost, and ghosts happens to each of you, all the time. You don't see it.

I said, "Well, it's like better than God. God does the good stuff, and he doesn't!" [*laughter*] He looked at me and goes, "Uhhh."

KITTY

BERDIE JOHN, B. 1965—RED WATER / CONEHATTA / STANDING PINE
TOLD ON MARCH 14, 1996

I remember we used to play games. They do piñata. We had just that candy, full in the paper bag that's hanging up there. They hit it. It was like piñata. We just use the regular paper bag.

We would play those games, and there was that cat game that we did. One was blindfolded. He used to go around the circle. The people would go around the circle. He would turn himself around and try to find a person. We used to call that "kitty." And that person would want to disguise himself. For him not to recognize who he is, he answered him, "Meow," but in a different tone of voice. If he recognized that person, he'll be it to be in that circle. If he can't recognize it three times, he'd go on to the next person. He'll say, "Kitty," or something like that. They'll say, "Meow."

COWBOYS AND INDIANS

CLAUDE YATES ALLEN, B. 1948—PEARL RIVER
TOLD ON DECEMBER 2, 1973

We had TV, and what I saw on TV, well, the White man was it, you know. He was making things happen. And, like when I was little, I used to play cowboy instead of Indian. I was a cowboy.

Samuel Proctor: And the Indians were bad people?

They were bad, right. When we played cowboys and Indians, we used to play cowboy, and we used to be chasing the Indians.

PLAYING TARZAN

MARK PATRICK, B. 1969—Q̱TOKLO (CONEHATTA)
TOLD ON JULY 7, 2021

When we were kids, we used to own a television, and we used to watch Tarzan and how he was swinging from tree to tree and all.

Anyway, we went out there, and there's plenty of vines that's hooked onto a tree. And we got so many gullies down there behind the church and then over there by the house and everything. So, what we would do is we would cut the end of the vine; at the bottom of the vine, we'd just cut it where we could just swing.

That thing would take us all the way over there, and we would come all the way back [*makes wide swinging motion with his arms*], but we didn't realize once you've cut the vine, after a few months, it starts to die. The vine is dying, and we didn't realize that.

So, I remember one time . . . and I know this sounds like I'm picking on my big brother, but you know what, what are the big brothers for?

So he had his hands wet. And for some reason his hands was either sweaty, or he got them wet from the little creek down there. And he said, "I'm fixing to go swing." So he grabbed that thing, and he took off. He got about halfway, he slipped. His hands slipped through. The vine just slipped right through his hands. And I mean, he just went down. [*laughter*]

And so I just remember those times.

And the ones that had the most experience, like me and Robert, we could do it fairly well. But these newer guys, newer girls, they just could not get the hang of it. But I remember they would go way out, and sometimes they would come back and slam into the tree.

ANT PILE

MARK PATRICK, B. 1969—O̱TOKLO (CONEHATTA)
TOLD ON JULY 12, 2021

We used to just run out of games that we could play because we didn't have electronic games or anything like that. We didn't have cell phones and all that. So we would see who would climb the highest tree and all this good stuff and swinging on vines.

But one of the things that some of us did—and some of us wouldn't do or couldn't—we would say, "Okay, let's go over here by the cow pond, and there's an ant bed. Let's see who can stand in that ant bed for the longest."

And there was really no awards. You just done it, and we would just stand there like, "Oh," and the ants would just cover your ankles and your legs. And it's like, "Oh, one, two, three." And I think the furthest that I've gone is maybe fifteen seconds, and that's a long fifteen seconds. And then you had to soak your ankles and stuff; you have to put rubbing alcohol. And another thing that we used to use is coal oil. Y'all ever heard of coal oil? It's like kerosene. That was good medicine.

GREEN SNAKES

MARTHA FERGUSON, B. 1949—STANDING PINE
TOLD ON JUNE 4, 2021

Once in a while, I find green snakes and catch that one, take it to the house. Mom would scream. She didn't like snakes. "Don't bring the snake in." That's all I hear.

I said, "It's friendly."

"I don't care how friendly it is. I'm going to kill it."

So I would have to take it back to the fruit [trees], during the season of that fruit. I guess they catch probably eggs from the birds. So they were there. I don't know, eat the bugs. I don't know, but they were green ones, that long [about two feet]. There were plenty of them. So I grabbed a whole bunch. I didn't know about snakes, but I grabbed that one, and it didn't hurt me. So it bit me, but it didn't hurt. I went, "Okay. You're a friend."

My mama always said, "You're lucky to not get bitten by poison."

I said, "I know poison. They don't look right when you see it."

Even when I was child, I seen cottonmouth and copperhead, and I know the colors. So when I looked at it, I went, "Ooh, they look mean." So I just go away 'til they go away. But the small ones like green snake, that is fun to touch him. My mother never did like it.

"Too bad you don't like the snake." [*laugh*]

She said, "I'll kill him." [*laughter*]

PRANKING THE NEIGHBOR

MARK PATRICK, B. 1969—Q̱TOKLO (CONEHATTA)
TOLD ON JULY 12, 2021

The man that had all that land around us, he had cows all the time. And me and my brother, we were so bad. We would go out there, and we'd shoot them cows with BB guns, and we would start a stampede! [*laughter*] Stuff like that.

And at one time we tried to ride one of them cows and got bucked off. We would just do all kinds of crazy things.

He had those round hay bales. He probably had two hundred of them. We would just jump from one bale to the other. That's all we would do until one of our cousins, he is crazy. He set one of them bales on fire and burned it up! [*laughter*]

PINCH FOR ENGLISH

SALLY ALLEN, B. 1959—CONEHATTA
TOLD ON JANUARY 10, 2000

My sisters and I used to play this game that no one speaks English, just Choctaw. Anything you going to say, just Choctaw. And whoever uses English, we used to pinch each other. [*laughter*]

This was before we got married, long time ago, probably in our teens, fourteen, fifteen.

When we're traveling somewhere, we'd sit in the back of the car, and then we'd talk; we'd say, "Anybody use English is going to get pinched." So we used to do that.

INDIAN MOVIES ON THE RESERVATION

LEONARD JIMMIE, B. 1957—PEARL RIVER
TOLD ON JULY 11, 2021

Every Friday and Saturday night, we would have a movie theater in the convenience center because the movie house in town had shut down for some reason or another. I think the owner passed away, and they were trying to gear up somebody to take charge of it. But it was an alternative to that because even after they opened up, we still had movies out here on the reservation for the locals to go to.

We would show Indian movies. My favorite was *Little Big Man*. I would always say, "Get *Little Big Man. Little Big Man*; they'll like it." It was tragic, but it was a comedy at the same time. One led to the other, but it struck a nerve with me because I always liked *Little Big Man*.

But then there was others like *Soldier Blue*. A number of other ones. And then of course *A Man Called Horse*. That was the big one. I think that's the one everybody would wait for and be like, "Wow. There it is."

That's what they did.

But the thing about it is, there was nothing about Choctaws. It was always about another tribe. And I think that was some of the stuff that we were doing in the late '60s, early '70s, and maybe some parts of the '80s, is looking for that identity that would be *here*. Period. Nothing else.

COMMUNITY EVENTS

IYYIKOWA

Before the Department of Social Services opened offices on the reservation to help those in need, before today's Tribal Council established formal programs for aiding the sick and elderly, before access to federal public assistance programs such as TANF and SNAP, there was *iyyikowa*.[1] *Iyyikowa* translates as "broken foot" and describes a custom of providing aid to those in need. It is an ethos that sits at the heart of the idea of community, where people are brought into relationships both social and economic, founded on the assumption that we need one another to survive the trials and tribulations of life.[2] Judy Billie explained:

> Long time ago when they called *iyyikowa*, they used to have neighbors coming in, helping out with one family if they get behind on sharecropping, if they were sharecroppers, or if the family is behind on getting the firewood for the woodstove or whatever the needs were. The neighbors came around from all over. The people that know each other, they contact each other, and they used to get together, and the women cook. And if it's a household cleaning, then they all help each other. But if it's like chopping wood, then the men do that, and the women cook for them.
>
> And in the afternoon, even the kids, they try to help, whatever that needs to happen. All the families get together, not telling each other what to do. They just knew what to do. There was no bossing around each other. It was fun helping each other. It's like you are so happy to help somebody in need.
>
> And we don't have that anymore.
>
> They call it *iyyikowa*. And in return, they don't get paid. The only thing they do is just get together with some food. If they have any, they bring them with them to be cooked. And the family would provide some of the items for cooking things.
>
> But they don't have that anymore. Now, just once in a while, some family does request that, but it's just in the family. Even though they do request, nobody comes out like they used to.

In the past, everyone pitched in—men, women, and children. Adhering to the division of labor followed throughout the year, men did most of the construction and repair, firewood chopping, grass mowing, and hay baling, while women cleaned the house, shelled the peas, canned the vegetables, and cooked the food. Children helped in the fields and in the house, again, often according to gender. *Iyyikowa* was called for any of a number of reasons: a broken foot, of course, but also any physical injury or illness, a change in family circumstances such as age, divorce, or death, or anything that resulted in the inability to keep up with the rigorous work in the fields, chores in the home, and hunting in the woods required for daily living.

Despite the focus on work, *iyyikowa* is remembered as fun. Like fishing and hunting, work with others offered a time for socializing, both during the work and after. "They'd just talk and laugh, just having a good time working," explains Gordon Sam. "You did it because you wanted to. That's the part I remember, and that's what I liked the best." Speaking back in 1997, Doyle Tubby also remembers the social bonds formed during *iyyikowa*, as well as the storytelling. "You could hear a lot of the stories being told. After they get tired or worn out and sit down, they go get a jug of ice-cold water or tea, sit under that tree. You see, those elders would tell you good stories, about animals or whatever. The women would, what they call *shokhannǫpa*, saying, 'The men are lying. *This* is what happened.' [*laughter*] They start telling their part—next thing you know, a lot of things that are happening with family, friends, and relatives."[3]

When the work was done, people ate, joked, and told stories, while the children played freely. If a fiddle player was around, there might be some house dancing. Longer ago, there might have been some social dancing. Shared work became shared enjoyment. Further, the shared work offered people stories that lived on well beyond the day's work. "It wasn't about the barn," Brian Billie explains. "It was coming together. Everybody would look at the barn and say, 'I remember that.' 'We remember so-and-so almost fell down,' or, 'Remember that cut me,' or, 'I was wondering how they were going to level it out.' Things like that. How it turned out." The new barn, cleared field, cleaned house, or full stack of firewood offers a physical reminder of the community spirit that brought people together.

While many mourn the loss of this community spirit, others note that the spirit of *iyyikowa* continues, partly though church groups who care for their elderly congregation, but primarily through family.[4] As noted in the introduction, the shift from community relations to family relations is apparent throughout the customs and traditions of the Choctaw. Families may not call for an *iyyikowa* to draw in their neighbors, but families put out a call for help for each other all the time.

Further, the spirit of *iyyikowa* extends beyond the formal custom and into smaller acts of generosity. Fish are dropped off at a widow's home; quilts are sewn for a family with a new child; official mail is translated and explained to elders who continue to feel more comfortable with the Choctaw language than English. The help given to families who have lost someone is considered a fundamental part of the Choctaw funerary traditions, but at least a few community members use the term *iyyikowa* for this work as well, when family or community members chop wood for the fire, help clean the house, box up the deceased's possessions, and cook food for the family and guests. This work continues today, as does the expectation of pitching in when there's work to be done. "If somebody's doing something, and if they show up at their house, they'll help them out," says Susie Alex. "I guess this is pretty much like *iyyikowa*."

This is exactly what happened in 1997, when Glenda and Meriva Williamson showed up at Odie Mae Anderson's home—their mother and mother-in-law, respectively—with me in tow to record stories from her and her sister Jeffie Solomon. The women were sitting on the front porch snapping beans. Without a word, they passed Glenda and Meriva a bowl and a pile of beans from the garden. I was exempt, whether because I was a guest, non-Choctaw, male, or because I had my hands full with the recording equipment.

The spirit of *iyyikowa* was on full display during the darkest days of the COVID-19 pandemic, when there were no vaccinations, and the death rate among the Choctaw was the highest in the state and one of the highest in the country (Mitchell, Finn, and Boudreau 2020). "Spirit warriors" emerged, bringing food and household supplies to families in quarantine (see "*Iyyikowa* during COVID"). There is no doubt that *iyyikowa* has shifted over the years, but the spirit of helping out families in need remains.

BROKEN FOOT

HAROLD COMBY, B. 1955—PEARL RIVER
TOLD ON JUNE 4, 1997

They used to call it *iyyikowa*. In English, it means "broken foot." That's what the Choctaw call when neighbors would come in and help another neighbor to do the harvest or to clean their yard or whatever when the occupants got sick or were unable to do things.

And this was volunteer work; they never got paid.

And that's one of the things we don't do any more.

SOME WORK, SOME FUN

BRADLEY ALEX, B. 1955—BOGUE HOMA / PEARL RIVER
TOLD ON JUNE 30, 2021

Iyyikowa was when somebody got sick or something like that and unable to work around their house, whatever, that needed help. And that when they announce *iyyikowa*, that people spread the word and whoever whose house it is, people came. They built barns; they finished what they were going to do, even planting a garden or harvesting it. Things that, whatever that need to be done that to help them, whoever was down.

I remember we went to one that we had to pick apples, pears—us kids—and also, the peas, butter beans, and all that stuff—us kids. The others, they help clean the house, paint something. I think it was a barn or something. Whatever that needs to be fixing. Cars, they worked on the cars. They came out, whatever they are able to do. Even the kids got involved to help.

I liked that because I got to see my cousins and to make new friends. Also, when we were kids, afterward, we were free to do whatever. We get to play. So for us it was good. The adults also, they brought foods and everything like that. So we ate all sorts of food they brought. So everybody shared too. So it was great. It was great.

HAULING WOOD

ESTELLINE TUBBY, B. 1928—PEARL RIVER
TOLD ON AUGUST 5, 1997

I was five or six years old. They used to use wood for the house. Well, these Indian people used to come and just saw a lot of wood and haul it to people who need it. And then my mom used to cook for them. Whenever they get through eating, they sit down and talk. But I was a little girl, and I just went and played with the other little girls.

But nowadays they don't have that. But that was the Indian ways a long time ago.

COMING TOGETHER

LINDA WILLIAMS, B. 1958—STANDING PINE
TOLD ON JUNE 15, 2021

I remember one lady was sick, and we were going to walk over there because it wasn't too far. And it was a dirt road too; it was not even highway. We were living in a frame house. There was no houses between our house and their house. But it wasn't too far, maybe like two, three miles.

So we had to walk over there, and I remember my mom packing up some stuff: what we're going to wear; we get dirty, whatever, change clothes, extra clothes and everything. Way back then they used to use that flour sack to put stuff in. So I remember she used to put everything in there. And in case we get nappy, like in the afternoon, she used to take us a little quilt where we can lay on it and sleep and all this stuff. And then we used to walk there.

So we went walking down the road to that house. And when we got there, there were some other ladies and men, all got together. And there was a few that was cooking outside.

But she was sick. She was sick bad.

And I remember they cleaned the house for her, and they were cooking, cleaning the yard for them and everything. And then when they were all done in the afternoon, everybody got together, sat down, and ate together. And they left.

But that's how they used to do it. Somebody is real sick, can't do anything around their house? They used to go wash dishes, clean the kitchen, clean the house, and wash their clothes, and clean their yard, and everything for them. But it was like the whole community coming together.

UNOFFICIAL HELP

MARK PATRICK, B. 1969—O̱TOKLO (CONEHATTA)
TOLD ON JULY 7, 2021

We'd done it, sort of, unofficially. We didn't really get the word out there, but whenever my grandmother needed something like a new porch or whatever, the porch is rotted, and somebody's going to get hurt because we was going to fall through it, we needed to build one. She would call some of the people that she knew or family, relatives, neighbors, and they would all come and pitch in and get it done. She'd cook a meal, and we'll all just have a good time.

HELPING EACH OTHER

WILLIAMSON ISAAC, B. 1947—PEARL RIVER
TOLD ON JUNE 27, 2021

My parents and their friends did. Men folks go out and chop some wood, and women were cooking.

And another time they'd clean the house, sweep and mop and all that.

And another Saturday, they said, "Let's go to our neighbor's house."

That's what they did. They were just moving around. Helping each other's neighbors. That's what you call *iyyikowa*. They're helping each other.

Even when working in the garden, that's what they did. They said, "You come over and help me with this garden, and I'll come over there next Saturday." That's rotating all that. I thought that was a good thing they did.

'TIL IT'S DONE

SUSIE COMBY ALEX, B. 1947—STANDING PINE / PEARL RIVER
TOLD ON JUNE 9, 2021

The main part of *iyyikowa* is if you had a big patch of corn that needed, or a big patch of peas or something, that they knew, "Oh, they need help," "She needs help," especially those without husbands, their husband has passed away or something. If she's there just with the children, then they would go over there and help her.

As soon as they were picking, the children and the ladies were shelling it.

Some would help her with what they call "canning." I'm pretty sure you have heard of it. At the time, we didn't have anything to freeze, so they canned. And they have to can. She'll have each farmer's wife, I guess; they had a little . . . now we call it "pantry." They have that and put the canned goods in there. When they decided to open up and cook it a little bit more, you feel like they just got it out of the garden and cooked it. It was that fresh.

At that time, they also had barns. Sometimes, if the roof needs fixing, I guess he would mention it to somebody, and then they said, "Oh, he's going to need help doing this, doing that," so they all come. Then, women will bring food to cook, and they'll cook outside. They all sit under the tree after. After the meal, they all sit under the tree and tell jokes or stories or whatever. If they didn't finish, they'll come back the next day.

BUILDING COMMUNITY, NOT JUST BARNS

BRIAN BILLIE, B. 1973—RED WATER
TOLD ON JUNE 30, 2021

We had one [*iyyikowa*] for our uncle.

That one, we had to build a car shed. That was one, two, three, four car sheds on poles, almost similar to a pole barn.

Iyyikowa. You don't go to think you're going to get paid. You're going because everybody's coming together to help someone.

My uncle's family cooked. And they had sandwiches and soup. But it wasn't about the barn; it was coming together. I remember every time we would have an eating at his house, everybody would look at the barn and say, "I remember that. We remember so-and-so so almost fell down," or, "Remember that cut me," or, "I was wondering how they were going to level it out," things like that. How it turned out.

I mean, it's good. *Iyyikowa* is what we were taught to understand why. But nowadays you all are told to help out. Your parents will say, "O̱t apilah," or, "Go help him."

You see an elder trying to get their groceries, or you see a parent with kids running away, and you go grab the kid and return the kid until the parents settle down and you're like, "Okay," and you go. That's helping out.

But as we get older, I start noticing people don't turn around to help each other sometimes. They're too busy trying to get to somewhere.

HELPING TO READ AND HELPING OUT

EDDIE JOHNSON, B. 1970—STANDING PINE / TUCKER
TOLD ON JUNE 11, 2021

An elder would come to our house. She lived just down the road, maybe about a mile and a half or so. She'd bring her mail and, "Yappa̱ am ittimanópolih akikkanoka̱." In other words, "Read that for me—I don't understand it—and interpret it for me."

So, that's what we used to do. Help out the elderly that way. I mean, nobody really knows about that now. Now they're going to know. That's the *iyyikowa*. *Iyyikowa* is not necessarily when you're in desperate need of help as in some kind of problem. *Iyyikowa* also encompass just a general help.

The bigger *iyyikowa* would be, like somebody broke their leg, and they can't go out and take care of the yard or making their income. People come say,

"So-and-so is hurt. On Saturday, we're going to come and help them with their yard cutting, chopping their wood. The gardening is just getting out of hand, and the kids are too small. The wife is struggling. So we're going to call for an *iyyikowa*. Y'all come. And if you can, and you want to bring something, we're going to do this." And then we'll eat together, leave or bring the food if we need to. And so they can have food for the week or something. Things like that.

I've heard one lady telling me that even blankets, quilting. I said, "blankets," but they were called "quilting." People help. And the women come together, and that was a form of it [*iyyikowa*]. And they just came together and talked and sat around and spit their snuff and enjoyed their conversation.

FISH FOR THE ELDERS

BRIAN BILLIE, B. 1973—RED WATER
TOLD ON JUNE 30, 2021

I went fishing with my brothers. Most of the fish we caught were just a small amount for our mom that liked the fish. But when we got older, there's people that knew you as you like to go fishing. So they would put in an order saying, "I want fish. Don't forget about me. I want some fish if you have extra." Then you're like, "Okay." Then you have a drive to want to go fishing for some more and not disappoint.

But there are some that wanted flatfish, and some wanted catfish, and some wanted smaller fish. The older ones would say they want the red bellies. And you had to find out where the red bellies are. Find out where the catfish are, where the perch and brims are.

Only when I got older, I understood their pride. Some people's prize fish is the biggest fish or something out of the ordinary. But growing up, you didn't see that. You just had fun, brought it back and the pride to feel like you accomplished helping somebody.

One lady used to say, "It don't matter what time you bring it, just wake me up." Those were the times that we went fishing far away and came back late. And we just drop off the bucket to them, and they would appreciate it.

I remember Mom and Dad said, "You just had fun. So there's no payment in it. They need it, and it just works out well."

SHOPIK FOR THE ELDERS

HAROLD COMBY, B. 1955—PEARL RIVER
TOLD IN 2017

Especially guys if they caught a lot of fish, they would give to elderly widow woman or elderly some fish.

I remember one time they gave Mom a big *shopik* [grindle or grinnel fish], and I looked in the trunk, and it was about this long [*indicates about three feet*] in the trunk. And my mom got it and cleaned it out and fried it, and we ate it.

COMMUNITY SERVICE

MAHLIH BOWDEN, B. 1991—PEARL RIVER
TOLD ON JULY 14, 2021

I want to say maybe about 2018, 2019, we were just noticing there's not too much community help just in general. And we were discussing how we can be more involved, being involved in our community development club, which they host fundraisers; they'll do community cleanups; they host other events just for the community, for fellowship and stuff like that. And so we decided, "Well, just for right now, let's just start picking up some trash."

So about every other weekend, if the weather permitted of course, we would pick a road in our community. We invited everyone out; you didn't even have to live here really. We just invited everyone to come out and just help us clean up. Keep your community clean because it is up to us. I mean, yeah, they have people to do it, but you got to do your part, too, sometimes.

And so from there we really enjoyed, of course, the fellowship that it brought, and just the positive feeling to just knowing you did something good makes you feel good.

IYYIKOWA DURING COVID

JAY WESLEY, B. 1975—STANDING PINE
TOLD ON JULY 28, 2022

At my house, when COVID hit, I got it. I brought it home. It was at a council meeting. For the most part, I think most of us got that.

In any case, we went into quarantine, the whole house. And I had to send my kids out to my oldest daughter's place, and they stayed over there. I isolated myself. But we put a table outside the house, and then we became pros of being in quarantine. We had family come by and drop off food and what else you need and basic necessities and water and all that stuff.

And we did that for others because it got pretty bad around here.

And then also you had the "spirit warriors." We had a group that actually got donations from everybody, anybody. And then if they find out the house that it's quarantined, then they would deliver these things to them: water, Gatorade, and whatever else they could get donated. Even Pampers for kids.

CEREMONIES, HOLIDAYS, AND FESTIVALS

"The elders use to say that there would be a gathering, where they would slaughter a cow for the feast. They would also play stickball all day. In the evening, they would start to dance the Choctaw dances. It was told to me that they would dance all night. They said they would dance so much that they left deep impressions on the ground they danced on." In an interview for the Choctaw Cultural Legacy website in 2017, Judie Lene Isaac laid out the general pattern for Choctaw social gatherings that encompasses informal weekend community gatherings and more formal tribal celebrations that link past and present.

In the past, as the corn ripened in late summer, Choctaw gathered to give thanks for the harvest and celebrate a new year. The old fires would be put out and new ones lit in a ritual referred to as *Lowak Moshólichi* or "Fire Extinguished." People feasted, danced, played stickball, and gave thanks. Historical records are at odds whether or not this was part of the Green Corn Ceremony practiced by other southeastern tribes,[5] but today, many elders draw a direct line from this ceremony to the annual Choctaw Indian Fair, once held in August, now held in July.

The Choctaw Indian Fair is perhaps the single biggest form of ambassadorship for the tribe. With midway rides, carnival food, and country music stars headlining the event, the fair is directed to Choctaw and non-Choctaw alike. Every year since 1949, with the exception of 2020 when COVID-19 kept the entire country shuttered at home, Choctaw families have gathered with their non-Indian neighbors to celebrate Choctaw culture and have fun.[6] While many events are intentionally inclusive such as the carnival rides and country music, distinctly Choctaw traditions are consistently highlighted and foregrounded.

The concept of dual significance is useful here.[7] The same event—cooking hominy, demonstrating blowguns, weaving baskets, playing stickball, or social dancing—can mean one thing for performers and another for their audiences, not to mention different things for different audience members. For a non-Choctaw, observing social dancing at the fair may be understood primarily as a formal dance performance of trained community members. For Choctaw elders, watching social dancing at the fair may offer them a chance to relive the tradition vicariously, remembering a time when these dances were performed socially for fun among entirely Choctaw groups. For the dancers themselves, social dancing offers not only a chance to earn some pocket money but also a chance to reinvest in one's traditions, reconnect with family and friends during dance practices leading up to the fair, and spiritually connect with their ancestors who have since passed.

As a public performance for audiences who may not be familiar with the tradition, each social dance is introduced with information about its origins and meaning.[8] Such educational outreach is not confined to the fair. Nearby non-Indian schools, chambers of commerce, and event planners often ask the tribe if they can send a dance troupe, storytellers, or drummers to their event. As director of the Department of Chahta Immi, Jay Wesley often fields these requests and accompanies Choctaw groups to presentations, parades, and festivals.[9] Not surprisingly, their groups are occasionally met with confusion from people unaware that there is a vibrant Native American community living nearby.

Festivals play an important role in maintaining cultural traditions, offering a venue and opportunity to participate in customs that are increasingly shifting from private practice to public performance. Tribal schools have followed suit, hosting festivals for their youth as both education and entertainment such as Native American Week in September that includes a Princess and Braves contest for each grade, a Green Corn Ceremony hosted by Head Start that rotates among the different communities, and a Spring Festival with social dancing. Some mourn the loss of community even during these events, however. "Part of the Spring Festival," explained Jay Wesley, was that "you get your plate; you hung out with friends, families; everybody got to know one another. That was a big community gathering. Nowadays, it's like your kid performs; you wait for the food; you get your food; and you're out of there. It's just grab and go." Yet there remains hope. Jay goes on to describe a young boy in Red Water who has become an excellent chanter thanks to school festivals. Further, the abundance of dance troupes vying for a spot to dance at the fair also suggests that public performances have helped keep the dancing, chanting, and drumming alive.

Schools have also been central in introducing the celebration of national holidays, a development that inspires mixed feelings in the community. Photos from the 1970s show White and Choctaw children sharing a Thanksgiving meal, with White children in pilgrim hats and Choctaw children in their traditional Choctaw clothing. Handmade pine cone turkeys decorate the cafeteria tables. Christmas parties were also held, both in the classroom and in facility buildings for the whole community.

For Christian holidays in particular, churches played a key role both in establishing the holiday and then hosting communal events to celebrate it. After church service on Easter, people describe their congregations gathering for a meal and an Easter egg hunt. Soon, Easter egg hunts were being hosted in communities among extended family and neighbors. The same was true for Christmas, as communities took aspects of the Christmas holiday, integrated them into their social complex, and transformed them into distinct Choctaw celebrations. Christmas celebrations at the beginning of the twentieth century, for example, included a big hunt by the men, followed by cooking by the women, and feasting by all. By midway through the twentieth century, Choctaw families began hosting communitywide celebrations called "Christmas Tree," where people would buy fruit or candy to hang in brown paper bags with their children's names on them.[10] As kids gathered around the tree, the sounds of an approaching throng could be heard as a dozen or so men in the community came marching towards them, shooting off firecrackers and singing and shouting their arrival. Either masked as *shilop* (spirits or ghosts) and monsters, or crossdressing in costumes that helped disguise their identities, men and women acted out loosely scripted roles or improvised entirely as they entertained the crowd with bawdy jokes and outrageous physical humor.[11] The scene alternately scared and delighted the children, who eventually received their piece of fruit from one of the costumed men. Over the years and from community to community, family to family, variations developed. Sometimes, Santa was the central character, with three to twelve *shilop* accompanying him. Sometimes, there were nuts and candy in addition to fruit for sale to give to their loved ones. Often, there was dancing afterwards, late into the evening.

The event eventually got adopted back into the institutional structure of Choctaw life, with development clubs hosting Christmas Tree events in their facility buildings or school gyms, replete with bags of fruit on the tree, scary *shilops*, and Santa. At times, a family might celebrate Christmas once at the facility building, again with their community hosted at someone's home, and on a smaller scale at home with their families. Today, the family reigns supreme, with most Christian and national holidays celebrated among a closer network of family, including Thanksgiving, Christmas, Easter, New Year's, and the Fourth of July, though the tribal government continues to play a central role in many of these, with a a communal feast for Thanksgiving and a firework show set off at the casino.

While Thanksgiving is celebrated by most Choctaw, Columbus Day is not. The Mississippi Choctaw celebrate Nanih Waiya Day instead.[12] The day commemorates the important role the Nanih Waiya Mound plays in their creation story, the ancestors who endured so much and persevered, and the political victory of the return of the mound to the tribe. Originating in 2008, Nanih Waiya Day was decreed by the Mississippi state legislature as the second Friday of August. During the 2022 event, the Choctaw Indian Princess opened the event with a formal welcome, a Choctaw Christian pastor offered a prayer, two young girls in traditional Choctaw dress sang "The Star-Spangled Banner" in the Choctaw language, and then tribal Chief Cyrus Ben offered the main remarks. When he finished, a dance troupe performed a series of traditional Choctaw dances, followed by a presentation of flags from each of the nine communities. The festivities concluded with the World Series of Stickball All-Star Games, where the best players from all the stickball teams split up into two teams to play each other.

Ceremonies and festive public events are constantly being revised, adapted, and created anew. However, the changes are made by drawing on recognizable patterns within Choctaw culture, whether structurally (for example, opening and closing events with prayer); thematically (for example, including references and gratitude to past ancestors); or symbolically (for example, using social dance as a representation of both community identity and shared ritual past). Some are developed institutionally by the tribe such as Nanih Waiya Day and the Choctaw Indian Princess Pageant; others are created by individuals. Both meet needs within the community to address shared challenges and celebrate shared successes. When three tribal members were murdered near the Nanih Waiya cave mound in 1996, Harold Comby developed and performed a ceremony at the mound to restore balance in the face of this terrible tragedy. When COVID-19 began to claim more and more lives, Harold's daughter Nikki Comby invited community members to gather in solidarity and prayer near Lake Pushmataha for a sunrise ceremony, where a cross has been placed to mark this devastating period in Choctaw history.

HONORING THE ORIGIN OF CORN

TERRY BEN, B. 1957—STANDING PINE
TOLD ON JUNE 3, 1996

Nineteen forty-nine, if I remember right, is when the Choctaw Indian Fair was officially born, but before that, it was basically the Green Corn Ceremony. One and the same.

As far as any ceremony, specifically you had Green Corn Ceremony. That Green Corn Ceremony was the time when the corn was this certain height, and the corncob was there, and this was just a celebration of the people to give thanks to the Great Spirit and the cause of this bounty time because of the season. So they'd make a big deal out of it and have dances and singing and storytelling. It was like a big old family gathering, and they just called it the "Green Corn Ceremony." And in the modern twentieth century, it's called the "Choctaw Indian Fair."

Supposedly, a long time ago, according to one legend, going back to Nanih Waiya, there were some hunters around Nanih Waiya at nighttime. And they saw or heard somebody crying; I think it was a lady, you know, crying.

The woman was real hungry and wanted food. And so, the hunt was not too well, but you know, they had a little game, and so they shared the meal they had with this woman, at the Nanih Waiya area.

And so the woman was so very thankful and told the hunters, "One month later, on the night of the full moon, come back."

And so, about a month later, the two men went to the same spot on the full moon night, and there, on Nanih Waiya area, the mound area, the cave mound area, were some strange seeds. They never saw that before. And of course, the item was corn—corn on the cob or whatever it was.

And this was a gift from the lady, who was maybe some kind of a legendary figure who was thankful. And this was a return gift.

And so that's how supposedly the Choctaws acquired corn, via the situation at Nanih Waiya.

NEW FIRES, NEW YEAR

HAROLD COMBY, B. 1955—PEARL RIVER
TOLD ON JUNE 1, 2021

In the first week of July or maybe second week, we have our celebration called Choctaw Indian Fair. But from oral tradition and written tradition they say it was our Green Corn Ceremony. This was a ceremony in which we would purify our bodies. And it would also be known as the new year, start of the new year. And at that time, we would eat the first harvest of the corn.

My mom used to tell me that during that time, there was the oldest man in the community that would stand up and tell about the laws on how people should treat each other. So this might have been something like New Year's resolution that usually talk about when New Year's comes in, in the modern society.

One of the things was that during this time of the year, we would forgive each other. Like now, somebody will carry a grudge throughout the whole year, maybe even through their whole lives. But during the Green Corn Ceremony, you're supposed to forgive that person, maybe other than homicide, but things like somebody starting a rumor about you, those are supposed to be forgiven.

Then there were dances, stickball games, so just having a good celebration.

I think one of the things is that this will be good for everybody. This basically came from my dad. He used to say that "I̱hitchali̱ noktalha̱ hicha." There was a third thing that he used to say. *I̱hitchali̱*, which means "vengeance," and *noktalha̱* is "jealousy." "Yakomikako̱ naksíka ish bohlicha ish a̱yak matoh achokma ish attana," which means that when you put these things aside, you will have a good life and live a good life.

So that would be, I think, good advice for everybody.

LOWAK MOSHÓLICHI

JESSE BEN, B. 1955—PEARL RIVER
TOLD ON APRIL 8, 2009

The fair, I think, originated from . . . In our custom, we had a time when people would get together called *lowak moshólichi* ["fire extinguished"]. And what they would do is come together and bring their fire, and they'd spend four or five days and celebrate and eat together and just have festivities: dance and . . . and that was called *lowak moshólichi*, and afterwards, it would begin a new year. And during that time, I think the Choctaws played . . . As far as I understand, that's when they met together and played stickball.

GOOD LUCK FOR THE NEW YEAR

MARTHA FERGUSON, B. 1949—STANDING PINE
TOLD ON JUNE 4, 2021

New Year's Day. Everybody cooks black-eyed peas. They always cooked that one. That was a tradition. I always wondered why. And they said, "That's to bring good luck for everybody." And that's what my uncle told me.

I said, "You mean we don't have food, and that's what they're cooking. Don't you think so?" That's what I said. [*laugh*]

He said, "No, it's supposed to give you good luck. Take a bite, and then they might have good luck."

I said, "Uh, I don't like that bean, so no. If I didn't have good luck last year, I'm still going to be the same. And it don't matter what you put good luck or this on. I don't guess so; I don't care for that bean."

So I never got into eating, even though when I got married, Bob was like that. "Well, I want you to. Open your mouth girl." I went ahead and opened my mouth, then he got one. "That's good luck for this year."

I went, "Bob, only God gave you your chances to have good luck. Bean don't." That's what I said to him.

"If you believe in Him, what do you need the beans for, for good luck? What do you need, this or that one. Life is given to you only one time, and He can take away anytime He wish to do so. And He's going to take away any minute, anytime, anywhere. It don't matter. If you're scared of tornado, tough luck. You can sleep through it, or all that will be taken away. So it's all up to you. Make sure you know how to pray and forgive things that you haven't done. Just look forward to living in enjoyment. But if you're scared all the time of everything, or getting good luck, it's not going to happen, when God decide to get you."

And I just walked away. That's the only advice I gave him.

Before we got married, he went, "That's a good lecture I got."

I said, "Yeah. You're going to keep getting it, too!" [*laughter*]

FALL FESTIVAL

LILLIE GIBSON, B. 1919—CONEHATTA
TOLD ON AUGUST 5, 1997

There was a place down there close to Lake Mississippi. That's where I saw all the dancing and all of that. They used to call it "campgrounds." It was sort of like this Neshoba County Fair they got on now. They'd have little houses built back there, some of them.

There'd be a lot of White people. Choctaw especially. My daddy, I guess he supervised it. He'd buy some cows, I guess about three or four of them and clean them. They used to put them on what they called a "rack." The meat. They put it up there. They roast it, I guess. They'd roast it, then it would turn red. They'd put them [the bones] in big paper sacks and keep them and make soup.

The women would cook that meat. There would be so many people, I don't think there would be enough for all of them. At least they liked that food.

Every year, fall of the year because they had some cotton to pick, so they couldn't stay over a week. The Choctaw would bring just like they were moving out there; they just put it under a tree, and they would stay there. That's where they'd cook; that's where they'd sleep.

We didn't have electricity then. And so my daddy, he was supervising it, so he built something like a table, and he put dirt on all that table. A big table. And it wouldn't be one table either; it'd be lot of them. And he'd haul pine from the woods and put it at each table where he going to have his fire. And he'd built that fire; he'd watch it, tend to it, and they'd be out there playing stickball. And they'd dance out there. And a lot of people from outside came in, outside of Mississippi too. So we had a lot of people out there. I can remember how we used to sleep under a tree. [*laughter*]

Our house wasn't too far from the camp where we were camping, but we had cows, and we had hogs and mules. Our daddy couldn't go out there to feed them, so me and my mom walk out there and feed them. My sisters would go with us, and we'd go feed them every evening.

And one day, there was a car coming down the road. I never had seen a car before, and I was scared. [*laughs*]

And well, whoever he was, he stopped, and he said, "I'll give y'all a ride."

But I wasn't going to get in there because I didn't know what it was. [*laughter*]

And so, Mama wasn't that scared, I guess. She said, "Yeah, he'll give us a lift."

"Well," I said, "I don't know, but I'm not going to get in there."

And so Mama told him, "No. We'll just walk."

And so we walked on over there and fed all the animals, and then we came back. And there's another car going the way we were going. Well, they wanted us to ride in their car.

I wouldn't get in that car.

Mama said, "Well, I don't think it'll hurt us."

And I said, "It might hurt us, though. We don't know." [*laughter*]

And so we walked back to the camp.

I'm still scared. I never got over it. [*laughter*]

TALK AND MORE TALK

TERRY BEN, B. 1957—STANDING PINE
TOLD ON JUNE 10, 2021

The Choctaw Indian Fair—my granddad was a big fan. When it was time to get things ready, to come on over, the big thing to him was to come over here and meet his friends and just talk. Talk, talk, talk, talk, talk, talk, talk. Then about midnight, time to go back home. Then the next day, about maybe three o'clock they'd come back, while the fair was going on, and meet with his buddies again, not necessarily the same ones, but talk and talk and talk. Talk would be about women; talk would be about politics; talk would be about crops.

CHOCTAW BURGERS

MARTHA FERGUSON, B. 1949—STANDING PINE
TOLD ON JULY 28, 2022

When the carnival was small, you could just walk through it.

One time, my grandma was selling hamburgers, drinks, and all of that. But the one that she did was a hamburger, add sausage to it, and mix it all up, and she'd call it a "Choctaw burger." And Bob [her husband] went ahead and got a taste of that one. He said, "This hamburger is not a really regular hamburger, is it?"

I said, "No, that's Grandma's dish, that hamburger is."

"Really? What she put in it?"

"Sausage and hamburger together and then put bread in it and then make a hamburger out of that one. That's what you're eating but had that good flavor."

And he went, "It has a good flavor. That's why I'll call it 'Choctaw hamburger' from now on."

ON DISPLAY

MELFORD FARVE, B. 1961—TUCKER
TOLD ON JUNE 1, 2021

At the fair, the carnival used to be at the old baseball field. And I remember Brother Mal, I don't know what he had in mind, but he built a little scaffold-looking thing with a thatched roof. Some kids would sit in there, paint their face a little bit, and take their shirt off and sit there with a drum.

You're sitting there beating on a drum, for fifty cents. Fifty cents can take you a long way at the fair back then. So kids would line up ready to go to that; it was like an attraction or something.

YOU SAY "HOLA"; I SAY "HALITOH"

JAY WESLEY, B. 1975—STANDING PINE
TOLD ON JULY 27, 2022

In Demopolis, Alabama, about Christmastime, they have a "Christmas on the River" parade, and it's a big thing over there. And they invited our group to come out. We took a group out there, and we're doing a parade. We were in our native Choctaw regalia and walking, and people on the side, during the parade, they're like, "¡Hola! ¡Hola! ¿Como estas?" Then that led me, from living in Arizona, to say, "¡Hola! ¿Como estas?" [*laughter*]

They say, "¡Hola! ¿Como estas?" [Hello! How are you?, in Spanish.]

And I'm like, "Muy bien, muy bien. Muchas gracias." [Very good, very good. Thanks very much, in Spanish.]

After a few, maybe fifty, yards, I stopped. I told the group, "Okay. Okay. Alright. I'll stop."

"Halitoh." Tell everyone how to respond. We're like, "Halitoh" [Hello], and you had some people looking at us confused. "Why are these Mexicans saying something else besides 'Hola'?" [*laughter*]

So the next year we had a sign that read "Mississippi Band of Choctaw Indians."

SCHOOL FESTIVALS

RAE NELL VAUGHN, B. 1964—PEARL RIVER
TOLD ON APRIL 22, 2020

In October and March and April we have school festivals. In October, we had the Green Corn Festival. The Green Corn Festival deals with the harvest, the fall harvest, or the end of the season. And we have dancing and eating and eating and dancing, and everybody comes together.

It has changed in the sense of we now have our Head Start and Early Childhood Program host this festival. And so we all come to watch the small children dance, and they rotate between the communities each year.

And then in March and April, we have Spring Festival. And again, this is where we dance and gather, and it's an opportunity to provide our young people. . . . Because this is from all of elementary school where they can dance and chant and learn the songs. They wear the traditional regalia—the Choctaw dress and the Choctaw shirt. Each class from each community, like I said with the Spring Festival, it rotates. They'll pick a day where they're going to have theirs in Conehatta; one will be in Bogue Chitto another day. So everybody has an opportunity because like with me, I've got relatives all over the place!

And our reservation is over thirty-three thousand acres. It's a checkerboard, meaning we have three communities in Neshoba County, two communities in Leake County. We have another community down in Jones County, which is ninety miles away from us. We also have a small community that's associated to Bogue Chitto, which is called Henning, Tennessee, in Lauderdale County, Tennessee; they moved up there during the relocation programs of the 1950s and '60s. And so there's a group of a hundred and fifty people. There's a number of houses in this small parcel of land. They also have a facility building and other support resources available to them there in Tennessee.

And so going back to the Spring Festival, we have family everywhere. So you can go and visit your family. Watch the children dance, eat together and fellowship.

So then in June and July, we have stickball and our Choctaw Fair. In June we partnered with the Mississippi State Games, and it's the version of the Olympics, so to speak, where we have a stickball tournament, just for our young children. And it's also coed because this goes up to twelve years old.

My daughter Brianna participated. But oh my gosh, we hear this story every year.

She complained that one of the opposing players was over age, and they lost. And she said, "If that player wasn't in there . . . "—because he obviously was a good player—"if that player wasn't in there, we would have won that game. We would have won the tournament."

Every year. She's twenty-what? Twenty-six, twenty-seven? Still hear that same story. [*laughter*]

A NEW GENERATION OF CHANTERS

JAY WESLEY, B. 1975—STANDING PINE
TOLD ON JULY 27, 2022

There's one in Red Water, and he was a kid chanter. He actually did the full nineteen songs for the Spring Festival now; fifteen songs the first time. But I was in the back, in case. Sometimes with these chants, it's like they're trying to get the tune right in the beginning. So I'm like behind the stage, and it's like, "Okay Jay, how do you start this?"

I tell him, and he's, "Okay." He's got it and says it. Goes back, and we got through it that way.

The next year, I'm still back there. I was like, "If you need me, I'm back here." A couple times he came back.

Third time, I'm still back of the stage, behind the stage. I was like, "Anytime." And nope, he didn't need me. I was like, "Awesome."

THANKSGIVING AT CHURCH

TERRY BEN, B. 1957—STANDING PINE
TOLD ON JUNE 10, 2021

Thanksgiving, a special service was done. Preachers do a special service a certain day. And people go out to the long table again [as they do for fellowship meals during the year], and somebody would be cooking hominy, and somebody would be doing fry bread. And the women in the community, church members, would bring in their dishes; they prepped dishes. Somebody would bring in desserts; somebody would bring turkey; somebody would bring ham and all that. Everybody would just enjoy themselves, you know, for a day of worship around Thanksgiving.

THANKSGIVING DAY

MELFORD FARVE, B. 1961—TUCKER
TOLD ON JUNE 1, 2021

For me, it was basically wake up to breakfast, and in the mornings, you watched Macy's Thanksgiving Day Parade. I think there was another parade, but, anyway, it was morning watching parades, then the Thanksgiving specials. Then football. Detroit had the opening . . . Detroit and whoever, and then Dallas and whoever in the afternoon. That was it.

Mom did most of the cooking, so being a small house, and a small kitchen, the smell of the food was all throughout the house. Then, I could remember the window was being fogged up because of the heat inside the house because of the food and things being cooked. And sometimes me and my brother would just go out and play a little tackle football before the games started.

It was nothing fancy. Just whatever. I don't think we had turkey back then. We weren't into the traditional turkey, probably just fried chicken and some others. Dressing and all that. But I didn't get into the turkey thing 'til much later in my life.

FIRST CHRISTMAS

MARY LOU FARMER, B. 1917—CONEHATTA
TOLD ON DECEMBER 3, 1973

My first Christmas, but we didn't have it at home. We had our Christmas at church. We had to come about ten miles in a wagon to the party, the Christmas party we had at church [Macedonia Baptist Church].

TREE IN THE CHURCHYARD

CARRIE TUBBY, B. 1914—RED WATER
TOLD ON NOVEMBER 1, 1973

They used to put up a tree a long time ago. Now they don't have it. They used to put it in front of the churchyard. A tree that has leaves that are shaped around it [cedar]. They would cut the tree down and take it to the church and put apples and some other good things that they had on the tree. When they finished, they called out our names, picked it from the tree, and gave it [to us]. That's the way they used to do it.

CANDIES FOR THE STOCKING

CHARLIE DENSON, B. 1923—CONEHATTA / STANDING PINE
TOLD ON DECEMBER 3, 1973

Just before Christmas, my daddy went to the store and buy the candy. I took care to put my stocking on the chimney so Santa Claus could put the candies in there. So we get up early, about four o'clock that morning. I had to get up to see what's in my socks.

COTTON, CANDIES

LORENA ALEX, B. 1952—HALLS, TN / BOGUE CHITTO / PEARL RIVER
TOLD ON JUNE 10, 2021

We would go out before Christmas. We couldn't afford anything like we do now here. So, we'd go out in the woods, get one of those cedar trees. And we couldn't afford ornaments, so since we got cotton, so we put cotton up there. Cotton for decoration.

And dad would get us a candy bar. That was our Christmas present.

And also, he would give us a bag of apple and oranges. And there were some walnut, pecan, maybe about two or three candies in there.

But that's what we'd get every year. That was the only time we would get candies. Other times we didn't.

ALL DAY, ALL NIGHT

DELAURA SAUNDERS, B. 1950—BOGUE CHITTO
TOLD ON JUNE 29, 2021

Another thing I remember was the old Choctaw Christmas gatherings.

Before all the Choctaw Christmas Tree ever start, I just remember that early in the morning all the men cousins would show up, get together, and they would go hunt. They would go hunt wild games.

And I remember the women of the family would show up together also. They would have their black pots. And to me just thinking back, these folks were well organized. You had some of the younger guys would be keeping the fire going for them. You had some folks that would have black pots and make sure water is in there.

As the men go hunting, they bring the wild games, and you had some that would skin them, gutted them out, and they would get it ready to be cooked. You had another set of families that would be inside doing the side dishes, the biscuits and whatnot. I just remember how things used to be. Of course, at evening times when the food would be prepared and ready, they all feasted. They all ate together.

Then the Choctaw Christmas Tree started. They had a holly tree. And I remember my grandpa would have fresh produce like apples, oranges, and maybe gum or candies. And people, what they did was, they'd buy it, wrap it around, and put their name on it, and hang it up on the tree.

When that all was done, you had different families that would be there and give them a chance to talk to each other, meet some old friends and those kinds of things. Just fellowship.

Then I remember at one community Christmas gathering, some of the men would come in with masks or painted faces and stuff that they used to wear. They used to call it *shilop* [spirit or ghost]. What their job was, they used to have a narrator that would tell stories about each one as they'd come in. They would pick, it didn't matter wherever if it was on the tree, they would get it and read the name and go after them to give them gifts. That was kind of like, to me, a discipline way, too. It kind of scared the kids but in a good way.

That took a while, but once that is done, I remember my grandpa used to go back and recount the apples, the oranges, the inventory. He would recount the inventory. He would say, "We have enough 'til morning," and the house dance would start.

Of course, you would have the fiddle, guitar players, and just like a square dance. They used to call them the "house dance," "Choctaw house dance." It would be way in the morning before everybody just finally go home. I didn't stay up that late.

But it was like a day of three parts. You had the feeding, you had the Choctaw Christmas Tree, then you have the house dance.

A CHRISTMAS STORY

HARLEY VAUGHN, B. 1961—HALLS, TN / BOGUE CHITTO
CAROLINE MORRIS, B. 1944—PEARL RIVER
TOLD ON MAY 31, 1996

Caroline Morris: The only time we ever got fruit was at Christmastime. Or the candy. Or anything from the elderlies. That's what we get for Christmas. Because we didn't have money. With Mom's family, on Sunday dinner or lunchtime, it was fried chicken. That's the only time we would eat fried chicken. That's the only time we would have fried chicken and fried pies or something extra. We don't eat like that during the week. For during the week, you might have cornbread and dried peas, black-eyed peas, field peas, nothing fancy. Or turnip greens and cornbread. It's something simple, but with a lot of kids, you have to cook a lot. But you can't have two or three different foods; otherwise, you're going to have to have a whole bunch of foods to cook.

Harley Vaughn: Same as what she said. We would have cornbread and beans and all that. Every now and then, we would have something sweet. Not all the time. That's why all these apples and oranges, you'll see these at Christmas. Kids would go crazy. We would go crazy. It was the only time we would get it. Christmas would be a lot. It was going to be good. It was something that they knew we would enjoy. I enjoy it. Shoot. I miss it now. [*laugh*]

Christmas was like the Twelve Days of Christmas, like the Christmas stories, like the ghost, like Scrooge, something like that. It's like the story of Scrooge. They all come and make Christmas to let them have a good time. Make it a story of Christmas, something like that. The way we, as far as I've known, the way they've been doing this, when it's Christmas, and they do that, it's like telling a story.

They would always go to Mary's house. They would get a holly tree, cut it, and put it in the middle of the yard, and they would sell apples and oranges for a nickel. You put the name on it, they tie it on the branch and all that.

They would do that while all these ghosts would come out and play together. And we would go to somebody's house and get dressed and they would throw a firecracker or whatever saying they're ready. "We're coming." [*laughter*]

And each ghost, they claim that they come from way off, like another state, to come and have Christmas with them, enjoy the Christmas Day and all that. That's why all these . . . it's about twelve of them. That's like the twelve days of Christmas.

It's really kind of a story. There's a man and a woman that says, "All these are my kids." The man dresses as a woman; the woman dresses as a man. It's just the opposite. They all say, "These are all my kids; they're here for Christmas." [*laugh*]

We dance all the traditional dances, we're singing, dancing and all that. We do all of it from that house all the way to the other house.

SO DIFFERENT FROM OKLAHOMA

SARAH JANE SAMPSON MCMILLAN, B. 1951—ARDMORE, OK / TUCKER TOLD ON DECEMBER 2, 1973

It's so different from my home in Ardmore than it is here. I'm beginning to feel like Christmas isn't here at all because I was raised knowing Christmas as the birth of Jesus and having all these Christmas plays that they put on in church, giving presents, and shopping even in October. But here, Christmas is here, and that's it. I haven't seen anyone exchange gifts.

We've been to something that they call "Christmas Tree." I guess it's a party or something, but the way they celebrate is some people comes up wearing Santa

Claus, being a Santa Claus, and he'll have three "helpers," they call them. But they wear Halloween masks. That's what's so odd about it. And they just clown around, making jokes, telling funny stories. And that's not Christmas to me.

Here they don't give presents like we exchange gifts down there [in Oklahoma]. Here they just give one apple, and that's it.

What they do is they take a cedar tree, and they bring it into the yard and stick it in the ground. And somewhere from the twenty-fifth to New Years, just anybody in that community can have, they call it a "Christmas Tree."

I guess it's a party. But they sell fruits; they sell nuts and all that, and whoever comes, buys those things and wrap it around newspaper and give it to whoever they want to give it to that's at the party.

They start on Christmas Eve. Just any house, any family can have one. They can have one from every night 'til that New Year's Eve

What I mean about that party is that like I said, a Santa Claus and three helpers. What's so funny is that they start somewhere around eight o'clock, and they say, "Here they come." And you hear firecrackers, and you can see a lot of fireworks up in the sky.

So these people, four people is going to be ready to perform or act. So they come, and the people are supposed to think of them as coming from the North Pole. And they walk. What they first do is drive them off somewhere and let them off around quarter mile, and they're going to walk back to the house. While they're walking back, they pop firecrackers and all that stuff. When they finally come to the house, they start telling their story about what happened when they were on their way to the house, and they just make up jokes like that. And people just have fun laughing.

When we first came down [to Mississippi] around '65, my brother-in-law said there was going to be a Christmas Tree at Tucker. So my grandmother, my aunt, and all my cousins, a lot of us came down. We didn't know what to expect, so when this came up, they got our names, everybody got our names. So we wrote all of our names on pieces of paper, and we thought, "We're going to get a present." And it turns out we got one orange. And that was a disappointment because we thought we was going to get a present.

SCARED OF THE *SHILOP*

LINDA WILLIAMS, B. 1958—STANDING PINE
TOLD ON JUNE 15, 2021

Standing Pine didn't have much of anything. But I remember when the Isaacs over here in Pearl River . . . Like I said, Elsie and my dad were close. So, Christmas, I remember coming to this Christmas. They call it "Christmas Tree."

"They're going to have Christmas Tree, so, we're going to go over there." That's what my dad said. So, we came. And back home, nobody had it. And this family here had it. So that's why he said, "We're going to go see." So we came over.

I remember they used to have apples and oranges wrapped with a paper sack, newspapers, or something. And they wrapped it up and tied it up and put it on the tree. But they put the names on there, so whoever they give, that's who they used to get.

They played little games, like they used to wear costumes and make them seem to look like an old woman or old man or just dress funny like that. And then, there's the one they used to call him *shilop* [spirit or ghost]. And they're the one who used to pass out the apples and oranges. And that's where I used to lock the doors and just sit in the car. And I said, "Even if they call my name," I said, "I'm not going to get it." But that's how scared I was! [*laughter*] And I never wanted them to come near me. And then, I used to say, "If I don't get it, Mom will get it anyway."

MASKING UP FOR CHRISTMAS

MARTHA FERGUSON, B. 1949—STANDING PINE
TOLD ON JUNE 4, 2021

Uncles on my father's side always had Christmas, but they sell orange. And then you wrap the orange in the paper bag and tie it to the holly tree. And whoever you wanted to give it to, it was just a nickel. And from there you paid, put the name on it, and hang it.

So I had about twenty cents, so I went ahead and put "Mom" and "Grandma," and hang it there at my uncle's place one time.

And first time I saw, they call it ghost, or *shilop* individual. It didn't matter who it was. Nobody knew who they were when they dressed up with a costume type, or any pillows with holes in it. And then they come with a different voice and tease you, and that's kind of like a Christmas spirit type, to me, when they were doing it. Since you read those Christmas story, those ghost that comes, acting out like that, teasing people. So that's the first time I saw a bunch of them.

Next year when we did that, "You going to be one of them."

I said, "Well, I'll get a costume, but I'll go ahead and get a mask." So I bought a mask, and went ahead and we did it, all three girls, and they all enjoyed themself, just doing an hour and that was it. Oh, we dressed up like that, and, "Change your voice if you can. Don't talk like yourself, they'll know who you are." So that's the type that was going on on Christmas.

Far as I know, that's first time Standing Pine did that.

WORRIED FOR SANTA

MELFORD FARVE, B. 1961—TUCKER
TOLD ON JUNE 1, 2021

They call it "*washówa*" [play]. Just a play kind of thing with people dressed up like monsters, something like that. But I've never been to one. I've heard of them but actually never been to one.

My family just stayed within the tradition of the gift giving, just things like that. Santa Claus. When I was young, I always wondered, you hear about him coming down the chimney and all that. Ours was a gas heater. So I was worried, how was he going to come down the chimney because the gas heater's there. And I'd be worried most of the night before Christmas. [*laughter*]

AN O̱TOKLO CHRISTMAS

MARK PATRICK, B. 1969—O̱TOKLO (CONEHATTA)
TOLD ON JULY 7, 2021

We would set up this holly tree, and they would string apples on them. Either you'd put their names on them or . . . I don't know how they did it, but you would pick a person that you want to give an apple to, and basically you go pull an apple and go give it to that person.

Then they would have what they call *anumpa ittimábi* ["to beat each other with words"]. It's sort of like a debate. It's almost like a debate team.

They would come up with a subject, and they would shift a lot of the different people on this side and then this side, and then they would have a judge that's sitting there, and they would say, "This is what we're going to talk about." It could be anything. What's better, a boat to travel in, or a horse? Or it could be a cat versus a dog. Whatever. It was designed to be real funny. When a person just gets up there and say, "What do you have to say about this?" and then they'd get up there, and they'd just start making up anything that they could possibly think of. We always had comedians in our family.

It was all laughter. Laughter and fun is what it was. That was around Christmastime we would do that.

COMMUNITY COOKING FOR THE HOLIDAYS

SUSIE COMBY ALEX, B. 1947—STANDING PINE / PEARL RIVER
TOLD ON JUNE 9, 2021

We used to have that in each community, like Christmas. The community development club, they would organize it. And then we would bring food, and we all get together, have the churches in the community to come and sing. Choctaw churches—Baptist, Methodist, Catholic—they bring their group to sing. And of course, we all used to play bingo at that time too. And we had lot of food.

Like Thanksgiving and Christmas before, coming to development here, they would assign you and bring you items to cook. I used to cook chicken dressing a lot. And so they'll bring you cornmeal to make the cornbread, and onions, and whatever you put in is what they bring you. So you tell them, and they'll bring it to you.

YOUNG BOY, WISE MAN

TERRY BEN, B. 1957—STANDING PINE
TOLD ON JUNE 10, 2021

Even at school, there would be nativity plays depicting the birth of Jesus Christ. We would take part. I'd be a Wise Man during that time period and took part in Christmas carol singings and all that, just like at church.

Santa Claus would come in and hand out presents and also fruit bags. Something about presents and fruit bags around Christmastime was done at church and at school during that time period. It was good. As far as just a young man growing up like that, I loved that time period.

CHRISTMAS AT SCHOOL

BRIAN BILLIE, B. 1973—RED WATER
TOLD ON JUNE 30, 2021

That would be like a school event. Each community has a grade that goes up to eighth, I think. About Christmastime, I think every one of them would remember meeting somebody and family at the school, at the gymnasium, where you see Santa Claus or you see the real Christmas tree, the cedar tree.

They would find the biggest cedar tree around the community and put it inside the gym. And you would wonder how they put the whole tree up there. You get to see it; then you're like, "Oh, okay." I was wondering how they get it through the door. What they did was wrap it up and let it loose inside.

But I remember long time ago, the classrooms had to do a section of popcorn strings. And I wondered why until they all put them all together, and it went around the big tree. So we could remember which section we did. It was popcorn. And popcorn was our treat, popcorn and juice or Kool-Aid. That was a treat.

Nowadays, they give kids popcorn and Kool-Aid, and they're like, "I wanted chips. I wanted Coke."

CHRISTMAS QUILT

DELAURA SAUNDERS, B. 1950—BOGUE CHITTO
TOLD ON JUNE 29, 2021

My mom was the center of our family, our relations, to have a big family get-together. Christmas was one of them.

One of the things I do remember is she hand-quilted quilts, made quilts, and handsewn quilts. It took half of the year to get one done at Christmas.

So we all anticipated, "Now, who's going to get it? Whose turn is it going to be?"

I think I have two of her quilts that had been made. But it's so old, it's faded.

That was one of the reasons, too, I think she had a purpose in having this big get-together with the brothers and sisters and the uncles or aunts. That was one of the ways also to keep everybody aware of who belongs to who, whose child this is, how is that child related to you.

HOMEMADE CHRISTMAS GIFT

TRAVIS WILLIS, B. 1958—PEARL RIVER
TOLD ON JUNE 14, 2021

The Christmas story. This actually happened when we were growing up as kids. Our father, he used to hand make stuff. We never actually got store-bought stuff.

One year, he made us a bat. It just looked like a regular baseball bat, with a knob on the end. All three of us got one.

And then that summer, that same baseball bat, my Christmas present . . . My cousin came down from Chicago, and I whopped him upside the head with it.

We were playing baseball, and we got into it. And I was standing there holding it so . . . [*laughter*]

But back then, my homemade bat Christmas present was a weapon.

EASTER AT CHURCH

TERRY BEN, B. 1957—STANDING PINE
TOLD ON JUNE 10, 2021

Easter time, early in the morning, sunrise service would be available. Then afterwards, breakfast early in the morning and fellowship hall. Then you had your regular preaching service, and then afterwards it was time for the Easter egg hunt. As kids, we looked forward to the Easter egg hunt. And when the hunt was over, everybody went home, and that was it for the day.

IMPOSSIBLE EGG HUNTS

MARK PATRICK, B. 1969—O̱TOKLO (CONEHATTA)
TOLD ON JULY 12, 2021

We had a long, outside table outside the church, and we would hunt all the eggs. And we wouldn't never find them all because there was guys that hid those eggs, and they would just bury them a foot in the ground or something. They would hide eggs in the trees and tailpipes of a car. We had an outside fire, and they'll dig a hole, and they would put it inside the ashes and stuff. And so we would never really just find all the eggs. But we would count them and find as many as we could.

And then they'll finally say, "Okay, every family will divide the eggs that they're going to take home." But we would just eat eggs. And we would eat eggs and dill pickles.

And the eggs. What we used to do is we used to hit each other's heads and crack the eggs like that. Just like, "Hey, come here, I got to tell you something," then pow! And just crack it open.

I don't know why pickles, but that's the way it was.

FUNDRAISERS

Community gatherings and fundraising go hand in hand in Choctaw customary life. Some events like the fair, community Christmas celebrations, and ball games are driven by entertainment but provide opportunities for fundraising, usually through food and drink sales. Other events like box suppers, raffles, garage sales, and bake sales work in reverse, driven by fundraising but providing ample opportunity for fun. The house dance sits squarely in the middle. Some families used to host them in order to raise money while others wanted to dance, which meant someone needed to sell drinks and treats to the dancers.

Some of the most common reasons for fundraising have been buying uniforms and equipment for ball teams; paying for dresses, baskets, and beadwork in order to participate in the annual Choctaw Indian Princess pageant; and funding school or family trips, though sometimes the financial need is far more mundane. "A lot of people that were selling usually needed income to pay electric bills or water bills," explains Martha Ferguson. "Whenever I'd see them there, they used to say, 'Buy some sausage and biscuit. A dollar.' I'd go ahead and buy it. I said, 'What are you guys . . . ' 'Oh, I'm trying to pay water bill.'" More direct fundraising such as a collection jar may appear on food counters when someone has faced a personal tragedy, such as an unexpected illness or accident.[13]

Sales of homemade cakes, cookies, and popcorn balls jump exponentially during December, partly to satisfy the demand for holiday treats and partly to raise money for Christmas presents, where the expectation has shifted from a piece of fruit hung from a community tree in a brown paper bag to the newest electronics, toys, and clothing marketed to youth across the country no matter their cultural heritage.

Raffles have become an increasingly popular way for Choctaw artisans to sell their work for a price worthy of its quality. The average person may not have $500 for a small, double-weave basket or bead set, but a lot of people have five or ten dollars to buy raffle tickets to try to win it. It is a gamble, of course, but Choctaw have traditionally coupled their social lives and culture with a competitive, wagering spirit.

In the past, people relied on phone calls, homemade signs staked into the front yard, and flyers posted around tribal offices to get the word out. Now social media dominates, even allowing some fundraisers like raffles to move well beyond the reservation, helping to solve a problem that often plagues small communities: how to raise money when most folks are in the same economic boat as their neighbor. When he was a young boy, Leonard Jimmie helped host chili sales in town outside the Cattlemen's Association to tap into the wallets of their non-Choctaw neighbors. Raffle sales today bring in dollars from distant acquaintances. However, the vast majority of fundraising continues to occur on the reservation, among fellow tribal members.

BOX SUPPER

CARMEN DENSON, B. 1956—STANDING PINE
TOLD ON JUNE 27, 2021

We called it the "box supper." The ladies' team, they would cook their dish and put it in a box and bring it. Usually, the emcee or whoever's auctioning the box, he would tell who made it. And all the guys that want to eat with her, they're going to auction it off; they're going to bid. And that's how they raised funds. They had fundraisers for the baseball teams.

RUNNING UP THE PRICE

BRADLEY ALEX, B. 1955—BOGUE HOMA / PEARL RIVER
TOLD ON JUNE 30, 2021

They used to have this box supper or something like that. They used to have an auction. That was the women or the girls. Majority was single, as far as I know; they had a supper, a box for two that it will share whoever buys it. And they share. If this guy likes this girl, he would buy that box.

I remember Linda's. I paid about fifteen dollars. That was a lot back then, about fifteen dollars. And I knew some of them that they were just doing that to me. They would raise it up. And she was, "You got some more money? You got some money?"

I remember she gave me some money, about three dollars. She was standing next to me, and she said, "You got some . . . ?" "That's all? Here."

That was fun. That was fun. I think that we should have that again for singles.

BIG BOX SUPPER

BRIAN BILLIE, B. 1973—RED WATER
TOLD ON JUNE 30, 2021

They had box suppers too. Box suppers were kind of like an auction.

Mom told me about a box supper in Tucker that one lady cooked a meal for, say, eight or ten people. It was a big box, and guys that were working in the field saved money for that time. And it was like, money *oklah ittahobbi, hikma̱ ittḭpaknah* [they gather the money, and they're competing], everybody's trying to outbid each other for that box. But they knew she made good pie, her chicken was good, and she doesn't disappoint you because she'll have biscuits, gravy, and everything else, just whatever can make a good meal.

And some young upcoming girls would take part of it and make their own too. And their fathers would buy it. And then whoever bought it would eat with the female that cooked it. They would buy the box so the family can eat. Another way of raising money.

UNCOMFORTABLE DINNER

LINDA WILLIAMS, B. 1958—STANDING PINE
TOLD ON JUNE 15, 2021

I never liked that box dinner. And my mom did a box for me, but I told her, "Why don't you do it yourself, Mom? You want to eat. You want somebody to buy your box. Why are you letting me eat with somebody?" You know? I kept on saying that to her during the time.

And then when somebody actually bought my box, I didn't want to eat with them because I was young. And then whoever it was, was an older man. And that just threw me off. I told Mama, "You can eat with him then."

SELLING CHILI IN TOWN

LEONARD JIMMIE, B. 1957—PEARL RIVER
TOLD ON JULY 11, 2021

Being what it was, people out here didn't have much money. We could raise some money, but it'd barely make maybe a hundred, two hundred dollars. We had to go into town to raise money. So we would have fundraisers up there.

That Boy Scout trip that we went to in Idaho. We always made a point of having a food sale right outside the Cattlemen's Association, the auction uptown on the north side. We always had a food stand out there. And they would come by and see what we had. We always had chili or something. And they would, "Oh, okay. Why go somewhere when we can have a quick bite here?"

And here we were selling those things.

FOOD SALES

LORENA ALEX, B. 1952—HALLS, TN / BOGUE CHITTO / PEARL RIVER
TOLD ON JUNE 10, 2021

When my daughter had to go to Hawaii for Winter Guard, we had to raise some money. So, selling food is what we did for maybe three months just to raise the money. And we did it, and she went.

But then that time she had to run for princess, so we had to do that, too. Raise some money. We didn't count on anybody else to help us out. We did that ourselves. My sisters and brother helped me out, and that was the good thing. I never forget that.

We had hominy, fried chicken, beans. I did biscuit. They love my biscuit now. And dessert like cake and drinks. That's what we did.

I think we did a sign where we sent it out and placed it on each department with their permission. Or we used the phone to let people know that we were going to do that. And we just let people know when we see them. And they would come during lunchtime. We used to start at eleven o'clock up to one o'clock. Hopefully, by that time everything was gone, too.

TRICKED INTO CHITLINS

LINDA WILLIAMS, B. 1958—STANDING PINE
TOLD ON JUNE 15, 2021

I never had chitlins in all my life. And they'd be there cleaning them. And especially when they're cleaning, I guess I used to run around and play around, and I could smell it. I think that smell got stuck with me, and I just never liked it. So, that's why I never took any interest in chitlins.

But I remember not too many years ago, Mary Morris was still alive, and so she was still up and cooking. So she said, "Linda." She called me one day. She said, "Linda, I'm going to be selling food plates." She said, "Bring your mom, and you all can come and buy a plate."

And I said, "Okay."

Mary and I took a ride way before that, prior to this time. And I told her, "I never eat chitlins." I said, "I never liked chitlins." And I was telling her my story about chitlins. And so, she knew it. Okay? And in her mind, she planned something for me. I didn't know.

But anyway, she invited me, so I told my mom. I said, "Mary says she's going to be selling plates, so let's go eat in Bogue Chitto today."

She said, "Okay." She said, "If it's Mary, she cooks good."

And I said, "Yeah, she does."

So, we drove all the way to Bogue Chitto. And she fixed my plate and gave it to me. And she had fried chitlins, put it in my plate. I didn't even notice it. The only thing I thought it was okra or something. So, I did eat it, and it was good and light with my biscuit so didn't think nothing of it.

And so, I finished whatever was on my plate until I got full. And then, that's when I came back and then sat down and started listening to her and my mom's conversation. And then later on, she said, "Well, did you like what you eat?"

And I said, "Yeah, it was good." And I said, "That okra? That fried okra? Was that fried okra?"

And she goes, "No."

And then, I said, "What was it? Whatever it was, it was good, because I ate it with my biscuit, and it was good."

And she told me that it was fried chitlins. That's when she told me, "I told you I can make you eat chitlins."

She got me good that day. [*laughter*]

And I laughed. I said, "So, today I can't say I never had chitlins." But I did eat her chitlins that day.

FUNDRAISERS

JAY WESLEY, B. 1975—STANDING PINE
TOLD ON JULY 28, 2022

Nowadays when they have washer tournaments at home, it's fundraising for something. Sometimes you have adult beverages involved, and they sell it, maybe a dollar or more each, and it's fundraising. But that association, kind of like the house dances, people think it has a negative connotation now.

So it's washers and tournaments.

I remember we used to go to those. My aunts and uncles would host a few of those. And I played growing up. I played when adults were done. We'd go out there and try our hand in it.

And then part of fundraising would be potluck. Everybody would sit down and switch out meals, and we'd all eat whatever, or you can purchase one. But it was all fundraising. Well, it was fun. It kind of made it more of a community gathering after a while. People would know, and it would be volleyball or whatever.

I think growing up it was more like volleyball, washers, and preparing food and boxed lunches and switching them out.

And food. As a group going out to France, we did a lot of traditional food. At one point, it was like Indian tacos. And then the other ones, frybread, hominy, *shokka nipi* [hog meat], fried chicken, green beans. And Phyllis [McMillan] likes to make that *walakshi*, the blueberry dumpling.

I remember at one time, my aunts and uncles and my grandma brought in the boxed lunches, and they just cooked and put together little meal kits. I guess we call it "bento" now. [*laugh*] But they brought it over during the volleyball game, and five dollars would get you a meal and a drink. So that was fundraising.

Or sometimes it was like potluck. Same setup except this time people brought their own boxed lunch, and they exchanged. So you didn't know what you were going to get. But it was fun. People got to exchange, and there was no cost involved. It's just people said, "Hey, we got a volleyball tournament going on. Just come on over and bring your food." And people bringing their own food to these things was always normal.

Nowadays, they do tournaments as fundraisers, they still do with gymnasium and stuff, but these were at people's homes. And then it's like, "OK. We're having a volleyball tournament. Bring a team in."

And then sometimes there's a fee involved, or sometimes they just get a team in, and we have food and drinks available for you from concessions. So that's the fundraising part. Or it could be both. But nowadays, I see a few here and there like washers tournaments. I see a few volleyball, and I find out it's a tournament. But a lot of times, it's part of a gym, and they do an entry fee and then bracket, and maybe if they have time, it's a bigger tournament, then it's trophies or half of the pot of the entry fees.

But it's always fundraising.

FUNDRAISING THROUGH SOCIAL MEDIA

MAHLIH BOWDEN, B. 1991—PEARL RIVER
TOLD ON JULY 14, 2021

This goes back to social media; it has its pros and cons, but I like to look more at the pros than the cons. We have . . . of course basketball is a really big sport. Choctaws love sports, especially basketball. And a lot of our youth, they do travel ball with other tribes. And so a way for them to raise money is they'll get on social media, and they'll do cake auctions. Either it's chocolate-covered strawberries, upside-down pineapple cake, cupcakes, just it's in a large quantity, and they'll start bids on it. And it'll be like starting bid fifteen dollars with one-dollar increments from now until whenever. It's a really good fundraiser.

Our current [princess pageant] contestants actually did that. Each contestant got their own specialized cake that represented them in a way. I believe one girl had the design of her bead set as the design of the cake. One girl had a basket with flowers. It was just all so unique and so beautiful, and it's a good way to raise money. Plus, when you have a sweet tooth, and you don't want to go anywhere, you don't want to cook anything, there it is.

DANCING

Stickball may be the favored sport of the Choctaw, but until recently, dancing was the favorite pastime. Community celebrations, ball games, festivals, and fairs all included dancing as the primary source of social activity. Young men and women were particularly fond of dancing as it offered them a chance to interact and meet eligible partners for marriage. Well into the twentieth century, people remember walking with their families to a weekend gathering and catching the first echoes of chanting and dancing filtering through the trees that would grow into loud, joyous music as they neared their destination. Dancing that began at night continued until morning.[14]

From the earliest written records in the eighteenth century, both men and women participated in the dancing, even the dances held before and after going to war, first to prepare, then to celebrate. War dances continue to be performed, but within the social context of public performances. The three traditional types of dance—social, animal, and war—are often casually lumped under the umbrella term *social dance* to distinguish it from the much more recent *house dance*.

In the middle of the twentieth century, house dancing began to nudge social dancing to the sidelines. The dance arena shifted from clearings in woods to cleared-out living rooms in wood-frame houses. Fiddle and guitar players took the place of chanters. Variations on French quadrilles and Anglo-American square dancing were adopted and adapted into these late-night house parties, following a common pattern of adaptation and integration. The Choctaw borrowed from their neighbors, and their neighbors borrowed from them. And just as settler colonists took stickball and created lacrosse, and corn to create the hushpuppy (among other things), the Choctaw took items from settler colonists and transformed them into Choctaw objects and traditions. "You know the Choctaw dresses?" Grady John asked back in 1998. "They copied them from the European women. So Choctaw got the idea. But they changed them. They added the stickball, the rattlesnake, the diamond designs." The black hat that accompanies traditional men's clothing came from the French and is still called a *shapo* in Choctaw from the French *chapeau* meaning "hat." The same process of inspiration and transformation is true of Choctaw house dancing. "Choctaw square dance now. Choctaw watched them. English was doing square dance. And French people, too. That's where they started." But Grady adds, "Ours is a little different."

> Square dancing has dos-a-dos, here we go, grab your partner, swinging dos.
>
> Well, Choctaw is this way, "Swayliii!" The woman promenades outside the big circle. One of them say, "Whoa." They stop. They start. They go round and round, dancing round. "Whoa." That's when he start dancing with his partner. Dancing and jump into the next, all way around.
>
> That's the way Choctaw did it.
>
> And when you finished, you promenade. Women goes inside; men, outside. He say, "Whoa back," and you'd go back. "Whoa," and he'd stop. With your girlfriend as partner, you're just dancing. But along again, he'd say, "Swing your partner," and you'd go to the next one. All the way around to the promenade home, they call "Buffalo." [*laughter*].
>
> Choctaw used to say, "Buffalo"; that means nickel.[15] And they'd have to buy apples, oranges, to give them [the women].
>
> The Indian, way back then, they didn't do that, but later, they changed up. And they'd make the partner buy apple, candy, give it to your lady. (February 22, 1998)

Just as the stickball games and social-dancing events were deemed sinful by Christian missionaries, and gambling at the games was outlawed by the state in 1898, driving the games underground when they were played at all, so too did house dancing come under fire for its ancillary vices: in this case, excessive drinking and fighting. Tribal police were tasked with breaking up house dances that got out of hand; many devout Christian Choctaw families barred their children from attending.

Today, both social and house dancing occur primarily in educational and performance spaces, including elementary school, where the dances are taught and then performed at fall and spring festivals; the Annual Choctaw Indian Fair, where dance troupes from across the various communities perform throughout the day; and public events for primarily non-Indian audiences, such as regional festivals, parades, and ceremonial events.[16] Occasionally, however, communities will host an event that invites dancing for fun, such as the Moccasin Boogie Woogie event hosted by the Cultural Affairs Program in the weeks leading up to the fair,[17] or to honor someone, such as at election parties or funerals.

SOCIAL DANCING

HENDERSON WILLIAMS, B. 1947—CONEHATTA
TOLD ON JULY 25, 1997

We learn from generation to generation. Some of us may be old enough to remember attending the old-time social dance that they used to have.

The one that I remember, I was a small child, went to social dance that they had. It was nighttime. In order to get to this field or clearing way in the woods, about a mile into the woods, we walked along this narrow footpath. There was hardly any light. I don't remember what kind of light we used to find our way through the woods, but we walked on this narrow footpath to that clearing. As you approach, I can vividly recall the sounds from the crickets and the bullfrogs in the woods and the surrounding swamps. But as you get nearer the field where they were dancing, you can hear the chanting, their dancing, and the foot thumping on the ground. And then here are these tall pine trees, and you're walking along, and all you can see because of the bonfire—they had a bonfire going, and they were dancing around the bonfire—and all you could see—you could hear the chanting and everybody's chanting real loud, and the lead chanter and then the ones that follow up behind the lead chanter and then here are these tall pine trees—and all you could see, the fire and these figures like silhouettes. But they were dancing all together. It was somewhat of an eerie, primitive feeling about that.

I remember I was a small child at that time. I used to have a lot of questions, and the grandparents that remembered those things used to tell me this dance was a snake dance. Snake dance is popular. But now the children I'm sure out there probably doing the snake dance.

Of course this is a tradition that goes back hundreds of years.

WALK DANCE

EDDIE GIBSON, B. 1953—CONEHATTA
TOLD ON JULY 1, 2021

These days you use the walk dance to honor people, like during fair sometimes. Somebody did something and died, and was a good leader, or like a VIP in the community or with the tribe, they do walk dance.

There was a professor at Mississippi State, John Peterson. And when he was still alive, one of his things was when he died, he wanted a walk dance at the fair to honor him.

So when he passed, I went to his funeral. I believe his funeral was in Louisville, and I went to that. And then during the fair, they did honor him by doing the walk dance. And people in the stands came out. They didn't even know John, probably never heard of him, but they all came out.

What intrigued me the most was that they have all these lights at the stage, and one of the light crew from Jackson, he got into it. And he made a comment. He said, "You know what? That walk dance was powerful." He said, "There's something powerful. It got to me."

And that's when I realized that dance could mean a lot.

CLASH WITH CHRISTIANITY

DELAURA SAUNDERS, B. 1950—BOGUE CHITTO
TOLD ON JUNE 29, 2021

Growing up, there was a lot of transitions from what would be culturally practiced, to the Christian faith, to getting back our cultural ways again. So there was a lot of transition. But as vaguely as I can remember in my childhood, I remember more of the transition of the Christian believers coming in and telling us that the way we do things was evil.

Then when my mom and dad became Christians, my mom especially.

One of the examples I can give you vividly. I guess the clearing we had lived in Bogue Chitto, my dad farmed—leased an area and farmed. We had whole acres of corn, or sometimes we'd have cotton. You guys [the YOP students] know what those are, right? Pick cotton? Panóla okla amoh? Then going through the fields, from our house, going through the field to get to my grandma and my auntie's house, we go through that way. It would be *sashki chaffa* [second mother or, literally, first other mother] in our side that we call my mom's sister or *sashki chaffa* and *pokni̱*, "grandma."

They would have a house dance. Or they would have dance practices. You could hear them at night. You could hear their footsteps on the ground, footsteps on the ground. You could hear it, and you could hear all the singing that was going on.

It's like if you wanted to go to a party or something where it's nearby, and you hear all this noise, and you wanted to go. But mom wouldn't let us go because of her Christian belief. But that was that kind of transition at that time.

But we did get to dance practices after, when I got older, a little older, still childhood, but a little older. And then we were all in dance groups, so we would practice where the old school grounds were. And then our relatives were some of the chanters, so we would practice chanting with them too.

HOUSE DANCING

MARTHA FERGUSON, B. 1949—STANDING PINE
TOLD ON JUNE 4, 2021

Friend of mine used to call me, back when I was seventh grade and eighth grade, in Conehatta area. "House dance?"

She always went. "No, no."

So finally, eighth grade, I asked Mom, and she said, "You want to go to that one?"

I said, "I don't know what house dance is. I don't know how to dance."

"And you want to learn?"

I said, "Yes." So I danced.

She went ahead, and I said, "What is house dance?"

"They going to buy something for you. It's a nickel or dime dance. They going to give you a gift after they finish dancing with you."

I said, "What kind of gift?"

"You'll learn. I'll take you."

And Grandfather said, "You really want to go?"

I said, "At least try it. A friend of mine is having one. So could we go?"

I went.

They cleaned up everything out of the living room. And they had a guitar player and a fiddle player. And they played that house dance. And that's the first time I walked in, and my mother grabbed a pillowcase. I said, "What are you bringing it for?"

"You'll see."

So once I started dancing, they came and gave me gum, apple, orange, and candy and more of that one. And finally, one of them bought a drink. He bought me two. And I didn't want to drink Coke, so I went to the car, gave it to Mom, and she put it in the bag and put it in back. "Now you found out what a house dance is."

"Yes. Looks like a big Christmas to me." [*laugh*] And she was laughing. It was a Coke, and then every time they give me Coke, I hand to my family that was sitting, waiting on me. And my aunt was there to dance. And my other aunt was there to dance. They could get that one, but no, they were doing their dance enough where they got fruits, whatever they wanted. And their bag, their pillow bag was this full [*indicates just a little at the bottom*]. Both of them.

I looked at her, and I said, "That's all you got here?" And mine was getting bigger and bigger. My aunt said, "How do you get all that?"

"I dance with the drunks too." [*laugh*] I did! But they don't want his money and just give you a whole bunch of candies, two at a time.

And then I told my grandfather, "As soon as it's one o'clock, let me know."

"Okay."

It's one o'clock. "Why one o'clock?" I said, "I'm ready to go home."

So we went home. But the problem was it was a school week. Church day next day; do that one. That same week, back to the sack that I filled up; I saw it that next day, it was full. Well, Monday came. The whole week, I forgot about it. And then all I saw was an empty bag. I said, "Who got the candies and other stuff?" And everybody's hushed up. "Who ate it all?" Nobody said anything. I didn't get the chance to eat nothing. Nothing. Nothing. [*laughter*]

"If you want to go to dance like house dance, let me know," Grandfather said. "I'll take you. Because I ate some. I liked the orange."

I said, "Oh, you're the one that . . . "

"Everybody else did. They're not saying."

I said, "Oh, because you're going to get after them."

"Did you get some?"

I said, "No."

"Well, next time hide it."

I said, "Yeah, that's what I did. And look what that got me. Empty bag." [*laughter*]

LEARNING THE RULES

LEONARD JIMMIE, B. 1957—PEARL RIVER
TOLD ON JULY 11, 2021

Back in the day when I was younger, house dancing is always associated with having a good time. And having a good time back in those days, you had to create your own fun. A lot of us associate it unfortunately with alcohol. But it was a good time.

The first house dance I went to was a place called Riley Phillips up here on west [Highway] 16. We were up there, and I was about thirteen or fourteen when

I first started partaking alcohol. And I just went along with the group. My aunt was the driver. So I was sitting in the back.

And then when we pulled up, I could hear the ting-ting-ting-ting-ting-ting-ting-ting. I said, "Hey, a square dance." It wasn't square dance. It was a house dance, a *abóha hilha*. "Ish ha̱kloho̱, abóha hilha," they say.

I said, "Oh, okay. All right. House dance."

I walked up. And back then they hardly had it during the wintertime. They would have it, but it would be kind of difficult because it's always in the house and some people are particular about their house. But in the summertime, Riley Phillips was wide open. And in those times, it would be crowded in the house, so you had to stand outside and look through the window. They would have open windows. And I was standing there watching and I'd say, "Hey, this is fun." And I would be watching them, and I'd see the fiddler and the guitar player and they go ting-ting-ting-ting-ting-ting-ting-ting.

And I said, "Yeah, I can get this."

So I went inside and then I saw some girls I knew, and I went like this [*gives small upward nod*], just give them a head nod. And they stood up and grabbed my hand, and here we are. Ting-ting-ting-ting-ting-ting-ting-ting.

After the dance we were walking off, and I went outside, and before I left, that girl that had grabbed my hand, she yanked on my hand. And I went, "Oh, I barely know you." And I went outside.

She did it for a reason. Anytime you ask a girl to dance, you're supposed to give her something.

And that's when—my friend's outside—she said, "You know why she did that, don't you?"

And I said, "Why?"

"She was expecting something."

I said, "What?"

Said, "Go give her something."

I said, "What?"

They said, "They got a table in there. Go get something."

So I went in there, went back into the house dance; off to the corner was a table, and they had goodies on there: candies, nickel candies, penny candies, whatever. And you could buy some. So I went over there and got a handful of peppermints, and I walked back to her, and I put my head down, and I just gave it to her. And then she just took it and looked at me. It's like paying for the dance.

And I went, "Wow, okay, I get it." But as time went along, when I asked her to come outside after a dance, I wasn't giving her candy, I was giving her a can of beer. And she was happy with that. So we'd go back in and ting-ting-ting-ting-ting-ting-ting-ting.

And there's a lot of stories about that. People will tell you about house dancing. Even some of them won't admit it, but they've been out there. I always thought the best ones were in Bogue Chitto. Every time I wanted to have a good time, I would always try to find my way to Bogue Chitto.

AN ORANGE FOR A DANCE

MELFORD FARVE, B. 1961—TUCKER
TOLD ON JUNE 1, 2021

The older days, from what they told me, it was a good social gathering. If you wanted to dance with a girl, you had to buy an apple and an orange or something and present to her. They said women need to bring little sack cloths to gather all their fruit or candy. There was candy, fruits, whatever the girls . . . If you wanted to dance with that girl, you've got to pay the price. You'd get that bag. You'd see a lot of girls going home with a bag full of stuff.

I didn't do that. That was way before my time. The ones I went to was . . . I hate to say it, but it was kind of alcohol-fueled a little bit.

I remember, I think me and Dorothy just pulled up; we parked our car in the yard, and we didn't even dance. We were just getting ready to go out, and there was a police raid, blue lights all over the place. I think Dorothy had already gone out to talk to her friend or something, and I was sitting there. When I saw the police, I pulled that thing down to make myself go back way down in the seat. I thought I was hiding because the security light was on the other side, so it was kind of dark, I thought. I guess it was enough light, but I was sitting there, and one of the policemen walks by. He says, "Hey, Melford," and just walked on. So I guess I didn't hide too well. [*laughter*]

I think most of the people in the house had already ran off and ran into the woods. So they didn't really catch anybody.

But yeah, in the old days, that's what they said, where a guy can meet a girl. That's how you can ask one out for an orange.

DANCING AND FIGHTING

TRAVIS WILLIS, B. 1958—PEARL RIVER
TOLD ON JUNE 14, 2021

A young man one time, he was from Red Water. And back then, the communities didn't care too much for each other. So if you got caught in, say, Conehatta, and you're from Pearl River or Red Water or got caught in any other community, there would be a big ol' fight.

And this one guy, he was from Red Water. They called him "Cat." I can't remember what his real name was, but I knew him. He was a friend. He died in a car accident many years ago.

One time we were at a house dance. We just got there about thirty minutes, and I saw him running toward the house. And then about an hour later, I saw him again. He was beaten up bad.

But it used to be like that, where the communities always had a fight with one another. They always had a fight.

One time, we were in Bogue Chitto, and some of my mama's kinfolks are from Bogue Chitto, or up that way.

One time, and this was at a house dance, one of the guys came up to me from Bogue Chitto, says, "Come here. I want to talk to you." So I went. He took me to the back, and he says, "Stay here." The next thing I heard, they were fighting. But just because it was my mom's kinfolks, they were saving my hide. I was with that bunch that got beaten up.

Like I said, the communities didn't care for each other.

LEARN BY DOING

LINDA WILLIAMS, B. 1958—STANDING PINE
TOLD ON JUNE 15, 2021

Probably Bogue Chitto and the other communities still had house dances, but that's something that I didn't go to. I wasn't participating in it, and I didn't have any interest, so I never did attend house dances.

But I remember Chief Martin, when he had something going on that night, we were in Conehatta. We were inside a gym, and he played that house dance. He said, "You all, dance." And I remember taking off. I didn't know how to dance. I just said, "I've kind of seen it, but I don't know how to dance," but I said, "I'm going to try."

So, I remember, I took off with the group.

And today, I still can do that. But I don't really dance, I don't know the steps of it, but I just follow somebody next to me.

COMMUNITY DANCE

BRADLEY ALEX, B. 1955—BOGUE HOMA / PEARL RIVER
TOLD ON JUNE 30, 2021

House dances. Yeah, I used to go. I was a teenager.

After I became a police officer, I came back, I had to stop those since they said to because they had alcohol, fights, and everything. We had to stop those. But if not, we let them enjoy it. Set a time, midnight, or something like that.

But when I was teenager, yeah, I used to go there. I used to dance with the older women. Man, you better watch out! They used to make you jump. [*laughter*] Swing. I thought they just did that, the older women, because I was a teenager. [*laughter*] No. Never seen that one before. "Let go!"

It used to be fun. They made it fun.

I thought about it, before COVID, having just a Choctaw dance somewhere—a baseball field, new ground. I thought about that. Invite Pearl River people. "Hey, we'll have chanters and let's just dress as you want to and just come. And let's have a dance, social dances."

I just enjoy being Choctaw.

That's when COVID hit. My wife and I, we were talking about it, but she passed away. She said, "That's a good idea."

And I said, "Really?" I said, "Yeah, let's do that." But we never got to do it.

PUBLIC PERFORMANCE

MELFORD FARVE, B. 1961—TUCKER
TOLD ON JUNE 1, 2021

Tucker was founded by the Catholic missionaries. So we had these people that helped us to participate in Boy Scouts and youth recreation. His name was Brother Mal. And he was a Brother. Then you had the Sisters. The Sisters were nuns.

Brother Mal was basically instrumental in forming a lot of activities for the youth. He took us to . . . at that time it was the Village Square Mall, the first mall in Meridian.

So he had us go there and dance over there. And the more people cheered for us, we were really into that dancing.

But we didn't know Miss Hand was in the audience.

So when we came back to school, Miss Hand admonished us. She's like, "Y'all didn't do what I taught you to do. Y'all were dancing . . . Your steps were too high." And she was showing us what we did wrong. She was more or less disappointed in what we should have learned and did.

She was right. We were just kind of cutting up for the audience, I guess. But it helped us to get better at it, anyway.

GETTING TOGETHER

Community-wide, organized events such as ball games and fairs brought people together in large groups, but daily life brought people together in smaller groups for fellowship. In the past, travel was difficult. Farming kept families tethered to animals that needed daily feeding and care; sharecropping ensured that families were spread out across the landscape far from one another; and lack of cars and paved roads ensured travel took days instead of minutes or hours. So when people visited, it was an event, remembered fondly by Choctaw elders today as a chance to play with other children, hear stories, and eat well.

Most visits were to family, but quilting bees brought women together in their local communities for shared work, and church activities brought neighbors together in fellowship. For Christian families, hymn singing was both a favorite pastime and a reason to gather in the first place. Storytelling and playing games such as washers and cards were also popular, though shared work like shelling peas was often expected as well.

As travel became easier, visits became more frequent but shorter in length. Eventually, the constriction of time would be matched with the constriction of the group, first from community to extended family and then extended family to nuclear family. Doris Bell notes this shift in how they celebrated birthday parties: "We would all gather there. It was more or less a community affair. But now it's a family affair." Speaking in 2000, Linda Willis remembered her grandfather Cameron Wesley organizing Easter egg hunts and other activities for the extended family. "He would get the family together on those days, and they all would be together. So, that was kind of fun. And, you would know who your family was, like your brothers and sisters or your aunts and uncles. That way you would find out who they were. Today, we don't do that, so our children don't know who their aunts or uncles or cousins are because we don't have a family get-together like he used to."

While family gatherings have grown smaller, they are no less vibrant. Birthdays and holidays are obvious occasions for gathering, but weekly dinners where grown children return to their parents' homes with their own kids in tow are common. So, too, are new customs, many adopted and adapted from mainstream American culture, such as gender-reveal parties, baby showers, and graduation parties, which open the social circle back up to friends as well as extended family members.

CHOCTAW TIME

HAROLD COMBY, B. 1955—PEARL RIVER
TOLD ON JUNE 4, 1997

We always say, "Indian time" or "Choctaw time."

A long time ago, my mom says they never followed the clock. It was when the leader of the group said that they were going to do something, that's what they did.

I think that's why. We carry this within ourselves subconsciously. That's why some of us are never on time.

RABBITS AND WASHERS

HENRY WILLIAMS, B. 1945—CONEHATTA
TOLD ON JUNE 24, 1997

We used to go out about nine o'clock in the morning. Come back around, before dark. If we hunt as a family, probably go half a day, probably about three or four hours then come home. But if we were to go out as a special occasion, Christmastime, Thanksgiving, we go all day and kill us about ten, twenty rabbits. And family—two or three families get together.

I used to get elected to bring rabbit in. I'll have rabbit full, about five rabbits around my waist, and three rabbits here [*points to shoulder*] and three rabbits here [*points to other shoulder*]. Carrying them home, dragging those rabbits, so those ladies can prepare when the men come home. Me and my brother and cousin used to bring rabbits home before dark. Two, three families was supposed to get together and have a feast, and ladies would be there to skin it and dress it and fry it and boil it. And then about dark time before sundown, just right at sundown, they'd be coming in bringing some more rabbits. But they save that for the next day.

They used to cook about two pots, two big pots.

And that time, we play washers or marbles, while women are preparing the meal.

Washer, about that big around [*indicates a half-dollar size*], and they have a hole there about two feet apart. You throw that washer in that hole, you get a point. One point or five points. Washer goes in, you get a point. But your opponent makes it with you, you lose your point. They both lose the point, no score. That's how they play. Twenty-five points is the game, I think. Anybody who can throw a washer.

Your partner would be standing over there [*indicates a short distance away*]. Five washer or ten washer, you throw it to that hole. When you've done that, your partner will throw it back. But you keep the same score. If you can't make the hole, it takes a little longer to finish up. Whoever gets twenty-five points wins the game.

You throw one washer at a time, but you get about ten times, ten throws. But if you make five washers in that throwing time, you win the game.

Sometimes they have tournament, once in a while.

QUILTING AND DIPPING

TERRY BEN, B. 1957—STANDING PINE
TOLD ON JUNE 10, 2021

Flour came in twenty-five-pound bags from cloth during that time period, and the people there, including my grandparents, were very poor. And those bags of flour cloth, where the flour came in, it was saved to make aprons, to make dresses, and to use as a cutout to make quilts.

The ladies of the church during that time period, sometimes they would gather on a certain appointed day on a Saturday, and they would have what they call "quilting bees." There would be about maybe ten or twelve women there, and they would sit around and sew using these pieces of cloth from the flour sacks and make a quilt for the purpose of fundraising for the church, or maybe some family struggling, somebody very bad sick, and they need help, maybe in the wintertime. They would do it that way to help people out in the community.

And so, that's the way it was.

My job was to hang around there with Grandma, and if somebody wanted snuff or whatever, "Hey, here's two dollars. Run up to the store and get it. You can get yourself a drink or whatever."

The ladies during that time period, they were bad snuff dippers! [*laugh*] Like that [*points to his lower lip, indicating where they would put the snuff*].

And so many times, they would give me money. I was about maybe ten, eleven, twelve years old, and Standing Pine store was about maybe two miles from the church. They gave me some money, actual money to get some drinks or whatever. So I had an incentive to go up there and back, and I would bring that something to a lady or whoever wanted, or sometimes it was chewing tobacco.

So that's the way it was. They worked all day, and they usually finished a quilt in one day because you had several ladies working together. So those are things that I grew up with at Standing Pine.

EXTRA FOOD

DELAURA SAUNDERS, B. 1950—BOGUE CHITTO
TOLD ON JUNE 29, 2021

When my mother ever cooked a meal at the house, she always cooked extra because she said, "You never know who's going to stop by. You never know." Especially Uncle Bob would always generally stop by or some of our other cousins. And our grandfather lived with us, too. I always set up an extra plate because you never know.

Then my mom, not so much as the big tradition of *iyyikowa*, but my mom believed in helping others. If you see people in need and people that are sick? Especially with her elder relatives. They would live out in Mashulaville, way out in Preston, little areas. You have to understand that the areas in these communities, the way they are built are so much different from what you see, where you have at least paved road to get to. And then the houses are together. But these were like in wooded areas, and it was like dirt road to get to the area. Mom would check on her elder cousin or her elder aunties. So we would go. When she started to learn to drive, we would all hop in the car.

Before that though, she would make us cook or help her cook a whole batch of food and stuff. So we would go around. She would always sing. She was a Christian, so she would sing some Choctaw songs, hymnal songs, and then do some verses. This was all in Choctaw.

So I remember those kinds of things that Mom taught us then to do.

COMMUNITY VISITING

EDDIE GIBSON, B. 1953—CONEHATTA
TOLD ON JULY 1, 2021

When I was coming up, now, there was a lot of visiting. Whether it was family or church people.

I remember church people used to come through our house all the time. And that's where these church hymns, singing would take place. And growing up, I'm like, "What's all these folks doing here?" But I didn't quite understand it. But as you grow, you keep looking and seeing these things happen, and you start thinking, "Okay, it's all right. It's okay."

And my mom, she was a good baker. She can whip up a cake in no time, a pie, or something. And a matter of fact, people used to ask her to bake them a cake. I can remember a cake she used to make all the time was "sock-it-to-me cake." And I don't know where that comes from; I don't know the stuff's name.

Or upside-down pineapple cake. She was good at making that. And people used to just come and say, "Lillie, can you make me a cake?" And she'd make them. And some people paid, and some people didn't. But it didn't matter back then.

So she'd make a cake, and they'd sit in for a couple hours. Two or three hours. And they'd take a break, and she'd bring out the cake and make coffee, and they'd sit around. And some of the storytelling would take place during that time.

GOSSIPING FOR THE GREATER GOOD

JAY WESLEY, B. 1975—STANDING PINE
TOLD ON JULY 27, 2022

Back then, we visited other people, they visited us, and to me, I was like, "Okay. They're just catching up on gossip." But they would know the community, basically the pulse of the community, knowing who's who, who's sick.

But as a child or just growing up, [I did] not really understand it. But that allowed *them* to understand that "Okay. Well, there's somebody sick, so we need to prepare some food and take it to them." My grandma used to be able to do all that. Then to me looking at it, "Okay. It's just old people talking. Just gossip." Because they would catch up on that side of their family and then totally come over and catch up on our side of the family.

So they knew what was going on around the communities, it be the sickness or wakes or funerals or any kind of celebrations or even newborns coming in and expectations and stuff like that. So, my grandma would have that in mind, and it would be sometimes with the church group or sometimes herself and being able to provide what they need. I always remembered that she said, "Okay, what would they need? What do you think would help them out?"

CHURCH FELLOWSHIP

TERRY BEN, B. 1957—STANDING PINE
TOLD ON JUNE 10, 2021

During that time period, Saturday, Sundays was morning worship, evening worship time. The women met in the afternoon for what they called WMU [Woman's Missionary Union] at the churches almost every day. And then on certain days, there was a lunch on the outside. If it was a pretty day, at the end of the service, people would bring their food out on those long wooden tables under the trees. People would gather after a church service and just have lunch, fellowship with each other. It was not an every day, every weekend thing, but every now and then, it was done.

REVIVALS AND BAPTISMS

TERRY BEN, B. 1957—STANDING PINE
TOLD ON JUNE 10, 2021

Our church tradition during that time period was to have what they called "winter revival," "summer revival." Usually, a preacher from the local other churches would come in and preach or somebody from Oklahoma. And during that time, it was a custom, it was a tradition for one of the families per night—usually the revival lasted one week, Monday through Friday nights—and families volunteered in the church to host that preacher one night for dinner.

And I looked forward to that. You know the reason why? Grandma's going to put out her best in terms of food. Grandma's going to do her best. She might even go to town and get pork chops, fresh from whatever store that was available during that time period, IGA or whatever. She did her best, and so I enjoyed those times when the preacher came to the house. It was a time of eating good, *actually* good food, and also lots of it, and also with just fellowship and all that. So that was one of the experiences I really enjoyed.

Then afterwards, when the revival ended for the saved new Christians, they would have to be baptized. And so, whenever you'd go to church, and churches have what they call "baptism places" inside the church, where people get immersed in water and all that to become Christians.

But during that time period, there was nothing like that at Hope Baptist Church. And so guess what? After the revival ended, if somebody became a new believer, they went to the pond at Standing Pine. Many new Christians baptized there. Many new. And some by the ponds in the other direction in which they used also.

And so, one of those things that's unusual, but I'm going to let you know anyway. Of course, you know, young ladies, women, also were baptized. And so, soon after somebody's immersed from the water, from the pond, when the preacher dunks that person in water, of course everybody's wet. And so, at any rate, the men would take their clothes and go up to the woods and change, but the women couldn't do that. And so, about maybe an hour or so before the baptism time, the women would go in with their sheets from home, and they would make a little tent, a little square, something like that tent, wrap it up couple times and tie it up. It was a custom, tradition to do that, so that women would have a place to take their wet clothes off and they'd get ready for the next part of the service of the baptism. So that was unique, but it was done. It's no longer done now.

PICNICS, EASTER EGG HUNTS, AND REUNIONS

LINDA WILLIS, B. 1953—CRYSTAL RIDGE
TOLD ON JANUARY 7, 2000

If my grandfather Cameron Wesley says there's going to be a picnic, a big picnic, and people's going to be coming from all over, and they'll bring lots of food, and all that stuff, and I don't know how he arranged it, but it would be done like that.

And they would play stickball or baseball or whatever. That was nice to see.

As he got older, things just stopped.

Like on Easter, he would have Easter egg hunt and all of that stuff. He would get the family together on those days, and they all would be together. So, that was kind of fun. And you would know who your family was, like your brothers and sisters or your aunts and uncles. That way you would find out who they were.

Today, we don't do that, so our children don't know who their aunts or uncles or cousins are because we don't have a family get-together like he used to.

VISITING

LOUISE WILSON, B. 1950—BOGUE CHITTO
TOLD ON JULY 29, 1999

Everybody lived in harmony. If somebody wanted to borrow something, you would share.

You also did a lot of visiting. Back then you didn't have TV that much or see all that was on TV. And a lot of people didn't have cars. But you still went to go visit. You got on the wagon or whatever. And visit wasn't just a one-day visit either. Visit was like staying there for the whole weekend, two, three nights or whatever. Those were good visits. And Grandpa said that was to show that is your family, that is your community, and you are still part of them. And that next weekend you invite them, and they come to your house and visit you.

And even when they visit, it wasn't like sitting around, not doing anything either. If they had a bunch of kids, they'd say, "OK. I'll send my kids out there to get the corn," or go help milk the cows or just have a good visit. Those were the ways the visits were back then.

And I miss those myself.

I remember Grandpa having this old truck, and we'd all get in. Only one time that I recall that we had overnight visitations. It was just overnight, now; it wasn't like a couple of days. But he said in his days, it was a couple of days.

We didn't do that that often. But I remember one time we did. I said, "Grandpa? Go to someone else's house?" It was strange because never did he hardly get away from home because we had cows, and we had hogs and all of that to feed. And you have to feed them twice a day, and you have to get someone in the community to do that if you were gone.

This particular time, I think he had somebody come in and do that for him. So he said if you don't do that, they'll get out of the pen, and they'll stray away. He was always making sure his animals were fed and everything like that.

HOST TO ALL

HAROLD COMBY, B. 1955—PEARL RIVER
TOLD ON JUNE 1, 2021

I remember one summer, back then the girls had a sleep in, but sometimes the boy or the girl would stay with us weeks at a time during the summertime. The other families would allow it, and our parents would just treat them like they were their own kids. Wherever we went, they went. Wherever we slept, they slept. Whatever we ate, they ate. It was like that back then.

Friends. Or sometimes even travelers. Sometimes they would come to the house, like four o'clock in the morning. If they were walking, Mom would say, "Hey, you guys get up; let him sleep in your bed." So we'd take a quilt or something and sleep on the floor.

I remember one time, there was a guy named Jacob Storm. He was a Seminole. He stayed with us one whole summer. He had a thumb missing. I said, "What happened to you?"

He said, "My brother alligator bit it off."

I said, "Your brother?"

He had one thumb missing. But he was proud of it. He said, "My brother alligator bit it off." [*laughter*]

ROAD-TRIP REUNION

AMANDA BELL, B. 1969—PEARL RIVER
WRITTEN ON MARCH 11, 2024

When I was a little girl, I spent my summer months with my grandparents, Frank Sr. and Ivenia (Lewis) Bell. One morning, Grandfather said we are going on a road trip. I replied, "Where?"

He responded, "Bogue Homa to visit grandmother's relatives." After breakfast, we hopped in my grandparents' Chevy Nova and drove off with the windows down. We stopped at a country store in Linwood, Mississippi, for gas and snacks.

My favorite was soda and potato sticks. Grandmother was shopping, and Grandfather was talking with his friend and bought a hoop of cheese. Afterwards, we continued our long journey. Suddenly, I realized the weather was hot and hotter passing through the little towns. The windows was down, but I can feel the hot air blowing in my face. Grandfather didn't have the luxurious air condition, and it was okay; we were on an adventure. We finally made it to the Bogue Homa community, and Grandmother was greeted by her relatives. They were delighted to see each other and Grandfather too. I was delighted to see kids as well, and we played. On that day, we fellowship with family and friends. I am grateful my grandparents encouraged me to visit families and friends who live far away to keep them close in our hearts and enjoy the road trips.

FAMILY REUNION

LORENA ALEX, B. 1952—HALLS, TN / BOGUE CHITTO / PEARL RIVER
TOLD ON JUNE 10, 2021

We had our family reunion twice on the Bell side. That's where we did.

The first one, I was the president for that one, so I gathered some people who could help me organize, get them to do the family tree, and ask them to gather some pictures or do some posters with pictures.

For example, like ours, I would put my picture and my kids' picture, my dad and mom, my sisters and brothers and their kids. And their names. Who they are and your mom and dad. If you've got a grandparent's picture, you put that on a poster and hang it up. Let everybody see.

Some didn't do that. Some just brought some pictures, put them on tables, so we looked at them or the family album.

We also had a cookout, so they ate breakfast, lunch, and supper.

WANDERING STORYTELLER

EDDIE JOHNSON, B. 1970—STANDING PINE / TUCKER
TOLD ON JUNE 11, 2021

I spent a lot of time with Zula towards the end of her life, maybe a few years before she passed away. She tried to show me how to make Choctaw baskets. I couldn't get it. [*laughter*]

Anyway, she told me that her great-grandfather, he was one of those wanderers who go from place to place. He would come occasionally. And she remembers when she was little, he would come, and then sometime later he would come again. But he used to come and tell stories.

And one of the things that he would tell about, that there would be . . . What you see now is not going to be the same, big cities, paved roads, railroads. And this is rural Mississippi.

I've heard older people: drinking water was not going to be as simple as dropping a bucket into the well and drawing water. So you're going to have to buy your water. That's what their parents and great-grandparents used to tell them.

And then changes are coming in.

And then even mixing of races and all that's going to happen and all that. And this is talking about the racism. But that's going to start changing more and more. And then you had the civil rights and all that.

LIFE CYCLE

PREGNANCY AND BIRTH

> A long time ago, the Great Spirit, God, created the mound, and had the opening. The five major civilized tribes of the southeast, one after another—one person came out, one person came out, and so forth. Eventually maybe the last person that came out of the cave mound was the Choctaw. And so this was his promised land. As far as all the others like the Seminole and Creeks and Chickasaws and Cherokees, they came out of the cave mound, but they moved to different areas of the southeast, as we know it, of the US. (Terry Ben, June 3, 1996)

In this emergence myth of the Choctaw told by Terry Ben in 1996, the Creator brings forth the Choctaw from the depths of the earth through a hole in the Nanih Waiya Cave Mound and into the light. It is no wonder that Nanih Waiya is referred to as the "mother mound."[1] From that first birth of the Choctaw people at Nanih Waiya to the daily births of Choctaw babies today, rituals and customs help ensure the health and safety of both mother and child. The vast majority of these customs pose restrictions on the behavior of pregnant women. Yet none of the many taboos surrounding pregnancy remembered in the stories in this collection or still practiced today are mentioned in the historical record save one: the fear of losing a child's spirit when crossing over water. Simpson Tubby reported that "they would not let a pregnant woman drive a wagon or cross a running stream. In the latter case it was because they thought she would leave the spirit of the child upon the other side and his life would be short" (Swanton 1931:118). Today, the taboo has shifted, expanding, on the one hand, to include babies and small children, but retracting, on the other, by offering a solution to keep up with contemporary life that includes frequent car travel across the many creeks, streams, and rivers in Mississippi. Terry Ben remembers his grandmother saying: "If you ever have a little baby, when you take that little baby and you're going to be crossing the bridge at Pearl River, always call out the baby's name. Call out the baby's name a couple times. The spirit of the young baby is not strong enough. You might lose the spirit and the baby might die. Baby may get sick and die" (May 30, 1996).

Most of the taboos are focused on protecting the unborn child, whether from physical deformity, illness, loss of spirit, anxiety, emotional distress, mental incapacitation, or even death. Others protect the pregnant woman, primarily from wild animals and snakes. Yet just as many protect men from these powerful women whose fertility is perceived to pose a risk to their ability to hunt and play sports. All of these taboos place restrictions on the woman: what she can look at, where she should go, what she should touch, how she can groom herself, and what activities she can participate in. However, women were not, for the most part, restricted from work.

Writing at the end of the nineteenth century, Horatio Cushman describes stories of women who worked throughout their pregnancies, gave birth at night, and were doing their chores the next morning (1962 [1899]:232–33). Recent memory suggests that while fishing was viewed as taboo for many, and gardening was viewed as taboo for some, the bulk of domestic chores remained for all.

Taboos against gardening extended to some women even before pregnancy. A French manuscript from the mid-eighteenth century describes customs that required women to leave the home during their menstrual period to protect their families (Swanton 1931:115–16). While these taboos are not practiced today, they are remembered. In 1996, Rae Nell Vaughn noted, "I can remember Grandpa telling me when he did gardening, when it was your time of the month, you couldn't go to the garden because you could burn the plants. You could kill the garden. You could kill all the crops." I mentioned this to Rae years later, in 2021, and she laughed: "We should have pretended it lasted a few weeks long!" We laughed all the harder a few years later, when her aunts accused each other of doing exactly this when they were growing up.

PREGNANCY CUSTOMS

LOUISE WILSON, B. 1950—BOGUE CHITTO
TOLD ON JULY 29, 1999

Grandma used to say if you don't listen, it's going to get to you. When you get older, you're going to feel it. And I never did know what she was talking about, but I remember being barefooted a lot, and she told me not to be barefooted that much; she says you're going to get hot feet.

If you walk on the dirt, it can be hot, hot on a day like this, barefooted. And if you're pregnant because she said you have different kind of blood in your system.

And that is true because doctors say that your chemicals change when you're pregnant. Because she said you've got different kind of blood in your system. So, when you go out there barefooted in that dirt—which I know a lot of women did—she said you're going to have hot feet. And sure enough, I did. [*laughter*] "When you get older, it's going to show up." And it has!

It could be coldest day, but the bottom of my feet will get hot, and I don't know what the cause of it is. And I'm not diabetic, you know, knock on wood [*she knocks on the tabletop*], but my feet will get hot. And she used to tell me those things—don't do that because your blood's going to get hot, and it's going to stay that way. Say, "Sometimes it will cool down, but then there'll be times you don't want it to get hot, and it's going to be real hot." And so, it does. The bottom of it will. And I don't know how they knew these things but, I guess, like I said, they were like wives' tales or whatever.

Women back then, they did not cut their hair. They always had long hair, braided hair. And if you had long hair, you always had to have it braided when you're pregnant. They said it would be less painful when you went into labor and things like that. And you never washed your hair.

And during the first trimesters of your pregnancy, you never did look at funny things. You never did look at animals that looked a little strange.

Or your husband wouldn't go hunting, especially if it was the season of hunting and, or killing animals and things like that—your first trimester. But your second or third was OK.

There was a lot of things like that I didn't know until I got pregnant. Well, anyway, they told me a lot of these, "No you don't."

I didn't believe it until now. My oldest daughter was five, and I was pregnant again, my son. And I wasn't aware that I was at that time. And my husband loved to go hunting. He'd go hunting rabbit, squirrel, deer, things like that during the season. But every December, they would ask him to come and shoot hogs. We kill hogs in November before Thanksgiving, so that you would have meat for the rest of the winter. And they'd ask him because they thought that he's always hunting, so he must be really sure, just shoot one time and he'd be dead.

So we went down there and got ready to kill the hog, and it was a whole-day event. You warm up the hot water and this and that, and everybody would get their knives sharpened, and everybody knows what they got to do. And he went.

I didn't know it, and it was not until later that my brother told me this. But he said, "When he [your husband] saw the hog, he just died laughing at it."

And I didn't know why. And after the killing of the hog, and he was telling me this, he said, "You know he was laughing at that hog."

And I said "Why?" because I didn't see it.

And, he said, "Because you know how this particular hog would get out of the pen, go run around, and the dogs would chase it? And the dogs we had loved to chase it where they would bite him on the ears. And it got to where one ear had a little bite of ear on there, you know, the lobe? But the other one was completely gone." And to him it was so funny. And here he was, going to shoot it.

Well, and like I said, I didn't know I was pregnant or anything.

So he was born. And he was born with a birth defect. And it was exactly the way that hog was. That's how he was. But I didn't think of it because all I could think of was the doctor said I was going through a delayed reaction of depression, I guess. And so all I knew was, "How am I going to make this child grow up? How am I going to handle this child?" I don't know if he's deaf because there's no openings or anything at all. And, "How am I going to speak to him?" To a young woman who is twenty-something years old, you just don't know.

So anyway, I didn't think nothing of it until I was at home, and I was still on maternity leave. And some elder folks came by, and they saw him; they wanted to see him. And he's such a pretty baby. And they said, "Ooh," you know. And she said, "Is there anything he did?"

You know, "He liked to go hunting all the time."

"Is there anything that he did that he wasn't aware of or you weren't aware of?"

And I said, "What do you mean?"

And she said, "Well, he might have seen something, or did he kill something that was similar to this?"

And then I thought back, and sure enough. And I thought, my brother, he told me about that.

And she said, "Well, maybe that's why the baby is like this."

Because see, they already told us you don't laugh at something funny, you don't be looking or staring at something funny.

Even to the point you don't even go to the funeral when you're pregnant, your first trimester. Those are the kinds of things that they told us not to do.

And ever since then, from then on, I believe whatever they said. So if I got pregnant again, which I did, I always abide by what they said.

Now of course the shampooing, I couldn't stand that, so I had to shampoo my hair when I took a bath. [*laughter*]

DON'T MAKE FUN

HAROLD COMBY, B. 1955—PEARL RIVER
TOLD JULY 23, 1999

Some of the things that, like when a woman is pregnant, you're not supposed to do. Like for example, someone that's crippled, you're not supposed to laugh at it because when the baby is born, they may be born in that way. Or if you laugh at the way someone is bald headed, the child will be born less hair.

Even when we were small, they told us, "Don't laugh at other people. Because when you have kids, your kids will be like that."

WATCH WHAT YOU SEE

LINDA WILLIAMS, B. 1958—STANDING PINE
TOLD ON JUNE 15, 2021

If you're pregnant, you're not supposed to see an accident or a car accident or if they found somebody dead or somebody drowned. You're not supposed to see those kinds of things. You're supposed to avoid because your child can have some kind of illness. That's what my dad used to say. When they're pregnant, they need to not want to see something or go run out there and see about everything. They just need to stay back. That's what he used to say.

STAY CALM

DAN ISAAC, B. 1968—PEARL RIVER
TOLD ON JUNE 27, 2021

If you are pregnant or with child, *alo̱si sha̱likma* [when you're carrying a baby], if you're carrying a baby in the womb, you can't—like modern day stuff, I'm going to tell you real quick—can't watch scary movies. Or like shock you physically or mentally, or even make you cry emotionally, or make you think of bad thoughts, which is mentally.

So when you think of not watching scary movies, one of the things I remember Mother-in-law used to say was, "You all, don't go to zoo and look at animals because *ish anokfillit ish atapánah hikma chim allat yohmi holbanah* [you would think about it too much, and then your child would look like that]."

It's just like, just don't look at anything that's out of the ordinary. Don't be going places where things are very different than what we call natural or nature. Anything natural is fine. But scary movies, a lot of them are what I call unnatural horror. So they would say things like that.

NO TURTLES

SUSIE COMBY ALEX, B. 1947—STANDING PINE / PEARL RIVER
TOLD ON JUNE 9, 2021

And, one time, I was pregnant. Momma told me, "Don't you fish," and said, "You might catch a turtle." I don't know. I never really asked her why. But, she said, "I don't want you to catch turtle."

I said, "Okay."

ATTRACTING SNAKES

SUSIE COMBY ALEX, B. 1947—STANDING PINE / PEARL RIVER
TOLD ON JUNE 9, 2021

On the other side of the road, there was a lot of blackberries. They were just huge. So, I was picking those. I said, "I'll take some to Mom, and I'll make some jelly out of it or something."

I was picking it. I had a little bucket in the pickup. I was doing that. I almost felt I had it full. When I reached to get the berries, there was a snake. It was a black-and-white snake. I said, "I've never seen . . . !" and I dropped that bucket. [*laugh*]

I was telling my husband what had happened. He says, "If you're in a blackberry field, you'll see snakes."

I kept picking blackberries, and I was standing by him. All of a sudden, he caught a fish and was pulling it in. Here comes the snake. That snake was headed towards me, and I ran! [*laughter*] Being pregnant, I jumped; the tailgate was open, so I jumped up there and was in the back. I told Mom that, and she said, "Yeah. Since you were pregnant, that snake was chasing you."

I said, "Well, I'm not going to go fishing." [*laugh*]

If I go with him, I would just stay in the pickup or take a chair like this [*points to the foldable chair she's sitting in*] in the back and climb up there, help me climb up there, and I'll sit up there and read a book or something.

POWER OF PREGNANT WOMEN

HAROLD COMBY, B. 1955—PEARL RIVER
TOLD ON JUNE 1, 2021

Well, one of the things is with the fair coming up, they used to say that they [pregnant women] don't go to the ball game because if their boyfriend or the potential dad is playing, it could weaken his play because of that extra life that he has made that the mother is carrying.

PREGNANCY TABOOS

LORENA ALEX, B. 1952—HALLS, TN / BOGUE CHITTO / PEARL RIVER
TOLD ON JUNE 10, 2021

When you're pregnant, you're not supposed to at all do any kind of beadwork. They say it's just not healthy for the baby. It's not healthy for the baby because something might go wrong. Her or the mama.

Also, same thing with playing ball. You're not supposed to play, but there are women that are pregnant that still plays. We would always ask each other before we start playing, we'd say, "Who's pregnant? If you're pregnant you can't play."

And they'd say, "Why?"

"Because if you're pregnant and play with us, we'd be losing the game every time." [*laughter*]

One time I was playing ball. I didn't know I was pregnant. I didn't. I thought it was just one of those normal things, or I was stressed out, but I was pregnant. It's a wonder. I went for a checkup, and the doctor said, "Did you know you're pregnant?"

"No."

I was about a week, so he told me to stay in bed for one week, and I did. Everything's fine.

I didn't play after that.

WORK BUT NO WOODS

MARK PATRICK, B. 1969—OTOKḺO (CONEHATTA)
TOLD ON JULY 7, 2021

When you're pregnant, you can't go off into the woods by yourself because the wolves or the coyotes would attack a pregnant woman just to get the milk from the pregnant woman. I've heard that. My grandmother shared that story with me. She said that's what her mother used to tell her.

But as far as work is concerned, they said they worked until basically a couple of days before they gave birth. They got in the garden, and they hoed, and they shoveled, and they raked, and they worked. They shelled peas. None of that just stopped.

NO GARDENING, NO FUNERALS

TRAVIS WILLIS, B. 1958—PEARL RIVER
TOLD ON JUNE 14, 2021

She [pregnant woman] couldn't go into the garden or attend a funeral. The saying was that the baby can be blinded. That's what they used to say if a woman is pregnant. They would say she couldn't attend a funeral, even if it was her own mother or father.

NO FUNERALS, NO CUTTING HAIR

RAE NELL VAUGHN, B. 1964—PEARL RIVER
TOLD ON APRIL 22, 2020

One of the things that happens as a pregnant woman, you're not allowed to go to any of the wakes or to funerals.

Our ceremonies, our death ceremonies, consist of a wake, which maybe takes about three days. And then we have a funeral. The body is brought home, and you sit with the dead in the home until the funeral. And so the belief is that because you have a new spirit in *you*, and this spirit that is in the process of leaving because we start a fire for the spirit to know that. So the spirit knows that we are here with them, and they're not by themselves. And so the spirit is with us, the soul of the person that has died is with us.

And so it's believed that a pregnant woman shouldn't be there because she has a new spirit, and they don't want the spirit that will be leaving to take the new spirit. So you never have women who are expecting to attend wakes and funerals. It's just not good for them.

Another thing that—and these are just a few things I wanted to share because Mahlih [one of Rae's daughters, who was pregnant at the time] and I were just talking about it. She has very long, straight, black hair. And she was fussing about her hair because it's brittle on the ends. It's very long. It's like right above her waist, and she said, "I know I can't cut it, but I want to cut it."

See, she's not allowed to do anything with her hair. I'm not quite sure exactly what that means, in the sense of not being able to do that, but you're just not supposed to do anything . . . You're not supposed to change anything.

So that's, a couple of things that during this time, when a woman is having her child or carrying her child, it's some of the things, the dos and don'ts.

PROTECTING THE UMBILICAL CORD

CASEY BIGPOND, B. 1983–
PEARL RIVER / MUSKOGEE CREEK / YUCHI LINEAGE
TOLD ON JUNE 24, 2021

They [pregnant women] can't tie knots because if they tie knots, their umbilical cord would be a knot. So, that's one.

They can't cut things. It's the same thing.

Everything revolved around umbilical cord, so knots, ropes, cutting things.

PATERNITY

HAROLD COMBY, B. 1955–PEARL RIVER
TOLD ON JUNE 4, 1997

And there's another thing. It says that when a husband denies that he's the father before the baby's born, the baby will look more like the father. Might be true.

CROSSING WATER

LINDA WILLIAMS, B. 1958—STANDING PINE
TOLD ON JUNE 15, 2021

If you were going to cross across a river, a big river, that's when, if it's kids, their mind can get, not confused, but lost. So you keep calling their name.

If you're going to, for example, Mississippi River. If they're going to cross a river like that, then they keep calling the child's name and just kind of wiping their face. Because they said that they can be carried or the minds can be carried out or away and that they can get confused.

That's what they say.

CARRIED AWAY

MARK PATRICK, B. 1969—O̱TOKLO (CONEHATTA)
TOLD ON JULY 7, 2021

I heard my grandmother and her sister telling me that when a baby is small, they said be careful about taking them to the Gulf Coast, to the ocean because their spirits would be carried away. They said you won't ever be able to get that spirit back. I've heard that before.

And then I know that they couldn't be around a dead person.

She said, "If you do get them to that water, the big waters or whatever, you have to keep calling that child's name and keep calling that spirit, so their spirit will stay with them."

GOING HOME

HAROLD COMBY, B. 1955—PEARL RIVER
TOLD JUNE 4, 1997, AND JUNE 1, 2021

I was told that whenever you go somewhere—let's say, for example you go on a trip to the zoo in Jackson—whenever you bring the baby back, you tell the baby, "We're going home. *Falámat* [To return]. We're going back home," and talk to the baby that way to bring the baby's spirit back.

It goes back to what we were talking about, bringing home the spirit. Anytime they were taken to Jackson, they would cross the stream or the Pearl River. On the way back, they would name that person and say, "Bebe. Chokka iliyah okih"

[Baby, we're going home]. "Mitih" [Come with us]. Because they say, if you don't do that, the baby will have anxiety, maybe start crying, will throw a fit.

We had an incident one time with Peggy's grandbaby. Before we got home, she started doing that. Although we did try, I guess we must've missed it somewhere. So when we got home, she cried herself to sleep. So while she was sleeping, I had some sage; I smoked her, and then she didn't even twitch the rest of the night. The next morning, she woke up and she was all right. She was the same old person.

NAMING

As with many Native American tribes, Choctaw names were derived not from parents or families but from events occurring at birth (Swanton 1931:119). As children grew up, they were given a name for some characteristic trait they displayed or for something they did. For men, those names were often replaced in adulthood as they earned a war name reflecting their achievements in battle. Stories of the famous Chief Pushmataha suggest he was given multiple names before his final name stuck (Lincecum 2004 [1906]:42–43, 61–64). Warriors were often given the common suffix *ubi*, *ubbee*, or *abbi*, derived from the word *abi* which means "killer" as in Choctaw chiefs Mushalatubbee and Apuckshunnubbe. Pushmataha's full name appears to have been Apushamatahahubi, translated as "Messenger of death, literally one whose rifle, tomahawk, or bow alike fatal in war or hunting" (Cushman 1962 [1899]:234). Today, the last name Tubby traces direct lineage to this tradition, seen clearly in Simpson Tubby's family tree: great-grandfather, Aliktábi; grandfather, Mashulatubbi; and father, Lewis Tubby (Swanton 1931:102).

However, as the US government worked to fully colonize and assimilate Native peoples, names that changed from youth to adulthood and that did not include surnames to allow tracking through bureaucratic channels came under attack. "The story of conquest, particularly in European settler colonies where the conquerors held overwhelming power, could be written as a vast project of renaming the natural world. . . . Nowhere is this hegemonic project more apparent than in the effort to rename the individual 'native subjects' of this colonial enterprise in a fashion that would allow the colonizers to identify each (male!) unambiguously as a legal person" (Scott, Tehranian, and Mathias 2002:18). How these new names would be ascribed, however, varied. Mistranslations and the whim of government agents can explain many of the surnames given to the Choctaw. In other cases, last names were given according to the last name of the landowner for whom a family sharecropped, a tradition that mirrors that of slavery. Charlie Denson explains that his father's name was Hitohgotobi (He used to be a killer), but his English name was Joe Denson, Denson being the last name of the White family for whom they sharecropped (1973). Other Choctaw tell stories of White doctors assigning children their own last name after delivering them and even store owners demanding a last name for purchases and choosing them at will. Official government and institutional recordkeeping eventually led Choctaw families to pass down last names in patriarchal fashion.

For a growing number of Choctaw today, however, middle names have offered a space for maintaining or revitalizing traditional naming practices. For most, those names are in the Choctaw language such as Ná Tana, meaning "Weaver," or Hopaii Osi, meaning "Little Prophet." A few others have reclaimed the first-name spot for a Choctaw name for their children. While using the Choctaw language is most common, Harold Comby notes, "On the stickball roster, I'll see some little Choctaw names, like One Arrow. It's English, but they're trying to become proud of who they are." While the task of naming a child is maintained by the parents, female relatives, frequently aunts, are often invited or allowed to offer names.

The tradition of naming people for some incident in their lives also continues, albeit informally, through nicknames. "You get a nickname when you do something, and they see you do it, it sticks with you," explains Harley Vaughn. "Like, I had a brother named Roger. Since he was a kid, he was kind of big, they called him Chitto. That's the word for big. [*laughter*] And Thomas, that's another brother of mine. He's got a nickname that just stuck to him. His name they call is Shila; White man word is 'dry.' Dry for bean." His mother-in-law, Caroline Morris, chimes in: "Bean is 'dry,' as in 'dried beans.'" Harley nods in agreement: "He's kind of skinny like that, and that's why they call him that. And it just stuck with him. So everywhere you see him you call him Shila, he'll turn around." [*laughter*] From the many stories of how people received their nicknames, it is clear that they are more likely to stick if they reference an embarrassing incident.[2]

Between the resurgence of using Choctaw-language names for middle names, and the use of nicknames that speak to a person's character or event in their lives, naming practices today reveal a continuity with older traditions that go unnoticed in informal conversations with non-Indians or formal surveys of entries in a phone book but that are a dynamic part of social life.

SHARECROPPING NAMING

EDDIE GIBSON, B. 1953—CONEHATTA
TOLD ON JULY 1, 2021

Real name on my birth certificate is Lloyd Edsel, and somewhere . . . I don't know who started calling me Eddie. As long as I can remember, I've been called Eddie.

If you want to know where in the heck they get Lloyd Edsel, it goes back to that sharecropping I was talking about a while ago. There my parents were, and they shared crop work for these non-Indians. One of the guys was Lloyd something, Lloyd Seal, I think was his name. Another guy was Edsel Brown or Edsel something. When these people started working for non-Indians, they get to know them. Sometimes they paid them good, but then they gave them fruits and vegetables and stuff like that.

So, that's where the names come from in my family. I mean, I think it's true with just about everybody, but that's how I got my name. I do appreciate if you ever start calling me Eddie. I appreciate that. I've used Lloyd a good bit lately, and I have to use that one when I do important papers like borrow money, or hospital or something like that.

Today, if you're having a kid, you can buy a book, go to Walmart, go to Books-a-Million or somewhere and buy a book that's thick with all kinds of names for your kid to choose from. But back then there was no books. People just shared names, or they heard people, and so that's how they got names.

LAST NAMES

LOUISE WILSON, B. 1950—BOGUE CHITTO
TOLD ON DECEMBER 4, 1973

My grandfather said we didn't get our last names. He told me that the names they used to have, they only had one name. They never did have a last name, the Choctaws didn't. But the White people, when they would go to the store or something, they said you have to have a last name. So they gave them such and such a last name, and that's how they started having last names. And my grandfather said that's how come they'd gotten the name Thompson, the last name.

OBLIGATIONS OF NAMING A BABY

SUSIE COMBY ALEX, B. 1947—STANDING PINE / PEARL RIVER
TOLD ON JUNE 9, 2021

One of our neighbor's sons was a doctor at Walnut Grove, and then he moved to Carthage, but his name was David Bowen. And he's the one that . . . my brother that died? His middle name was Bowen. He was the doctor that delivered him. So he named him Dean Bowen after himself.

If somebody wants to give names, they used to say, "If you name a baby, each birthday, you have to give him something. You have to give him a gift."

Then the baby that you named, you give him maybe money or something to play with or even groceries for the family to use but gave it in honor of the baby.

He [Dr. Bowen] used to give him a check. Gave him a check, so Daddy had to go cash it for him. And he'll go get clothes or shoes, things like that. He would give him like two hundred dollars and all.

So, at that time, shoes and clothes didn't cost that much. And then he would give some and say, "Tell Mama to get groceries with it."

That's what they used to do.

I named one, and she has passed on now. And so that's why I used to take her shopping, so she can shop what she wants.

It was Cynthia Denise Willis. That was my aunt's daughter. For some reason I like the word Cynthia. And so I told my aunt, I said, "I'm going to name her." And she went, and she found that she was going to have a girl. I said, "I'm going to name her. So I gave her Cynthia Denise."

BEAR AND THUNDERSTRUCK

HUBERT WESLEY, B. 1933—MASHULAVILLE / BOGUE CHITTO
DECEMBER 18, 1992

My name is Hillohambee, "Thunderstruck" in English. Dad's is Nitta, which is "Bear."

My dad gave that name. I imagine his daddy give his name. Back in old days, they used to name names after animal things. That's why his name was Nitta.

In fact, lot of the Choctaws used that name up 'til I was a young man. I remember that. They never did call him Cameron. His name was Cameron in English, but they always called him Nitta.

ENGLISH NAME

HAYWARD BELL, B. 1948—BOGUE CHITTO
TOLD ON JUNE 30, 2021

I want to see the Choctaws maintain the names, the old names.

When I was about forty, I saw that there were some Choctaw names still used. A lot of the older ones were using Choctaw names, but it never was recorded because nobody put it into the birth certificate.

So I said, "Well, I'm going to have to lead the pack, I guess."

And so that's why my son, his name is Craig Tushka Nayukpah Bell. *Tushka nayukpah* means "proud warrior." *Tushka* means "warrior," and *nayukpah* means "proud."

And then my second son, now I didn't have a problem with this name, but Motabi, the nurse said that, when I gave him the name it was just Motabi, and they said, "You got to have English name."

I said, "What?"

"Got to have English name, or else they ain't going to let you go."

I said, "Why?"

"It's just that way."

I said, "I'll come back."

So the next day, I went over there. I gave the nurse, I put letter *A* period, Momit Abi Bell. [*laugh*] They said, "What's the *A* stand for?"

I said, "You wanted it. You tell me." [*laughter*]

CHOCTAW NAME

DAN ISAAC, B. 1968—PEARL RIVER
TOLD ON JUNE 23, 2021

We had so many different, beautiful names. The girls would have like flower, *ná paka̱li* [flower]. My granddaughter, I have one granddaughter. Her first name is Rose. Middle name is Paka̱li Halhpa̱sha. *Paka̱li* means a flower. But *Halhpa̱sha* means it's blooming. A Blooming Flower is what her name is.

That's my granddaughter. That's Push's daughter. So we have names, and it's important because you got to live up to the name. If they give you a name that means this, you got to kind of live up to it.

So I told my son, Pushmataha, I said, "I gave you that name because Pushmataha was way back." And when he was born, that was the year 2000, the new millennia. And I said, "The name had to come back." I said, "I gave you . . . "—my first name is William—"you're William. Your middle name is Pushmataha. That's who you are. One day if you go to service or go in war or something and you come back, we're going to name you *abi* on the last part."

And he said, "I don't know if I'm going to service."

"It's okay. You don't have to. But the name Pushmataha means a messenger. 'He who brings a message.' And that means he loved his people more than anyone."

NEW NAME

CASEY BIGPOND, B. 1983–
PEARL RIVER / MUSKOGEE CREEK / YUCHI LINEAGE
TOLD ON JUNE 24, 2021

When they're born, they name them. Because you don't want to name a baby before they're born. It's a superstition, I guess.

They name them, and then when they come of age, like twelve, thirteenish, whenever they start their puberty or whatever, they change their name that fits them, whatever they're good at or something that describes that person. That's what they name them.

Mine was Ná Ikkanah, which means like "To Learn, Willing to Learn"—rough translation. And then, I named my son Ná Ikkanat Ikbi, which means "He Likes to Learn It and Build It," because that describes him.

NAMING CEREMONY

CASEY BIGPOND, B. 1983–
PEARL RIVER / MUSKOGEE CREEK / YUCHI LINEAGE
TOLD ON JUNE 28, 2021, AND JUNE 1, 2023

I read it in one of the books. I can't remember which one, but the way I read it is if someone wants to give out a name, Choctaw name, to an individual, they would have a crowd of five or more. And then he would tell the crowd to recite the name of that person that they're naming at least three times. And then it's basically a short ceremony. It's not too long; it's just they recite the name three times, and then that's the new name. It's not very much ceremonial, but it's just a process that they go through.

And that's kind of the same way I did for my son when we did his naming ceremony. But the way I did mine is I invited the chief over to come and do it. Because out of respect, he's the chief. So the chief should be able to do stuff like that because they're for the people. So that's the way I approached it. And if the chief wasn't available, I had other councilmen that I could have asked to do it because they were elected and selected, however you want to put it.

The day that we did it was right on his birthday. And for us personally, we all fasted the day before we started our own fasting journey. We had fasted for twenty-four hours: no food, no water. We cleansed ourselves before the naming ceremony, which is how a lot of things used to be done to purify yourself; you fast and bless yourself. That's one of the ways that they did things.

I invited the chief to come over and give out the name. Our current chief, Cyrus Ben, came over and presented the name to him in that fashion, after I taught Chief the way to do it.

My son's name was given to him by the chief, chief of the Choctaw, Mississippi Band of Choctaws, which hasn't been done in probably a long time.

It was a good response. At the beginning. I don't think people understood what was going on, but we did it a couple of times, and they caught on of what was going on. I expected that because not many people have done naming ceremonies in that fashion, I expected some people was going to wonder what's going on. Now, a few people know it, and hopefully in the future, more people do it and more people know the protocols of doing naming ceremonies. It starts somewhere.

NICKNAMES

DELAURA SAUNDERS, B. 1950—BOGUE CHITTO
TOLD ON JUNE 29, 2021

There was a lot of storytellers in our family. My *afo* [grandfather] liked to tell stories; my Auntie Mila liked to tell stories. They like to tease each other, too.

To give you an illustration, an example of how some person would get their names or they found them, okay?

On the dirt road, where we lived, the houses were far apart from each other, and sitting out in the yard was really nice. There was a tree with the shade.

So that's where Afo and one of our cousins, Chanter Mussen, it's Prentiss Mussen [would sit].

So we call in Chahta what their names were.

Then there was this guy, English name Will.

People didn't have a lot of transportation that we have now. So they walked wherever they would. So they knew, because this guy, he comes generally every day that way, and then stops by. They sit around, and then they chat, and they talk. They tell stories on each other, all that stuff.

So when they saw this guy coming, one of the comments that would be made was like, "Ma pí—la mítih, yakah mi̱tika. Ma pí—la mítih." They would say, "Look, he's coming, he's coming way off. Can you see he's coming?"

So eventually he got his name Píla (Far Away).

EMBARRASSING NICKNAMES

LORENA ALEX, B. 1952—HALLS, TN / BOGUE CHITTO / PEARL RIVER TOLD ON JUNE 10, 2021

When we lived in Tennessee, there was these White people [last name Hearn] lived close to us, and this woman, this family used to have a White girl. She had blonde hair. She was pretty. I think he liked her, and that's why we call him Mr. Hearn. He probably wouldn't say it, but we would! [*laughter*]

DOC

SUSIE COMBY ALEX, B. 1947—STANDING PINE / PEARL RIVER TOLD ON JUNE 10, 2021

At that time, when we first moved to Pearl River, we used to live in a big house on the campus [of the high school]. It was just three of us and a brother. I had a brother from my mother's previous marriage. He was our half brother. Daddy raised him up. We all came out of the same womb, so we're brothers and sisters.

At that time, when he was growing up, a little bit older than a toddler, we used to have—now it's a baseball field, at the school around the baseball field. It used to be trees all over before they fixed the baseball field—they had a cabin. I don't know what they used it for, but there was a cabin there.

One night, Doc told Daddy, he says, "I want to go play with my friends."

Daddy said, "It's dark. Where are you going to play with your friends?"

He looked at Daddy and said, "Do you see that light over there?"

And Daddy said, "Ah, I don't want you to go."

After that, they had to keep a watch on him. But he would jump out the window and go over there. He said there were little boys, that he plays with them. They had to watch when it sort of gets dark. One of them would come and meet him or something. And then Daddy said some of them might steal the children. They were afraid to let him go. But he used to go over there, and what they did was, they wanted Doc to be a doctor. Choctaw medicine man. So that's what they were helping him and teaching him.

When we moved away from that area into another house, he got real sick. Daddy took him to Bob Henry at Bogue Chitto. He asked Daddy, he says, "Do you want me to just clear him? 'I don't want to be a doctor?' Or do you want me to help him?"

Daddy says, "Well, he's just a baby." Not a baby, but, he says, "He's just a small . . . So, why don't you just . . . " What he said was *moshólichih*. It means "just take it away."

So, he did that, wash him and all this.

He was destined to be a doctor. I think that's where he got the name Doc. He never did. I guess that's why he's so interested in learning whatever he can.

NO NAMES FOR THE DECEASED

MARTHA FERGUSON, B. 1949—STANDING PINE
TOLD ON JUNE 14, 2021

Grandma usually goes to a church conference, where a lot of them get together.

I heard them talking; three of them was talking. They haven't seen each other for quite a while. So, all of them were just talking away, and then, "You still have your kids?"

And she goes, "Let me count again." And then she start naming the kids that's living. She went ahead and named . . . She had eight, so she start naming each one, one by one, as she put her fingers down. [*She has her hands up, fingers splayed, and then closes one for each name/child.*] One, one. And then the child that she lost, she just bring it down, never mentioned the name or anything, "I lost that child," nothing. She'd just bring it down and the one that's living, finish it off.

And when they talk about their kids, that's just only one that say, "Am alla iksho," and that means the child that passed away. I think she was talking about it when they says *iksho* because she didn't use her finger, and she named all that are still alive. Some of them are married. Some of them live elsewhere, like in Greenville, picking cotton. They just keep on talking. And that's how I found that they don't mention the name after they passed away.

All they going to say is Mama and Daddy *ikshǫ* [not here]. The old one. They always say, "aki ikshǫ sashki iksho" [my father who's not here, my mother who's not here]. Kin folks who have passed away, they don't name that one either. Especially the elders. All they say is, "He used to live over there, but he's gone now. Kaniyatok" [He's gone].

And I always thought, "Did he go away? Or what?" And then I always said, "Illitok" [He died]. That's what I kept hearing. So I thought, if the generation goes by, they might forget all this. So I'm just adding to something that needs to be add on. So that at least they can go ahead and say, so that one has been said. And teaching their kids along the way, this is what they used to say. Because a lot of stuff, some of their parents that's gone, one that's my age group, they always say, "My mom *iksho* said this and this and this." But some of them don't name their parents at all. They said, "Mom *iksho*." That means "my mother's gone."

COMING OF AGE

"Let's go." Hayward Bell remembers growing up sharecropping beside his parents. There were no lectures or formal instructions; he learned by watching and doing. "Choctaws teach Choctaw how to do things, but not in a step-by-step type thing. Just show you how to do it is simpler than just trying to explain. He didn't say a word. So I just saw it and did it. That's the best way of learning things I know."

Writing at the end of the nineteenth century, Henry Halbert, who not only documented Choctaw history, geography, and culture but also taught in tribal schools at the time, described a similar process where parents taught by example. This training was gendered. Boys followed their fathers into the woods to learn to hunt; girls stayed with their mothers to learn to cook.[3] However, more formal instruction also occurred as elders gathered the youth around fires and on front porches to share the stories of the past imbued with the values of the present (see Mould and Vaughn 2025). Many of the stories guided young Choctaw in how to be safe and maintain their culture in a world where threats lurked behind every pine tree and around every street corner.

During both formal and informal instruction, children were taught what *not* to do as often as what *to* do. Don't play outside after dark; don't point at rainbows; don't say the name of the deceased; don't walk over someone lying down; don't go to the cemetery after dark; don't garden when it's your time of the month; don't hit women. These interdictions extend beyond childhood and are shared among adults as reminders of appropriate behavior. Don't let others touch your stickball sticks or baseball bat; don't mock others or look at scary or upsetting things when you or your wife is pregnant; don't let children look on the face of the deceased. People often refer to them in English as "no you don'ts." Harold Comby remembers a Choctaw version as well. "Well, my mom uses the phrase 'Ish mihchay kiyoh okih,' which means 'You're not supposed to do it.' That's all she uses. Or she would say, 'Nána ish mihchay kiyoh okih' or 'Nana ish mihchay kiyoh alhpisah.'" Harold sums her words up succinctly: "What not to do."

Listening to the elders was the key. In the past, those elders were grandparents, great aunts and uncles, and elderly people within one's community. By the nineteenth century, however, there were new authorities who expected to be listened to: Anglo missionaries and teachers. Choctaw schools emerged as early as 1819 as a result of the 1816 Treaty of Fort Adams, which established money for schools for Choctaw youth. Chief Mushalatubbee had particularly high hopes for the schools: "When I was young, such a thing was not known here. I have heard of it, but never expected to see it. I rejoice that I have lived to see it. You must be obedient to your teachers and learn all you can. I hope I shall live to see my council filled with the boys who are now in school; and that you will know much more than we know and do much better than we do" (Cushman 1962 [1899]:84).

By the end of the nineteenth century, six schools had been established for the Choctaw with two in Neshoba County and one each in Kemper, Leake, Newton, and Jasper Counties (Halbert 1896). Segregation, the need for children to help parents in the fields, and the lack of resources meant that education typically ended early for tribal youth. By the middle of the twentieth century, the only way for Choctaw youth to complete high school was to leave the state and attend one of a handful of Indian boarding schools.[4]

Boarding-school experiences were mixed. Many remember boarding school as the only option in a segregated South where educational opportunities for Choctaw were limited for primary school and nonexistent for high school until Choctaw Central High School was completed in 1963. Many learned vocational skills they could bring back to Mississippi; a few continued their education and earned associate's degrees. But Native American students were not allowed to speak their language, and their traditions and customs were often banned. The devastating impact of Indian boarding schools has been documented increasingly in recent years.[5] To date, the schools most Choctaw students went to have not been found to have perpetrated the worst of these crimes, such as physical abuse, sexual abuse, and mass graves hidden on property, but corporal punishment and forced assimilation practices were common.

Some parents encouraged their children to go to boarding school and continue their education; others, like Necey York, were far more conflicted. Writing about future tribal leaders Emmett and Baxter York, Bill Brescia notes, "In the early teens, the York boys were taken, along with many others their age, to the BIA operated Chilocco Indian School in Oklahoma. Watching their children leave was a painful experience for the Choctaw mothers. They gathered at the home of Neesey [*sic*] York for a 'cry,' the Choctaw ritual of mourning for the dead. But Neesey's grief was tempered by the hope that education would, in the future, be of value to both her children and the tribe." She was not wrong—Emmett and Baxter York helped draft and pass the constitution that established the current tribal government of the Mississippi Band. Both served on the first ever Tribal Council, with Emmett serving as chairman from 1955 through 1969 (Brescia 1982:21).

When schools in Mississippi were finally forced to integrate in 1970, options for Choctaw youth opened up, but resources remained unfairly divided. Further, many of the newly accessible schools in Mississippi continued the same discriminatory practices as Indian boarding schools. The Choctaw language, for example, was forbidden in public school as well as by BIA teachers in the new Choctaw Central High School.[6] Many of the non-Indian teachers seemed to agree with the philosophy of Richard Henry Pratt, founder of the influential Carlisle Indian Industrial School to "Kill the Indian, save the man," articulated more than a hundred years earlier.[7] Deeply entrenched racism against Choctaw language and culture resulted in teachers punishing Choctaw students for speaking their own language in their Choctaw-only schools. But speaking in 1982, Jackson Isaac remembered they resisted all the same: "I was about twenty or twenty-two years old, and I told the teacher, 'You can't change the native tongue because you're not a God. God give us our language, so we're going to keep it.'"

Because the Choctaw language is one of the most powerful symbols of Choctaw identity, it has often been the primary target of assimilation efforts. Many parents worked hard to ensure their children spoke Choctaw, recognizing that English would be spoken at school but requiring Choctaw to be spoken in the home. Yer the constant attack on the language from non-Indians in institutional settings worried some parents that their children could not succeed unless they embraced English more fully. Together, the impact of being punished and called "dumb" for speaking Choctaw, and being told their children would not get jobs if they continued to speak their native language was powerful and led some parents to dissuade their children from speaking Choctaw even at home. Despite these factors, the Choctaw language remained spoken by the vast majority of the Mississippi Choctaw well into the 1980s. By 1997, however, only 3 percent of Choctaw children were fluent in the language. By 2000, that number had dropped to 1 percent.[8]

For more than four decades, however, the Tribal Language Program has led concerted efforts to reverse this trend and teach Choctaw in and outside the classroom. Further, many adults and elders continue to speak Choctaw at home and at work, embracing the most common mandate heard in the context of cultural preservation: "Keep the language!"

BRAVES CEREMONY

HUBERT WESLEY, B. 1933—MASHULVAILLE / BOGUE CHITTO
TOLD ON DECEMBER 18, 1992

This is something they used to do, from what I understand.

When we was living in this area, when my daddy was chief—I don't know how old I was—I was small boy anyway. They set aside a day—I don't know whether it was on Saturday or Sunday; must have been Saturday—going to make us boys a brave. And they had a whole bunch of Choctaw people meet and give us a little old stick with all different color ribbons on it and painted our face up.

And where the log house was, across the road from there was where we had this thing going.

They told us we going to have to go east all day long, traveling, never stop and never turn. To face east. And these men carried us out there in the woods and turned us loose and told us go straight. When the sun goes down, camp out. Then next day go south. Then make another day going south. Then from there to west. And then from west back to where we start off.

And then when we got back, when make that trip, we're supposed to be a brave, some kind of special little guys then.

So what we did, we boys was small, and we was scared going out in them woods. So what we done, we just went so far, and we watched these guys going back, so we just laid down there in the woods. We laid there until they went out of sight. We just laid around there until the end of the day, and next day of course we went direction we supposed to go, but we didn't go but very little and laid around there, too, next day, then made our round like we was supposed to do, but we didn't go but maybe mile or so away from home. [*laughter*] But if we had followed the rules there ain't no telling how far we had to go all day long.

I never told the older people about it, what we did. So I don't know what the others did or not.

I would imagine somewhere around ten years old when that happened, and all of us was close to that age. We were just little fellows and send us out like that thinking we going to do that. But we had a little sack with different little things in it. Mostly cornbread and potatoes. I don't know what all was in that sack. I don't remember too good on that. We had little sack; each one of us did. What would have actually happened, I don't know. We made it back, and they were proud of us. I remember that. [*laughter*]

EDUCATION THROUGH STORYTELLING

CARMEN DENSON, B. 1956—STANDING PINE
TOLD ON JANUARY 12, 2000

Years and years before I was born, we had prophets, back before any other races came, other than Native Americans living. We had prophets that prophesized long time ago that these things were going to happen. Elders would tell, and this is the way that they put it, when they tell, they would say, "It was said, and said, and said, and said, and that's why I say it." And that's the way that they say it. And I don't know when it was originally started. In Choctaw terms, I would say, "Makato, makato, makato, achili." *Maka* means "it was said," *to* means "at the time." "It was said at the time, it was said at the time, it was said at the time; now I say it."

And that's the way it was passed on. There was no school; there was no education; there was nothing. Even back in 1950s, '40s, Choctaws were sharecropping on their own. And there was no government intervention, no school education. So late at night, then, before when we get to bed, or when we're in bed, our parents would talk to us then. That's where the schooling was, kind of Choctaw school, elders, how it was; to me it was that way.

CIRCLING UP WITH THE ELDERS

BRADLEY ALEX, B. 1955—BOGUE HOMA / PEARL RIVER
TOLD ON JUNE 30, 2021

Once in a while, we had elders come. There was a gathering at our home. And Conehatta, we went there. And last time I went to a gathering like that it was in Standing Pine.

Anyway, the elders, after we had eaten and everything, by the end of the day, they had a bonfire going on inside of the yard. They got elders, one or two individuals. They cater to them, to the elders. At least as many as from three to five, I think was, but at different times. But they sat them down so that they would be talking. And whenever they are ready, they said, "We're ready. Get everybody together."

What everybody was doing, it didn't matter how old you were, everybody quit doing what they were doing, and they came. And they were in kind of a semicircle already, the elders, and the younger ones, they're pretty young. And I sat in front. We sat in front, and the teenagers be kneeling behind us just all the way to the elders. The grownups standing or sitting, but they make that a complete circle.

And that's where they taught what our responsibility, what are we supposed to do.

Let's say you are parents. They instructed them, what their part is and how to raise kids—that you never spank to discipline a child unless that child's been told or taught what to do or what not to do. You never spank them until they understood, or if they do something bad, then discipline.

The women from a teenager on up, the elders will be some women and men, both elders. The elder woman would talk to the females, even how to sit, that you're not supposed to sit a certain way, but always decent. That men have different perspective of women, they used to say. And there was a word that they use also that they will consider you as that.

Anyway, the children were always, as the teenagers and everything, all of them were instructed not to talk back to their parents or to elders in the community. It didn't have to be your parents, your relative, but in the community. You never got away with it. You never get away with anything. [*laugh*] And that if you did something out there where you thought your parents aren't going to find out, a tribal member, the elder, whoever's there that saw you, they could give you a whipping or spank you, and they would go and tell your parents, and you get a whipping again. You'd be corrected. And they would speak to you and tell your parents what happened. So, you never get away with it. Anything, everything in community.

So you never said bad words. It was easy for kids to hear some from somewhere, teenagers, especially. And if they said something, they ask you, "Where'd you learn that? Where'd you hear that from?"

And my mother . . . I had said something. I don't remember who I heard it from, what I heard. And I was shouting it out. And my grandmother, she was sitting on the porch. She called me. So I came, and she told me what I was saying, and my face was red. [*laughter*] And she said, "No, don't say that yet!"

So I said, "Yes, ma'am." [*laughter*] It was embarrassing in front of my grandma. [*laughter*]

TEACHING BOYS AND GIRLS

ESTELLINE TUBBY, B. 1928—PEARL RIVER
TOLD ON JULY 22, 1999

Well, a long time ago, when the boys get a little bit older, the father takes them out for hunting. That's for the food. And maybe the animal skin would be our clothing. And that's how the boys looked forward to the father side. Be a good hunter and all of that.

And the girls would be teached by their mother. And well, it was good stories; some of them were good stories about what long time ago was. It was a good story.

But today, we are all mixed people in this world. I don't think they can do this anymore. Except go out and hunt for deer. And like today's world, they been teached, but I don't think the older men do that anymore.

DON'T CUT HAIR

HAROLD COMBY, B. 1955—PEARL RIVER
TOLD ON JANUARY 10, 2000

You're not supposed to cut the hair of your child for the first year. That's one of the things that's taboo. You're not supposed to do it.

Something about the teeth. If you do it, they won't come in right.

DON'T TOUCH HAIR

SUSIE COMBY ALEX, B. 1947—STANDING PINE / PEARL RIVER
TOLD ON JUNE 10, 2021

And I'm trying to now instill in my granddaughters, the little one, every time it [her hair] goes longer, her dad cuts it off.

And they said, "Don't let men touch your hair because then the growing would stop." Even if you wanted long hair, if you let a guy play with your hair, they say it would stop growing and things like that. So they said don't.

So Mama used to say if we go to the beauty salon to have our hair fixed, they said, "Don't let a guy do it; let a woman do it."

But then, now it's getting thinner. I said, "I'm going to turn to be a bald lady." [*laughter*]

DON'T PLAY AFTER DARK

MARTHA FERGUSON, B. 1949—STANDING PINE
TOLD ON JUNE 4, 2021

Oh, Grandmother was always telling us not to play after dark or go in at dark, not to play.

And from that one, I played basketball a lot. Start off at seventh grade. So when they had them play basketball, Mom bought a basketball, and Uncle found a ring, and he fixed it up. He said, "This is what you practice in."

Uncle Charles, he's always in trouble, okay? He's the one who's always okay about playing. "See if you can beat me." Every time I get in a shot, he pushed me. But anyway, he played.

They went out of town to Jackson or somewhere because somebody got sick. All of them went, and kids were there and told we're not supposed to be playing in the dark.

We played.

And once they all got back, Grandmother went, "Everybody, lights off, go to sleep." So I slept outside. It was summer. And the first thing I heard was a basketball. It was laying there; you could see it with that bright moon. You could see it real clear. And the basketball was hitting that thing, where I played, shooting. You hear that basketball hit, and then it gets down; it bounce. But the basketball is laying there, but what's doing that, and what's making that sound? You could see that nobody's there.

And Grandmother said, "I told you not to play. Instead, it's going to keep going."

And sure enough, it just keep on until about three or four o'clock in the morning.

There was nobody there.
She never told us what it is.
She always said, "Don't play after dark. That's why we say, 'Don't play.'"

CLEAN UP THE TOYS

HAROLD COMBY, B. 1955—PEARL RIVER
TOLD ON JUNE 4, 1997

And a long time ago, we were told never to play outside and to bring all the toys in because if you leave the toys outside, you're leaving the spirits of the kids outside, and the spirits of the deceased are going to come and play with the kids' spirits and the toys.

So what they would do is they would bring all the toys inside the house or kind of stack it up inside the porch, kind of push it together.

Tom Mould: Is that practiced anymore?

No. But some of the older people, they will do that.

Let's say, for example, I was playing with my child, and she left her tennis shoes outside in the yard. And at night, the elders think that the spirit is not happy, so the child will probably cry or not go to sleep, have nightmares and such. What you need to do is bring all that stuff in.

POINTING AT RAINBOWS

TRAVIS WILLIS, B. 1958—PEARL RIVER
TOLD ON JUNE 14, 2021

There's a lot of taboos along with dos and don'ts. This one part is a Christian thing. They used to say, "Don't point at the rainbow."

That was God's gift. In the Bible it talks about how God promised Noah and his generations that he would never flood the earth again. That's the symbol of his peace between man and himself.

We used to hear, "Don't point at the rainbow."

What they used to say was, "Your finger is going to fall off."

STAYING SAFE

MARK PATRICK, B. 1969—O̱TOKLO (CONEHATTA)
TOLD ON JULY 7, 2021

I'm a pastor, so sometimes I tell my congregation some of the stories that I've heard, and some of the things that I believed, that I don't quite believe now.

One of them is, if a toad peed on your hand, you would have warts. They just didn't want us to play with toads because most of them were afraid of them. They would say, "Get that thing [away] . . . !" They say, "If it pees on your hand, you're going to get warts."

Or if they say, "Stop playing with that fire . . . " We've always had a fire out in the yard, almost. Summer and winter. Most days, most evenings, or whatever, because my grandmother, she would gather up leaves and twigs and branches and stuff like that. She would just burn it, just to deter the mosquitoes and bugs so we could sit outside for a while before we went inside. But once we went inside, she didn't want us back outside. Because in the summertime, snakes come in the yard or whatever. But instead of saying, "We're doing this for your safety; we don't want you to get hurt; we have no access to go to the hospital," because we're way back . . . Back in those days, we were lucky to have one car, the whole family. And then we had to have somebody to drive. If that person wasn't there, then we were just stuck.

So instead of saying, "This is why we tell you these things." Instead of doing that, they were bad about just making up stories. So they would say, "Don't play with that fire." Instead of saying, "You're going to get burned. It's going to hurt, and you're going to be crying all night, and you're going to get infection," they would say, "You keep playing with that fire, you going to pee in your bed," is what they would say.

And we would believe that.

"You going to pee in your sleep. I'm telling you, that's what's going to happen."

And we would actually believe that.

DIVISION OF LABOR

HAROLD COMBY, B. 1955—PEARL RIVER
TOLD ON JUNE 1, 2021

There were certain roles [for men and women].

Getting us up at sunrise, he [my father] used to say, "You guys get cleaned up, eat breakfast, go outside and do man things," like cut grass or cut wood or whatever needed to be done outside. Clean the car, wash the car.

And then she [my mom] used to tell the girls, "Get up; learn how to cook because when you start having kids, they're going to want to eat. When they're kids, they can't take care of themselves. You've got to take care of them, and it's your responsibility."

So these are things that was taught to us.

HARD WORK, INSIDE AND OUT

JAY WESLEY, B. 1975—STANDING PINE
TOLD ON JULY 27, 2022

My grandma used to kind of harp on us that women, the females, do the inside work, and then guys do the outside work. And there's a lot of labor, hard labor at times because she had a large land area because we had a big garden. And we did the work in the hot sun.

And she loved wood heaters, woodstove, cooking that way. So that means we had to get a lot of firewood, and we had to go out there and haul the wood all day. And I'd see my friends go out there and say, "Hey, we're going to go to the pool. We're going to go shoot basketball."

And my grandma was like, "You can't go out there until you're done." And we learned the value of hard work, and then play afterwards.

A lot of times, as I'm looking back, I could see that; I understood I had to get work done before I played. And then it rolled over into what I do nowadays or instill in my kids. It's like, "Oh, you have chores? Those things get done before you do what you want to do," and different activities, leisurely activities for them. But that hard work was instilled.

And it was hard work, especially in the heat.

"Grandma? Today I want to be a girl. I want to stay inside in the air conditioning, watch TV. [*laughter*] If you want me to sweep, I'll sweep."

Grandma was like, "No, you're going out there; you're going to chop that wood. You're going out there; you're going to haul that wood. You're going out there; you're going to pick up that rake, and you going to rake."

And then, "Oh, Grandma, how come you can't get that electric stove? How come you don't get them gas stove?" because it didn't matter when it was. In the wintertime, it's cold so someone had to get up and go get that wood to get the heat going.

And vegetables. I was like, "Grandma, vegetables are canned nowadays already. Just got to go to Walmart. Piggly Wiggly."

But she was like, "No, I love fresh vegetables." And I didn't really appreciate that until later. It's like nowadays, *I* love fresh vegetables.

SUMMER SCHOOL "BREAKS" IN THE FIELDS

JUDIE LENE ISAAC, B. 1942—PEARL RIVER
TOLD IN 2017

Someone else would plant cotton. We would go work for a White man when that time came. And we would go to the Delta to stay there and pick cotton. That's how we were able to get our clothing to wear for school. When school was about to start, we would return [home], and we would go to school when it started.

SHARECROP AND SURVIVE OR GO TO SCHOOL

HAYWARD BELL, B. 1948—BOGUE CHITTO
TOLD ON JUNE 30, 2021

Sharecropping was a big deal. Part of the education process too. Most Choctaw families are large because you got to have that labor to survive, having a house to live in, and be able to do the sharecropping process.

One school year, the principal . . . You can't miss so many days or you fail. It's not that you didn't learn it, it's just there's so many days you can't miss according to the federal school system.

Anyway, so I was working in the field, and the principal came and talked to my mom. My mom would send him to my dad, and he went and speak to my dad. They talked for about an hour or two. He left, and I didn't go to school.

Next day, I was curious, and I asked Mom. I said, "Mom, what did Dad say to the principal?"

She said, "The principal said you're going to have to go to school, or you're going to fail."

"What did Dad tell him?" I said.

"What Dad said, I explained to them about labor. I got to work there for us keep a house," and all that stuff.

At the end, he told the principal, "Okay. If my son goes to school, you stay here and help me." And he just left. [*laugh*] That was the end of the problem.

SENT AWAY TO BOARDING SCHOOL

JASPER HENRY, B. 1917—BOGUE CHITTO
TOLD ON DECEMBER 3, 1973

While I was little, we been living on a sharecropper to the White people. And in my community where I'm living now, they built up a school there in I think it was about 1930, somewhere along in there, maybe a little later. I was pretty well grown-up kid then, somewhere around fourteen years old. That's when I went to school there.

And I finished . . . well, actually, I don't know whether I finished or not, but I went to sixth grade and considered, and they sent me to Cherokee, North Carolina. At that time, within the vicinity, Choctaws didn't have no higher school than sixth grade. That was just the highest they had was sixth grade. And so if there was anybody wanted to go any farther in their education, well, they had to go to Oklahoma or to Cherokee at that time.

SCHOOL LIKE THE MILITARY

RUSSELL JAMES (R. J.) WILLIS, B. 1940—RED WATER / STANDING PINE
TOLD ON NOVEMBER 4, 1973

When we were living the sharecropping, I don't hardly go to school around here; not 'til I was about eighteen years old. So when I was about twelve, twelve years old to eighteen, I could just speak a little English back then. But I was not too good then.

But anyway, when I was about eighteen years old, I decided to go out of state somewhere. I then said to myself, "I want to go to school. Then maybe I can learn more English."

And I just keep on saying it.

So I finally talked to a schoolteacher in that Standing Pine school. And I just asked him if I go to school somewhere, maybe I could learn some more English and learn some more.

So that schoolteacher was agreed with me to talk to somebody. I don't know who was he talking to. So finally, they fixed the papers up for me to go to Sequoyah, Oklahoma, and Tahlequah. So they fixed it up for me, and I went over there about two years and stayed over there, and that's where I learned some more of the English.

There was a lot of Indians over there, but they were all mixed up; they got there from every place, so speak English over there. So that's where I learned English, picked English up.

But I was lonely. I never been in the military or anything. I don't know much about it, but some of them said it looks like military. So about four o'clock somebody come along, blow the whistle down the hall, and wake everybody. But myself I liked that. Wake me up.

CUTTING THEIR HAIR

HAROLD COMBY, B. 1955—PEARL RIVER
TOLD ON JULY 23, 1999

Another thing, this young lady told me that when she went to Sequoyah back in the '60s there was a girl from here that had long, black hair.

Our tribe was noted for long hairs. So they cut her hair, and this lady said this other girl cried. She just broke down because they cut her long hair. That was a sign of strength. The only time you would cut your long hair was when you were in mourning.

NO OTHER OPTION

EDDIE GIBSON, B. 1953—CONEHATTA
TOLD ON JULY 1, 2021

I think it's a well-known story here that Choctaws could not go to public school here until a certain year, but I can't remember what the year is now. And so you had to go somewhere else.

I had brothers, two brothers, getting their high school at Haskell and one in Sequoyah in Oklahoma. And so these guys went out early. And so they got to learn how to live, how to get by, how to communicate with the other side of the world, other people.

So these guys left because they couldn't go to high school around here. But they just stayed away; there was nothing to come back to in Conehatta.

A CHANGE IN PLANS

CALVIN GIBSON, B. 1940—CONEHATTA
TOLD ON DECEMBER 4, 1973

My father and mother strongly wanted us to get an education, and if we went to a boarding school, then we would get it. See, we stayed at the school, at the boarding school, and you could take the type of education you wanted. And if you wanted, these schools had vocations with it. And what my father had said was that "If you're not college material, then you can take some of this vocation and learn some skill so you can fall back on that skill."

I took a vocation. Baking. I took welding for a while, but my eye . . .

When I was thirteen years old, I was fixing a fence, and I took that nail out, you know, this U-type nail? And I wasn't holding the wire, and it popped out, and it hit my eye on this side, this right eye. Ever since then, I can't use it very well. I mean, I use it pretty good sometimes, but then, like welding, when I was welding, the sparks and all, my eye got affected on it, and I couldn't see as well in order to weld. So I had to change vocation, and when I did, I just took bakery.

TRIBAL SCHOOL

TERRY BEN, B. 1957—STANDING PINE
TOLD ON JUNE 10, 2021

Even in the old days, education was very, very important. Very important. The more education you have, the better knowledge of the Bible you would have. And so in the Standing Pine community, you know where the facility they're building is? The gym? Right above it, that high hill, that was the old wooden-framed school. That's where I attended school. At max, maybe there might've been sixty-five students or so.

When I went there, it was first grade onwards, but later on, they added kindergarten. It was operated by the Bureau of Indian Affairs and not from the tribe. The principal, during that time period, had all the power in the world. There was no school board, no Tribal Council acting as a school board during that time period. There was no bus run; there was no breakfast, anything like that during that time period. But eventually, it came to be, as parents organized, and they worked with the principal, they had meetings. I think they had monthly meetings at the school to express any concerns they had. And so eventually, Standing Pine got a school bus, and eventually, white milk and chocolate milk was served at breakfast during that time period—not the full meal that's found in schools nowadays.

For whatever reason, the head cook kind of liked me, and so if I wanted extra food, whatever it may be—there was no such thing as pizza during that time period, but they had things like maybe a hot dog, whatever—if they had some extra, and if I asked for it, I went back again, and she gave me something extra for whatever reason. And so those were good food during that time period, way better than what I was used to back home with Grandma, even though Grandma did it best, and she always had good food. In some ways we had more, greater amounts of food at school.

One of the things also that I want you to remember during that time period, when I was going to school at Standing Pine Elementary, the principal and the teacher did not want us to talk Choctaw. If we did, there was some kind of punishment coming. And I saw that also.

One of my peers accidentally talked Choctaw, and some teacher, the person who was the offender was sitting at the desk, and teacher said, "Get your hand out."

And the student got their hand out, and she got a paddle and just hit it right here [*points to knuckles*], about maybe, oh, I don't know, maybe ten times right here. You could hear that smacking right there.

When something like that happened, then eventually it was not to be done anymore because the parent meetings with the principal and all that. So eventually that was not done anymore.

Also during that time period, there was no such thing as a library. Every two weeks, there would be a bookmobile that came around visiting all the schools. I would enjoy those times at the bookmobile.

Now, all of you know, at Choctaw Middle School, do you all know Susie Alex? Okay, she was a librarian assistant on that bookmobile. The librarian was an old White lady. She was about maybe seventy years old. Her name was Inez Allen, and Susie was her assistant. They would come around every two weeks, kind of like those big bloodmobiles, something that big, but it had books lined up and all that. We would line up and go check out a book every two weeks, and then we'd take the book back and get some more other books.

ENGLISH IN SCHOOL, CHOCTAW AT HOME

DELAURA SAUNDERS, B. 1950—BOGUE CHITTO
TOLD ON JUNE 29, 2021

After being in the service, when my dad came back, he was really for education for the kids. My mom wasn't. My mom, I don't know if it was because she feared that it would take us away or that we would lose who we were. But the school that we went to starting when they built the day schools, I think first grade is when we had started.

So Mom relented. But she always had this rule: house and her yard. When you come into her yard, English is kept out; you can't bring English in the homes. You can't bring English in the yard, that kind of thing.

ENGLISH ONLY

THERON "DUKE" DENSON, B. 1956—PEARL RIVER
TOLD ON JUNE 15, 2021

They [my parents] spoke Choctaw all the time. But they didn't want me to speak any Choctaw. They would say, if I tried to say something in Choctaw, they'd say, "Well, just try to speak English. Just so you're learning only English."

So I did.

But I wanted to be a rock star, movie star, so I knew I couldn't get that far unless I knew the language. Or if I wanted to be a doctor, lawyer, I got to learn the language. So they said, "You're just going to learn the English."

Years later, I asked my mother, "I wish you had taught me to speak Choctaw." I said, "Why did you want me to only speak English?"

She said, because when she was going to school, she was a non-English speaker, and she couldn't learn the academics. It was hard for her to learn how to read and write. So she didn't want that for me. She wanted me to be better than her.

But I think she was better than me because I never finished high school. I got a GED.

TATTLETALES

HAROLD COMBY, B. 1955—PEARL RIVER
TOLD JANUARY 10, 2000

My mom said there was a girl that was a tattletale. Whenever they spoke their Choctaw language, they would get punished for that. She said they beat her up.

She [the tattletale] said, "How come you did it?"

She [Harold's mother] said, "Well, we're going to get punished anyway so might as well as get something for being punished."

Those were some of the things we were taught. We were taught to be ashamed of who we are. I think some of us still carry on that wound that we need to heal.

PRANKING THE TEACHER

HENRY WILLIAMS, B. 1945—CONEHATTA
TOLD ON JUNE 24, 1997

One time we got mad with our science teacher.

He had this Volkswagen. He parked it facing against the gym wall. We had that thing turned around. This guy went crazy. We watched him after school.

We live in dormitory, you know. There was six of us. I think he gave us D on our science projects. We did pretty good. Somehow, we had different projects. Mine was a still—how to make whiskey. We never saw a still, but he kind of tell us how to do it. So we put it together; we made a still to make whiskey. I thought that was pretty good.

But we were smoking in the restroom and all that. I guess that's the reason he gave us D. And these other guys, they had another project, and they got a D.

So we got mad at him.

I think it was, we went to play ball in the gym. We decided to do something about that D. So we looked at that Volkswagen. I said, "Let's let the air out of his tires."

One said, "No. Let's flip it over."

One said, "No."

So, "What do we do now?"

I wanted to let the air out. One guy wanted to flip it over. We decided we didn't want that. So we decided to face the other, you know; it was facing that gym wall. Well, maybe we'll turn it around.

After school, we watched this guy, science teacher, what he's going to do. He was kind of like in a hurry to go to his car. When he got there, he went like this [*he looks back and forth, pointing with his index finger back and forth, as if gesturing to the front and back of his car*]. He just went like this [*repeats perplexed looking around*].

He knows that he has it faced to the wall, but it was facing the other way. So he went [*repeats looking*]; stand there like this [*repeats looking*]. He looked up, you know. [*laughter*]

SCHOOL MEMORIES

FRANK BELL JOE, B. 1951—BOGUE CHITTO
TOLD ON APRIL 16, 1975

One time I was in the seventh grade, and the teacher was Mrs. Carson. She wanted to pull out my grey hair, which I had. That was the only grey hair I had when she wanted to pull that. I didn't want her to, and she kind of got ticklish on that. So that's the thing that I remember on that.

Then the eighth grade, Mrs. Dubrowski was my teacher. I had one boy sit in front of me who shot me with the rubber band. I kind of got mad at him, so I had to find me a rubber band, chewed up all the papers I had, and rolled it into one, and I was going to shoot at him. He ducked on me, so the spitball I had went on through and hit my teacher. And the teacher came down there and slapped this boy's face in front of me even though it wasn't his fault. But I guess that's the only thing I remember from my eighth grade.

Then in ninth grade we took a trip down to New Orleans one time, and down there I went up to this fellow and asked him where I can find a trash can. He was a Frenchman, and he didn't know anything about English. I asked him where the trash can was; he talked in French, and I didn't understand. So I just got out, and I just speak to him what I can.

COURTSHIP

The isolation of rural Mississippi farming communities, sharecropping, and long distances between traditional Choctaw communities meant dating was not easy. Jay Wesley points out, "If you lived in a community, that means you're related to almost everybody in that community." So people looked outside their communities to help ensure they were dating beyond their extended family trees. In the past, families were careful to marry outside their *iksa* or clan (Halbert 1899:230). Yet as movement among communities increased, keeping track of one's relatives became all the more important. Today, the clan system has been replaced with a web of familial relations tracked by memory using community identity, last name, parentage, and household. Speaking in 1996, Louise Wilson remembers her grandfather telling her, "When you have children, make sure you let your kids know who they're related to." It is a mandate that continues today.

In both the past and present, sporting events offered ideal opportunities for meeting people outside one's clan or family. Families once traveled days for stickball games that involved social dancing, including such dances as the "stealing-partners" dance that offers a perfect guise for meeting new people or rekindling old connections. Baseball and softball games operated similarly in the more recent past, with teams from different communities gathering to play and socialize, ending the evening with car lights pointed in a circle to light a spot for social dancing.

Dancing was key.[9] While the ball games were competitive and divisive, the dancing was social and communal. Church fundraisers such as box dinners where men bid on women's prepared food baskets and the creation of Choctaw Central High School that brought students together from across the various communities also offered opportunities for people to meet, date, and marry. Such avenues did not keep some family members from trying to arrange marriages for their children, however, even into the late twentieth century. To ensure the laws of exogamy kept relatives from marrying, and to ensure financial viability for the families as well as the future couple, parents and aunties were heavily motivated to participate in the matchmaking process.

As with larger shifts in courtship throughout the country, however, couples have taken back this process for themselves. One result is increased intermarriage outside the tribe, despite a host of factors discouraging it, including ethnic pride, continued racial divisions in the US South, tribal prophecies warning of the loss of Choctaw culture through intermarriage, and the fact that children who are less than 50 percent Choctaw by blood cannot currently enroll as a tribal member. For many elders today, finding a suitable partner, therefore, requires a delicate balance between not marrying too close to one's family and not too far from one's tribe.

FIXED MARRIAGES

LOUISE WILSON, B. 1950—BOGUE CHITTO
TOLD ON JULY 29, 1999

Years ago, Grandpa said that when a boy and a girl talked to each other, that was it. They got married. But even prior to that, they used to have weddings that were already fixed. If a child was born in one clan that was a female, and a child born in another clan was a male, then that family would already have that particular marriage set up, so they always knew from the time they were little 'til they grew up, the whole clan, they knew, these two are going to be married at one time or another when they eventually get old enough to get married.

And years back then, and even back in my days, there would be quite a few people get married at the age of twelve, thirteen years old. And I never could get over that because when I was in the third or fourth grade, there will be some people in there that got married.

And I thought, "No, you don't get married . . . " I just didn't understand that. And here I was, still playing with dolls and making mud pies, and I just didn't understand that.

But now looking back, I can see the necessity, or it really wasn't necessary for them but what it was a lot of families had maybe ten, twelve kids, and it would be one less mouth to feed. However, if that happened, and they had families and kids, that family would be all together in order to pick cotton, in order to pick fruits or whatever to get the farming done for that particular year. So the more you had, like the saying goes, the more the merrier. But in this case, the more you had, the more those kids would be working out there in the farming things.

COURTSHIP

LOUISE WILSON, B. 1950—BOGUE CHITTO
TOLD ON JUNE 10, 1997

Nowadays, young people, when you date, when you go out with girls or boys, we say, "Find out. Go out with several, and if you like somebody or whatever, you'll meet somebody eventually." That's what we say. I mean, that's what I say to my kids.

Back then, they said that if you found and meet somebody, then that's it. You can't go out and try to meet somebody else again. I was thinking to myself when I was thirteen, fourteen, "Well," I said, "Well, how am I going to know if somebody else could have been better for me instead of this one person," who I might have liked now? But then, this is called dating. Back in my mind, that's what it was, it's dating. That's how you date other people that you finally find somebody that you want to be with for the rest of your life.

Well, in Grandpa and Grandma's day, uh-uh. You just found one person, and that was it. Because he said the main thing was there's too much gossip in the community. So when you're going out with this one person, then that's going to be it. It's more like courtship. You have courtship, but that means it's more or less that that's it. And you're not going to be going out with anybody else because now if you start seeing somebody else, then somebody else will gossip about you. This will come back to them, to the family. The family's not going to like it is what he was saying to us.

And he was talking about the other thing is that if you do go out to different people, he said you don't know when you might catch something, which is an illness he said that the non-Indians brought to us.

He was wise. As young people, we didn't know these things. Fourteen-, fifteen-year-old. He was wise because he knew that nowadays maybe there's sexual promiscuity. But back then, he said you have to be careful. He said, "That's why when you find somebody that you think that you like, yes, you can have a courtship with that person, but that person only. And then we will have a wedding." That's what he said.

So we were like [*shaking her head*], "Uh-uh." [*loud laughter*]

DATING

JACKSON ISAAC, B. 1902—PEARL RIVER
TOLD IN FEBRUARY 1982

The girls and boys, they had rules, and some of them, they go by their parents; you got to get permission from your parent to go to dance or somewhere. Or if you don't but decided to go, they all go together in groups and dance through the night that way.

When I got older, I was about eighteen years old, I wanted to go too. My grandpa, my aunt, or my daddy-in-law, he gave me permission every Saturday morning but to be back exactly before sundown Sunday in the evening.

So I go down there and stay there. About Sunday afternoon, I head on back.

Then the next time I want to go somewhere, I get permission easy. If I don't do what they say, I had a hard time to get permission. If I don't come down, about nine o'clock, he would come, and I would sit down and answer the question. I go down the line: aunts over there. And I went to their place, and I get whipping. They furnish ride and go with them.

And girls do the same thing. Girls did the same thing.

And when I was old enough to get close to girls, the parents pick out the girl. They like it; then parents think they are good and the family over there and the girl, and the boys over there talking well together, all the family of the girl and judging this way. They're watching all the time and listen in on the conversation. If they heard you had tuberculosis, cancer, they don't want you to marry their daughter. And then the same thing for the boys; don't want you to marry them.

DATING

CARMEN DENSON, B. 1956—STANDING PINE
TOLD ON JUNE 27, 2021

The social dance shifted to house dance, and that's where they did their socializing, finding the girls or whatever. Before, it was a social dance. We even have a social dance that they call "stealing partners." You try to get the girl you like; if she's dancing, you go and get her.

> **Tom Mould:** I've always thought that the stealing-partners dance was just a recipe for a brawl.

Well, the elder that was there, he would be like a preacher. He'd tell people not to get angry, jealous, whatever if they're talking to them while they're participating, but it was calm.

But when somebody started bringing some alcohol into it, then it started getting out of hand.

And a lot of people went to church, and they stopped going to house dances and social dances, so Christianity had a lot of influence in our ways.

YOU'RE RELATED

HAROLD COMBY, B. 1955—PEARL RIVER
TOLD JUNE 1, 2021

You never married within your clan. See, ours is matrilineal. Everything goes through the female side. So for us, they would tell us if they sensed that we were talking to this girl regularly.

During the pandemic, one of the guys came out with a caricature. It was like those cartoon figures that move, and it talks about this guy comes in with a bouquet of flowers, and the grandma says, "Napakalima allatikmá ish imáchih ish ílabi kiyo akiniha? Hash ittikanomi kiyo!" Which means, "You're not going to give flowers to that girl, are you? You are related!" [*laughter*]

And she says, "Chipoknit Bók Chito míti hicha Koni Hata ámíti!" "Your grandmother is from Bogue Chitto and Conehatta!" [*laughter*].

ALL RELATED

LOUISE WILSON, B. 1950—BOGUE CHITTO
TOLD ON JUNE 10, 1997

They don't want you to marry your cousin or somebody who's closely related to you. So he [my grandfather] said, when you have children, make sure you let your kids know who they're related to.

And so, I've learned that, and I have done that with my kids. They're all fully grown. The youngest is twenty-one years old now. But I still tell them who they're kin to, as far as closely related. Because they need to know.

I remember my young son, when he was in middle school, he liked this little girl, and someone teased him. And I heard about it, and I said, "Well, who is this little girl? Where is she from? What's her last name?" and all this kind of stuff. Sure enough, it was my first cousin's daughter. And I said, "Wait a minute."

And so I had to set him down and talk to him. And I said, "Look. We're related."

He said, "You mean we're related to everybody in Bogue Chitto?"

I said, "Yes, just about." [*laughter*]

So from then, he never messed with anybody from Bogue Chitto.

ALL RELATED UNTIL EIGHTEEN

JAY WESLEY, B. 1975—STANDING PINE
TOLD ON JULY 28, 2022

Understanding who your family is has always been a big thing. Even with my daughters nowadays, they tell me, "Dad, I met this boy, and so can you tell me if we're related?"

I'm like, "OK. Tell me the name. OK. Let me see and ask my wife." And "OK, we know the parents, and then yep, you're related. And then yep, you're related. And then yep, you're related."

And she comes back and says, "Dad, I'm related to all the boys in school?"

I'm like, "You're right. When you're eighteen and older, that relationship stops there; we'll get you out in the world." [*laughter*]

WINNING A BRIDE WITH TURKEYS

JIM GARDNER, B. 1895—PEARL RIVER
DATE TOLD UNKNOWN

When Choctaws were to have a wedding, they used to challenge [the suitor] to kill something, a deer or I mean a turkey.

When they had the wedding, they would adorn and shower the couple with gifts. The woman's uncle and her brother would stand behind the seated bride, over her head holding a woven blanket or a large handkerchief. They used to stand there behind the seats and would hold it on top like this on top of the head. And whoever brought a gift, they placed it there [on top of the head]. That's how they use to have it.

For the man, they had a *walakshi* [grape dumpling] set out for him. That's the way it used to be. That was the way they had weddings in the past that I remember seeing. These Choctaw traditions are no longer practiced anymore.

So there was this young man. After many days, this young man had a desire to marry a particular girl. He went and spoke to her father to ask his permission to marry her. He asked him, and the woman's father told him, "If you could go out and kill some turkeys and bring them to me, I might consider giving her to you. You could marry her then."

He set him the day and time to do so. But the man knew about him, that the young man was lazy; he did not do anything at all. He was very aware that the man just stayed at home. I think he just wanted to see what he would do.

The young man had some relatives. At the appointed time they gathered together and strategized a plan. They said, "You go there, and we will go this way." And they knew where they were to meet. They told the young man to go on ahead to the appointed place. The men went on their way to kill the turkeys. They kept going, going, and going until they met at the place they agreed upon to help him with the turkeys. The men brought in their kill and loaded them up on the young man's shoulders.

Although he didn't kill any at all, there he was full of turkeys.

And so, the father had to give his daughter to him.

ALL IN THE FAMILY

LOUISE WILSON, B. 1950—BOGUE CHITTO
TOLD ON JUNE 10, 1997

John Hunter Thompson is the one that raised us. But his brother is my real grandpa. This is on my mom's side: Tommy Thompson. That was his name. But he died.

This is what my grandpa said. Now this was kind of funny, and he said it in a funny way, too, so I don't know whether to believe him or not.

He said that when his brother died, he said, here he saw this woman with all these little kids. And he said that in the family, they believe in helping other family members. And he said, "Since this is my brother's kids," he said that "I felt like I should step in and help raise those kids." And that's why he married her.

He said, "But I think she really wanted me," he said. "But I think she really wanted to marry me first anyway." [*laughter*]

And I don't know which was older, whether it was Tommy, my real grandfather, or John, my stepgrandpa. But like I said, he's the one that raised us, so I always call him Grandpa.

MARRIAGE AND TRIBAL IDENTITY

RAE NELL VAUGHN, B. 1964—PEARL RIVER
TOLD ON APRIL 22, 2020

My father was non-Indian. Let me tell you about that love story.

My mother and my father met down on the Mississippi Gulf Coast. He was an airman. She had left home to go down to the coast. We had family down on the coast, so she went to work as a housekeeper at one of the hotels. And they met each other down there and fell in love and ended up getting married.

And then he left Mississippi, and they moved to Massachusetts. And like everything else, I remember my mother telling me about the racism in Boston in Massachusetts.

So things didn't quite work out, and she moved us back home. It was me and my brother. And so we came back to my grandmother's house.

So I am half.

My mother is full blood: four-fourths. My great-grandmother, Sweeny Willis, who was a renowned basket maker, her name is on the Dawes Rolls; and her signature is on there, as well as my grandfather's signature and my grandmother's signature. So that's our base roll.

So if your family is listed on this roll, then you were deemed a tribal member.

WEDDINGS

Choctaw weddings today are mostly indistinguishable from other Christian weddings in the United States. Brides wear white gowns and assemble female friends and family as bridesmaids; grooms wear suits or tuxedos and assemble male friends and family as groomsmen. Family and friends gather for the wedding ceremony, where the couple is sealed in marriage by a pastor of their church unless they have a family member or friend who can fill the role. A reception follows with food, music, and dancing.

Flipping through family photo albums, however, reveals some of the ways contemporary Choctaw couples continue to express their ethnic identity. The groom's father in one photo wears a vest decorated with traditional Choctaw ribbon work. The bride's mother in another photo wears a beaded necklace with Choctaw designs. A three-tiered wedding cake is decorated with red and black diamonds, the most pervasive and iconic Choctaw design in use today. No Choctaw celebration would be complete without hominy. Eddie Gibson explains, "It was my father who married us. We had just got a house on the reservation on Lagoon Road, and back of the house, there on the side where it was shaded, that's where we got married. And some of our relatives came and cooked hominy, and we ate good; we ate big. That's one thing about Choctaw people is when they eat, they don't mess around."

However, most older members of the community remember attending traditional Choctaw weddings, and occasionally a couple will choose to follow the old ways.[10] Bogue Chitto, one of the last communities to adopt Christianity, maintained the Choctaw wedding the longest, and the majority of the people recalling those weddings attended them in Bogue Chitto. In 1974, Peggy Thompson attended a traditional wedding and wrote about it for the high school magazine *Nanih Waiya*. In her article, she describes many of the key elements of traditional weddings, all of which can be traced to historical records from the nineteenth and twentieth centuries.

Although the planning and cooking starts long before the actual ceremony, the day of the wedding begins with the *ittafáma*, when the groom and his relatives march behind a drum to the appointed place for the wedding. The bride's family is already there, preparing for the event. When the groom arrives, the *ittilhiyohlih*, or chase, begins, where the bride takes off running, and the groom must catch her. Once he does, the bride and groom are seated side by side while the *ishtika* speaks to the families and marries the couple. The two families then begin the gift giving, laying ribbon, cloth, money, and other gifts on top of the heads of the couple—the bride's family giving gifts to the groom, and the groom's family to the bride. The gifts are then gathered up and redistributed to each family, a sign both of gratitude to the families for all the work they put into the festivities but also of unity that goes beyond the couple to their extended family as well. The families then enjoy the feast, with the bride's family eating first, followed by the groom's. Social dancing follows, and in the more distant past, a stickball game.[11]

In between these three ritual stages are a host of additional rituals performed by some couples but not others, as well as variations that speak to the rich, diverse, and dynamic tradition of the Choctaw wedding as performed over the past century or two. Pervasive in these traditions, however, are themes of mock competition and sport that include chasing the bride, bestowing the most gifts, identifying the groom and bride, claiming the presents, and occasionally a stickball game at the end of the festivities, as well as expressions of unity between the bride and groom's families that include formal greetings of acceptance, sharing dinner plates, sharing food, and social dancing. Through it all, family groups are brought together on each side as the groom's extended family contributes meat and other food to be cooked and gathers to usher the groom to the wedding site, while the bride's family cooks much of the food and prepares for the ceremonies, securing the *ishtika* to preside over the ceremony. Both families contribute gifts to the event, which are then redistributed in gratitude for their help.

CHOCTAW WEDDING

HUBERT WESLEY, B. 1933—MASHULAVILLE / BOGUE CHITTO
GARA WESLEY—MASHULAVILLE / BOGUE CHITTO
DECEMBER 18, 1992

The wedding used to be the same as funeral arrangements, about same length of time as a funeral.

The way they used to do was a couple going to get married. First week, the young lady would go live with the boy's family first week. And what that means, his parents approve of it or what. She lived with boy's parents first week, and she goes back home. And the boy and the girl not supposed to see each at all until the time of the wedding, maybe like six weeks.

And that length of time, the boy and his family would buy hog or beef or whatever they going to have for the feast. Then they meet at the girl's house, and the girl won't come out of the house. The other girls would kind of chaperone her in the house, and she stays in the house. And this boy, his family would come close—maybe quarter mile from her house, and they would group and stay there until peoples in charge of that wedding, when they get set up and everything, they managed to come to tell the bride they're ready.

Always have it at twelve o'clock. Then here comes the girl's brother or nephew, some close to her kin. Two guys would come there and to find this guy was going to marry the girl; he be in that crowd somewhere. They have to come in that crowd and find him. And they grab him by the arm and carry him to the girl's house. And they set two chairs side by side out in the yard and set him down. And then they would get the girl and set her right by side of him.

Then whoever's to do the ceremony—the man, always man, perform the ceremony—he would make a speech over it, telling this couple how to live together and what they should do for each other and all of that. Used to be the chiefs who would do it, but now I think they pick ones think he can do the most or something.

When he gets through talking about the ceremony, then the couple, they be the first people goes to table to be served, and everybody else go and serve themselves. But like girl's side would eat meat, and the boy's side would eat hominy or other things, but they wasn't allowed to eat meat. And if it was any left, then they could eat; the boy's side could eat. But most of time took all day to do that.

Hardly ever have that anymore. But every now and then they have that somewhere. That kind of ceremony has kind of changed up some too.

Gara: Nowadays they take and put ribbons across the girl's head and on her shoulders. But back then they gave money or something that they could use instead of ribbons and all.

UNITING FAMILIES

SUSIE COMBY ALEX, B. 1947—STANDING PINE / PEARL RIVER
TOLD ON JUNE 9, 2021

I've been to several. They went from Bogue Chitto. We got invited, so we went over there. The two that I've seen, they were just both similar.

The woman side, they bring what they call "*walakshi*," it's like a chicken dumpling or something like that. They put it in a little container, little bucket with handle on it, and they'll take it to one of the rooms where the bride had stayed, one of the rooms.

And then the relatives of the male would do the cooking. They had to buy hog, kill it, slaughter it, and all of this, and cook it. Help cook hominy, whatever. They cooked the whole meal in the father's side of the family.

And then when the man had to chase that woman, if they catch her, then they were married. But I guess if she didn't want to get married, I guess she can run away from him. But I guess she wouldn't wear heels. [*laughter*] She'll slow down, and the guy would catch it. [*laughter*]

And we started off with like the man's side of the family. They have what they call "leader" or the "speaker" for the group. So when they were coming down the road, they would holler, "We're coming." They were coming, things like that.

And they came, and then the lady's family met them. And then the sisters of the groom would escort the bride to a chair. It was put together. So they would put her, and then the brother of the groom would take the husband to be, and then sat him down. And they both wore Choctaw traditional dress. And the aunt of the bride would stand there. We went around congratulating them.

At that time when they invited you, they gave you a scarf, a handkerchief, a piece of jewelry, anything. When they invited you, they gave you this. And then in turn, you have to give it to the bride, put it on her head, and the aunt would be standing there to pick it up.

And then after the ceremony, they distributed out to the group. If they didn't have enough, that was it. But they used to try to give it to all that was there.

And the bride's family eats first.

And nowadays they wouldn't want to do that with COVID going on, but when they finished with the plate, they'll put it on the table. And then the groom's family comes and picks up that plate—it's not washed—and fill it with food and eat from the same plate. Now with COVID, they want to wash it, sterilize it. But that's what they used to do.

They used to get the minister to do all of this. And so that's what he tells them. He says, "You're now one." And that each family becomes the whole family.

FAMILY WEDDINGS

LORENA ALEX, B. 1952—HALLS, TN / BOGUE CHITTO / PEARL RIVER TOLD ON JUNE 10, 2021

We had two [traditional Choctaw weddings] in our family. Granny [Lorena's younger sister, Pauline], she was the last one. It took about maybe a week for us to sit down and talk about when it's going to start, how we're going to do it, and who's going to do it. We had to get the hog. Who's going to do it? Who's going to cook? When it's going to start? And they're not supposed to see each other at certain how many days?

As far as dresses, I gave her my dress, and I gave her my set of neck beadworks so where she can wear it. And as far as I think the other side were doing that for him.

Also, it rained. I'll tell you, it rained. Nobody stopped. They just kept on doing what they needed to do because time just flies when you do things like that.

And they also danced like the wedding dance and a house dance. Everybody was dancing. It was nice. It was nice.

Since we were having it at my sister's house, Rosalie, and the neighbor was Lucy Morris, which she lived maybe as far as the bank [*points to the nearby bank about a hundred yards away*]. So, they just come from a distance from that far. From Lucy's house, that's where the guy was coming from.

As far as Pauline, she had to be at my sister's house, so when they were ready, they would hide her. She would be inside. They all would come out, but she would be inside the group of women, and nobody else would see her.

So, on the guy's side, two guys would come over and ask if they're ready. And they said they are, and they'd go back.

And the two women would go and find out if they're ready. And they said they are.

And as time goes on, that side, the men, would play the drum, saying that they're coming. They're ready and coming, so they all come.

On the women's side, they would come and pick the guy and take him to the house. The same thing with the woman. Then they sit them in a chair. Everybody would gather around, and the chanter or the preacher would speak in Choctaw language.

All of that I really didn't pick up myself. My son did, but not all of what he was saying. So everybody would do what they say, and we'd just follow because I didn't know exactly what you had to say after you shook their hand.

But after that they would take them to the table, serve them their food. They would eat first, and everybody would come in and eat. After that they would all get together and dance.

WEDDING KINSHIP

DELAURA SAUNDERS, B. 1950—BOGUE CHITTO
TOLD ON JUNE 29, 2021

Chahta *ittawáya*? [Choctaw wedding]. We teach you [YOP students] that in class too. Knowing whose kin to you, it's really, really important. Because in a family, how it's done or in a family, if you are the elder aunties or elder female cousins, then they would have specific responsibility of what their task is, if a wedding is to happen.

They call the three different types. Sometimes all of those three steps or three things can happen in one wedding, depending on how elaborate and fun the family wants the whole day to be. One is *ittafáma* [to meet]. The other is *ittilhiyohlih* [to chase each other], and one I think it's called *loma* [to hide]. Okay, *ittafáma, ittilhiyohlih*, and *loma*.

Within the wedding step, there are a couple of other steps too that they used to say, what happened. *Ittafáma* is on that day, the bride side, the groom side, when the drums start, they would meet and all that. Could be that and nothing else. That's the *ittafáma*.

Whoever the *ishtika* is, I guess what's close to the announcer or emcee right now. The *ishtika* would announce or tell about what's [going on]. The *ishtika* was also the one that married them. That person that they choose had to have a good, good position, reputation in the community to be chosen to do that. A good orator, I guess.

The first step is *ittafáma*. You can hear the drumming, they said. Then the group that surround the groom's cousins or uncles that surround him and brings him. The bride's cousins and uncles bring the bride over to meet. It's called *ittafáma*.

Then the *ishtika* tells what's going to happen next and what's going on and what they say. Then from this, to recognize from this day forward, that these are a couple, these are mister and missus now. Then in order to recognize that, each family to recognize, then they are moved from where they were sitting or standing, depending.

Then they moved a little bit further. Then they have what they call *ittiyappachi* [to greet each other]. They are to be welcomed by the family. So the groom's family welcomes the bride. By welcoming them, like okay, say if I'm the auntie or . . . I mean, it wouldn't be the same auntie that you say in English. If I'm the *hokni* of the groom, which means I'm the groom's father's sister. Then I'm *hokni*. Okay? But if I were the groom's mother's sister, I would be *ishki chaffa* [first other mother or, colloquially, second mom]. So by knowing these terms, it also lets you know which side your blood runs, which side it is, your mom or your dad.

Anyway, so they would have to introduce themselves. I would say, "I'm your *hokni*. You can call me *hokni*, as a welcome." So that you are telling them your position. That's why knowing kinship terms is really . . . was important. Then the bride's family would welcome the groom into their family by introducing themselves and say, "I'm a cousin, and this is what you can call me."

The other steps to the *ittafáma*, like I said, if they wanted to elaborate and have a little bit more fun or make it not so easy for the groom or bride was *ittilhiyohlih*. I always said that this part also gives the bride a chance, if she changes her mind, to run as fast and as far away as she can. Because in this part, this part is where the groom has to chase the bride to catch her in order for the wedding still to continue.

But some of the stories that they had said was, if the bride really ran away, and the guy, the groom couldn't catch, she was forever banished. [*laugh*]

But that's it.

Then the other step too, it is *loma*. This can either be with the groom or the bride, depending on sometimes the families. Families like to joke a lot, right? I guess in order to see what kind of family you're getting yourself into, right? But the bride, they can have the bride dressed like maybe the sister or the cousin. The actual bride . . . but they can make them dress exactly alike because you have to have that scarf on. Okay. You have to have that scarf on. So you won't see. The cousin, especially the male cousins, will bring the bride, the look-alike, not the real bride. Then try to give that one away to the groom. [*laughter*] They call that *loma*. So the groom has to look and search and find the real one.

THE RUNAWAY BRIDE

GRADY JOHN, B. 1934—HENNING, TN
TOLD ON FEBRUARY 22, 1998

Way back 1800 and before, they said that when you want to get married, time they talk it over, and then they set up what day they're going to chase that woman.

So one day my uncle was fixing to marry that woman. He liked that woman, so they talked it over, and then they [got engaged].

Okay, so there's certain days you put up, maybe Saturday. And then, they have to chase that woman.

So that house, they were there. That woman in there, she knows where, how to hide. They turn them loose, and they wait thirty minutes.

Okay, all their relatives, they got to help chase them. They went all over, tear up their shirts, tear up their . . . scratched up, you know, try to help them find them.

You know what that woman did?

She didn't go too far, from here to that end of that road right there [about a hundred yards]. Had a big hole in it, in there and laid in there. They could not find her. [*laughter*]

And so they hunt all day. And so, that girl, they hollered at them and beat the stick.

And they got out and come on down.

So, next day, one of my uncle's cousins, said, "I'm going to see that woman, where—I act like I ain't coming. I'm going to see where that woman goes," you know.

So they turned her loose again.

They didn't come. He watched that woman, make a circle, make a circle, make a turn.

Then they take that stick, and they started gathering around. My uncle didn't tell nobody he saw where she went.

So after a while, they walked around; after a while, he know where the girl laid down at. He waved [*pantomimes waving with one hand, the other with a finger to his lips to be quiet*], and everyone started coming in, coming in, closer. So they jumped over the ditch and kind of closed in. And that's when they caught her!

When they caught her, he thought he was going to sleep with her that night. But he got messed up; they said he had to wait two more days. He was so mad! He wanted to sleep with her right away, when he caught her. [*laughter*]

You see, he had to wait. That would give them the chance to get her clothes and everything straightened out to come home.

WEDDING FOOD

LOUISE WILSON, B. 1950—BOGUE CHITTO
TOLD ON JUNE 10, 1997

Choctaw wedding is a beautiful thing to see. Very colorful. I really don't know why they don't do more of it. Nowadays, even, even though they do the license, they can still go through the ceremonies and all of that. That's just something beautiful to see.

The first time I went, it scared me half to death; I didn't know what was going on. But when it came to eating time, there was plenty of food and stuff like that. I asked questions. My aunt, she was patient with me. So she answered my questions; whereas my grandmother, she had all twelve or fifteen of us out there, so she didn't even have patience because she knew she had to watch over us and everything like that. So my aunt was more patient. So she would answer questions that I might have.

So I remember the day before the wedding; we would be making sweet biscuits, and we'd have these flour bags; she got five-pound flour sacks and had them and made the sweet biscuits.

And I saw how they made them and things like that. And my grandma and aunts and them would be talking about it in the kitchen. And I said, "Well, how come you know?" I said, "How come this is all we're going to eat?" you know, like that because it was just sweet biscuits.

And it's, "Oh, you don't know," they said. "Other family members going to bring peas and *banaha*."

And all the other families, which they mentioned, woman's family or man's family, one of them did biscuits, and the other family did the meat or something like that; it's divided up. It's divided up.

But I remember we were making sweet biscuits, and I used to sneak off a couple of them. They were good. I mean, they're like biscuits, but really like big cookies, like tea cakes now, okay? Almost kind of like that, but she put vanilla and some milk and eggs, and sugar was in it. And they make big sackful, and they put ribbons on it.

And we carry that. And I remember we take that. Back then, they had lard cans, and now they have plastic buckets of lard. Bryan lard—I've seen that in grocery stores. They used to have cans, had a lid on it. And we would take it. And they would have peas or hominy or *banaha* and those. Whatever we took would have ribbons on them. We also take handkerchiefs. That was the other thing we would take. By noontime, seemed like it would take all day long. Just with the ceremony. But see, all I thought about was eating. [*laughter*]

So I've been there, and they were in this old house. And then the men are coming down the road, you know, walking, coming down the road.

And they have the person who's doing the whole speech, and he's yelling and hollering, and he's making the speech about this family and this girl and all of this. And this is supposedly after he had caught her when she ran. You know the story of where the girl is supposed to run, he's supposed to catch her? Well, this event started after he supposedly caught her.

So now here's the wedding ceremony that's going on. And there's these two old chairs, and he's talking, and he had the two chairs inside the house. And as he talked, he'd move one chair and then the other. And he continues to talk and talk and talk and finally ends up on the porch, and he continues to talk, and everybody's standing around listening. And of course, the women who's in the back continue to cook, the ones supposed to be cooking.

And he finally has those two chairs, keeps moving and moving them on the front of the lawn of the house. And finally, about that time, the men are there right there at the foot of the lawn. The men are there. So the women bring the woman out there, and of course she's got the scarf on there, and she's, you know, comes out with the Choctaw dress, and they put her in the chair, and then he says something, and then the men bring the young man, and he sits down, and he goes and continues to talk and talk and talk.

And I don't know what all he said. I mean, I know what he's saying at the time, but I can't remember any of the stuff. He goes, continues to talk.

And then finally, the people start coming out. One family comes up there, and they bring monies like fifty cents, quarters, or they bring the ribbons or the handkerchiefs or towels. The last time, I remember they used towels. And they put it on the head of the woman. As they go by, shake hands, whatever, and go by. And what they do with all that ribbon, and all of that stuff . . .

But what I found was that he continues to talk. And someone from the family goes and picks up all of those and goes. And when they get through with the buckets and the flour sacks with the biscuits and peas and all the other stuff that was brought in, they go and lay it down. They have it all lined up—the buckets and the sacks and everything lined up on the ground—and they go lay down the ribbons and scarves on each one of those.

And so after they get through eating and the family that owned that, they go by and pick whatever it is on their sacks. And it was more of like a thank-you thing I guess. There'd be beautiful scarves and stuff like that to take home. And they had the option, they could either give it back to her or either take it with them as part of the ceremony.

And I remember seeing that. And that was something I hadn't seen.

The other thing was, and it was to me, when I think about it, maybe unsanitary. But the plate that's left on the table, whatever someone ate out of, when you got through eating, you go up there with your plate, you got your hog meat, hominy, and whatever, and you ate out of the same plate. And it's like uniting the whole family.

I remember that because I asked my grandma. She got mad at me. "Don't ask questions in public like that!" And when I asked my aunt later on, she said that was just part of it.

But I really would like to go to another one if somebody would have one. [*laughter*]

RICE ATTACK

JAY WESLEY, B. 1975—STANDING PINE
TOLD ON JULY 27, 2022

Wedding has been a church-based, Christian wedding, which is not too different from non-Choctaw.

One time that's funny—my uncle got married, and then after they came out, they gave us bags of rice to sprinkle when they came out.

They came out after the ceremony, and then next thing I knew, we had the whole bags. [*laughter*] Because they didn't understand that they're supposed to open . . . No one told them they were to open it and toss the rice. So they had cannons being thrown at the new couple. [*laughter*]

I thought it was funny as anything.

MARRIAGE AND PARENTING

Marriage and parenting are ubiquitous; stories about them are less so, at least for the Mississippi Choctaw. As Bradley Alex points out from his vantage point as peacekeeper for the tribe, marriage has its ups and downs. He describes his own forty-two-year marriage as an adventure. Stories of married life are often deeply personal, rarely shared in contexts outside the home. Yet those that capture images of married life are reflected throughout a person's repertoire of stories, with spouses appearing as protagonists, antagonists, foils, and partners throughout this book.

The same is true for parenting. Stories about sharecropping, chores, ball games, and growing up reflect relationships between parents and children that paint a dynamic picture of parenting styles shifting through the generations. Parenting at a distance, with firm expectations of hard work and no complaining have shifted to one where children appear to have more of a voice. Where a seat in the lap of a parent was a sign of the greatest affection in the past, today hugs, kisses, and frequent "I love yous" have become commonplace. Parenting was shared among grandparents. Summer meant long visits at great aunts' and uncles' homes, providing informal opportunities for kids to learn from a wider range of elders, connecting the parenting of the nuclear family with education by community elders described in stories of coming of age.

Labor is a common theme in both marriage and parenting. Gender often dictates the kinds of work expected of each. Those roles were described as firmer in the past, but even in the historical record, the permeability of gender boundaries appears.[12] Traditional roles placed men in the woods hunting, at the council fires governing, or at war fighting. But while stories of hunting encountered earlier suggest men may have been the ones to throw the rabbit stick or pull the trigger, women were often nearby ready to dress and cook the game. Fishing blurred these lines even further, with women often taking up the fishing pole, both for food and recreation.

Children were a valued source of labor too, both in the fields and at home. In this section, however, the stories focus mostly on discipline. Many people describe corporal punishment as a regular part of parenting. Harold Comby says simply, "There was a lot of spanking." He notes that has changed dramatically in the past few decades and that kids today have much more freedom from the strict rules of his generation. Yet those rules remain important. "It was explained to me by my parents—teach a person how to act responsibly. If they don't act right, then it's them. You have done your part. You have told them how to act within a certain realm. But the example that she used to use was that 'if you don't listen to what I tell you, you're going to end up in a jail, where you won't have a place to turn around.'" Then I don't want you to sit there and say, 'Nobody told me this.' She said, 'I'm telling you now. If you get in jail, I'm not going to get you out.' That was tough love."

MARRIAGE-NIGHT FRIGHT

BRADLEY ALEX, B. 1955—BOGUE HOMA / PEARL RIVER
TOLD ON JUNE 30, 2021

But living together was something else, was getting to know each other. We didn't live together or anything. We dated. She was my high school sweetheart. We broke up about a year and a half or something. Then we got back together, and within seven days we were married.

I proposed to her; I think it was on a Saturday. We came, and that following Friday, we got married. We were supposed to have counseling, but I was going to go overseas.

But a funny thing happened. I think I told you [*indicates his granddaughter, Makaylin Alex*] about the horse, right? [*Makaylin shakes her head.*] No? Okay.

That Friday, we got married, and we left. We didn't really have time to go out anywhere. So we went to Meridian, and we came back that following night to my mom's house. We were going to buy this old tribal frame house and build it up that belonged to my mother-in-law.

Anyway, we winded up at staying at my mom's house in my bedroom. And we all talked late and was tired. So we all went, "Good night"; everybody said, "Good night." And we went to our bedroom, and she got in bed and everything, and I was about ready to take my shoes off, and I notice it's two big window, double window. And there's a security light or the moonlight, I think it was.

Anyway, when I looked out, there was a big shadow, and I looked, and that shadow had gone this way [*points to his left*]. So I put my shoes back on, and I said, "I'll be right back."

She said, "Why? What's wrong?"

"I think somebody was by the window."

So I got up, and as I was leaving, my sisters and my mom and my stepfather . . . My stepfather hardly talked. He was an older man. Anyway, Mom said, "What's wrong? Where are you going?"

I said, "I think somebody's at the back of the house."

And so I went out the front door, slowly opened the door, the screen door. And I started going to the side of the house. And all the way, slowly. I went to the corner, and I heard him breathing kind of pretty heavy. And so I stopped, and he stopped right there where the corner of that house. And I was hearing him breathing. And he stopped. And so I stood there for a while, not making a move. I guess I was going to flip him over or something [*small laugh*]. So I would take a peek. I went like that [*leans forward*], and the biggest pair of eyes I ever saw came right there [*motions close to his face*].

I guess I was surprised. I went like this [*thrusts head back and opens eyes wide*], and *his* eyes went [*opens eyes wide again*], and I guess both of us screamed or something. Something came out of my mouth. But his eyes just went up, and he fell kind of backward. That was the biggest thing I ever saw. It rose up, and my legs started running. And before I got to . . . I saw my family at the door; my wife is there. They had come out, and they were shouting, "What is it? What is it?" in Choctaw.

Anyway, I heard a gallop. I knew who it was, but my legs didn't want to quit. I passed by them. [*laughter*] I passed by them and met the horse at the other side of the house. And we almost hit each other. And that horse took off. He made a weird noise, and he went like this [*indicates a pivot motion with his hands*] and went the other way.

There's a persimmon tree there. I tell you, if anybody got frightened, or sometimes that they say that you can't control your body? I couldn't control my body. There's a persimmon tree that I wind up hanged onto it. My leg was still going like this [*quick hand motions back and forth*].

It was a horse that I met face to face . . . eye to eyeball anyway. [*laughter*] I finally got a hold, and I stopped, and I was sweating like a big dog. The horse was gone and everything. I looked and nobody was there.

I heard some noise inside. I went inside. Well, I opened the screen door, and my sister, my wife, they were all scattered. My stepfather was in the corner, standing there. He didn't say nothing. They all looked at me, and they started laughing. So they were laughing; they were pounding . . . [*laughter*]

Oh my God. That was the most embarrassing thing. They couldn't stop laughing. They could not stop laughing.

I said, "Y'all quit." And they all stopped.

But then one would make a little noise or something; they started again. [*laughter*] And Mom was pounding the chair that she was in. My new bride, she was doing the same thing. My sister was on the floor. They were screaming, boy. [*laughing*] They were laughing.

So eventually, they calmed down, and we all went to bed. And one would laugh, and everybody in the whole house started laughing again. [*laughter*]

"Y'all go to sleep!"

It went on and on through the night. My new bride right there. No romance. I gave up. I said, "All right." I went to sleep. [*laughter*]

Next morning, I woke up. My mother was cooking; I smelled bacon. I'll always remember it. And I got up. Linda was still asleep. So I don't know what time they went to sleep. I ignored them and put the pillow and went to sleep. And next morning, when I woke up and went down the hallway, and there's my sister and my brother-in-law. And my mom was sitting there. They all looked at me, and they started laughing. And my sister started pounding on the table. [*laughter*] My brother-in-law, he just pointed at me. He just laughed. I said, "Ma, you didn't have to tell him." I said, "When did you come?"

They said, "Mom called us over, so we came. She had to tell us. She said she had something to tell us." [*laughter*]

PROTECTING THE FAMILY

HAROLD COMBY, B. 1955—PEARL RIVER
TOLD ON JUNE 1, 2021

In traveling, I learned that warriors ate first and rode the horses. We're mobile first because if the village got attacked, they had to fight while the woman and the kids ran for cover. So they have to be strong.

And in our tradition, we used to walk to town. I didn't, but other folks did. And you'd see the man walking up front, and that was it. He was the protector of the family. In case something happens, he had to fight them off while the ladies and the kids ran and hid. So that's why the man walks up front.

SIDE BY SIDE

LOUISE WILSON, B. 1950—BOGUE CHITTO
TOLD ON DECEMBER 4, 1973

That's the way it used to be a long time ago. I can still remember my grandparents, and they were that way. When they walked in town, the woman would always walk behind her husband.

It's not so any longer. The younger women just walk side by side their husbands. I think the younger people had decided that the man is not going to have so much say-so in the family. The women and the men will be equal when they're married.

GRANDPARENTING

CASEY BIGPOND, B. 1983—
PEARL RIVER / MUSKOGEE CREEK / YUCHI LINEAGE
TOLD ON JUNE 24, 2021

Some people say the kids don't respect their grandparents anymore. I hear that a lot.

But I always tell them, "Well, the grandparents were the ones raising kids. Back in those days, the grandparents were the ones raising babies."

The reason why is because the able-bodied ones, the teenagers, adults, they were the ones going out and hunting and fishing. They were doing all the young stuff. They were having babies, but they couldn't take them with them. So who was going to take care of them?

Let's just say, if the able-bodied adult women had babies and stayed home, and all they did was watch the baby, who would cook? Who would wash? Who would clean the hides? Who would take care of the house? Who would weave clothes, and who would knit? Because the grandparents wouldn't do it because their hands are brittle, you know?

It became the duty of the older ones to take care of the young ones, to raise them up to a certain age, which was thirteen, or twelve, to raise them up, get them up to the age. And then, by that time, they're able-bodied, and they just start going in with the males, and adults. When they turn thirteen, fourteen, they start going hunting with the adults.

It was like a rotation. By that time, the older adults, they started being in elder age, and then they're the ones that start raising the babies up.

But now, everything is reversed. Now, the parents are the ones raising the kids. And, a lot of parents aren't ready to raise kids.

WAKE-UP CALL

BRADLEY ALEX, B. 1955—BOGUE HOMA / PEARL RIVER
TOLD ON JUNE 30, 2021

I had a lot of respect for two of my aunts, my father's sisters. One was a very patient one, and the other one, she was strict. But eventually I found out why. My sister was the one who told me, my older sister. I used to be afraid of her, Esbie. And whenever I went, she said, "I want to say it one time." And, "Do what I say."

We had to spend a whole, I think it was a week or two weeks or something, me and my brother. My mother and my father, they said, "It's time for you to go spend time with your Aunt Esbie."

So we did, and she told us exactly what she expected of us, that, "Whenever I tell you to do something, don't ask. Just do it. And if I tell you to wake up at what time, you get up; and go to sleep at a certain time, I'll tell you to go to sleep. And it's usually at nine o'clock!" [*laughter*]

I always remember because she had a little TV, and one of the movies she always liked to watch was . . . she'd been married, and her kids had grown up and everything, but she used to say, "I will go and watch my future husband." It was Cannon the detective she liked. But anyway, she told us the first morning for us to get up and get ready, "It's morning."

So we got up, and she told us to go feed the dogs, the pig, and chicken. We were still sleepy. But we got all what she had already by the door. We took it, and we went outside. The dogs were still asleep, and the pig was still asleep. We look for the chickens, couldn't find them. But they were up in the trees asleep. And it was still dark, so we went inside. I told her, I said, "They're all asleep." The sun was not up.

And she said, "Oh, okay."

I guess after leaving, I always think that she tested us on that.

But next morning, it got a little harder for my brother to wake up. And he said, "No." Eventually he said, "I'm not waking up. She ain't going to do anything."

I told her, I said, "He's still asleep."

And she said, "Tell him to wake up."

I went and told him about twice, and I said, "He's not getting up."

She said, "Okay, I'll fix that."

And she had a cold ice water in a refrigerator. She got it, and I heard my brother just scream. I went and took a look at him; he was at the corner of the bed. He was all just, "Don't pour that on me." [*laughter*]

SHOWING AFFECTION

JUDY BILLIE, B. 1946—PEARL RIVER
TOLD ON JUNE 3, 1997

My father used to hold us or either put us on his lap and talk to us in a gentle way. My grandfather used to tell him that this is how you teach your kids that you care about them because we didn't have these expressive ways like kissing and hugging. We didn't have that. But you hold them on your lap, and you talk to them.

And that's what he did with my brother. So he didn't used to say, "I love you," but instead, the way of him expressing his love is by putting them on his lap and holding them on his lap and talk to them.

SAYING "I LOVE YOU"

BRIAN BILLIE, B. 1973—RED WATER
TOLD ON JUNE 30, 2021

People in the old days never said, "I love you."

I realized that with my dad. I asked my mama. Said, "You know, he don't say that."

And she goes, "He's not from that time."

I asked her, "Am I going to be that way?"

She goes, "You don't have to be if you don't want to be."

That's why I start telling my children, "I love you." My grandchildren, I hug them, tell them, "I love you."

I did that to my dad, and the first time I did it, he had that shocked look, the kind that he had to hold himself not to react, like hug you back or say a response. It took him about two years to get to say, “I love you too,” which was simple. Doesn’t make you less than a person. It just makes you more confident, I guess.

A PROMISE OF FRUIT

RAE NELL VAUGHN, B. 1964—PEARL RIVER
TOLD ON MARCH 14, 1996

I remember Afo Tubby—that’s Grandma’s daddy—I remember the way he used to get us to do stuff for him. He would say, “If you do it for me, I’ll give you an orange and apple for Christmas.” And it would always be in July! [*laughter*]

“OK! An orange and apple for Christmas!”

INCENTIVE TO GO TO CHURCH

TERRY BEN, B. 1957—STANDING PINE
TOLD ON JUNE 10, 2021

It was very, very important to Grandma, in particular, for me to go to church. I had no choice. If I didn’t want to go, another way Grandma made certain I went to church is—or if I gave her attitude and I don’t want to go to church, right in front of the house, there was some bushes with them little, small sticks growing up inside the bushes. And if I had an attitude showing to Grandma that I didn’t want to go to church or school, “All right, you go over there and get me a little switch. You break it off yourself.”

Grandma would tell me that when I was about maybe ten years old, and I knew what’s happening. I knew what’s coming. I would go there and come back. Grandma would trim it up real good. She would say, “Take your pants down.”

I took my pants down, all the way right here [*points to thigh*], and she would whip me right here [*points to backside*], and she would whip me right here [*points to back of thighs*]. And after that, I wanted to go to church. And I *did* go to church. I should be going to church anyway, but she made sure I went to church that way.

And other things, other situations where I didn’t want to do it, I got whipping or switched right here. Nowadays, people will call it child abuse, but it’s not child abuse. Not to them.

DISCIPLINING KIDS

EDDIE GIBSON, B. 1953—CONEHATTA
TOLD ON JULY 1, 2021

Let me say a little bit about discipline. My parents believed in discipline, back then.

Parents can get a flyswatter or switch and go like that [*makes a swatting motion*], and the kids would say, "I'm going to call social service. I'm going to call the police for child abuse." People say that today.

But back then, I wouldn't say there was no child abuse, but it wasn't child abuse back then. It was called "discipline." And probably it was good; it was that way in my family. With eleven of us, you had to be good.

But today, when you raise your hand at a kid, they're going to say, "I'm going to call the police for child abuse." And y'all heard that, right? [*directed to the YOP students*] That is a true statement. And I think we all need to go back to discipline.

I disciplined my kids, and my grandboys, but I swat them in the rear end. I don't go and beat them in the head, or anything. But discipline was important back then, long time ago. A long time ago. I don't think people know what discipline is today.

CORPORAL PUNISHMENT

HAYWARD BELL, B. 1948—BOGUE CHITTO
TOLD ON JUNE 30, 2021

I was raised on corporal punishment. And I said my child is going to be on corporal punishment, too. But the thing you got to know about that, the thing is the teachers also know that the federal guidelines don't permit corporal punishment in the school system. So what they do is tell them, tell the kids, said, "We're not supposed to whip you, but your parent wants us to whip you."

And then when there's no corporal punishment, then discipline goes out of whack. They said Choctaw parents are not a good disciplinary type of people.

Now that burned me up. I told the judge, I said, "Judge," one of the judges I know, I said, "Hey, if I whip my child and then come to your court, I'm going to tell them that I'm not an alcoholic. I'm not a drug person. When I whip my kids, I'm sober. If my child messes up, I'm going to whip him. If I whip him, then you're going to lock me up?"

He said, "Well, I know you, so I would use discretion, maybe separate from any other decision made. And I'll check you out some more." But he said, "I wouldn't arrest you or anything."

And I said, "That's the way all parents should be treated."

He agreed.

I appreciate that. Parents need to hear that. When I was growing up, that's what our parents did. And so did other kids' parents. But now, we can't, and the teachers turn around and blame Choctaw parents for not disciplining their kids. I think the teachers complain to get out of teaching.

DEATH, WAKES, AND FUNERALS

Death is universal; how people deal with death is anything but. For the Choctaw, funerary customs have shifted dramatically over the past few centuries, keeping pace with shifts in religious and spiritual beliefs, social networks, and resources, not to mention the impact of pandemics such as COVID-19. Some of the earliest accounts of Choctaw burial customs at the end of the eighteenth century describe a process of building wooden scaffolds for their dead. Once the bodies had deteriorated sufficiently, the *hattak fullih nipi foni*,[13] or bone pickers, would be called to clean the bones of their remaining flesh and either bury it or burn it, then preserve the bones first in a specially made box, then in a "bone house" or ossuary used throughout the community. When the bone house was full, it was covered over, resulting in small burial mounds.[14]

As Christianity began to spread among the tribe, however, the practice began to wane so that by the first decade of the nineteenth century, scaffolds, bone pickers, and ossuaries had been replaced by the Cry Ceremony. Bone pickers were replaced by pole pullers, removing the poles erected at the initial burial to mark the graves and signaling the end of the mourning process. During *Yáyah Osi* or the Little Cry, families mourned their dead daily. Men stopped cutting their hair; women stopped wearing shoes. Both stopped wearing any ornament at all. When the family decided the mourning process was over, the *Yáyah Chito* or Big Cry was called. The entire community gathered to feast, dance, and cry.[15]

The ceremony ensured that the deceased could leave this world for the next and that the living could heal from their loss. Such important functions meant the Cry was not something easily dismissed or ignored. Publishing in 1880, John F. H. Claiborne recounts the story of a Choctaw woman who seems more upset about the prospect of not being able to finish the Cry ceremony for her daughter than about getting kicked out of her home and off her land. He describes the woman as a "full-blooded Choctaw, supposed to be seventy years of age," who presented her legal claim.

> *An-na-le-ta* deposed that at date of treaty, claimant occupied, with her family, three cabins; had a good corn-field; their land was yock-a-na-chic-a-ma [yakni achukma] (good land); some time thereafter a White

> man named Wilkinson, ordered her off, saying that he had bought the land. Claimant had just lost a daughter, and she first remonstrated, and then begged that she might stay until she cried over the grave. Wilkinson angrily refused. Witness knew a friendly White man named Johnson. He, the witness, went to him, and he wrote to Wilkinson to let them stay till the cry was over. He consented, and when they had cried they all moved about a mile off, and built a cha-pa-chook-cha [chabli chuka?] (bark house) where they have resided ever since, not wishing to go too far from the dead. (Claiborne 1880:493, cited by Swanton 1931:181, who added the bracketed notes)

By the end of nineteenth century, however, this tradition, too, had mostly died out, replaced with funeral practices that more closely resembled Christian practices of a wake at the home of the deceased, visitation and viewing of the body at the funeral home, and then burial in a church graveyard. However, as the stories that follow attest, cultural beliefs about appropriate ways to mourn the dead, spiritual beliefs about the nature of a person's ghost or spirit, and religious beliefs about the afterlife continue to shift and shape the dynamic and creative customs of dealing with death. Maintaining a fire from the time of a person's death until they are buried or cremated, for example, has become a fundamental part of the wake as a central space for gathering, whether to tell stories, sing Choctaw hymns, drum, or just sit silently in reflection. In the spirit of *iyyikowa*, community members and extended family members ensure there is sufficient wood, part of the expectation that nuclear family members should do no work but focus solely on mourning. The custom of maintaining a fire has become so integral that the tribal government has also helped procure the necessary firewood so that no family has to forego the tradition because of a lack of resources.

Rituals, customs, and ceremonies surrounding funerary practices, however, are all preceded by death itself. Old age and current illness offer some hint that death may be near, but many Choctaw beliefs offer additional signs that death may be imminent. Those signs may be tied to the natural world, suggesting a holistic system that operates without malice. Others, however, such as the recurring presence of an owl, suggest much darker intent, often linked to witchcraft.[16] For the former, death is inevitable. For the latter, some Choctaw hope the omen may be a warning rather than a death sentence and seek out a Chahta *alikchi* or Choctaw doctor in hopes of counteracting any work being done to harm them. Either way, many find the warning useful to prepare themselves for bad news.

HARBINGERS OF DEATH AND DANGER

SIMPSON TUBBY, B. 1867—NESHOBA COUNTY
PUBLISHED IN 1931

Ishkitini, the horned owl, was believed to prowl about at night killing men and animals. This sinister character was undoubtedly due to the association of the bird with witchcraft.

He [Simpson Tubby] said that when the horned owl (*ishkitini*) screeched, it meant a sudden death, such as a murder. If the screech owl (*ofunlo*) was heard, it was a sign that a child under seven among the connections of that family was going to die because in size this is a baby owl. If a common owl (*opa*) alighted on a barn or on trees near the house and hooted, it foreboded death among the near relatives.

The sapsucker (*biskinik*) is the "news bird." He brings news both bad and good. If he lights on a tree in your lot early in the morning, some "hasty" news will come before noon. If he does this late at night, the news will come before morning.

They believed that the chicken had been put into their yards to give them a friendly warning of danger. If a chicken crows outside of its usual time, it is because it foresees bad weather. If one comes up to the doorstep or into the gallery and crows, it means hasty news. If a chicken flies up on the roost and crows after reaching it, there will be trouble in the family. If a hen crows, that means that the women of the neighborhood are going to fall out.

BURN IT OUT

EDDIE JOHNSON, B. 1970—STANDING PINE / TUCKER
TOLD ON JUNE 11, 2021

If an owl was present, what they would do was take peppers and anything that could be hot and burn it. I've seen them take a foil of embers, break it up, and put it in some kind of little fire and walk around.

I said, "What are you doing?"

And they said, "Nishkin abá chi̱ho michilih," which means "I'm trying to burn out their eyes," where they can't see, so they'll leave.

WARNING OF DEATH

HAROLD COMBY, B. 1955—PEARL RIVER
TOLD ON JUNE 4, 1997

Choctaws are a very superstitious people. They believe in spirits and bad omens, especially bad omens. They say the owl is an indicator of bad omen. Whenever an owl hits the front of your windshield, somebody that you know is going to die.

Like the spider. She said if there's a spiderweb in the corner of your house, or like sometimes there will be like strings, hanging from the roof, she said that's an indicator of a relative dying.

If you find a snake inside the house, it means that your relative is going to die.

BEWARE PART 1

STAFF OF THE *NANIH WAIYA* MAGAZINE
PUBLISHED IN WINTER 1974

When an owl comes to your yard and hoots, it means there will be a death in your family or a relative or a friend will die.

If a young man should kill an owl which comes to your yard or near your yard, one of his elders will die.

If a child kills a frog, one of his parents will die, and the child will be full of warts.

When a mole makes trail in your yard, one of the members of your family will die.

If a woman is bearing a child, and her husband goes about doing the wrong things, their child will be deformed.

BEWARE PART 2

STAFF OF THE *NANIH WAIYA* MAGAZINE
PUBLISHED IN SPRING 1974

The first time a young hunter goes out with his bow and arrow, he should kill a snake. He then should carry the arrow along with him on all future hunting expeditions. It should not be used again for game, but it should be kept only as a good-luck piece.

A fisherman who walks over his cane pole won't catch any fish.

If a bird gets into a house, a relative will die.

When a tooth comes out and a crow is seen, throw the tooth over a house; otherwise, it won't grow back again.

BEWARE PART 3

STAFF OF THE *NANIH WAIYA* MAGAZINE
PUBLISHED IN WINTER 1975

You'll die when you walk on a dead tree which has been hit by lightning.

When two persons wash their hands together, they will always get mad or have a fuss with each other.

You'll have visitors if you drop a dish cloth.

When a person is sweeping and sweeps on another, the latter won't get married.

If somebody has a funeral, and you play around with shovels, banging them together, deaths will follow the funeral.

If you play with a little bird, a large wind will come upon you.

HOLISSO INCHUWA AND BELIEFS!

STAFF OF THE *NANIH WAIYA* MAGAZINE
PUBLISHED IN SUMMER 1975

If you have a nightmare, put a fork under your pillow before going back to sleep, if you wake up!

Never try to kill a snake with a freshly cut stick or branch. The snake will be more dangerous to you.

Someone is talking about you when there is ringing in your ears.

Never fight or quarrel over a girl before marrying her. If you do, she won't be faithful to you after you get married.

When you burn a biscuit, it will rain, or you will have company.

When you point at a rainbow, your finger will rot off.

Never point at a watermelon; it will rot.

If you dream of fish, you will receive money.

If you wear a shirt backward, you will never get married.

If you count the stars and don't finish, you will die.

When you have a continuous itch, you will have company.

OWL OMEN

LOUISE WILSON, B. 1950—BOGUE CHITTO
TOLD ON JANUARY 11, 2000

For a long time, I didn't believe in a lot of these things that was told to me. And until I actually had gone through or actually saw it, whatever it might have been told to me. And there had to have been a reason why there were myths or there are stories or there are these things that are handed down to us. There had to be a reason why. But with me, until I personally went through it, that's when I began to start believing.

It's just like here recently, my daughter's uncle, which was my former brother-in-law, passed away. We had a funeral two weeks ago. My grandma always told us that if an owl comes to your yard and sits there, and he makes this sounds, you know, "Whoooo," right there in your yard, that you need to get rid of it as soon as possible or try to get it out of your yard. Now if he's far away in the forest, and you hear it, well, it doesn't bother you. But when it comes actually into your yard, that is a bad sign that something's going to happen.

Well, I didn't know if a lot of people get these signs anymore. But as I was at the wake and talking to some of the sisters there, sure enough, that's what had happened, in their yard. One of those came in the yard, and he was doing that. So these things still happen.

And the other thing is, one of the sisters said they were driving along, and one of the owls was just sitting on the side of the road and that those are signs that you just look for. I mean you don't look for it, but it happens. And you think, "Well, I'm going to hear something."

Well, here recently, I saw it myself: an owl. It just came, and it flew from nowhere, I don't know where. And it came and landed as I was going past this section of road. And so I was thinking, that just happened the other day. And then I hear this bad news about Grandma [losing the function of the left side of her body]. And now I think, "Well, those are things that just go hand in hand, I guess; it's part of it."

So I always say, "Is there going to be any more bad signs that I'm going to get, before?" But Grandma always used to say that those were signs just to let you know, to prepare you mentally, that you're not going to go into a whole big shock when you find out something had happened. She always said that "Oh, something's going to happen," and "OK, I'm going to prepare myself mentally and emotionally. Something's going to happen, but I don't know what." But if I hear something, at least I got the message before it actually happened. That way we don't just, you know, crack up or whatever. So that's how I feel like these things happen.

SQUIRREL OMEN

HAROLD COMBY, B. 1955—PEARL RIVER
TOLD ON JANUARY 10, 2000

They used to tell me that if a squirrel runs across the road while you're driving, somebody is going to die.

And me and Peggy has kind of kept count, and it's almost like 95 percent. May not die the same day, but maybe two or three days after that.

It's odd. One time we were going to Red Lake, Minnesota, which is like four lanes. We were in the fourth lane, and the tree line is way back thataway [*points to the far right*]. But a squirrel went across the road, and I was thinking, "Dang, how did it get here?"

But on the way back, they called me and said this person died.

I said, "Well, we were told."

TEMPTING DEATH

HAROLD COMBY, B. 1955—PEARL RIVER
TOLD ON JANUARY 10, 2000

If somebody is laying down on the floor, you're not supposed to walk over them. They say that death would soon follow. But if you do it, you can come back, and I guess that neutralizes whatever.

When my mom, when she goes out to the cemetery, she never walks on the graves; she walks around it. That's just respect, I guess.

BONE PICKERS

FRANK HENRY, B. 1927—BOGUE CHITTO / TUCKER
TOLD ON JULY 23, 1997

Going back hundreds of years, I guess, Choctaws, when somebody dies, they build a scaffold and put that body on top of that scaffold and let it sit out there in the sun. And they had a special person, one person, bone picker, that we read in the history.

And the bone picker would come and pick the bones; that was her craft. She took care of the bones and put it in the sack or something. Wherever they move to, they carry that bones with them.

In the early '30s, missionaries, Baptists came through and helped us build us a church, and people started going to church. Things just changed all of a sudden.

MISSIONARY INFLUENCE

HAROLD COMBY, B. 1955—PEARL RIVER
TOLD ON JUNE 4, 1997

What they used to do was put the deceased in some type of robe, buffalo or bear hide, and put them on scaffolds and let the weather and the animals kind of decompose the meat. And then once almost all of it was gone, they used to have a bone picker, pick up excess meat from the bones, and then the relatives would carry the bones with them.

I read in books that when the missionaries came, they saw that, and they said, "That's a heathen way," you know. "Our way is the best way, so you should do it like our way." So I think gradually some of them became Christians and changed.

PUTTING TO REST

HUBERT WESLEY, B. 1933—MASHULAVILLE / BOGUE CHITTO
GARA WESLEY—MASHULAVILLE / BOGUE CHITTO
TOLD ON DECEMBER 18, 1992

They kept it [the deceased's body] in the house. Back then, they never did have a church in this area, so they kept in the house. And they always got together. Just as soon as they found out somebody died, they're making arrangements. Like, say, some of them in a pine box. Some of the men got together and built a box, then put him in the house, and he or she is there for maybe so many days, and then they put them in the ground.

Gara: The women's job during this time was to make new outfit. They never buried them in old outfit. They always buried them in new outfit—new dress or new shirt and all of this. The women did this while the men were preparing the box.

Hubert: That's still going on. That tradition, that part, is still going on now on reservation or off reservation, still doing that now. Women get together and make new dress, for especially a woman. Man hardly ever bury in Choctaw outfit, but women, they still bury Choctaw women in outfit.

Gara: And another of the tradition and all that's going on is the Cry after the funeral.

Hubert: Used to be six weeks [after the funeral], but they cut it down to about like four weeks. Used to be six weeks. They put a cross usually behind the house. This crosspiece of wood laid there for six weeks after the funeral, and they get back together and go over same kind, just like a funeral happened first time. Then of course, they always had beef or pork cooked for everybody to eat after the funeral.

Gara: This was at the Cry.

Hubert: That's when they would eat and have that Cry; they call it "Indian Cry." They still have it every once in a while, but not too often.

Gara: Way I understand about the Cry is the six weeks was their mourning for the one that had passed on. And that ended the mourning, at the Cry and all. And the one had died, their family wore their head covered all during this time after the ceremony. Then they could uncover their head; the mourning was over.

Hubert: The men wasn't allowed to get a haircut or dress up fancy during that month.

WAILING

EDDIE JOHNSON, B. 1970—STANDING PINE / TUCKER
TOLD ON JUNE 14, 2021

Those who would mourn, they didn't cut their hair, they didn't actually bathe or anything like that. It was an act of mourning. They were all out, and they would be wailing. There would be actual wailing, and they'd be scary. I've had some funeral experience where there was actual wailing. A lot of the times we'd see sniffling and crying, but wailing is a little different. If you've never seen it, it's scary.

That was one of the old practices. I think it's practiced along the way and for expressing their sorrow. When you talk about Choctaw Cry, that's part of it. What Choctaw Cry has become now because it's not really practiced now; it's an old practice. But there's more contemporary wakes and funerals now.

And the thing about it, I don't think anybody's exempt from that. The thing about it, when it comes to the funeral, bringing the body home was even practiced among non-Choctaws. Bringing it home from the funeral home and placing it. But the wailing thing still continued. And this is words from older people I've talked to, how they used to do. My mother talked about it one time; she remembers there were like professional wailers. They came for that purpose: to wail. She said that they would cover their heads at the home and sit around on the outside, not in front of the door, but near it, and they would actually wail. And she said, "It's scary."

And they'll go, "Aaaaaaahhhhhhhh!" like they're really hurting. Crying, hurting. And I think part of it was . . . To me, it sounded like they were encouraging them to cry for the one that passed. It's not just doing it just to be done but to help these people to express their sorrow.

I said "professional," but that's probably not the best way to say it. They just encouraged the people to mourn, express their sorrow because a lot of people hang on to their sorrows, bottled up on the inside, and then it's after the fact. It's when they're alone, that's when it's tough.

BIG AND LITTLE CRY

HAROLD COMBY, B. 1955—PEARL RIVER
TOLD ON JUNE 4, 1997

A long time ago, they used to have *Yáyah Osi*, which means "Little Cry" during the actual wake, and then they would have the Big Cry, which is *Yáyah Chito*, "Big Cry." It's like a memorial after the burial has happened.

My mom told me the Big Cry is two weeks after the burial. The uncle of the deceased would cut down a pine tree and split it in half, about the length of the size of the grave, I guess like this, into this [*indicates how the flat part of the log would lie against the ground to keep the "bench" from moving*]. People would go and sit on that split log and put a shawl over their heads, and actually cry, actually shed tears.

And she had mentioned something about the elderly making some kind of speech, trying to carry on the tradition. Either that or memorializing the deceased, telling his background information.

And then after that anybody who wanted to mourn, sit on there and cry.

And after that was over, they would have a big feast.

She says that when that mourning was over, the uncle would take the piece of wood and go into the woods and either hide it or throw it away. They said nobody else was allowed to accompany him. And he was the only one that took care of that duty.

She says she remembers her mother mourning the death of her relative, maybe two or three months after the death. And what they would do was don't even take a bath, wear the same clothes, and don't even comb their hair. I mean, they go by doing the same duties as cleaning the house or washing the dishes, but they never took care of themselves until three months later. And then they would start cleaning themselves up and saying that the mourning was over.

Another thing is, when a deceased died, you know the Choctaw tribe was recognized as long hairs. They used to call them *pashi falaya* [long hair] because both the women and the men, both had long hair. And whenever somebody died, they [close relatives] used to chop it off and put it into the coffin or the grave.

CRY CEREMONY

JACKSON ISAAC, B. 1902—PEARL RIVER
TOLD IN FEBRUARY 1982

In the early days, when people died, they used to call for a Cry Ceremony. They proposed to have a Cry on the same day, right after they buried the deceased's body. They placed a piece of wood [representing the deceased], and they would begin the Cry. They cried together, then they ceased and would go their separate ways.

Then, for about a whole month, they would continue their mourning together. From morning to morning, the people would come and help the grieving ones by crying with them for thirty days.

Then at the end of the ceremony, on the day when the wood was to be taken away, a great many people would gather on that one night in order to place the ceremonial scarf on the mourners [signifying the end of the Cry]. The mourners stayed together but did not do anything else, but the others would dance in the great dance.

The mourners remained together 'til the morning, and then they came out to the end of the log to get ready to go forward with the taking away of the log. They all gathered for this purpose and took away the wood. When that happened, they signaled the end of the mourning by taking the log away for the mourners.

If a child had died, they held a Cry in mourning for him; the father and mother would both be in mourning. All the mourning, brothers and sisters of the deceased, when the numbered days for mourning were finished, at that point and onward, they stood at the edge of the wood facing the west as appointed, they eulogized the deceased. When that happened the Cry Ceremony was considered complete. The speaker would continue to console them, how they should live in the days to come, to be at peace. He would tell them to be happy. They would have a celebration and bless them. They would go through a joyous time, the Choctaws.

If it were a woman, the mourning woman at the beginning of the Cry would be given a green handkerchief to wear [around the neck]. The same would be done for the man if it was their child that passed away. And then on the day arrived when the log would be taken away, if the father's hair had gotten long, it was cut, and a red scarf was placed around his neck. And for the woman, when the wood-removal ceremony was complete, a red scarf was placed around her neck. Then a larger scarf, that was very red, was taken, and they wrapped her with it.

These practices were ordained practices. The deceased would be buried, and after many days, many would come together to honor them.

Now, they just bury them, and that's the end; it's over quickly. They used to think on the deceased for days; that is how they buried people in the past. Nowadays, the younger generation, many of them don't understand, but they think they do. But we keep on telling this; from the start that's how it used to be . . . That's all.

WAKES IN TRANSITION

TRAVIS WILLIS, B. 1958—PEARL RIVER
TOLD ON JUNE 14, 2021

My little sister, she died at five days old, just five days. Norma Jean was her name, Norma Jean. She was still a baby when she died. But that was the first time I came into contact with that. It was the traditional, the three-day wake. That third morning, it was the funeral in the morning.

But everybody's talking about the *Yáyah*. It's the Crying.

See, this was an old tradition that is not used anymore that I know of. I've seen it once or twice when I was a kid. But after the death of a person, they would have the wake. And that's what they do.

A year, one year to the date of that person's passing, they would go out. I think they went back into the woods, and they would lay down a log in the middle. And it was mainly women. Daughter, in-laws, if he had a wife, his wife, and other women from the family. They would gather around this piece of log and sit there and cry. And as they were crying, they would have a veil over their face. That was a symbol of saying goodbye.

Today, when they have their wakes, even now, when they're just a couple days that they appear in the home, they'll burn wood. That's not tradition. That's not the way things were done. That fire don't mean anything. That fire, during the wake, it was to cook with. That was the purpose of that fire, to cook with. But they went overboard and said it was to guide the spirits. It was not for that purpose. It never was.

I figured they got it from some other tribe.

But that's just recent, in the last, I'd say, ten years or so. But that's not Choctaw tradition.

CLEANING AND SMOKING

LINDA WILLIAMS, B. 1958—STANDING PINE
TOLD ON JUNE 15, 2021

That's what my grandma used to say, that when somebody dies, they can hang around. And so that's the reason why she used to use that cedar tree, burned it, and then smoke it real good and then smoke it around the house.

But before she did that, I remember they used to put up their stuff and then wash the house where they had the wake at, wash it real clean. And then they used to smoke it. So it took a day's job.

But this is where what they called *iyyikowa* comes in. When something like that happened, they used to help each other. Community people used to help each other out. So, "Ladies, let's go help her out. She's going to wash the house today." And that's where they used to go and help her clean and wash the floor. And they wash the whole room.

I remember they used to do—it wasn't really a mop then—but they used to put an old T-shirt, or whatever, and they used to just pour the water on the floor, even though it's a frame house, and the floors are wood. They used to pour the water and the soap on the floor and then just wash whatever they can. The walls and ceilings if they could get to it, and clean. Get it clean. And it used to be clean.

That was after they buried the deceased. And then when they come back home, they don't do anything that same day, but it's the next day that they plan on doing that. And so that's when they get up the next day, they're ready to move everything and wash and clean the house.

And then I remember, like I said, my grandma used to smoke. She used to come back with that cedar tree and smoke. So that's why she used to have cedar tree in her yard. But she did a lot of things with it. And even around the yard, she would smoke it in the evenings. But that's what she said, to get the bad spirit away, or she said that they would bother you.

That doesn't happen anymore. I mean, if it's a wake, yeah. Families, relatives get together, and they come up with helping as far as cooking and meals and all this stuff. But as far as cleaning the house and everything after the wake and all this stuff, they don't do that. I think it's because of these newer houses. There's a sheet rock too and paneling and all this stuff goes on. So you can't wash them like you used to. So, they just do what they can on the floor or cleaning up maybe, but that's as far as they do.

COMMUNAL EVENT

MARTHA FERGUSON, B. 1949—STANDING PINE
TOLD ON JUNE 4, 2021

Family passed away. A lot of time, they made me stay home and cook for them too, so they could come back and eat. And a lot of them, I didn't go. But they did take it to the church.

And then from that funeral, what I know about, the old way, I never got to see it 'til, gosh, back in '94, where they did the Cry. That's the first time I ever went.

I wanted to see it. So Bob took me over there.

What they did was cook. And then out of that plate, the same plate, they feed that person. And then they leave the food along the plate, along same plate, they go ahead and put food on it. Then the next person eats. And that's what I saw.

Where they cry, they put logs here, here, here, circle. And they did the Cry.

And that's all. I never seen that before in my whole life and that's what I saw.

TAKING TIME TO MOURN

FRANK HENRY, B. 1927—BOGUE CHITTO / TUCKER
TOLD ON JULY 23, 1997

I seen a little bit of it when I was just a kid. When someone died, they'll have what they call a "Cry." After the funeral, six weeks later, they'll have a Cry. They'll build a fire and put a log all the way around this fire, and they'll all come and cry. They'll cry; they actually do cry.

A whole year. I think six months, they'll have a Cry and then after that, end of that one year, they're going to have one more Cry, and that was it.

In the meantime, if a man dies, young man, his wife never dresses up for a whole year, never looks at another man for a whole year. And they cut their hair. I'm not sure if this was a good rule or not, but that was the tradition at that time.

I would think it was a pretty good tradition because today, a man loses his wife, within six months, he'll be with somebody else. I guess, to me, I think it was pretty good, I think. At least they had some kind of ruling. Same way with the husband. A man loses his wife, he can't court no one until the end of that Cry, one year.

I've been to a Cry when I was just a kid, when Grandma demanded that. My grandma. And they had it. But they don't have it anymore.

I saw it two times and that was it. Gradually, they got away from that.

BURYING THE DEAD

TERRY BEN, B. 1957—STANDING PINE
TOLD ON JUNE 10, 2021

From time to time, people would pass from this world, and the whole community during that time period would be in grieving for the family of the deceased. And during that time period, there were no machines like bulldozers from John Stephens to go in and scoop the ground to dig up the grave. There was nothing like that. You know who dug the grave? The men of the church. They would come together.

I dug many a grave during that time period with the older men. You had to go six feet down. And so it was not one of those things that is enjoyable, but you did it to help out.

And then at the bottom, you would leave about maybe one foot. It was a tradition to leave about one foot undone for that day, until the day of the funeral.

So those are just things that was done.

And then after the service is over, the casket is lowered. Then we would get our shovels and close everything up, refill the grave, put the deceased inside the bought area. And so, it was not one of those things that was pleasant, but it had to be done. I've been on many of those grave-digging holes when somebody was deceased.

And the women would take the food to the family of the deceased, and that was just tradition. It was just one of those things where people helped each other out during time of grieving. And the men, some of the men were what they call "firekeepers." They would keep the fire during the duration of the wake, usually about three days.

And so those are things that people did to help each other out during that time period. They did not get paid; it was just done. People just helped each other during that time period.

HIGHLIGHTING THE GOOD LIFE

BRIAN BILLIE, B. 1973—RED WATER
TOLD ON JUNE 30, 2021

Our people have laughter to overcome bad things.

At a wake, you'll see them all be by the fire and laughing. Sounds disrespectful, but really they're highlighting the good life of the past of a person that's passed away.

But then I noticed more kids sit in the car and just turn on the radio and on the phone. But they're missing out on history, where they're from, and who their family are. The history comes by the fire. Laughter, because when you laugh about a lot of things, you remember. It kind of imprints on your mind; good memories that you can pull from.

BURIAL GROUND

HARLEY VAUGHN, B. 1961—HALLS, TN / BOGUE CHITTO
TOLD ON MAY 31, 1996

Take the [Nanih Waiya] mound. They say it's a burial ground. Bodies after bodies after years and years, they build up.

As far as I know, the elderly say never disturb a graveyard. They'll say, "You disturb it, take something that does not belong to you, or belongs to the person that died, he'll haunt you as long as you keep whatever is his." That's why they really don't dig up graves and all that.

LET THE DEAD REST IN PEACE

HAROLD COMBY, B. 1955—PEARL RIVER
TOLD ON JUNE 4, 1997

There are other stories that my mother has told. She has told me that you cannot go into the [Nanih Waiya] cave because once you start going in there, even if you have a new flashlight, new batteries, the light will go out on you.

And I've heard stories where people say they hear voices or somebody singing.

I think that's the way it should be. It's a taboo to deal with buried persons. Once they get buried, they should be left there; I don't think we should disturb it.

BURIED POSSESSIONS

HAROLD COMBY, B. 1955—PEARL RIVER
TOLD ON JUNE 4, 1997

About the spirits. If the deceased had wanted a certain type of funeral or wanted to give something to another person, you have to follow their wishes. If not, they say the spirit will never leave. They'll never be happy.

My mom says a long time ago, they used to bury certain . . . let's say, for example, I loved a certain gun. So when I die, they would bury the gun with me. "Prized possession," I guess you would call it.

That's one of the things that I've read in books where other Native tribes used to do that too. And I guess one of the rationales is that they would use that in the afterlife or hunting, put the bow and arrow in.

My mom said that they put my grandmother's favorite beads and Choctaw dress and stuff with her when she was buried.

I see that now. Some people will put sage or tobacco or eagle feather or their favorite beaded belt or whatever with them.

COMING HOME

HAROLD COMBY, B. 1955—PEARL RIVER
TOLD ON JUNE 4, 1997

I've always wondered why if a Mississippi Band member dies somewhere, even in LA, they would do whatever they could to bring that body back. And I always wondered why. Why spend all that money? They could bury that person in LA or cremate the body. But the thing was, they need to bring that body back so the spirit would be happy back home. It even describes that in one of the books, historically, if a Choctaw warrior died in battle, they would do whatever they can to bring that body back.

Like the other day, this guy was involved in a hit-and-run, and he died. The family asked for the clothes back. The investigator, who is a non-Indian, said, "Why do they want it?" It was bloody and stuff.

But the thing he doesn't understand is that if that person's blood is still around, the person is still around. It hadn't gone to the next world. So that's the reason they wanted it back.

They'll probably go to the grave and bury the clothes with him. Or they could probably take it to the medicine man and let him bless it, put medicine on it.

NO KIDS AT FUNERALS

TERRY BEN, B. 1957—STANDING PINE
TOLD ON MAY 30, 1996

I remember my grandparents saying a funeral, a wake, never take a small child or a baby to look on the face of the dead person because the spirit of that young person or that baby is too young, and the dead person's spirit, something may happen, intertwine, and baby might get sick and die.

You had that superstitious belief. And even now, I guess this got stuck in my mind, so I don't allow my kids. I've got a girl, maybe fifth grade, and three-year-old girl, too. If you go to a wake and whatever, or actual funeral, I don't let them look inside. I don't. It's just ingrained in me, instilled in me. I've got one ten years old, and one three. I've got one seventeen, but she's seventeen. [*laughter*] Just things like that. They were so very, very superstitious. Could be true, could not be true, but because of the teachings of the elders, I've stuck to a lot of things too as far as with my own.

BAD OMENS

HAROLD COMBY, B. 1955—PEARL RIVER
TOLD ON JUNE 4, 1997

My mom has mentioned something about spirits protecting you, warning you of impending danger. But mainly it's like the bad things, like bad omens, it's going to bring you bad luck or just a sign of bad things to come.

Like about the child who was hit by a truck and died violently without being sick. My mom says that when a death like that occurs, it's going to take some other people with him. Maybe all the families know that when a Choctaw dies that two or three follow.

She had also mentioned that when a person's buried late in the evening, that means that the spirits are active and that they want to take somebody with them. Like a relative. In fact, that happened.

I told her it [a funeral] was going to happen at three o'clock in the afternoon. She said that's too late to have a funeral. They should have it earlier. She said now it's going to take some relatives with her. Soon after that, those two kids got killed in that pickup wreck. They were relatives. It was a girl that was hit by a car or a van. She stayed in the hospital maybe four days and was brain dead, so they pulled the plug.

On the other hand, when a couple are fighting, and they're fighting over a child, over divorce, and each of them are pulling on the child, my mom says that you should never do that because the Creator might take the baby away, teach you a lesson.

Maybe they were fighting over that little baby, the mother and the grandmother.

AFTERNOON FUNERAL TABOO

HAROLD COMBY, B. 1955—PEARL RIVER
TOLD ON JUNE 1, 2021

You're supposed to do a burial when the sun is straight up because you don't want yourself to see your shadow. They say your shadow is part of your spirit, your *shilombish*.

So that's why burial is supposed to be [*points to the sun*] straight up. But we can't convince the funeral people, who are non-Indians, to do at noontime. I guess they have so many burials that they have to do.

Because one time—this is what happened—one time, I was the pallbearer for one of our relatives, and we were still at the cemetery at 5:30. The sun was setting, which you're not supposed to stay in the cemetery, or the ghost will follow you home.

So we were standing there and said, I told him, "I don't feel right," because this is what I've been taught. And most of them, they knew about it, but they didn't say nothing. [*small laugh*] So we went and sat in the van.

And what it is, is that if you bury somebody after the sun is set, there will be a relative following that person.

And sure enough, two weeks later, her sister died in a car wreck.

UNNATURAL DEATH

GRADY JOHN, B. 1934—HENNING, TN
TOLD ON JANUARY 15, 2000

Grandpa used to, way back when we were kids, the elder people would tell stories, ghosts, what Choctaw used to do. We used to stay up and listen. Sometimes scare you because Indian people, they believe in spirits.

For instance, somebody died, he just died, maybe tree fall on him. Or the guy got sick and died. He said, "The guy got sick and died, not going to bother you. But it's different here. Tree fall on him, he'll stay longer."

I said, "Where?"

He said, "Where his home. You'll hear him walking, but you can't see him. He's like wind."

BURN IT ALL

SUSIE COMBY ALEX, B. 1947—STANDING PINE / PEARL RIVER
TOLD ON JUNE 9, 2021

At that time, they didn't allow people, the family, to do anything. People would show up to do what needs to be done. During the night, they'll sweep the floor, mop the floor, or cooked. Things like this. The family didn't do anything, they just sit with the body.

If, when somebody's died, they're going to have a wake, this time of year, the forest provides the wood for the fire. But before, a man would go out in the woods and cut trees and bring it in. Whatever, the amount of wood they had, they say for you to burn it all; you can't keep it.

"If there's some left, I'll use it later." It says you can't do that. Whatever they brought you, the wood, you have to burn all of it. Even if you're going to have to burn it after the funeral, but you have to burn all of it, burn it all.

SPIRIT RETURNS

SUSIE COMBY ALEX, B. 1947—STANDING PINE / PEARL RIVER
TOLD ON JUNE 9, 2021

They said the spirit will come by to check on his or her belongings.

Well, the first night, what they did was put it in a box or laundry hamper or even trash bag. They'll put his favorite clothes, or the ones he wears the most, by the casket. At the end of the casket, they put that. After they get buried, they clean all of it, what belongs to them, and pack it.

That first night, they leave the bedroom where the person sleeps; they just left it. Put all their clothes in it, whatever belongings like medicine and all of that. They said the spirit will come around to check, so that's what they used to do.

One time, when my husband passed away, I tried to do that. But I missed one medicine. After he was buried, he never left me alone. When I'm asleep, it seems like. I'll call it a dream, but Momma said, "No, you had missed something."

She said, "You need to check around and see if he had left a medicine or even razorblades or razor. Whatever belongs to him, you need to go throughout the house and see if you had left his belongings to put it with the other stuff."

When I go to sleep, I would . . . I guess, it wasn't a dream; it seems like I would see him trying to get in the house. At the time, we didn't have air conditioning, so he would poke his head in the dining room. That's what I told Momma. They said, "Well, just tell him. You have to, even if you're dreaming, you have to tell him that he no longer lives here," and things like this.

He finally stopped.

At that time, my daughter and my grandson's father stayed with us.

I thought, in my dream, he was chasing me around the house. I thought I was hollering and screaming. I knew. I asked my daughter, I said, "Did y'all hear me hollering?"

She said, "I thought you were just having nightmares or something."

I said, "I did have nightmares!" [*laugh*]

HEALING A HAUNTING

TERRY BEN, B. 1957—STANDING PINE
TOLD ON MAY 30, 1996

If somebody dies, there's a strong belief that immediately, as soon as possible, when somebody dies, you're supposed to go in and clean out their bedroom. Clean out all the clothes, store them up, clean up the bedroom, put it outside on the porch immediately after somebody dies. Relatives and friends would go to somebody's house and do some house cleaning. Because you know about the Choctaw custom. There's going to be a wake; it's going to be at somebody's house, not usually at the funeral home. And so the reason for that was, my elders, my grandparents always told me that if you don't do that, the spirit of the dead person is going to hang around for about maybe three days. This is tied into Christianity, Christ, three days. Then there might be a haunting if you don't do that. If you take things that belong to the person who died, the bed, linens, clothing, shoes, and all that, take them outside onto the porch, within that three-day period, the spirit would come by and pick up these things, spiritually, I guess, and go to wherever the spirits going to be going, and there's going to be no harm.

But then if you don't do that, within that three-day span, the spirit will come inside the house, and a haunting might take place. So, this is something that people don't really talk about, but any family you go to, just about 98 percent of Choctaw families, they'll tell you the same thing.

If there's a haunting, go to the Choctaw doctor, tell him what the situation is. As far as that situation is, what I've heard is the doctor would go to the house site and spread medicine inside the house and outside the house to keep the spirit away, to keep evil away from that house. He would spread medicine outside. For a fee. [*laugh*] So that's what I've heard.

If somebody has dreams of the dead person that just happens over and over and over in terms of nightmares, some people have problems with that, can have problems. So what the usual Choctaw custom is, go visit the grave of the dead person. So just go visit, and they'll take care of it. Somehow the spirit of the dead person is reaching out. Supposedly, that's why the person is maybe having nightmares of the dead person.

They might not actually see a face, but it's usually the person who just recently died. So just go visit the grave of that dead person.

SPIRIT AT THE WAKE

TERRY BEN, B. 1957—STANDING PINE
TOLD ON MAY 30, 1996

I remember this from Standing Pine about ten years ago.

A woman's dad had just died, and this man said he was sitting out on the porch late at night, a wake situation, one o'clock in the morning. There was a gate. He said he was just sitting out there; there was nobody sitting out there except him. People were on the inside; I guess they were talking or semi-asleep or asleep and whatever on the inside, but he was the only one outside at that point.

And he told me the gate on the outside just opened by itself, the latch, on the outside.

So he was sitting there. As he was sitting there, the door to the house just opened by itself and closed; and there was nobody that he saw, was there, at that point.

You know things like that I hear, every time I go to a wake. Especially from the older men. They tell little things like that that supposedly happened to them or that they've heard.

WAIT A YEAR

LINDA WILLIAMS, B. 1958—STANDING PINE
TOLD ON JUNE 15, 2021

If there was a casket right here, like on this side of the wall here, they used to gather it [the deceased's things] up and put it all together and put it in this corner, right above their head, where the head is. That's the way that Grandma used to do. Get all their clothes, all their belongings. She said that they're going to come back and get it, so leave it up to where they can get it. Put it up somewhere like in storage or somewhere and, for a year, keep it. And then after that, then you can give it away.

For that matter, when my dad passed away, I remember I didn't want to move anything from his room. I left his room alone. I didn't even touch the bed, nothing.

One year after, finally, I went in there, and I said, "It's time to move on. It's time we're going to clean this room up, and we're going to move everything out."

So I started getting everything, his clothes and everything, out. We washed them, dry-cleaned it, and everything, the suits and all he had. And we gathered them all together, and then we started selling them at a yard sale. And that's how we did my dad's.

TAKE IT BACK: THE CANE

SUSIE COMBY ALEX, B. 1947—STANDING PINE / PEARL RIVER
TOLD ON JUNE 9, 2021

When we were growing up, my parents were what they call "sharecroppers." So we had to go even to the Delta to pick cotton. They gave us a cabin for us to stay.

And so we were walking from the cotton field, walking back to that cabin we lived in, we used to pass a cemetery. And there was a walking cane at the edge of that cemetery. Mama picked it up, and Daddy said, "Put it back." He said, "Whoever put it there," he said, "you have their walking cane, so it's going to follow you over there to the cabin."

Well, she pretended she was hobbling on this, and Daddy said, "Oh, it's going to be a laughing matter when . . . "

So, well, it wasn't long. We had finished supper and were sitting there talking and things like this. And there was a knock at the door. And Daddy said, "Who is coming? This is the middle of the night?" He opened the door, nobody. So when he sat down, he said, "Well, better sleep. We're going to have to get up, cook, have breakfast and . . . "

And there was another knock, again. And Mama said, "Whoever it belongs to is coming for the cane. You better take it back." Mama opened the door and throw it out.

And he said, "You have to take it to where you got it."

So we all had to hold each other and went to the cemetery. We stood not a little bit farther, and Daddy told Mama, he says, "Go put it where you found it." So she went and put it in, and it quit.

And that's what he said. You don't pick anything off the cemetery.

TAKE IT BACK: THE POT AND THE RING

SUSIE COMBY ALEX, B. 1947—STANDING PINE / PEARL RIVER TOLD ON JUNE 9, 2021

My aunt and her husband lived in a little shack. And when Mama's sister passed away, her husband told us we could live there. So we moved over there. Well, the brother-in-law told him, he says, "If you all want something, she said for me to let you all have it."

Well, this was at night. So my aunt said she wanted a pot with the lid on it. At that time, they loved to cook outside, so she wanted that. And their sister had told them they can take what they want. There were four of them.

And so Mom and her sister, they went to that house and got a flashlight. He had already turned off their electricity, so they took a flashlight, and my aunt got the pot, and my mother got a ring that she liked. So she put the ring on her finger, and Daddy said, "I thought you all just came to look. I say you all better not take those."

Well, they put it in the car, and off we went. And her sister was, at that time, staying with us. After the funeral, she decided she'll stay a little bit. She was from Red Water, though. So it happened like that too.

So Daddy said, "Your sister's here to pick up her stuff." And they thought that she was there physically. So they looked at each other and told my daddy to go give it to her, and he said, "No." He said, "You all got it. You all have to take it back. That's why I told you not to." He was telling my mom. He said, "That's why I told you not to take anything, not at this moment."

If you're going to give away something after a person dies, in Choctaw, they wait six months to a year. That's what Mama told us because she had a lot of clothes. We had to buy her blouse, and she wore mainly blouse and pants, so we'll get her . . . And it seems like there are certain ones that were just her favorite. She wore those out first. And there were some new blouses and all that was hanging in the closet. So we says, "Who is in need of clothes? Just give it to them but wait until over six months."

So, that's what my dad was saying. That you all should have waited until six months to pick it up, then nothing would have bothered you all.

So, we all had to go pack up the car and go back. They put it on the porch, and Daddy said, "Go put where you found it."

So they had to go inside. Mama wanted Daddy to go with, and Daddy said, "It's yours." He said, "It's your doing."

So we all sat in a car, and then they went and put it up and locked back the door. Her brother-in-law gave her the key. So they locked the door, and he said, "This is not the first time that's happened to you."

So Mama said, "Ah, no. But it does happen."

TRAVEL AND RETURN

MARTHA FERGUSON, B. 1949—STANDING PINE
TOLD ON JULY 28, 2022

Grandma's uncle passed away. They live in an old house that's one room, one bed, one living room, no bedroom, and one kitchen. But it was a big house.

When he passed away, what they did was get a sheet and then put all his stuff in it that belongs to him, what he wore, what he had in his pocket, if he had a songbook, Social Security, anything that belongs to him was put in that one big bag and just tie a knot and put it in the center of that room.

And from there, that's why it was coming into my head, "What's going on?"

That's when Mama said, "I'll tell you later." And this what she said. "All the stuff that you see, that you've been seeing, what they put in after he passed away, that means wherever he's been, if he's been in military overseas, he can be out of state, he could just live here alone, but he'll be traveling. He's going to travel all over and then come back home.

"Once he gets back, he's going to come and claim everything that's in there. Once he's done, then you can go ahead and get rid of it or give it away to an individual that belongs to him that he plans to give out, or the wife plans to give it to somebody."

So that's just how it's done.

From that, I went, "How do you know that he's coming back to gather all this stuff?"

She said, "Oh, you'll know. He'll walk in, and you can see his spirit. Some people will see it, and some. . . . Once his spirit has come through, and that person that's seeing it is going to say, 'I saw him come to gather his stuff, and then he left. He went back out to the door and left.' Or however it left. Or, 'He just disappeared once he stand there gathering his stuff.'"

I said, "How do they go through this stuff?"

"Oh, all they to do is they know what they want out of it, and then from there they're gone. And then the spirit goes back to where it was going. Don't ask me where because I don't know."

That's what my mom said. But that's how it was told to me when Grandma's uncle passed away. So that's what I remember out of that.

And from that one, when I married Bob: "Where's the White people go?"

And Mom said, "I don't know."

"Does he travel just like us? Just like the Choctaw does, or I wonder how is it done?"

And when Bob passed away, that's when I found out about something nice and great that happened the day he passed away. You know, before he passed away, this large angel walked in, and from there on to the end of his foot, where he was located at the hospital, there was smoke—white, pure smoke. You could see it. It just comes out. And then that angel just stand there, just collected it, all the smoke, just blend right into it, and it turned around and left.

From there I went, "What is that just sitting on there?"

And then the phone rang, and it turned out to be my mom, and she said, "How are you doing?"

I said, "I'm doing fine."

"Are you eating?"

I said, "Yes, but I've got something great to tell you." And that's what I told her. "This angel walked in."

"How do you know?"

I said, "Well, I saw the wings."

But gosh, it was shiny, just like the sun hitting those glitter type. It was silver and gold and shiny as can be. And here's Bob's spirit, the smoke came up and just blend in with it, and that thing just walked out, and I just, "Wow." That's all I could say was, "Wow."

She was like, "Well, since that kind of stuff happened, that means in three days, Bob's going to pass away. He's going to die. Because anything like that happen, that's when He is giving him three days."

So, "Oh." I didn't know that. And so that's how I found that out. And from three days, he did pass away on the third day just like what she said.

And not only that, right after Mom talked a few minutes and let go, a few minutes later, his friend called up, "How's Bob?" I told him the same thing and they went, "Wow. Ferg. So he's really going."

I said, "Yes. Yes, sir. He is. Looks like an angel picked him up, so we probably won't see him until the end of our days, probably."

"Yeah. I agree. Wow. Ferg." That's what he called Bob all the time, Ferg. A bunch of his buddies.

"Make sure your other two friend knows about Bob. Just want to let you know about that."

"Well, I'm glad to hear that he's going to the best place he can go."

And from there, that's when I said, "Mom, I guess we get a chance to see what Bob's going to do." It was July 22nd when he died, so September 21st or 22nd, I saw his spirit walking by at the house.

I was just laying there resting before, "Okay, I'm going to eat and go to bed." I had collapsed on the couch, and that was it. And then first thing I saw was him going by. I went, "What is that? That looks like Bob's shadow." And then he turned around and looked and then went right to his den.

So all the stuff that's there, I just left it alone; so that's what he came to collect, I guess.

And after that, I didn't see him anymore or his spirit. So that was interesting. Awesome. I thought, "Gosh." I couldn't believe what I saw. Couldn't believe it.

GUARDIAN ANGEL

SUSIE COMBY ALEX, B. 1947—STANDING PINE / PEARL RIVER TOLD ON JUNE 9, 2021

My mom and dad had passed away, and my husband had passed away, too. I had my daughter's two kids, oldest one, Trinity and Hannaniah. They [Susie's daughter and husband] were going somewhere. They said, "Can they stay with you?"

I said, "Yeah."

I was cooking in the kitchen. They were used to turning on the living-room light to watch TV. One day, I had them make a pallet and got them a quilt to sit on. They said they wanted to sit on the floor to watch it, so I got them a quilt to sit on. They were watching, and then I would go in and stare and check on them if they were sleepy. They were so interested in this TV that they were watching it.

I had stared at it and turned around. There stood Mom and Dad. Momma had her legs, Daddy's arthritic arms wasn't arthritic no more. They just startled me. I didn't say anything, but Mom says, "We just came to check," in Choctaw, says, "We just came to check." She said, "You're doing a good job with the family."

One of my bottles was bubbling, so I was going to turn it down. When I turned around, they were gone. I guess Daddy used to say, "When I die, I'll be y'all's guardian angel. I'm going to come and watch out."

So I says, "I guess that's what he means by that."

DEATH AND LOSS

THERON "DUKE" DENSON, B. 1956—PEARL RIVER
TOLD ON JUNE 15, 2021

My cousin that lived here, he said he had tested positive for it [COVID-19]. And I said, "Oh my God. If he's testing positive for it, and we live together here, I must have got it too."

And two days later, he passed away. He went somewhere and collapsed and died.

He was a double amputee, and he was going to dialysis. So that morning, he was okay, like nothing happened. We were talking; he was fixing breakfast, getting ready to go somewhere. And I came back here, and I went to sleep for about three, four hours. Got up. Telephone rang. Lady said she was from the hospital. She asked me, "Does Travis Isaac live there?"

And I said, "Yes, he does."

She goes, "What is he to you?"

I said, "Well, he's my cousin." And I asked her, I said, "Well, how's he doing over there at the hospital?"

Said, "Sir, he just passed away."

So the next day, I got sick. All I wanted to do was sleep. But I could tell there was something wrong with my whole body. They tried to get ahold of me. I was laying on the couch out there. I heard somebody talking, and I just couldn't get up. I had no strength to get up or . . . I couldn't talk.

They left. They came back later. I heard a man say, "Well, the door's locked. Nobody's home."

Said, "He is home. Open up the window."

So he opens up the window, stuck his hand inside, and opened the door. "He's here."

I'm laying there. They put me on a stretcher, took me to the hospital. They gave me X-ray. And one of them says, "You got double pneumonia." They carry me to Jackson, Mississippi, where I spent a month there.

What I heard was they didn't expect me to live. Because they looked at my X-ray pictures. Said this is the worst case that he'd ever seen.

"Well, what do you see? Is he going to code?" something or other.

But I hung in there. I told them, "I want to stay alive."

So I put all of my energy into staying alive.

Next thing you know, there's a bunch of people came over to look at me. The nurse said, "This is our special, special patient."

So I wasn't expected to live, but I came through because they called me the "special patient."

DEATH WITHOUT CEREMONIES

RAE NELL VAUGHN, B. 1964—PEARL RIVER
TOLD ON APRIL 22, 2020

Unfortunately, with the COVID-19 virus, it has really put a halt to a lot of things, our ceremonies or death ceremony. It has really changed life on the reservation here in regards to our practices. Only the immediate family can go to the funeral home and be with them. And they're buried the next day!

And I reference my own experience. My father was non-Indian.

When my grandmother, his mother, passed away . . . She lived in Oklahoma City. I had to go up there with my family, and we went to pay our respects. And I remember that was the hardest thing because we went to a funeral home, and I felt like I needed to stay and to sit, that desire, that need to sit with her. And of course, the other family members who live there were with us. They were like, "Okay. You've viewed," you know? "We can go back." And I just . . . it was hard for me. It was hard for all of us—my mother and my brother. I felt lost.

And so I can only imagine what these families, our tribal families, are going through because you don't have the ability to grieve with each other and to laugh, to talk about stories of who this person was and what they meant to you. And just not having that grieving process that I've known all my life—I just, I cannot imagine. I can't imagine what they're going through right now.

I know we have one death that they're not going to be able to do anything for the family because the husband died, the wife tested positive, and they can't do anything until May 1st, that they're not able to do anything until then. And I just, I can't even fathom it.

And you know, as community members, you go out, and you support the family. You bring them food, and you sit with them, and you talk with them, and it just, I don't know. It's just been the most impactful that I have seen. It's really, it's really changed a lot of things.

WAKES IN THE TIME OF COVID

JAY WESLEY, B. 1975—STANDING PINE
TOLD ON JULY 28, 2022

Another way it [COVID-19] affected our tradition is like our funerary process of having the deceased in the home and having the family get-togethers and family meals and family and friends and community members coming down to pay their respects. And having a fire to light a path, all our normal processes of honoring our loved one was taken away. We were going through the funeral-home process, and even then, with very limited people. So, for a lot of people before COVID, funeral process was normal because it's unexpected, and it's spaced out from one death to another, whereas during the pandemic, there were a lot of loved ones passing in a short amount of time and the prevalent risk of infection in gatherings. So it wasn't what we were used to. I mean, staff members would ask me, and say, "Can I go?"

I'd say, "That's up to you; that's your call."

And maybe you put whatever leave you want to put in, but you got to watch yourself and sanitize. And even we had to have emergency management go over there and bring masks and hand sanitizers and kind of remind people.

It was hard. And some people still trying to keep a fire going at their own homes for that wake ceremony, the fire ceremony. So I think after finally it came down, then they had that *lowak moshólichi* ceremony, which is lighting the fire and then having a fire, putting a fire out. It hails back to the Green Corn Ceremony and the lighting up the new start of the new year. And then having the deceased to have a path to go. And so they had it at Pushmataha Lake, and anybody that wanted to come in and dedicate the name of their loved one was invited for that.

HEALTH AND HEALING

On April 8, 1974, as the school year was coming to a close, a group of Choctaw high school students were working to finish their spring edition of the student-run *Nanih Waiya* magazine and sought out an interview with Frank Henry, the service unit director for the Choctaw Hospital. Their first question was a straightforward one: "When and how was the Indian hospital first established?"[1] The second, however, cut to the heart of a dilemma facing the community for the past century or more: "Did the Indians have any difficulties changing from the Indian doctor to the regular doctor at the hospital?"

"Choctaws' adherence to traditional custom, moral attitudes, and belief is very strong," Frank Henry replied.

> Change is something not to be taken lightly. The old ways are deeply entrenched. Thus, if a person has a pain, he may have more faith in the traditional medicine man—or Choctaw doctor—than the service unit physicians. The medicine man possesses an extensive knowledge of native herbs, which definitely have medicinal properties similar to those drugs prepared by a pharmacist. Further, the medicine men realize, as do modern physicians, that many diseases and ailments are psychological, and must be treated accordingly. Thus the medicine man is often as effective, or in many instances even more effective, than the service unit physicians dealing with illness of this nature.

Why should people abandon their own medical practices when they felt their medicine worked as well or better than those of Western doctors? It was a question whose answer was made all the clearer by the racism institutionalized in the Jim Crow South. "Most Choctaw feel that the Philadelphia Indian hospital is inferior in every respect to medical facilities in surrounding areas," Mr. Henry said, launching into a litany of complaints his fellow tribespeople made about the hospital: the doctors are young and inexperienced; the medicines are out of date; you have to wait all day to see a doctor, and when you do see one, they have to send you an hour away to Meridian for real care; they don't have any privacy for visitors or patients; and most important of all, "I go there, but I don't get well." Despite improvements to the medical facilities in the area and the building of a new Choctaw Health Center in 2015, many of these views remain. As one elder complained in 2021, "If something happens, I would rather go to a Chahta *alikchi* than go to Choctaw Center. Sometimes you have to wait half a day to see a doctor."

Not surprisingly, the critique runs both ways. Early chroniclers of the Choctaw were divided on the efficacy of Choctaw medicine. Some recorded sincere stories of Choctaw doctors healing bloody noses, snake bites, leprosy, and blindness not just among their own, but among French, Spanish, and English colonists as well. Others, however, summarily dismissed Choctaw doctors as frauds who use sleight of hand to make it appear they are drawing out bits of fur, antler, and other foreign objects from a patient's body, and who blame fate, witchcraft, or some hapless elderly neighbor when their doctoring has been ineffective.[2]

Diseases brought from Europe, such as measles, smallpox, and tuberculosis, posed a particularly dire challenge to Choctaw medicine. Tribal prophecies that are still told today describe epidemics that will reappear among them, once again decimating their population. In the 1950s, some believed the prophecy was partially fulfilled with the influenza pandemic known as the Spanish flu; in the 1970s, some believed the prophecy was fulfilled with outbreaks of whooping cough and influenza, as well as tuberculosis and diabetes. In the 1990s, some pointed to the AIDS epidemic. And in 2020, the prophecies were once again reinterpreted and this time applied to COVID-19.[3]

Between the dismissive attitude by non-Choctaw towards their medicine and belief systems and the lack of access to quality biomedical care, it is no wonder many Choctaw have long distrusted Western medicine and of speaking openly about their own health practices. Tension about what is and is not acceptable to speak about continues today. For the most part, general discussion of the types of medical practices used by Choctaw doctors is acceptable, but not the specific herbs used by doctors to make their medicine. It is also generally acceptable to acknowledge the integral role *bohpoli*—the little people—play in both training doctors and helping them heal their patients but not to discuss the exact nature of the relationship doctors have with the specific *bohpoli* who help them. Witchcraft is acknowledged as a very real threat still today, but naming people who might be witches or describing the specific nature of their process and medicine is too dangerous to speak about freely. Further, sharing information meant only for trained doctors, even with other Choctaw, may violate the trust established between a doctor and the *bohpoli* with whom the doctor is working, as well as risk harm if a person attempts to imitate the doctor without proper training. When Choctaw high school students in the 1970s asked Choctaw doctor Pete Dyer what herbs he used the most, his reply was clear and direct: "I'm not supposed to tell you that." When they ask what he does with the blood he extracts, he replies, "That's *my* business" (November 4, 1975).[4] But stories of becoming a doctor, healing patients, working with *bohpoli*, and warding off witchcraft could be shared, and still are. So are stories of home remedies that describe knowledge that all Choctaw should have in order to ensure good health.

BECOMING A DOCTOR

Serving one's community as a Chahta *alikchi* or traditional Choctaw doctor is not taken lightly. The job is twenty-four hours, seven days a week. People may show up on your doorstep at all hours of the night. Pay is often minimal and in the recent past, was as likely to be a chicken, a day's labor, or a bushel of corn as cash. In the more distant past, skeptical non-Indian writers painted Choctaw doctors of the eighteenth and nineteenth centuries to be greedy and unethical, bleeding their patients both literally—through bloodletting—and figuratively—by requiring excessive payments and cutting off care when the person ran dry.[5]

Then and now, however, doctors put themselves at social and physical risk in accepting the role of *alikchi*. For one, they attract the attention of other doctors, including bad ones often referred to as witches who might attempt to harm them to avoid the competition. Also, the mystery surrounding the work, the power involved in interacting with the *bohpoli* and other supernatural forces, and the ambiguity of whether a person practices only good medicine or whether they also practice witchcraft, causes many people to view doctors warily. The oral tradition is full of stories of children who were chosen by *bohpoli* to become doctors, only to have their parents have the process halted, fearful of the life that awaited them.

People describe two main ways to become a doctor: being trained by the *bohpoli* and having it passed down through the family. When a person is young, *bohpoli* will seek them out, try to get the child to play with them, and lure them into the woods to begin their training.[6] Because so many parents do not want their children to become doctors, they warn children not to play alone, not to leave toys outside that might attract *bohpoli*, and not to play near areas known to be inhabited by *bohpoli*. Pete Dyer explained how he knew he was supposed to be a doctor. "That's easy. I played with them [the little men] all the time when I was a little boy!" He also says, however, that his ability to heal was "a gift to me before I was born," adding, "I was born with a veil over my head," referencing a common folk belief found in many cultures around the globe that babies born with a caul or veil—a piece of the amniotic sac attached to the baby's head—are gifted with second sight, preternatural intuition, or other spiritual or supernatural abilities.

The power to be a doctor can also be passed down from a direct relative. In some cases, this may involve intentional training; in others, the gift is passed more effortlessly. Children who have never met their fathers may also be gifted with healing power. But according to some, there is no guarantee. "You have to be given the gift in some way, or it has to come to you," says DeLaura Saunders, whose uncle, Bob Henry, was a medicine man. "Uncle Bob could take one of his sons with him to do all this medicine in hopes that he would carry. That son could get all that training and knowledge from that. But if that gift doesn't come to him, if the spirits don't give him that, he may know how to practice it, and he may know all the knowledge, but it's not going to work if that gift didn't come to him, or if the spirit didn't come to him. Only the *alikchi* person knows; it comes in different ways to them."

MEDICINE WOMAN

ESTELLINE TUBBY, B. 1928—PEARL RIVER
TOLD IN 1976

My mother used to talk about my grandmother and how she became a medicine woman. Her name was Louisa Phillips, and she lived to be a hundred and four years old before she died. When she was a little girl, she used to roam around a lot in the fields and other places that were isolated.

One day, a strange thing happened to her. While she was walking in the woods, she heard people laughing. It became louder and louder as she approached it. She got very scared.

Then a strange thing happened. Out of nowhere, a cloud of dust forming a funnel-like shape as if it was a tornado appeared. It hurled around with great speed and went in a thicket of bushes.

The cloud of dust disappeared.

At least that's what my grandmother thought.

She then started toward the bushes where the cloud had vanished. The thorn bushes were making a lot of noises, as if they were alive or something. For some reason or another, she happened to look in front of her, and there stood an old woman, carrying a pipe, coming her way.

After she saw her coming, she did not stay. She ran home like she never ran before in her life.

When she got home, she was still in a daze and told her mother. Her mother told her that it was a sign informing her that as long as she lived, she would never be hungry or poor.

From then on, my grandmother knew what was to be done. She had to become a medicine woman.

WAYS OF BECOMING A DOCTOR

TERRY BEN, B. 1957—STANDING PINE
TOLD ON MAY 30, 1996

From what I've been told, it comes down two ways. Say a woman was a doctor during that time period. She may teach maybe her daughter or son how to do things, how to go out in the woods, get some roots and all that, what to look for, flowers and different things like that. And she would pass it on that way, from mother to son, mother to daughter. That's one way I've heard.

The other way is meeting these little people in the woods. According to the old people, some people have an ability, a gift, and these little people know.

And at some point during their life, usually when they're kind of young, maybe teens, twenties, whatever, they make contact with usually young men because usually they're in the woods. They make contact with the young men, young boys, and they teach them a lot of things. Show them this, that, and all of that.

So that's the second way that I've heard people have learned to be a Choctaw doctor. These little people sometimes go with medicine, just be around, kind of like an assistant to these doctors.

There was a herbal doctor that lived in Tucker, years ago. His name was Pete Dyer. He was one of the better-known herbal doctors. Probably someone has told you about him? He died about maybe about eight years ago. He used to be a part-time worker up here, too, at the health center.

Anyway, when my grandmother was still alive, she would go to Tucker, and Pete would always do bloodletting or give some sort of salve medicine. Whenever he got through maybe talking with my grandma, he would go out in the back, go out in the back of the house. And I never did ask in that time period, but I've heard that maybe he went outside and maybe talked to the little people to maybe go get medicine for him.

In later years, I've heard things that that Pete Dyer told other people. So he was probably the best known, at least in the last twenty years, of the herbal doctors around here. He was very popular. He was so popular that the health center people said, "Let's go out and give him a job." I think he had an office up here where, especially, the older Choctaws who didn't want to really see a White doctor, would go in and see a Choctaw herbal doctor. He's one of the better persons to talk about as far as this area and Choctaw health.

LOST: A PERSONAL EXPERIENCE STORY

CAROLINE MORRIS, B. 1944—PEARL RIVER
TOLD ON MAY 31, 1996

Note: The next three stories all describe the same event, first from the person it happened to, then from her mother, who witnessed it, and finally from her daughter, who heard the stories about it.

In the old days when I was growing up, we lived in an old frame house on Willis Road. And when we were growing up, we didn't have TV or radio, or have no electricity. And after supper, we would sit outside to give the house time to get cool from the stove wood. We cook and make the house hot, so we sit outside until finally the house get cooled down a little bit. Then maybe ten thirty, eleven we go to sleep.

Then at that time, we sit outside, we used to see pine, lighted pine. You would just see off in the distance, the hill where we were at, and you would see it. And my dad would say, "That's the little people. *Bohpoli*."

We used to see that. But dad always tell us, "Don't mess with it. Don't do anything. Don't go near it."

Somewhere along the line, prior to us growing up, when I was like about two years old, Mom said I got lost in the woods. I got lost in the woods. We lived close to that wood; I didn't go that far into the wood, but I got lost, and they hunted, and they hunted me, and they finally find me, sitting on a stump.

And mom said they got a medicine man to come out to see what was going on. And by that time, I think everybody in the neighborhood searched and searched, but the medicine man was there. Mom talked to him to see what was going on with me, why was I sitting like that in a daze. And that was a process of the little man trying to get me to be the medicine woman. And Mom says, "Uh-uh." So the medicine man fixed it up where I wouldn't remember anything to be prepared to be a medicine woman.

In those days, we have a good medicine doctor and a bad one. If they don't like it, they will kill you. And that was one reason Mom did not want it.

I'm glad I don't know anything about medicine.

I never sit outside to look for the little man with the torch anymore, but I'm sure it's still out there. But I don't know.

LOST: A MOTHER'S STORY

GLADYS WILLIS, B. 1926—PEARL RIVER
TOLD ON MAY 23, 1996

I don't know how we missed her, but we was out in front, probably. I called her, but she didn't answer. So I went around the back; she wasn't there. So we looked all over, call for her. She didn't answer. And Nannie and them used to live in the white house up there. Grandma or somebody called and said she was going behind the house. We believed it was all over. Didn't see her. But all of a sudden, she was sitting right there on the stump.

We used to have, it's called "medicine doctor," or "Chahta *alikchi*." They went and got him, and he came and looked around, and he said it was them *bohpoli* that had took her away. And she just came back, and we found her. I don't know how it happened, but it did.

Well, they said sometimes they can keep them for two or three days. And he or she will be well-fed, well taken care of. But she didn't have a thing to tell him. That's the way she was. Asked her where she was, and she said she didn't know.

"Where did you go?"

"I don't know."

Her daddy got on her. "When you going to go somewhere, tell us where you're going!"

While the Choctaw doctor was sitting there, he was investigating what happened. After that, that was the one who came and got her.

I think he said when they do that, they will turn him or her into medicine man. After, Chahta *alikchi* said she was too little. He said he would take off whatever spell they had left on her. They would take what they left on her. I think he said to watch her on full moons because she might walk off again.

LOST: A DAUGHTER'S STORY

RAE NELL VAUGHN, B. 1964—PEARL RIVER
TOLD ON MARCH 14, 1996

Going back to my grandmother, I remember them telling me that my mother had gotten lost. I think she was about two or three, around that age. She was lost for some time. She said she was only outside in the backyard playing. From the backyard to the woods, it's a good stretch. I can't see how she could have all of a sudden been there and not been there. She was lost for some time.

There was a Chahta *alikchi* there. Chahta *alikchi* is a Choctaw doctor. He was there.

They looked for her. They had been looking for her. They looked everywhere for her.

All of a sudden, she was there sitting on the stump between the barn and the house. There was a tree stump, and she was just sitting there. My grandfather asked her, "Where have you been?"

She said, "I don't know. I don't know where I've been."

The Chahta *alikchi* told them that this is probably what had happened: that the *bohpoli*—my grandmother said she thinks this is the only reason why *bohpoli* would take children, take anyone or any child because of the fact that they're just trying to let them be a doctor, to teach them or to give them the power to become a Choctaw doctor.

Anyway, this Choctaw doctor, Jack Tubby, sat with her for a while, stayed with her for a while, and said, "She'll be fine. She'll be all right."

I don't know why. Either they didn't want to give it to her, give her the power, or what happened. And it didn't happen because my mother is not a Choctaw doctor.

HEALING AND PROTECTION

The primary task of a doctor is to heal the sick. Chahta *alikchi* do this primarily through herbal medicines and bloodletting and cupping. Herbs are gathered from the nearby woods and processed most often into herbal teas and salves, though also by burning them and using the smoke to help purify and heal. Knowledge of which plants to use is typically guarded by doctors; some say this is to protect people from using them inappropriately, ineffectively, or dangerously, while others say it is because the *bohpoli* have entrusted this knowledge to them as part of a reciprocal relationship, and it is not theirs to share.

Like the use of herbal remedies, bloodletting and cupping is practiced around the world, though in diverse ways. Choctaw doctors practice cupping most often with the use of small horns, typically from a cow, to create suction to draw out the illness through the blood.

The term Chahta *alikchi* or "Choctaw doctor" is typically used for both types of doctor, though sometimes men and women who only make herbal remedies are called "herb doctors." But there is another type of medical practitioner, the *hattak holhkonna*, or witch. The *alikchi* works to "heal, divine, or otherwise improve the lot of his patients. The witch, on the other hand, exploits, debilitates, and destroys. . . . Either type of practitioner can be good or bad, depending on whether he uses magic, medicine, or both and to what extent" (Blanchard 1981:148). Distinguishing a good doctor from a bad one, then, may be simply a matter of perspective since the same doctor who helped cure one person has the power to do harm to another. Kendall Blanchard recorded the story of a young woman who had hurt her foot walking in the woods. The doctors at the hospital were ineffective in treating her, so her mother took her to an *alikchi*. He knew when and where she was hurt without her telling him. More importantly, he knew what caused it and how to cure it. "He also told me it was not an accident. Another doctor had done it to me. Some girl was jealous of me because the boy she liked had a crush on me, so she had him do it to me." The doctor applied boiled roots to her ankle and healed her, but then he shifted gears. "He asked me if I wanted to do something to that girl, but I told him 'no'" (1981:153).

Jealousy is a common motivation for witchcraft, which is why children are told not to brag, and personal successes may be kept within the family rather than publicized more broadly. But success is not shied away from. Medicine is also used to influence the outcome in one's favor, an effort that some view as doctoring, others witchcraft. In the past, such work was commonplace. Men variously referred to in the written record as "*hopáyyi*," "prophets," "ball-play witches," "witch doctors," "conjurers," "sorcerers," or "medicine men" were described as pacing the sidelines of stickball games and working their magic to help their team win, either by strengthening their own players or weaking the opposing ones. Such practices have been driven underground today, where such doctoring or witchcraft is not openly admitted to, but accusations and suspicions continue, particularly when a game's outcome is unusual or unexpected.[7]

MULE AND A RATTLESNAKE

HUBERT WESLEY, B. 1933—MASHULAVILLE / BOGUE CHITTO
DECEMBER 18, 1992

Cameron Wesley's daddy is supposed to have been raised up somewhere around Tucker. Sydney Wesley. He was a herb doctor. I don't know whether we got a picture of him or not, but my family's got it anyway. He has long hair and wearing overalls, and he wore a black hat, you know, round top. And from what I been told, he always rode a mule to making his rounds doctoring people. He had a tote sack that he carried his rattlesnake with him everywhere he went.

After Grandmother passed on, he was living by himself. He had a three-room little house somewhere Tucker over there. The mule was on one side and the rattlesnake on the other side [*laughter*], and he was in the middle. So lot of people were scared of him. I think they was scared of the snake more than him, but I understand that a lot of people . . . He was kind of weird because he had long hair and all that. He was kind of unusual in those days.

HEALING HIS NEIGHBORS

HUBERT WESLEY, B. 1933—MASHULAVILLE / BOGUE CHITTO DECEMBER 18, 1992

Cameron Wesley was herb doctor, too. He tried his best to teach me how to be a doctor when I grow up, and he showed me a lot of herbs and what they're used for and some of the roots that he dug up. I used to go out in the woods with him. I just never get interested in it, and I never did learn, but I seen him working with people and how he done things. I remember all of that. It just never did grow in me, I guess.

He knew about herbs, what herbs used for whatever's wrong with the person, way my daddy done. I've seen him working on patients. For instance, somebody's got some kind of thing wrong with him. He would talk to them; then he would feel his head, put his hand on his head, and talking to them some way or another, figure out what this problem is, you know, pain somewhere on body, like back or somewhere.

He had his wooden thing built like hospital bed, shaped where you lay down and fit right into it. Then he had this cow horn cut off almost to the point, and then had a little hole on top of it where air suction would come through it. And he would take broken piece of glass, and he would cut across the skin, just break the skin where it bleed, move that cow horn on top of it, and move it around until friction builds up. Then he put a hand across the top. Thing set on there certain length of time, and then when he takes it off, he takes blood in pot and dumps water in pan of water and takes stick, and he stirs and look at until he figure out what's wrong with that person and what kind of medication they need. And he goes out in the woods and gets what's supposed to take care of that.

That's way he done a lot of them, I seen.

I know one lady that she had one of those epileptic fits quite often. In fact, she had one bad one way back here in the woods, and we had to go out and get her in the wagon, brought her over to our place, and she stayed with us for two weeks, and Daddy treated her. And from there on, she never did have another one. And she lived 'til about five years ago. She got to be an old woman when she went on got blind, where she can't see. Never did have another one [epileptic fit].

So also, he worked on one case that little boy had been bitten by a rattlesnake. He walked like about five or six miles when this boy come told him. We were living right in this area. My daddy was plowing in the field when this boy come up and told him what happened. So he left; he goes over there, and I went with him. And when he got there, he got his pocketknife and split that where the snake had bit him. Swelling done got big. He got some kind of herb and beat it up in a handkerchief, and when that thing got sort of like milky looking, he set that on top of that before he did cutting, and the boy lived. And he's still living.

So, some of the things, I guess, he was good. He was called on by different people. All time people come see him. Way they paid him was they give him a chicken or pig, any small thing, you know, or basket. Sometimes they give him a dollar or two, something like that. That's how he was paid. He never asked for how much he charged for his work. People just give him whatever they wanted to.

A HOG FOR A CURE

LINDA WILLIS, B. 1953—CRYSTAL RIDGE
TOLD ON JANUARY 7, 2000

They would come to my grandfather Cameron Wesley from all over, seeking medical help. They would go to the hospital and try to get medicine to help them. If it doesn't help them, they would come waaaaay in the middle of the night, two or three o'clock in the morning. But still he had time to get up and doctor them.

And to show their appreciation, sometimes they would stay and help with the farming and all of that. So he got his pay that way.

I remember this real old lady, I don't know where she was from, but she was all wrinkled up. I guess she was about half dead when they brought her over. So, my grandfather said, "She's got to stay here couple of days. By the time y'all pick her up, she'll be well and walking, and y'all can take her home."

And he did that.

And to show their appreciation, they brought a hog for my grandfather, as sort of a payment. And I guess they gave him money, I don't know. I never saw the money part. But they used to do that. And whatever my grandfather would tell them, they would believe him and did just what he would say.

And the nonbelievers used to just want to beat him up or kill him and just do away with him because they said he was more powerful than he was. I don't know what you call these people, but they were not doctors. But they said they would put a curse on him. I guess they would study voodoos and do all of that junk to him. Then if one of us gets sick, real sick, he would say "Yep, that's what that man said he was going to do, and he made y'all sick. I'm going to get you all better."

And he used to get us better. And he used to go and get those herbal medicine and give it to us. Then we'll be all right. Like, medicine for high fever. He used to have that on hand. If we come down with a high fever, he would just boil that, and it tasted like tea. But we drank it. And next thing we know, we were up and running. [*laugh*]

BACK FROM THE DEAD

JESSICA MILLER, B. 1984—CRYSTAL RIDGE
TOLD ON APRIL 11, 2024

Cameron Wesley used to be a medicine man. He was a good medicine man. And he used to try to help people. Back then, they didn't have nothing; they didn't have no money.

One time, when my grandmother passed away, he came and asked the family to give him money to wake my grandmother back up. And they didn't have no money, but somebody came in and gave him a penny for my grandma to wake back up.

So, this is a story that my mom told me. She said they gave him a penny; they gave the penny to my great-great-grandpa, and he woke up my grandma while she passed. She was already gone, and her body was already frozen; it was outside and cold. And he came in and woke her up. So but then they didn't have no money then, so somebody came and paid for it.

HELPING PEOPLE

PETE DAVIS DYER, B. 1912—OKLAHOMA / TUCKER
TOLD ON NOVEMBER 4, 1975

I have a good friend right here. You know what "vegetable" is?

There's a church house on the other side. This boy lost his mind. He lost his mind, and he was . . . I guess it last him about two year. And I tease him, and I said to this friend of mine, I said, "Now, it's going to take me one year, and you watch," and he did. He put down in his memory book, and this guy come to himself, exactly to that date. Year.

And now he's teaching for the Choctaws. I think that's good. I'm glad I can say I helped him.

There's another friend of mine he had met. Well, he was down, and he couldn't walk, and they said he was going to die that way. I got him on his feet, and he's doing just fine.

PROCESS OF HEALING

PETE DAVIS DYER, B. 1912—OKLAHOMA / TUCKER
TOLD ON NOVEMBER 4, 1975

Note: Choctaw Central High School students interviewed Pete Dyer for their high school magazine. He regularly addresses the young men during his storytelling.

I get all my herb out in the woods. I bring my herbs in, put it up thinking it'll last me a week, and sometimes it lasts me an hour. That's how many I make.

What you boys want to know?

I use this right here, this buffalo horn to do blood outlet. This buffalo horn is what I use. This is buffalo horn, and I got a cow's horn, and I got one deer horn. Just work with three of them.

Now what else you want to know? You want to know if I do any dance to heal the people like they do around the other places and call themselves "medicine man"? They wear that big old mask and then they got that rattler shaking and saying, "Howwa waw a, how wa wa." I don't do that. No, I don't do that. But I set down and talk with them. And then I use this horn; people out here use a razor blade. I don't. I use a glass, and I sterilize my horn every time I use it.

Another thing is this: I don't drink when I'm using this horn, so therefore, I don't let people come here drinking. And if anybody going to drink here at all, I'd rather do it myself, and I don't do it!

BARTERING FOR A CURE

TERRY BEN, B. 1957—STANDING PINE
TOLD ON MAY 30, 1996

Around maybe 1920, I think the health facility was built downtown Philadelphia as far as the Choctaws in this area.

It took a little while for the Choctaws to fully trust the doctors in that facility for a lot of reasons. And the primary reason would be that, of course, Choctaws have their own health practitioners, Chahta *alikchi*, or Choctaw doctor.

Before 1920s primarily, if somebody got sick, they would go to . . . Way back then, there were a lot of doctors per community. There were just a lot of them. I know Standing Pine, Red Water, whomever they trusted, they would go up, tell them of their ailments.

Then the doctor would give medicine, herbal medicine or whatever, draw some pictures and give directions about how long to drink it or maybe come back at a certain date and check up on you.

Of course, some kind of deal would be arrived at during that time period, maybe monetary, those with money available, maybe money might be given to the doctor for services. Or if not, barter something of value, maybe eggs or whatever might be bartered in exchange for the doctor's services.

Then the patient, who would take up the medicine or whatever it was, if it was the drinking kind, you would drink the medicine. Or maybe a salve might be put on some kind of wound. Or it might be what they call "bleeding off." A lot of those doctors at that time period did: create a wound with a sharp object, go into the vein of the area where the person has an ailment, and then just cut the vein in that area, put a little horn, maybe a cow's horn, with a little hole on top, make a little suction there, let the bad blood be taken out. It's called bloodletting.

And so primarily, as far as before the health center was built, that's the way, in terms of health, the Choctaw at that time period, maybe about 1920 and before, that's how they lived and survived: by going to these Choctaw doctors.

LAPISH

GLADYS WILLIS, B. 1926—PEARL RIVER
TOLD ON MAY 23, 1996

Nowadays, they just go to the hospital and get Tylenol. But when the Tylenol wears off, it's still there.

He [Choctaw doctor] put a *lapish* on there. It's a small horn of a cow. They cut a small skin and put a small *lapish* on it. That's what was causing them to be sick. If they didn't get it all, then he would say, "Come back and I'll do it again."

They had all kind of medicine with herbs. They didn't have Tylenol.

Nowadays, people don't know how to go get herbs.

BLOODLETTING

EDDIE GIBSON, B. 1953—CONEHATTA
TOLD ON JULY 1, 2021

My father really believed in Choctaw Indian doctors, where they'd cut you. They take a razor, and they put about three cuts about this long [*indicates about an inch*]. Three cuts. And they take a horn and put that horn on top of that place that you've been hurting.

My father used to be hurting on his shoulder, on the back, all over his back. And then we'd go. Used to be a doctor in Tucker; I think he passed a long time ago. And we used to go over there, and he wanted to go get cut. He really believed in that. And he believed that it helped him, after he got cut. And he says, "I feel better."

And the guy would put that horn on top of where he was hurting and suck the bad blood out. He'd suck it out. And then he'd let it sit there for a while, let the horn suck it up itself. And after he did that, he'd put it in a piece of paper, and you could see the blood there. And it's a big old blood clot. And it was dark, and he said that was the bad stuff that somebody did to him. It was the bad blood. And my father really didn't have a clear spot on his back, because he got cut a lot by the Indian doctor.

Even little kids, when they get a little rowdy, or can't behave, they would used to say, "He needs a cutting. He needs a good cut." And they would take the little kid to the doctor and take the bad stuff out, and he was okay. A kid would be crying, rowdy, or rambunctious, or whatever. And he'd settle down after that.

And I know people don't believe Indian doctors. Well, for one thing, you can't find one, anyway. I don't think there's none. There might be one or two left, but basically, there's nobody to go to.

BACK PROBLEMS

HAROLD COMBY, B. 1955—PEARL RIVER
TOLD ON JULY 23, 1999

I went to the hospital, and they wouldn't help me. I had stayed up most of the night, and it was like a muscle spasm, and it hurt so much. Every time I moved, it would grab ahold of me. So I went to a hospital, and they just gave me some painkillers, and they said it's going to go away, just give it time.

So I said if they're only going to give me this, I'll go. And I went to see this medicine man. I went to his house and said this is the problem that I'm having. And I said my mom told me if I come see a medicine man, maybe it might help.

So he invited me in, and he told me to take off my shirt, and I sat there. And I told him my back was what was causing the problem. And without me telling exactly where, he tested and said, "Is this where it is?"

And I said, "Yeah."

And then he went around to where all the pain was at, and he said I need to be cut three times, but he only cut me two because it was getting late. And he said, "There's still something in there. I didn't take everything out, so you might need to come back."

Tom Mould: Did you go back?

Uh-uh [*negative*]. Every now and then I can feel that little . . . it's like a pain, pulling.

HERBAL CURE

FRANK BELL JOE, B. 1951—BOGUE CHITTO
TOLD ON APRIL 16, 1975

My father had some type of . . . There was something wrong with his urine. And one of the witch doctors—he died several years back now—came down there one time and made up these remedies for him. And few days later, he was back to normal without going to the hospital. So whatever they're making now is still working.

THE BETTER DOCTOR

PETE DAVIS DYER, B. 1912—OKLAHOMA / TUCKER
TOLD ON NOVEMBER 4, 1975

Even like that guy come see me. He lived at Fair River Community come see me one time, and you know what he said? He said, the doctor, she told him, she says, "Now you are fixed to have this headache and die with it." And that scared him. And she told him, she says, "Now, I can cure you if you'll pay me a hundred and sixty dollars . . . now."

Well, he didn't have the hundred and sixty dollars, and he came over, and somebody's talking to him about it, and he says, "Well," says, "You go over and see him."

So he comes see me. It didn't even cost him a hundred dollars. It didn't even cost him sixty. Just proving to him, I just give it to him. I used this right here.

His headache was gone.

See a lot of people do that in order to get money. The money is what they're after. I'm after their health, not their money. I can't see no sense in that.

REMOVING THE PAIN

PETE DAVIS DYER, B. 1912—OKLAHOMA / TUCKER
TOLD ON JUNE 23, 1976

On example, Bob. He always complained about his shoulder. I would always have to do a little bloodletting and give him the herbs. Now he's doing just fine.

Once upon a time, he had sugar so bad the doctor told him he would have to lose weight—put him on a diet. And then he was starving to death, and he lost a lot of weight, and he couldn't hardly even go. And he had to lose time at work. Well, when he know I was here, he come to me, and I gave him herbs and told him, I said, "If you've got diabetes, I've got TB."

He said, "What do you mean?"

I said, "If I had TB, I'd have a rash on both sides of the nose."

He said, "Alright," and took my herbs.

Today, that guy can work all day long, and it won't bother him.

You take Linda working at the hospital. She was in bad condition when I first come here. She couldn't hardly work.

OK, they had to lay her off on that account. Now, she went back to work, and she's fine.

You take Annie. She couldn't hardly walk. Doctor told her she had arthritis. I treated her, and today she can run, walk, do anything she want to. Still working at the hospital.

I believe a lot of these doctors over at the hospital kind of hated me because I tell them . . . I take a lot of patients off his hands, to keep them off the payroll.

LITTLE HELPERS

TERRY BEN, B. 1957—STANDING PINE
TOLD ON JUNE 10, 2021

Bohpoli love to get little rocks or whatever and throw it against trees and make that knocking sound. They love to do that. And they will turn into a ball of light about that size [*indicates about six inches in diameter*], kind of a dull color. And then, if you go near it, it's going to go like this [*waves hands apart*] and disappear. Sometimes it'll be by itself; sometimes they'll have friends.

At the old Choctaw Health Center—the one that was vacated; we have a new Choctaw Health Center—at the old Choctaw Health Center, they had a man from Oklahoma. His name was Pete Dyer, and he was from Oklahoma, and he was a medicine man and a rainmaker. And people respected him so much that they gave him an office at the Choctaw Health Center.

At any rate, Grandma had problems with her foot. And so, we're going to go see Pete Dyer. And so, we got in the truck. Granddaddy drove, and I hopped on. And Grandma went to Pete Dyer's house in Tucker community. And we drove into the house, and Grandma said, "Go see if he can see me."

And so, I went up there, and Pete came out, "Hey, come on in. Come on, come on in."

"Hey, Pete, Grandma has a problem with her feet. Can you help her out?"

"Yeah, ask her to come in."

And so, we went up to the house in the living room, and Pete said, "What's wrong?" talking to my grandma and all that. And Grandma said this.

"Oh yeah, I got the cure for you." And so, Pete said he's going to go to the woods in the back of his house and go get the medicine because he said he don't have it right there, what's needed for her leg. But before he turned out, he said, "I've got some people who could help me out. They're in the hallway there. They're jumping up and down and laughing. You see them?"

And I looked down the hallway at Pete Dyer's house, and I see nothing. Didn't hear nothing. Didn't see nothing down the hallway.

"Hey, Pete, what you talking about? I don't see anything." And he just laughed.

"These are my little workers. Don't you see them? These are my little workers. They help me out. When I go up, go into the woods and find the correct medicine, the roots, herbs from certain trees and all that, that I'm going to dig out and bring back, and that's going to be the medicine." And he just laughed. And he walked out the back door, kitchen. He said, "I'll be back in a few minutes. Give me about maybe thirty minutes or so, and I'll be back. You all just sit and watch TV."

And we did. And about thirty minutes later, he comes back with something in his hand, roots or whatever. Then he stuck those inside a milk jug, gallon milk jug, and put some whatever in it, put some water in and said, "Put it on your leg," whatever times a day and all that, "and eventually it's going to get well."

And so, we left. And before we left to go, I asked Pete Dyer, "Those little guys that you say that you have helping you? How long do they live?" And he said that it be a thousand years at a time, but they eventually die.

So, that's what he told me, Pete Dyer himself. Those little guys lived to be about a thousand years at a time. Long time.

DIVINATION

DOLPHUS HENRY, B. 1919—BOGUE CHITTO
TOLD IN 1985

My brother was sick in the hospital with pneumonia. And my dad said he's going to try to use his methods. And I believe at that time, those doctors had just about given up.

So my daddy went in there. He tried his method using this needle. I don't know how long the needle was. He used that needle right on top of his back where the bones are, and on the bones [that] run back there. And he stuck that needle right in a bone.

He said that if that needle stands up, he's going to live. If this needle falls down, he's going to die.

I don't know how long it was but found out that needle stood up.

So he says, "My son's going to live."

HELP

SUSIE COMBY ALEX, B. 1947—STANDING PINE / PEARL RIVER
TOLD ON JUNE 9, 2021

One time, they were fixing up my parents' house. They were paneling their houses inside. Daddy said it was time to take a nap, and they couldn't with them hammering and sawing and all this. So I said, "All right. Do you want to go to the house and stay?"

He said, "Okay."

So, I took him to the house. And my two girls, Nancy and Natalie, they were small girls. I told him, I said, "Do you need anything?"

He said, "No, I'm comfortable right here."

He was in one of the bedrooms, so I thought, "Well, okay, we're going to go to the store and get something."

At the time it was Sunflower; it was along here [*points towards Highway 16*] somewhere. So I said, "We're going to go to the store and get something. I need something to cook."

He said, "Okay."

So we came, did our shopping, and came back home. Then, I went into the bedroom to check on him. He said, "Did the girls stay?"

I said, "No, they went with me."

Mother said there were tiny little children in the bedroom with him. One of them came up, and he had that arm. So he said, "You're hurting right here, aren't you?" in Choctaw, I guess.

He [one of the boys] said, "Yeah."

He'd just rub it and did all the massage and all that.

He [her father] said it felt so good.

By the time we got there, they were gone, I guess. I said, "No, I took the girls with me."

And he said, "But there were three boys."

I says, "Well, I don't know."

But those big, white stones, whatever. When they were making this house, this industrial road, they broke those stones. That was *bohpoli*'s house. So, I guess they all disappeared or found somewhere else to go.

I've never really seen them, but Daddy told us. He said there were three of them. "Children," he said.

I said, "Well, I guess *bohpoli* is sitting there on the other side of the line, and I don't even know!"

SLEEP MEDICINE

GRADY JOHN, B. 1934—HENNING, TN
TOLD ON FEBRUARY 22, 1998

My granddaddy used to tell a lot of good stories. He used to talk about medicine man.

He said one day they were living in a house, and the dog was barking, coming back and forth, back and forth. So, they thought they saw something, but they went to bed.

Well, our people, we got a sort of Indian doctor.

"How about coming over to my house, spending the night with me?"

"I'm certain that I can come. You'll have something cooked for me."

So medicine man came over. And he was laying on the porch, edge of the porch. He said, "Just give me a pillow."

That dog was barking. So my uncle said, "You'll have to hit his foot."

Boy, he jumped. He was at the edge of the porch. He fell down. [*laughter*]

He said he cracked up. He's supposed to watch; instead, he went to sleep. And he fall down.

He said, "Hey, boy!" That cracked him up.

He come back right up, he said, "Well, I went to sleep."

But, "OK. I'm going back to bed. If you get tired, there's a bed out there."

But, "No. I'm going to try to catch him."

He went back to sleep.

He said, "You know, last night I caught him." He said, "That was another medicine man, come in your house."

He asked him why.

He said, "You have beautiful daughters. He wants to marry one of your daughters. But he played that medicine on you so you can sleep and get to you, as close as he can. So that's what happened. That's why he's coming closer: to put you to sleep. Next day, he'd be start coming in, trying to meet up with you, he's going to start—marry your daughter. So, that's what happens," said the medicine man.

HEALING TENDONITIS

HAYWARD BELL, B. 1948—BOGUE CHITTO
TOLD ON JUNE 30, 2021

I played baseball, and my arm got hurt. My elbow got tendonitis and stuff. The medicine man went and picked up some herbs and he said, "We're going to go and boil these herbs in water."

So we did, and he said, "Put your arm over where the steam hits it, right there on your arm." And he said, "Don't get it too hot. If it gets warm, move it back and forth." But he said, "You can be able to just keep it like that. If you get warm, do that for thirty or forty minutes, stop, and then do it the next day and so forth."

He said it would go away. So it did go away. So I know it worked.

CHILDREN'S DOCTOR

SUSIE COMBY ALEX, B. 1947—STANDING PINE / PEARL RIVER
TOLD ON JUNE 9, 2021

Momma, she didn't really consider her as a doctor. She used to treat little kids, like toddlers on down. Throat thrush, she used to treat them. We didn't know how she did it because she'd take him to the bathroom to do whatever she was going to do. Whatever medicine that she made, she didn't tell us what tree it was from, what leaves, but she would boil it and all of this and have it.

Sometimes she knew if somebody's going to come. So, she would make enough to wash it out and then give it to the parents so they could do that, to clear up the thrush.

Nowadays, this one lady, she said my mom treated her child when he was a baby. So she has grandchildren that was like that, so she wanted to know how she did it. I said, I have no idea. She didn't tell us how she did it. I knew she used some kind of tree bark and then some leaves, but I pretty much thought, because we had a persimmon tree in our yard, I thought maybe that's what she's using. I never did ask. She used to do that, and they would ask.

Now, we call it like "acid reflux."

I could find it, but it's hardly around no more. She taught me, and I could find it, the type of leaves. There was one that used to be on the side of my yard, but it's not there no more. It's dying out. I guess, when you don't use it, it just dies out, I guess.

TURNED ANKLE

CARMEN DENSON, B. 1956—STANDING PINE
TOLD ON JANUARY 12, 2000

In my time, I've gone to a couple of medicine men. I had my ankles keep turning on me. When athletes play, they turn ankles or turn their knees. My ankle keep turning on me. Even I be walking down the street, all of a sudden, little pebble, I step on it, I turn my leg, ankle.

One time, I turned my ankles about three times in one month. And when my ankle turns, it's like a big egg on it. Takes about two weeks to bring it down and heal it. So I got really tired of it, really sick of it. And I was what you call . . . I wasn't a skeptic, but I wanted help bad, you know.

I went to this doctor, and he told me to come back a week later. He gave me something to rub on it. I did that. Went back week later.

Usually, when a medicine man talks to you or works on you, he'll look at you and know what kind of person you are. And if you are, you know, if you like to be joking around, he's going to know you. If you're serious, he's going to adapt to your attitude.

So he was talking to me and everything. Sometimes they do tell, and sometimes they won't say nothing. And this guy told me that he was going to cut it and put a horn on it. He said he was looking at it, said, "Both of your ankles." Said I turned both of my ankles.

And he did that, and it felt pretty good when he did that. And he sucked all the blood and whatever they want to suck out of it. And he told me, "You like to play ball."

I said, "Yeah." He said, "This woman got you long time ago," he told me. "It's a spit," he said. Yeah. He put it in a pan, like, put the blood and things in there. It looked different, kind of. He said, "It's a spit. A woman did it to you a long time ago," he told me. I knew it was. I started turning my ankle when I was about fourteen years old. I was about eighteen, twenty when he was doing this to me. He said it'll be alright now. Ever since then, yeah, sure enough.

Tom Mould: Did you know who it was?

No, no. He said it was an older woman, probably gone now.
There's something to it.

HERBAL STEAM CURE

LILLIE GIBSON, B. 1919—CONEHATTA
TOLD ON AUGUST 5, 1997

My daddy used to be an Indian doctor. There used to be a lot of them, but you can't hardly find any now. I can't when I need one.

My daddy's house used to be like a hospital. People would come in. He'd use herbs, medicine. I know a little about it because I used to sneak around and try to see what he was doing. [*laughter*]

He would see his patients first, whatever's wrong with them. And then I guess he knows what's wrong with them after he examined them and all of that. So he took to the woods and bring little sticks; I used to think they were little sticks, but that was the herbs. And he'd come home, and he would cut it up about so long [*indicates a couple of inches*] and bundle them up and tie them. He hardly ever cut them like these doctors.

He'd used to just boil the medicine, and he'd dig a hole in the ground. Mama would have some quilts; she'd just put it around the patients. And he had these little sticks across there to cover that pot. He don't really cover it because he needs holes where that steam will come out. The patient would have to lay there for either an hour or two hours. Then have them, whatever's wrong with the person—I don't know why he did this, but I saw him do this—he'd keep that person for a week. He went in their home.

My husband's brother, he was never able to walk since he was born. He came and stayed with us. We had to pull him in a little red wagon, pull him around because he couldn't walk.

All of us, well, there were three girls, my older sister, middle sister, I'm the little one, and he's the baby. We used to pull him in the little red wagon and pull it to where, well, my daddy had a little house built out there where he could doctor anytime, whether it's raining.

So when he laid that person down, he put them on a sheet, a plain sheet. So he got all right for two weeks. And he begin to walk. And my daddy kept him another week because he wanted him to be strong enough to walk. And so he did walk.

JEALOUSY

HAROLD COMBY, B. 1955—PEARL RIVER
TOLD JUNE 4, 1997

Some of the elderly will say, "Don't brag." "*Isht ilawata*," which is actually bragging. Never brag because people will get jealous and put a hex on you or whatever.

Because one experience I had was this.

I was working here back in the '80s. I'm divorced now, but at that time, my wife called up here crying, and she said somebody's trying to get into the house. So, me and this other officer went to our house and checked around, but we couldn't find nothing. So we came back.

And about thirty minutes later, she called again, and she was crying. She said there's somebody on top of the house trying to, you know, get in. So we went out there again but couldn't find nothing. She explained to me that whatever it was, it was like jumping up and down on the roof. So, my partner said, "Well, why don't you . . . it's kind of quiet anyway, why don't you just go on and leave and stay at home?" So I did, and we kind of discussed it.

And then, there was a bird. It sounded like [*whistle/blow sound*], like that. And it was at night. And I've always been told that birds don't chirp at night. That's what my mom says. So then my ex-wife said, "You know, it's been like that for almost two weeks." I didn't hear it.

So I went out and checked, and it stopped. I came in, and it started up again. So I turned the lights back on, and it stopped. So after that, we just turned the lights off and just stayed inside the house. And that thing kept chirping all night long.

So finally, whatever it was, my mom said it wasn't real. So we went to see a medicine man. And I don't know what he did. He came to the house and did something; I don't know what it was. And he told me, "You know, people are jealous of you and your wife," because she was a registered nurse, and I had just finished college and got my degree, and we were doing OK. And he said that was his reason for someone trying to put the hex on us.

So he made some kind of potion, and he went around the house and did some I don't know what. And he said, "Tomorrow . . . tonight, he's . . . whatever it is is going to be in that tree. And the next night, it's going to be beyond the road. And the next night, it's just going to get on further and further. And then about four days from now, it's going to be gone."

And it sure happened that way. Seemed like it just kept on going further each night. And by the fourth night, we didn't hear it anymore.

That's why I say we live in two worlds. I bet you if I went and talked to Neshoba Central [High School], one of their classes, they'd laugh at me.

BAD MEDICINE

HENRY WILLIAMS, B. 1945—CONEHATTA
TOLD ON JUNE 24, 1997

Growing up, I used to like baseball. And I used to hit pretty good too. Sometimes, one home run a game, two home runs a game, hit it way over there. And I didn't have no problem. But some players would act like somebody cursed on them and got sick. But I never have. So I don't have experience on somebody cursing me. Maybe they tried, but I don't know.

And also, using that herb to be a better player, I never used it.

My uncle, you know, found this root in the wood one time. We was going to go play ball. We walked through the woods. So he found this herb that's supposed to be something to make you a better player or something. It made me sick.

I hit the ball pretty good, so I didn't think I was having problems, but he told me I could do better if I take that stuff. So he give it to me, and I chew it and swallow it. At the game's start, I felt dizzy, vomiting. I can't catch a fly ball either. Dropped it, strike out two or three times in that game.

So when we got home, my daddy said, "What the hell wrong with you?"

I told him about it. Soon as I finished telling him that he made me eat that stuff, he took his belt out and whipped me. Toss and turned. He told me never, never use that type of thing just to become better. I can be a better person without it, he said. So, every time they talk about it, I slip away; you know, I don't want to listen to it.

PROTECTIVE MEDICINE

HAROLD COMBY, B. 1955—PEARL RIVER
TOLD JUNE 4, 1997

If you have a spirit in your house and seems like it's taking over, and you can't get rid of it any other way, my mom says confront it, speak to it like there's another person in the room. Say, "Hey. This is my house. Get out of my house." And open the door for that spirit.

And I've had people tell me that it has worked. I've never seen it done; I'd be scared anyway. But my mom says talk to him; scold him; tell him to get out of the house. "You no longer live here. This isn't your house anymore."

There's another way, long time ago, we used to call it "*shobochih*," which means "to smoke," smoke the house. I guess that's what medicine men used to do: take cedar and smoke each house. And I know that some people still do that, using tobacco, cedar, or the rabbit tobacco, sage. That's just to bless the house, drive out the spirits and bless the house.

The best thing is try to prevent it [bad medicine]. Some people will use hot pepper to warn, keep bad spirits away, hexes, things like that.

I know some people that will put salt in their shoe when they play ball. So that will keep the bad medicine away from them.

Now, I see some people, like stickball teams, they'll smoke themselves with sage or cedar to protect themselves. And like during the powwow, that's what they'll use to bless the grounds.

BARKING AT SPIRITS

MELFORD FARVE, B. 1961—TUCKER
TOLD ON JUNE 1, 2021

I keep remembering this story.

There was a little old . . . they said he was a medicine man. My dad told me one time he was probably about ninety-eight years old. And they were sitting—his mom, my grandma—they were sitting on the porch. At that time, they were being cooled off by the night too. So he said that . . . They saw him pass by, and they said they saw him. I don't know what his name was, but they called him over. "Come sit with us for a while. Come rest." So he comes over there and sits with them.

They're telling each other stories.

And all of a sudden—there was a pack of dogs that they had—and for some reason, the dogs started going to one part of the yard, and they were barking, crazy.

And they were like, "What are they barking at?"

And that medicine man kind of looked, and he said, "There's a spirit . . . " or dead people, or spirits, ghosts . . . I don't know what he saw. He said, "They're over there, and they're trying to get through the yard."

But I don't know if the dogs were holding them back or if the dogs were just barking. So that old man said, "You want me to take care of them for you?"

So they said, "Yeah. Yeah."

So he went over there, and he started making these gestures, like his hands, to go this way. He was just making . . . using his hands. So after a while, the dogs actually started following something because they were barking at the woods, but then they started following and barking to a different direction. Like if somebody was walking by your house, and the dogs bark, and they're going to follow that person for a while 'til they're out of that little territory. They followed whatever, and they were barking along the way.

He said, "I got rid of them for you." But then he told my dad, "Do you want to see what they look like?" He put his hands together like this [*makes a hole between his two hands*], and he said, "Come over here and look through here. I'll show you what they look like."

And my dad being curious, he wanted to go, but my grandma snatched his shirt and said, "Don't you do that. If you look at them, you're going to die." So she pulled him back.

But I remember him telling me that story one time.

HOME REMEDIES

Although naming the specific herbs used by doctors in their medicine is generally not shared, the herbs used in home remedies were intended to be shared widely. People needed to be able to administer basic healthcare to their families, and so people shared their recipes for treating colds, fever, aches and pains, sore throat, teething, body odor, warts, insect bites, snake bites, and bad dreams. Some of these remedies follow the basic principles of homeopathy, where a person treats "like with like" so that a snake will draw out its own poison, a scratch with a quail feather will make a person a faster runner, and whipping a person with an eel will make them strong.[8]

As with medicines made by Chahta *alikchi*, herbal remedies are made with local plants found in the woods nearby. Further, both the woods and nearby fields offer animal products for ensuring health and comfort as well. Squirrel brains are used to treat teething, cow fat is used for aches and pains, and snake skins are used to cure warts. As many stories humorously attest, medicines were created for efficacy rather than taste.

RATTLESNAKE BITE

PETE DAVIS DYER, B. 1912—OKLAHOMA / TUCKER
TOLD ON NOVEMBER 4, 1975

If a rattlesnake bites you, kill that rattlesnake, cut off a piece about this long [*indicates eight to ten inches*], tear it open and lance where it bit you, and slap that on there and tie it. Let it go for about an hour and a half or two hours and then take it off, and it'll just draw its own poison out.

Remember that always. Always remember that.

You boys get snake bit, you kill that snake, cut off a piece that's about this long, about eight or ten inches long, just cut it open, guts and all—and this is where that snake bit you—then slap that on there. Just put it on there and get your handkerchief or something and wrap that on there real tight. And that snake will draw its own poison out.

CURE FOR WARTS

TRAVIS WILLIS, B. 1958—PEARL RIVER
TOLD ON JUNE 14, 2021

A lot of the time, it was Grandpa. Henderson Tubby. He would do warts. He would take a snakeskin and rub it all over the hand or whatever it is. And he'll tell you to go that way, whichever way, either left or right. But he would say, "Go that way. Don't look back. Get rid of it."

But it actually worked.

TRADITIONAL REMEDIES

STAFF OF THE *NANIH WAIYA* MAGAZINE
PUBLISHED IN WINTER 1974

For Warts

1. There is a plant (milkweed) which is about two feet high and which was used for making warts disappear. This plant gives out a milky, white juice when cut. The juice is put on the wart that has been cut and bled. The wart will go away soon after this is done.
2. Rub cornbread or biscuit over the wart and throw it to a black hen. The hen will eat the biscuit or cornbread, and the wart will soon disappear.
3. Take a straight pin and get it red hot and stick it through a wart that has appeared.

For Diarrhea

The roots of blackberries, when dug up, washed, and eaten, will help diarrhea.

CURE FOR THE COMMON COLD

PETE DAVIS DYER, B. 1912—OKLAHOMA / TUCKER
TOLD ON NOVEMBER 4, 1975

If you got a cold, I'll tell you what you do. Get you a lemon. Squeeze lemon; you don't have to squeeze them unless you want to. Cut the lemon up and put about this much water, let it boil, and while it's still warm, put it in a glass and then put some sugar in to your taste. Not too sweet. Just bitter enough where it'll cut those flames out of your throat. You drink that or either suck a lemon.

CAMPHOR TREE

CARRIE TUBBY, B. 1914—RED WATER
TOLD ON NOVEMBER 1, 1973

The camphor tree grew up in the forest or along the riverside. The tree leaf is real dark green; it's tall. The old people used to say that the tree leaves were for cold medicine. They used to give the medicine to their children.

BLACK JUICE

DELAURA SAUNDERS, B. 1950—BOGUE CHITTO
TOLD ON JUNE 29, 2021

They had a lot of home remedies that my mom didn't take us to the hospital. But I do remember this jar of black juice that she had all the time that we would have to drink. It tasted like awful tea. [*laugh*]

BLACK DRAUGHT

TERRY BEN, B. 1957—STANDING PINE
TOLD ON JUNE 10, 2021

Grandma made me go to church unless I was sick. And if I was sick, this is how she knew I was sick. There was a medicine called "black draught" during that time period. If I didn't want to go to church for whatever reason, or even school, Grandma would come in with that bottle and say, "Hey, if you're sick, let me give you that." And if I was sick, I would take it. And if I didn't want to take it, she knew I wasn't sick. So she'd made me go to church or school.

NATURAL BATHS

LOUISE WILSON, B. 1950—BOGUE CHITTO
TOLD ON JULY 29, 1999

They said "Don't shampoo your hair too much. If you do, when you get older, you're going to get real cold."

And you know how a lot of women get cold, old women, they have to wear a sweater or something? She said that's what causes a lot of that. You don't take care of your body. My grandmother says we have natural oils that come out of the system. And she said, long time ago, they used to get in the dirt and really rub it in good. And it's just like taking a bath, and you get rid of that oil. And she said, "If you notice, there's not that many full-blood Indians who have body odor. It's because if they do these things, like going into the dirt, cleaning themselves real good, it's just like being clean. It's just a natural thing. But you don't want to smell either," she said. [*laugh*]

So the young kids, she didn't mind if they went playing in the dirt and all that. But once a week, you'll give them a bath. But that was fine to them.

I always wondered, "Why don't you give them a bath every day?" But she said that's why they're healthier. I didn't know.

Still to this day, I question that in my mind because I give my grandbaby a bath every day. That's one good thing: they're washable. They'll get sick real often, too. So I said, "Well, does that have anything to do with it, too?" I don't know. But I can't stand them to be dirty, so I don't do that. [*laughter*]

But back then, they didn't have bathrooms and all of that. You go into the creek. But if you're working out in the field or kids are out there playing that they get in that dirt and rub it, she said. But the older people, that's one of the things they used to do: they just get out there and rub with the dirt. She said we're made of dirt, but that will take care of a lot of that oil that secretes from our body, which makes the smell.

COLD OR COUGH

HAROLD COMBY, B. 1955—PEARL RIVER
TOLD ON JUNE 1, 2021

I hadn't had it in a long time, but one of the things that she used to make was, we call it *ashíla*. It's cornmeal. They mix it up, maybe about a cup, mix it up, and then you have the squirrel boiling, and they would pour it in and stir it. They would put in cayenne peppers and seasoned it with black pepper. That's some good stuff now. And especially they would serve it to us when we got cold or cough during the wintertime.

STRONG MEDICINE

HAROLD COMBY, B. 1955—PEARL RIVER
TOLD ON JUNE 1, 2021

We had a relative. Sometimes he would come to the house, like Sunday morning, intoxicated, and he would just come and tell stories about Mom. And my mom would get pissed off. It's like, "Hey, Chį chokka iyá. Go home."

We'd have a good laugh.

But then sometimes he would leave his whiskey bottle full or half full. Then mom would take that and put a peppermint stick in it and make a cough syrup. But if we needed it, she only gave us one teaspoon.

But now people say if you have a cold, drink peppermint schnapps, and it'll clear your sinuses up.

TEETHING NECKLACE

RAE NELL VAUGHN, B. 1964—PEARL RIVER
TOLD ON MARCH 14, 1996

There's one [Choctaw doctor] in Bogue Chitto that's a baby doctor that knows about teething and stuff like that. Even my grandmother knows a little bit about that.

They used to wear a necklace. It was made of little twigs. I can remember back in the mid '70s, they were still doing this. They don't do it anymore.

It's just not any twig you go and pick up. It's a particular plant. I think you boil it. I can't remember. Anyways, thread it up, and it's a necklace.

They wear it during the times when they're having a tooth . . . and even longer! They wear it until I think all their teeth come in. I can't remember. I know they wear it for a long time. We used to see babies wear it. You don't see that anymore.

TEETHING REMEDY WITH SQUIRREL

BERDIE JOHN, B. 1965—RED WATER / CONEHATTA / STANDING PINE
TOLD ON MARCH 14, 1996

What my dad did on mine was he killed a squirrel and got some . . . I don't know which part. The inside part. I think the brain part. I think that's what it was. He took it, and he boiled it and everything and then just rubbed it, and that's on their gums when they were babies before they start teething. They didn't have no problem with it.

WÁK BILA

RAE NELL VAUGHN, B. 1964—PEARL RIVER TOLD ON MARCH 14, 1996

I remember, now that we're talking about babies, using *wák bila* [beef tallow]. You would heat it up. It was for fever. I remember she said to heat it up and with my thumb, put it on the belly button. That was supposed to help with that when they get sick.

And in Mama's refrigerator, that *wák bila* is still in there in the cup, and that's what she uses.

ACHES AND PAINS

MARK PATRICK, B. 1969—O̱TOKLO (CONEHATTA) TOLD ON JULY 12, 2021

We used to use *wák bila*, which is beef fat off of beef. And they would put it in a mayonnaise jar. And they might add a little bit of liniment, a little bit of rubbing alcohol, or whatever. And they'll mix it up and then just rub it on your arthritis and cramps or whatever.

Or if you got a cold, you'd put that *wák bila* right here on your neck. And then you might want to put a handkerchief or something around it, and it'll cure the sore throat, things like that.

CURE FOR SORES

LORENA ALEX, B. 1952—HALLS, TN / BOGUE CHITTO / PEARL RIVER TOLD ON JUNE 10, 2021

My sister, when she was little, maybe ten years old, she used to have these big sores on her leg. I mean big ones. And Mom would go out in the woods. There was this certain grass, leaf, that she would go out and pick it and boil it, let it cool off, and use it on her leg.

You never questioned Mama what it is. I don't know if it was secret or what, but she used to use that on her leg, and it [the sores] would go away.

To this day you can't tell she had big sores.

SMOKE HEALING

RAE NELL VAUGHN, B. 1964—PEARL RIVER
TOLD ON MARCH 14, 1996

When you get a cut—I don't know if it's necessarily your foot—but I know my mother got a cut, and I remember my grandfather digging a small hole in the ground and did a smoldering where it was smoking. She had to put her foot over it and keep it like that to get the infection or whatever to help it heal.

I can remember it was during the summer because we all sat under the shade tree while she was doing that. I can remember them doing that. It was just the burning. I can't remember exactly what he was burning, but I know they were burning something.

It's like when you play washers—that size hole.

MOSQUITO HANDLER

MELFORD FARVE, B. 1961—TUCKER
TOLD ON JUNE 1, 2021

The social way for us was nights. When it was so hot, we didn't have an air conditioner, so we had box fans in the windows. In the day, the house is pretty hot. So we would go outside and sit outside, just like we're doing now. And my job was to be the mosquito handler.

Mom would get some of her old cloth rags and stuff and tie it on the end of one of these limbs or something. So my job was to walk around waving the smoke . . . We'd put it on fire, and smoke so the mosquitoes would stay away. And then they started telling stories.

BAD DREAMS

BRIAN BILLIE, B. 1973—RED WATER
TOLD ON JUNE 30, 2021

My sister-in-law would say, "Get an old timer knife, one with a wooden handle. Nanohmi makalika̱ ish ka̱naho̱? Hopaki? [Do you know the kind I'm talking about? A long time ago?] It's not the shiny ones.

It's the old . . . looks like old metal, black. Y'all know what kind of knife I'm talking about? The kind your mom cuts up chicken. Your grandma would call it "old timer knife."

Put it under the bed if you have bad dreams that just can't go away. Or if you have a kid that's having those kind of bad dreams, you don't tell them, but you just put it under their bed, and something about it, it works.

Now if your chim allat yot dream, ish anokfillit atapakma, ishi̲ tryat mah. [Now if your child dreams a dream like that, if you think about it too much, try it for them.] Maybe it'll work. Give it a try.

How to soothe things like a *nishkin halbah* [sore eyes]. That is the medicine man as well.

FASTER, STRONGER

HAROLD COMBY, B. 1955—PEARL RIVER
TOLD ON JUNE 4, 1997

When you want your child to run fast, you can scratch their sole with quail [quill], and they'll be fast runners. If you want them to be strong and stout, whip them with the skin of an eel.

It seems like it's true. Because one of my sisters is real fast, and that's what they did to her. And one of my brothers, he is small, but he's stout, and they said they whipped him with an eel skin when he was small.

RITUALS, CUSTOMS, AND LAWS

When tornados threaten Choctaw lands, the elders used to say you could split the storm in half with an ax so that the storm would go around them. When the world seems out of balance, people may seek the solace of the woods, or the healing vapors of the sweat lodge. More mundane customs also offer people a way to connect with one another, whether by establishing familial relations through formulaic greetings or by maintaining the expectation of future interactions by never saying goodbye. These traditions are linked through habitual performance to the many other rituals and customs developed as part of other aspects of daily life already explored in this book. Most of the rituals and customs are performed as a cultural norm based in social expectation. Some, however, are part of a more formal system that can accurately be understood as law.

The Cameron Wesley murder trial, for example, remains a common narrative shared within the community, often used to explain the traditional Choctaw judicial system in contrast with Western court systems and laws. The murder and trial took place in 1940, recent enough to remain in people's memories but long enough ago that traditional Choctaw laws were still being practiced. The stories are clear: Cameron Wesley was tried in a court by a White judge and jury in Noxubee County. He was found innocent; the killing was declared self-defense. But Wesley was famously quoted as saying that while he had been acquitted in the White man's court, he still needed to face the judicial system of his tribe. Dan Isaac explained: "When he was found innocent, he told the judge, 'You find me innocent, but now I got to go to my people, and they have to find me innocent. This is White man's laws. But when I get back, I'm still going back to my people to see if they find me innocent.' And the judge didn't understand what he's talking about. But he called it his blood for blood law, the Choctaw blood for blood law." The Choctaw, too, found Cameron Wesley innocent.

It was the last time the traditional Choctaw legal system was used to handle an accusation of murder. By the 1970s, the Choctaw had adopted a judicial system modeled on Mississippi state and federal legal systems, a move strongly encouraged by local BIA agents. By the 1990s, however, as the tribe gained increasing autonomy from the BIA, the tribe began to revise and expand their judicial system. By 2000, they added a peacemaking court system called "*ittikana ikbi*," or "to make new again." Modeled on the Navajo peacemaking system and rooted in the ancestral Choctaw cultural norms of peacemaking by community elders, *ittikana ikbi* is a mediation court offering a restorative system that many see as more fitting with Choctaw culture, which seeks balance and social harmony, rather than the punitive system favored by state and federal court systems.[9]

AVOIDING TORNADOS

BRIAN BILLIE, B. 1973—RED WATER
TOLD ON JUNE 30, 2021

The old people used to say, "Chahta alhiha ano pano ámiti atokósh oklah nana, 'Ná, pishnano, pishnano a̱tiyachi̱h,' oklah áchit biliya áttok. Ná kanimay kiyo, a̱t iyachi̱h, hikma kanimi katoh Chahta alikchi atoh," kind of like folklore. Ohmiho̱ oklak makáchaykattok mato. Nana, ax ishicha mitima tikba ishmichichakma palhlhalanah tokloh tobanah tornados. [Because the Choctaw people come from here, they always said, "It will go over us. It won't do anything. It will pass." And some say it's the medicine man, kind of like folklore. Like that, is what they used to say. They just say they (the medicine men) take the ax, put it in front of the one coming, it splits it and can turn into two tornados.]

I took it as folklore. *Hikma*, [and] the tornado, it went over Red Water, it went over Pearl River. Chahta aki̱ni kano ikissoh ki̱sha I mean kiyoh amawah [The Choctaws themselves have not been hit yet. I mean, I don't think so] because the last one that, before the sirens were put up, there's one that went over the Health Center and landed on . . . Remember that park in town that messed up all the backstop of the softball [field]? That one jumped over Pearl River. It came down away from Pearl River. The old school, one went over that one, a tornado.

Sacred. Chíhówat pisht a̱ya chi̱nih tokósh oklah pi̱nokhakloh hitoko̱ pa̱ makálíka̱ people at hapi̱ kaniyah aki̱ni kakósh hapi̱ kaníyak ma nanash achokma kato tikba ma i̱lat tikba mitish tikba hachi̱ hiyowachi̱h. [Because God will take care of us. He has mercy on us. So I say this: even though we lost people, when we lose people, what is good is ahead. There are others coming forward to come stand before you all.]

LISTENING TO NATURE

BOBBY JOE, B. 1953—BOGUE CHITTO
TOLD ON JULY 30, 1999

Myself, I'm proud to be a Choctaw. I'm proud to speak my own language.

Sometimes I go the woods, and I find the spring water somewhere where it's cool. I sit out there and just thinking; listen to birds singing, listening to the winds blowing, making that sound of that trees. Sometimes, if you understand, that tree can talk to you. Sometimes, the birds can talk to you. Even if you go somewhere, little stream, water stream, if you hear that water, if you think hard, you be understanding. Even that water can talk to you, too.

ANSWERED PRAYERS

HENRY WILLIAMS, B. 1945—CONEHATTA
TOLD ON JUNE 24, 1997

You ask for guidance, a better life. I think that part is true. It clears your mind, and you think better. You do things right.

I pray for my house. I was living in a trailer. A hundred-year-old trailer. I tried to change my life in better ways. Start going to sweat lodge. I prayed for the house that I want; I prayed to God in the sweat lodge. The guy who teached me how to run the sweat lodge—you pray to God but don't expect miracle the same night. Just sweat and be prepared, he says. Whatever you ask for, just be prepared, it'll come to you.

I started sweating about three years ago. I started praying about a house. It finally came. He said God will use other people to give me answer. I think that's what it was. I was calling superintendent's office for somebody. I told him, "I need a house. I'm going to look for a double-wide trailer."

He says, “No, no, no. Go see Jim Walter.”

At that time, I didn’t think about it. But it seems like God told him to tell me to go to see Jim Walter. It’s no down payment; it’s no question about how much money you got in bank. Nothing. I just filled out an application one Saturday morning. They told me to call back Monday morning. They told me it was approved. And now I’m living in there now. So that’s a miracle for me. Because we tried double-wide trailer, and they wanted two thousand dollars down payment. We didn’t have no down payment money. We could borrow money, but it’s going to be a rough time paying loan and house. I was worried about that. They was ready to sell us double-wide trailer. But I have to borrow two thousand dollars. I didn’t want to have to do that.

I think that’s what I was telling him about. We was talking about school, but I wind up talking to him about house, and he said, “Go see Jim Walter,” on the phone. I think this was Friday.

And I called over there to Jim Walter in Meridian.

Say, “Come on over in the morning and fill out an application.”

And I did.

And Monday, we was dancing, my wife and I. [*laughter*]

So that was true to me. In sweat lodge, in our ways, prayed in our language. So I got my answer.

And I got my other answer: I got elected to Tribal Council. I told God if I don’t get it, no hard feelings, I said. [*laughter*]

If a guy better than me representing our community, he deserves the position. If it’s me, get me on that council. [*laughter*] That’s my second miracle.

SHARED VISION IN THE SWEAT LODGE

JAKE YORK, B. 1950—PEARL RIVER / CONEHATTA
TOLD ON JULY 29, 1997

The sweat lodge they built recently, I mean, this is a recent sweat lodge by the spring where I’m telling you about. They just built that thing about two or three years ago.

These young fellas that used to hang around there when it was first built, they said they were all around that sweat lodge and decided to sleep. Either they all had the same dream, or they were put to sleep or saw the same thing.

This one guy was the one who told me—him, and I think he mentioned about three or four others that stayed with them at that sweat lodge.

He said he thought they all went to sleep. And they said there’s a ball of fire started swinging around where they were out there, around that sweat lodge. Kept going around, around.

He woke up; he said others woke up too. He didn't want to say anything because he thought he was the only one who experienced it. They were all kind of quiet sitting around because they all were awake until something like three o'clock in the morning. He said he couldn't resist no more, so he told, "Hey, I just had a weird dream." He said, "I thought we were all here, and there was a red ball of light going around us, this area."

And the guy that he was telling it to said, "You know something? Hey. I saw the same thing."

And pretty soon, all of them had either the same dream or saw the same thing.

But one boy told me he thought he was asleep; he thought he dreamt it. They all had the same experience. And they all thought that they were asleep.

And I said, "How could they have the same dream?"

They said they left out of there; they didn't spend the whole night. [*laughter*] Whatever it was startled them or scared some of them. They said they left out of there.

TOBACCO AS THANKS

DAN ISAAC, B. 1968—PEARL RIVER
TOLD ON JUNE 27, 2021

There was an elder in Bogue Chitto, and I stopped by her house one day, and I gave her some tobacco because I wanted to know about stickball.

And I actually stopped at Carmen's house one time. This is years ago and gave his dad some tobacco because I wanted to know about the ball, the *towa*. And his dad had told me that sometimes they would use the skin of a frog to cover the ball because it would make it bounce more.

GREETINGS

JAY WESLEY, B. 1975—STANDING PINE
TOLD ON JULY 27, 2022

Generally, when we're greeting people or introducing ourselves, we usually say it in Choctaw, and it's, "Halito sa hohchifo yat Jay Wesley." Basically what I've said, a little, "Hello, my name's Jay Wesley. I'm from the Standing Pine community. My mother's Rita Frazier; my father's the late Danny Wesley." The reason for that is so that way, it's our ancestry, people would know who is who, and then where you belong, and if you get in trouble who they can tell. [*laughter*]

GOODBYES

BRIAN BILLIE, B. 1973—RED WATER
TOLD ON JUNE 30, 2021

Just give them a hug, and you tell them, "Chi pisaláchíni." You tell them, "I'll see you later."

Then one day I realized there was no goodbyes, and I asked Mom and Dad, I said, "What's the word for goodbye?"

"We don't have one. You can say, 'I'm leaving.'"

But you know, "Iyalih ókih." I'm going. "Chi pisaláchíni" [See you later]. And the elder would say, "Hm. Omih" [Alright], and let you go on.

RETURNING TO NANIH WAIYA

DAN ISAAC, B. 1968—PEARL RIVER
TOLD ON JUNE 23, 2021

I don't really call it a "ritual." I call it a "ceremony." They're coming home to reconnect, find out where they're from. This is the homeland if they're Choctaw.

Let's say they're Oklahoma Choctaw, and they say, "I want to come home."

"Come on, I'll take you to Nanih Waiya." I've done this for twenty years.

We had Native American workshops here in the Casino Convention Center. I had a guy named Charlie Tailfeathers. He said, "Where's your sacred area?"

I said, "Oh, you've never heard of Nanih Waiya." He goes, "No."

Well, this guy's an older powwow guy, and I took him to Nanih Waiya. And I told him the story, and man, the guy just had tears. He said, "This is awesome because my grandfather told me that I would see a place like this one day."

And he said back then, he was like five years old, and his grandpa told him about a sacred place and described it. He said, "My grandpa described this place to a T." He said, "I'm an old man. I don't care if I die today. My grandfather's prophecy for me is fulfilled. I saw your sacred site, and it may be our sacred site."

I said, "We're all one, so yeah, it's yours too." He just cried. I was like, "Wow."

I thought he fell down because he got on his knees real quick. "Are you okay?" I was like, "Are you alright?"

He was like, "No, I am fine. I'm just going to pray." And so, he prayed, and he cried. He told the story. It was very emotional at that time. It was very good.

One guy was Cherokee. He said he's Cherokee, and I said, "If you say you're Cherokee, let's go." I took him to Nanih Waiya.

And he said, "Man, this is the best time I ever had in my life. I can't believe you just brought me. You didn't even question, and you didn't look for my card."

I said, "What card?"

He said, "My Cherokee card." He was going to show me.

I'm like, "No, don't worry about it. We're Natives. We don't care about cards, and paperwork, CDIB [Certificate of Degree of Indian Blood]. What did you think I was going to do, check your blood?"

He just started laughing, but those are the kind of people that Creator brings to me. And as a warrior, I have to do what I'm supposed to do.

One of the prophecies the elders had told me is when the Creeks or Muskogee, when the Cherokees, when the Chickasaws, when they come back and say, "Where's our mother?" we're the last. We're the Choctaw. We're the baby of the group. We're supposed to take our big brothers back to Mama.

They come home and say, "Where's Nanih Waiya?" I say, "Come on, I'll show you."

And that was one of the responsibilities I believe we're supposed to have is take them home. It was good. There's a lot more I can say on that because I've done this for years.

We were in Greenville, Mississippi. Cherokee guys all walk in with their outfits. They're all . . . got the turbans. They've got the silver. They've got their nose ring, earrings. I'm like, "Wow, you guys are cool. Look like you stepped out of the movie set."

And he goes, "No, we're Cherokee."

I said, "Well, what are you going to do?"

"Well, we're going to tell stories. We're going to dance."

I'm sitting in the front. I'm like a little kid, "Cherokees!" They start telling a story, and I'm like, "Wow, I know this story, but what's the beginning?"

He said, "The beginning is unknown, but the part that we can tell you, we're from somewhere in the South and that we were told to go to the mountains and the lands where the mountains seem to be on fire because they're smoky."

I'm like, "I know the first part to this story." So after it was over, I walk up to them. I'm like, "Hey, guys, 'Siyo, siyo,' because I know how to say *siyo* [hello], greetings in their language. "Hey." I said, "Hey, man, where's the leader?"

The leader steps up.

"What's your name?

He was like, "Oh, I'm Sonny."

I was like, "Oh, okay. Well, hey, you was talking about your story, and you said somewhere deep in the South where you originated, right?"

He said, "Yeah, we don't have the whole story, but we know that as our beginning, somewhere deep in the South."

"I know where it is. I can take you."

"What are you talking about, 'You know where it is'?"

"There is a story." And I said, "Let me tell you the story."

Okay, so here's my one story: Back in the beginning of time, the Creator himself, Great Spirit, wanted to make man. He said, "I will make man. I will build a mound, and the mound will be in the shape of a woman when she lays down, and she's pregnant. And on the east side, I will make an opening. And from that opening, I will bring four brothers."

And the Cherokees were like, "Wow, this is good." They're all sitting back, all noble, all cool. Kind of a stereotype, but I love it.

In that opening, the Great Spirit called forth, "Muskogee, Kocha mitih!" [Muskogee, come outside!] He called forth Muskogee, the brother. A warrior, all wet, brand new, walked out. All muscles, and all wet, he walked out. His name was Muskogee, a full-fledged warrior ready for battle. Behind him were people walking out of that Nanih Waiya Cave. There were elders. There were women, children. There were what we call "medicine people," holy people. All came out, and they laid out in the sun, and they dried their bodies.

And they looked up because Muskogee says . . . He puts down tobacco, *hakchoma*, on the ground. And the Creator says to him, "Muskogee, chishnato hashi imma ish iyachi̱h." [Muskogee, you will go towards the east, towards the sun.] You must travel east, where the rising sun . . . and there, I will show you where you will become a great nation."

Muskogee takes his people, and they travel.

And the Creator says to the second warrior . . . He beckons him to come out. "Cherokee ho mitih!" [Cherokee, come out!] Out steps this warrior, Cherokee, all wet but brand new and strong, tall. His people come out, the elders, the young people, the medicine people, the holy people. They all dry their bodies, and they see the footprints of their brother to the east. They put tobacco down, and they pray. And the Great Spirit says, "Cherokee, you travel north, a little bit more northeast to where you will see the mountains that seem to be on fire." AKA Smoky Mountains, Blue Ridge Mountains. "There you will be a great nation, and I will show you." So, they walk out.

The Creator says, "Chikása. Chishnak kiya ho mitih!" [Chickasaw. You, too, come out. Come out.]

Chikása comes out, full-fledged warrior, a man. A warrior with his people, the elders, the young people, the teenagers, the infants, the youth, all of them with their holy people and their medicine people. They see the footprints of their eldest brother, the next brother. They put tobacco down, pray to the Creator, "Katimma pi nato ílhkolih?" [Where do we go?]

And the Creator says, "Chikása, you see the footprints of your brother, Cherokee. Follow that footprint 'til you get to a certain point where I will show you. And there, you will be a strong, mighty nation." Chikása follows to a certain area where there's a place where the Cherokees had stopped and made fire. "This will be your home."

So the last warrior that the Creator says, "Ishtayopih amalla, mitih Chahta." [Last of my children, Choctaw, come out.] He calls the final warrior, the name is Chahta, the last one.

Ishtayopih means last. When you have children, the first one is the first one, but the last one is called *ishtayopih*, meaning the last one.

Ishtayopih comes out. His name is Chahta, full-fledged warrior. All his people, the adults, the youth, the infants, the medicine people, the holy people . . . They all dry their bodies, and they see the footprints. Muskogee, Cherokee, Chikása . . . and they put down tobacco. Chahta puts down tobacco and says, "Aba abiníli chiya mah, pishnato katimmak ilhkólih?" [You who sits above, where do we go?] "Creator, our father, where do we travel to? We see the footprints of our brothers."

And he says, "Chahta, chishnato pakini pako̱ hash ma̱ ya chi̱h hicha hash akanallinah!" [You will stay right here. You all do not move away!] "Pakini hash ma̱ya billiya chikih. Nanih Waiya pat chishki hikma anato chi̱ki siyah." [You are to stay right here forever. This Nanih Waiya is your mother, and I am your father.] "Chahta, you are the last. You must stay here always around your mother, for Nanih Waiya is your mother, and I am your father."

And again, the elders say, and I believe, Chahta was also instructed when that eldest brother, elder *brothers* come, bring them here to see their mother.

And so, that's what I do. And when I see a Muskogee, I say, "Hey, eldest brother."

And they're like, "What?"

"I'm Chahta. It's me."

"What are you talking about?"

"We all came from one place, man. We came from Nanih Waiya."

And they say, "Tell me the story." And I tell them the story.

"That makes sense. I've heard that before, but I never knew all the details. You can take me there?"

"I'm *supposed* to take you there. Come home. You come to Mississippi. I'll take you to Nanih Waiya, where we come from, Nanih Waiya Cave."

I wanted to tell you guys [YOP Choctaw youth] this story because I'm supposed to tell it to Choctaw. I'm supposed to tell it to Creeks—which is known as Muskogee—Cherokees, and Chickasaws. Those are who I'm supposed to tell it to, but I wanted to tell that story because every chance I get, I have to. I have to do my best every day to pass that on, so you know who you are, who your relatives are, where you come from. Why you're here.

There's a reason on the Trail of Tears. When they removed 90-something percent of our people, there was a group that said, "Wait, we're not supposed to go. We're never supposed to leave our mother."

People can say, "Oh, they loved the land, and they stayed."

Yeah, we loved the land, but it was mainly because of our promise, Chahta's promise to stay, guard the mother. But that part, I wanted to make sure I tell you guys, and I tell anyone, anytime I get in front of Choctaw, Chahta people, I have to tell it.

RITUALIZED PROTECTION

HAROLD COMBY, B. 1955—PEARL RIVER
TOLD ON JULY 23, 1999

Some of the things she [my mother] has told me is that during wartime, you're supposed to hang out your Choctaw shirt on the porch or have those kettles in the yard so that the people fighting knows that there is a Choctaw family lives here, and they were supposed to not bother them.

Just recently, somebody told me that during the Civil War, same thing happened. When Sherman came through, they said they would burn the Southerners' houses, but they would leave the Choctaws' dwellings alone.

CHOCTAW JUSTICE

CARMEN DENSON, B. 1956—STANDING PINE
TOLD ON JANUARY 12, 2000

The Choctaw, when you kill somebody, then you sing, and you sing to indicate that you killed somebody. Everybody comes out to find out if the person is truly dead, and there is an investigation about it.

If it was self-defense, you're off the hook. But if you killed him just for the sake of killing him or whatever, then they would determine you have to die too.

And they would go get some expert arrowhead shooters, bow and arrow, and they would set a date for you to die. And before that date, if they danced, you danced with them; if they ate, you ate with them, like nothing happened.

But that date comes, you're going to go stand there, and you're going to be executed because of what you did.

Then your uncle, on your mother's side, if you run away, you get scared, he says, "I'll do it," and he goes there, and they execute him. And you can come back, and they won't even think anything of it. That's the way the culture's different from other cultures,

So, that's what my father told me, that it's a tradition. But if you didn't run away and get executed, everything was evened out then; it would go back to the same it was before.

That's one of the traditions he told me, that if you murder somebody, if it was self-defense, you can go free, but if not, if found guilty, you're going to be executed. And that date comes, and you get executed. And the grave, you go lay down, they measure you, and that's the way it was.

SELF-DEFENSE

CARMEN DENSON, B. 1956—STANDING PINE
TOLD ON JANUARY 12, 2000

Cameron Wesley was also a medicine man.

You probably heard the story about his trial and everything. His son, Barney Wesley, told me. He was talking about Cameron when he was young and that this guy, neighbor of his, got jealous because of what he can do. But this other guy was also into that medicine and stuff. And he got jealous, and he got drunk, and I think he had a gun. And this is the way he told me.

He came into Cameron's house to shoot him, but he was drunk, half drunk maybe. They went out the back when he was at the front trying to get in, and they ran. It was an open field, somewhere through a pasture that had a fence around it. And they were going into the woods after they crossed that fence. And the man that was after them noticed that they were taking off the other way, and he went after them. And they went under the fence to get through it. And Cameron, he was the last to try to get through it, he caught up; that guy caught up to him, and they struggled, and he shot him. And he died.

And they had a trial after that. And I don't know if you know, but this John Stennis used to be a senator for a long time in Congress. He knew Cameron Wesley. He was the judge at the trial. And probably that's one of the reasons why, being Choctaw in those days, when you kill somebody, there was no such thing as manslaughter. [*small laugh*] But he knew John Stennis, and he was the judge, and that's probably one of the reasons why he got off on self-defense.

That's how Barney Wesley told me.

MURDER TRIAL

HUBERT WESLEY, B. 1933—MASHULAVILLE / BOGUE CHITTO
GARA WESLEY—MASHULAVILLE / BOGUE CHITTO
TOLD ON DECEMBER 18, 1992

Gara: This is the man [*pointing to the grave of Evans Tubbee*] that Hubert's father accidently killed, and they had two trials on it. They had a White man's trial, and then they had a Choctaw trial, and Stennis was the judge at that time.

Hubert: That was the old ways, old traditions. They had to have their own trial. Although they called it the "White man's trial," that's what the newspaper said when they acquitted him because he had to go through the trial laws.

They had not written anything like that. But that was their beliefs, and that's what they did. Brought him [Cameron Wesley] over here. The sheriff had to bring him to Macon because the little chief was in charge then when they had the trial. If Choctaw people find him guilty, then he's supposed to have killed himself, digging his own grave and kill himself. But if he wouldn't kill himself after digging his own grave, then one of the oldest sons supposed to have.

But it didn't turn out that way because the Choctaw people acquitted him, too, and because little chief [John Cotton] recommend—worked more or less just like a judge—and he recommended that he done this thing in self-defense.

They acquitted him.

Of course, my dad didn't mean to do what he did; he just protect himself and us. And he set the flower on his grave and everything. Picture of it, we got newspaper piece. It was on a Sunday afternoon, sunny day just like today. I was small then, but I seen what happened. I was with him when it happened.

He [Evans Tubbee] was I guess about quarter of a mile from us. His family lived up the hill, and there was a trail from his house to our house. It was Sunday afternoon, and we heard a lot of racket. What he done, Tubbee, he got drunk and beat up his wife and children. And we seen him running towards our house, running just as hard as he could run, come running. He was behind them [his wife and children], raising all kind of cane.

When they got to our house, Daddy let them on in the house and shut the door.

So he talked to Tubbee when he got up to the house, tried to talk him into calming down, try to get hold of himself. Well, he got worse, so he just slammed the door.

Then he started throwing rocks and anything he could through the window. All that time he done that, Daddy told the womenfolks, my mother and all of them, says, "Y'all go out the back door." And there was a ribbon cane patch. "Go through a cotton patch, little hill up there. Y'all go on back to the house, go through that ribbon cane patch and go fishing. Just get out somewhere and go fishing." So they did.

I stayed with my daddy in the house. Another boy I used to run around with—we were little fellows—and after he let the women leave the house where it was safe, he told us, "OK, let's leave."

So he picked up a single .22 rifle and said, "We're going to hunt. Let's go hunt squirrel."

We hit the back door, went through the ribbon cane patch, and as we come up the rise there, he seen us. Here he come.

Back then, they had a fence pole—make a fence that was like about eight foot long, pine; they were green—and he had one of them. And he followed us. Just when we got to barbwire fence, edge of pasture, and he got closer and closer to us, and he was raising all kind of cane. My daddy said hurry and run and get under the fence. So we run under fence, and just as I got under the fence, and I looked back—I was still on my knees—when I looked up, and I seen daddy throw that rifle, that single rifle, on his shoulder. Kind of glanced back, but he wasn't aiming, and pulled the trigger.

I think he meant to scare him. I've always thought he meant to scare him. But he pulled the trigger. This guy just dropped the pole down and laughed like I don't know what, you know. He said, "I wasn't going to hurt you. I was just playing."

But in the meantime, he'd done beat up his wife and kids. So what he meant there, we don't know. But anyway, he laughed and walked back few yards, just fell down. And we thought he went to sleep. But my oldest brother come over there and went over there and looked at him and seen blood and turned him over. He had shot through the split pine. The bullet went through there and splattered, I guess knocked a big hole right in his heart because they accused him of shooting him with a .45 pistol. It wasn't. It was a big old single-shot rifle.

And they come got him and put him in jail in Macon. Noxubee County jail. And he stayed there, I don't know how long. That was in '40.

Gara: 1940. Happened in June. Stayed in there until they had trial in September.

Hubert: John Stennis was judge then, and Daddy's lawyer was Lucas. And he always carried me in where he was at and left me in there with my daddy lots of time. And I spend lots of time with him in the jail. He would come and pick me up and carry me different places. It come a rain. It rained for days and days and days, and the water—backwater off of Noxubee River—come out on the bank almost to the courthouse, where nobody can't cross at all. So we was on the other side of the river for so many days.

Gara: During the trial.

Hubert: During the trial. Then, course, when the trial was over, it was at night. The Choctaws lived there on the courthouse grounds for days and days, just sleep out there. It was a lot of news media was there and lot of thing was going on there that Choctaws never did leave the court grounds until it was over.

After that when they acquitted, they brought him over here, have another trial.

PEACEMAKING THROUGH STORYTELLING

BRADLEY ALEX, B. 1955—BOGUE HOMA / PEARL RIVER
TOLD ON JUNE 30, 2021

The court up here is the European type. And there's no forgiveness. There is no forgiveness. If you're guilty, you're guilty. You still have that record on you for the rest of your life.

But that's not the way the Choctaws used to deal with any kind of disputes, arguments, and such. It was through talking. And you resolve things. If not, sometimes, if it was very serious or something, there used to be some people or family, they were banned from the tribe. But anyway, that was back then.

When they brought this [peacemaker court] in, they have three things that we're able to use as a peacemaker.

A judge.

The tradition and customs that teaches.

And current religion. It's in the [peacemaker] code.

So I am a Christian, and I use the Scriptures in here. The third thing is, in biblical form anyway, that you can use stories or illustration or life experience, in order to reach to them, to open their eyes and such.

So that's where this peacemaker court is, that what they're trying to reach is that apology and forgiveness truly from the heart. I like to especially work with married couples. Each of the courts, if they believe that it can be handled here, or sometimes they have a hard time or something like that, especially in a child custody or something on that, they send it here. Divorce.

Even without court, they can come. If they have some sort of a disagreement or something on it, they can come. And they have—at least about since I've been here, about two or three times—money problem, they resolve through here.

Youth court, they could . . .

One example is one kid, very destructive, had damaged property and such. So police officers had to . . . Youth court wind up taking them, and they said that he wouldn't talk. The mother was here also.

Anyway, I got to talk to him, and he wouldn't talk. He wouldn't talk. And so I sat by him, and I said, "What's going on? You won't talk or anything. What's bothering you?" I said.

So I went back to my childhood, and I said, "I had this one girl I had a crush on. She broke my heart," I told him. I said, "I was so upset, my stomach was in knots and everything. I couldn't eat, couldn't sleep and everything."

He looked up, and he said, "You went through the same thing I did?"

I said, "Is that what's wrong?"

He said, "Yeah."

I said, "That's what you were upset about?"

He said, "Yeah."

And I told him, I said, "Can't you talk to your mom or your dad?"

And he said, "My dad don't live here. He lives somewhere else."

I said, "What about your mom?"

"I don't know if she would understand."

I said, "Anybody that's in your family? Your sister or somebody?"

"My sisters, no way. Uhm-hm [*negative*]. Uhm-hm [*negative*]."

"What about your friends?" I said, "Somebody that you can . . . "

"My friends? Uh-uh [*negative*]. They pick on me. They wouldn't . . . "

I said, "Okay. Yeah, I know. Okay. I believe you."

So he said, "Yeah, I don't have nobody to talk to."

And I said, "So that's what it was?" I said, "You didn't know how to act right?"

And he said, "No, I just got angry." And he said she fell for somebody else or something like that, so she was just, "Bye," and he didn't know how to get the rejection. He couldn't handle the rejection. He just said, just anger came out and hurt.

And so we talked, and I told his mom what was going to happen. I said, "Just remember, you probably had gone through the same thing."

And she kind of said, "Oh, that's what it was. Oh, yeah."

So I reminded her, "You probably had gone through something like that. Just be sensitive to him," and such. "And if you can, let him talk to you."

And she said, "Okay."

And later on, when I saw her, the mom, she's like, "Oh, he is so helpful at home. He has completely changed."

And I've seen him. He's a lot better. And I told him, "Hey, there's going to be more girlfriends in your life." He is only fourteen years old right now. So I said that "Probably, this was your first crush."

He said, "Yeah."

I said, "Yeah." I told him, I said, "I still have that first crush here just a little bit. I remember."

FAMILY INTERVENTION

BRADLEY ALEX, B. 1955—BOGUE HOMA / PEARL RIVER
TOLD ON JUNE 30, 2021

The men, we're not supposed to hit a female, physically abusing, or manhandle a female. If you did, you're considered not a man. If you stole something, you were considered a thief; if you had assaulted a woman, and so a woman beater.

I was about seven years old. One of our oldest cousins, she got married to a guy, someone I don't know where he came from, but I've known him after that.

We lived off the reservation. And when we moved on the rez, there was a couple of us that they were sharecroppers. So they came out. Some of them stayed off the reservation until later on, but we were all a group; families were grouped together. And so when we moved on the reservation, my oldest cousin, she had got married. Everybody liked him. He was a hard worker. He worked with my father. They worked in the forest. Pulpwood, I think they call it. And I don't know if they were hauling it or whatever, but they went and sometimes the women would go help them also.

But anyway, this man later, probably about within a year or something, he beat her, and we got the word to come to my aunt's house. When we got there, we were almost the last one; the dirt road leading to the house was pretty long. We got there. Anyway, there was cars all over, and they were parked on both sides. And when we got there, there were our family; they were all from on my father's side. And they were all there. And so, my aunt was the one who was speaking, and she said, "Is this everybody"?

And everybody looked and said, "Yes," within the vicinity within the community.

The husband was standing in front of the porch, by the steps. He was standing there; he had his head down.

My uncle, my cousin's stepfather, actually, he was a gentle man. He was a gentle man. I used to like him. I had never seen him raise his voice. Anyway, as a father, he's supposed to speak on what he [his son-in-law] had done, but he couldn't; he got choked up. He said, "I can't speak what he had done."

And my aunt kind of got upset with him, but so she told what the husband had done, their son-in-law. I don't remember what all it was, but I just could not understand that anybody what could do that.

After she told them what he had done, she said from then on, he is considered not a man, and "Hattak kiyoh okih himaka̱ isht hikit iyaka̱" [He's not a man starting from now on]. And everybody turned their back.

They shunned him. And our parents turned us around.

But me, I always get in trouble for some reason, but I turned around, and I looked at him to see what was wrong with him. I thought his appearance or something would be changed, I guess. That always stick to my mind. But my mother turned my head, and she told me, "Don't speak to him. Don't look at him until we tell you."

"Okay."

And I remember they told us, "Y'all can go home. That's what we wanted to let y'all know."

So everybody started leaving. But they started calling out the men to come back with some certain men. I don't know how many men they call back, but one of them was my father. And my father said, "Y'all go wait at the car. I'll be there."

So we went, and later, the men started coming, family started leaving. We were the last one, and my father came over and said, "He's going with us." And

I had a problem with that. I'm not supposed to look or talk to him. Okay. How do I do that? But he came with his belongings or clothes or bundle of clothes, I don't know what he had. I think it was a pillowcase or something and his clothes stuffed up in there. So he came and sat next to me. And he always used to rub my hair all the time. So, he came in and rubbed my hair. What am I supposed to do? I would get a spanking if I talked to him.

But we all went home. And we had a barn at the back of the house; all the tribal homes had barns back then. And so there was a stall. One stall had a floor in, and it had a gap that the wall to it had a slat, and you can see through it. And it had a door also. And I guess you might say, just turn it to close it. But that was my responsibility of keeping that stall clean. That was one of my chores.

And so when we got there, my father said, "Help me to get it ready." And my responsibility was to turn around and teach my younger brother. He was about a year younger than I was. So there was a cot. So put that . . . well, *he* did. And we got a pillowcase, sheets, blankets, water to wash his face. We had a little table, a wooden chair, broken mirror, oil lamp. Everything he needed, it was there.

And it was not cold. I don't know if it was springtime or fall or something, but it was nice weather during that time. And whenever they were going to eat, they let us know. They were supposed to eat first. But if not, my father would tell, "Y'all eat first that we will eat later." But whenever they came home from work, they sat under the big oak tree we had in the back of the house, and there was a sitting area that every day there was other men came and join, I guess they already had picked whoever's [cotton or crops]. They're supposed to come. So they came and spoke to him. They spoke to the husband. And it went on for about a week, week and a half, it was less than two weeks, but it was on a weekend. Whenever they got through, it was before noon, I remember. They said, "Y'all get ready. We're going to go." And the rest had already went and told the other families.

So, when we got there, we were the last ones there. Everybody was there. And I think it was my father was the one that spoke on his behalf. And I don't remember the husband speaking, but it was my father that spoke on his behalf. And then my cousin, the wife, agreed to talk with him. And she came out. That's when we saw the bruises and such still. Both eyes was . . . I mean, it was just a bruise all over her face and everything.

I always remembered that.

I asked my mother, "Did he do that"?

And she said, "Yes, that's why we're here."

And she had a Choctaw dress. She was slender. And she had long Choctaw dress all the time. All my aunts, cousins, they wore Choctaw dress, and she did all the time.

And then when she stepped out, her sleeve was up here [*indicates just up from the wrist*]. That's the way it was made. And so we saw the bruises on her wrist.

And it was just, she had gotten beat up, I guess kicked in some way. When she stepped down, even her ankle area, it was bruised. And it was like, everybody got mad. I know that everybody got mad when they saw that. But she was willing to speak with him. So they went to the back of the house, and some men and women went to the back kitchen area, keep an eye on them and for us kids not to go to the back. And we were instructed, "Don't be looking or anything." Guess who looked? [*small laugh*] They told me I'll get a whipping if I don't keep away, and, "You going to get a whipping."

But eventually—forty-five minutes to an hour, so it was a long time, and they were holding hands. They came, and when they came, that's when everybody . . . we came back, and she spoke of all the promises that he made to her, and he will never, ever do that again and such. So, everybody went and congratulate them and pat them on the back and shook their hands and everything. And that the instruction from, I don't know who gave, but he said from this day forward, nobody speaks about it, that everything has been taken care of. So, forget this ever it happened. And the majority, if you forgive somebody, you cannot go back and use it. You never talk about it again once it's been settled.

And that's what's a peacemaking court is about, is to settle it. Whatever that issue was, it's dead and gone. But the effect of it is here, sometimes fear, guilt, both of them, have hurt feelings and unforgiveness and such. But that's our aim at peacemaker court is to find apology and forgiveness, really from the heart.

And I remember, I was probably in my late thirties or something, and then it always bothered me. "Why did they say that once a man hits a woman or manhandles or push her or beat her or something, they were considered not a man no more? How do you make it right?"

That's where my mother had to set me straight, sat me down and said, "Do you remember this?"—[*then, to the YOP students*] what I just told you.

I said, "Yeah."

She said, "That's where he had to be taught again or had to be taught because he was from a different family, and maybe he was never taught that way or raised that way."

So basically, she told me that, "Well, he was not a man when he did that, or he was not really mature, and he didn't understand a female, a woman." He was not ready and that he was not mature enough to have a woman. And that he didn't have a control of his anger or that he didn't have patience also.

And as she was telling me this, I always thought, "Okay, you now understand that we follow the instruction of our elders." The old men, they had responsibility as a grandparent, what their responsibility was as the grandmother, and also the aunts and uncles, they were a part of their niece and nephew's life. They were the second parent.

INFIDELITY

LOUISE WILSON, B. 1950—BOGUE CHITTO
TOLD ON JUNE 10, 1997

My grandfather talked about punishment that was done. The punishment were if a man who was married was found with another woman, or vice versa. He talked about that. And he said that what usually happened was if a man was found with another woman, the woman that he was found with was more or less kicked out of the family where she was from.

And he said that the man was taken and was beaten up by the women, her kinfolks, the wife's kinfolk. And they had a right to do that. Now the wife may or may not be involved in doing the beating, but he said it was the wives, sisters, aunts, grandmother, mother-in-law, all of them, he said. They had a right to beat him. Once they got him, they beat him up. And usually, he said, they didn't do it again because they got beaten up pretty bad, he said.

But now the woman that he was messing around with was kicked out of the family and the clan. It was hard for her to find a place to be. But now if she was married, that was even worse, he said. Sometimes, he said, a long time ago, his father told him that women were killed, even then. But now, I don't know if that's written in history or what, but that's what he said, what my grandfather told me, was back then, women were killed. But to his recollection, he said it was worse because each clan or each area that the woman who had been caught with a married man, she was going from one place to another. And she might could stay a day or so, but then it was like she was lost; she was kicked out. They all knew, said, "Well, oh, she did this." She was treated worse than . . . I don't know which was worse, whether it was the man or the woman. [*small laugh*]

But he said that's the way it was then. She was shunned from any of the community people. But the man, since he's the sole hunter and food provider, he got beat up, but he got a chance to stay within that family. But most of the time, very rarely after that would he try to leave the home again.

ADVICE FROM THE ELDERS

Throughout this book, there is a genre of traditional lore sometimes referred to in English as "no you don'ts," in Choctaw as "*nána ish mihchay kiyoh okih.*" But parents and elders teach more often what one *should* do, rather than what they should *not*. People remember practical tasks being taught by example. The same was true of good behavior, but rarely did elders leave it up to eyewitness alone to ensure the youth recognized and applied important values to lead to a good life.

During my many conversations with elders over the past thirty years, I rarely asked explicitly what people wanted the youth to know. Instead, I asked about origin myths, *shokhannǫpa*, and all the stories they heard and retold that made up their shared oral tradition. Yet whenever I was with the YOP students, and sometimes even when I was not, elders talked about the things that youth needed to know, offering advice not only for how to be happy but also how to live in harmony with others. Like older generations the world over, many opined that the youth were not being taught these values, instead living in ways that would shock and sadden their ancestors. Others took a proactive approach, offering advice rather than critique. Finally, in 2021, after elders made it clear that sharing these values was of paramount importance to them, that it was in fact their job as elders, we started asking them directly what they wanted the youth to hear.

The need to record the advice from elders, and heed it, has been particularly acute following the devasting losses the tribe faced during COVID-19. "So as far as the tribe here recently, we've been through a lot, and a lot of our elders passing because of the virus," Terry Ben said, turning to speak directly to YOP students Lakylee Martin, Thomas Saunders, Meka Willis, and his own daughter, Taylor Ben. "So if you know of any elder, your family members, people up in age, get with them, learn from them, their life experiences, their tradition because there are not that many anymore now."

The Mississippi Choctaw have proven their resilience again and again in the face of disasters both natural and manmade. They have done so again in the face of COVID-19. New elders will replace old. But Terry Ben is also right that as old generations die out, especially so quickly and in such numbers, inevitably, so too does some of the knowledge individuals built over a lifetime, an accumulation that includes knowledge from their ancestors that extends their understanding of Choctaw life by centuries. New generations will keep adding to this history with their own stories, their own advice, their own wisdom. There is change, and life goes on. As Brian Billie reminds us, in Choctaw, there is no word for goodbye in Choctaw. "Just give them a hug and you tell them, 'Chi pi̱saláchíni.' You tell them, 'I'll see you later.'"

ONE TIME TO LIVE

MARTHA FERGUSON, B. 1949—STANDING PINE
TOLD ON JUNE 4, 2021

I always want to try different things. So mine is, I go in there to learn whatever they teach me instead of fighting back. Advice from my Grandfather Whitman, he always says, "You got one time to live. So go learn; learn everything you can. Then you can say, 'I lived it, learned it. And I know how it's done.' That way you'll see it and believe it. But don't be afraid to ask questions either. If you don't ask questions, you're never going to learn." So that's his advice.

BE FRIENDS

PETE DAVIS DYER, B. 1912—OKLAHOMA / TUCKER
TOLD ON NOVEMBER 4, 1975

I want you boys to know that this is one thing we all ought to learn to do is be friends to each other and not hate one another. Be friends so that we will work together.

TALK IT OUT

SALLY ALLEN, B. 1959—CONEHATTA
TOLD ON JANUARY 10, 2000

My dad was never prejudiced, never, at least not with races.

As far as our siblings, there were four of us kids. He taught us not to fight. "There's just four of you. You get mad at each other, who's going to be there to help you? Always stick together. We're a close-knit family. We don't believe in pouting. [*laughter*] We fight, but we don't get mad and stay mad, like some families do."

And he used to tell us if a person treats you wrong, you go talk to them. If they don't want to talk to you, you just go talk to them and say, "Hi." They don't talk? You still try.

You don't ever treat anybody different or bad. At times that's hard to do. [*laughter*]

PREDICTING SUCCESS

GRADY JOHN, B. 1934—HENNING, TN
TOLD ON JANUARY 15, 2000

We can succeed if we work hard more. This is going to happen. My prediction: we can educate more our Choctaw kids; we can do more. These younger generations coming up, they're a lot greater than when I was coming up. They're thinking more and better than we do because they're going to school.

RESPECT NATURE

HENDERSON WILLIAMS, B. 1947—CONEHATTA
TOLD ON JULY 25, 1997

As far as the dances, the tribal members respect the animals. Nowadays, it's not a point of worship anymore, but just to respect animals.

A lot of people will just come out and kill a snake, any snake. Some of the people I know would tell me—and I would do the same thing—if you see a snake somewhere, you learn to identify it. If you see a rattlesnake, if you see a cottonmouth, water moccasin, if you see a copperhead, you kill them because they're poisonous. But if you see these other snakes, the ones I know that's not poisonous, I leave them alone. Why? Well, because they have a useful purpose.

Like the king snake. They kill rats and mice. Rats and mice can invade your house. And those are useful creatures, that king snake. So why kill a useful creature?

That's something that I believe might have been passed on from generation to generation also. Just a small fraction of the total Choctaw culture I know is to have respect for the creature if one is not harmful.

RESPECT YOUR ELDERS

MARTHA FERGUSON, B. 1949—STANDING PINE
TOLD ON JUNE 4, 2021

Grandfather said, "Don't say nothing; just go do it. Whatever's been asked you to do, go do it no matter who it is. The older people are the one that ask you to do something, you go do it, whether you like it or not. Don't be saying, 'Why? What for?' Forget it; just go do it. That way, they will all respect you from then on. And they will start trusting you."

PEOPLE FIRST

HAROLD COMBY, B. 1955—PEARL RIVER
TOLD IN 2016

My parents used to say, "If it's material things, it's going to deteriorate, so why fight over it? Always put people first. You can always replace a chair, or a pickup truck, but you can't replace a person."

I think these are things we need to teach our folks, especially the young, so they will have an identity of who they are and be proud of who they are.

OTHER PEOPLE FIRST

HAROLD COMBY, B. 1955—PEARL RIVER
TOLD ON JUNE 1, 2021

I had a question one time, and I asked my mom; at the time she was alive. She said, "If we're going to talk about death, we need to talk about the living first." She said, "If you have a spouse, you take care of that person; you work for that person. If you have any kids, you take care of them. You work for them, you provide essential things like shelter, food, clothes, stuff like that. Your wants or needs come second because your kids, they're small, they can't take care of themselves."

I think that a lot of our people have lost that responsibility, or they never been taught. So they don't know how to carry it out.

STAY OUT OF TROUBLE

FRANK BELL JOE, B. 1951—BOGUE CHITTO
TOLD ON APRIL 16, 1975

The only thing my parents told me to stay out of trouble as much as I can, and don't go around drinking. But that was the only thing that they offered me as a suggestion, and that they told me to take care of my family when I got married.

SMILE

AMANDA BELL, B. 1969—PEARL RIVER
TOLD ON JULY 1, 2021

Grandma Anderson, Thelma Ben Anderson, she was confined in the wheelchair. I remember her wearing a flower-pattern dress. We would play with my dolls. We would talk, talk, and talk. One thing that stood out from her was her smile. I mean, she *smiled*, literally. Therefore, I can say that when you face life's challenges, smile. Even when it hurts. So with that said, smile. That's what she bestowed upon me.

KEEP THE PAST ALIVE AND KEEP GOING

CARMEN DENSON, B. 1956—STANDING PINE
TOLD ON JUNE 27, 2021

My great grandfather, his name was Willie Solomon. His Choctaw name was Mosholi̱t abi̱, and he was a medicine man as a senior. He did not have an education, and he is right from the root of the Choctaw culture. And he said, "Get as much education as you can, but don't forget your language."

That's how I think about it today. It should be instilled to our young people. You don't forget the past, but you go on, you know?

TEACH THE LANGUAGE

BERDIE JOHN, B. 1965—RED WATER / CONEHATTA / STANDING PINE TOLD ON MARCH 14, 1996

That's what my grandpa used to tell me: don't ever lose the Choctaw language. They could speak English and all that, but that was given to you. That was a gift. Don't ever lose it. If you ever have kids, always teach them Choctaw.

KEEP YOUR LANGUAGE AND YOUR CULTURE

MARK PATRICK, B. 1969—O̲TOKLO (CONEHATTA) TOLD ON JULY 12, 2021

Don't be an apple. You know what that means, right? Red on the outside; white on the inside. Don't lose everything that you've learned and has been passed down from generation to generation. Continue to grasp and continue to practice your specialty, what identifies you.

And I mean this with sincerity, hold on to your language. That's what gives you your identity. It's not your hair; it's not your skin; it's not the way you walk or what you eat. Fry bread is not what makes you Choctaw. It's not eating hominy that makes you Choctaw. The number one identity is your language and your Choctaw songs.

That's what makes you Choctaw, so don't lose that. Don't lose that identity. Struggle to hold onto it or strive, I should say, to hold onto it. And that's a way that you honor your ancestors and our forefathers who were here before us, who fought so hard so we could sit around this table and talk about the things that they've said, the things that they believed and what they stood for. So hold onto those things.

KEEP IT ALIVE

DAN ISAAC, B. 1968—PEARL RIVER TOLD ON JUNE 27, 2021

Let's respect the people that lived before us, *hicha Chahta imanno̲paha̲ ikhapi̲ kaniyo kiya* [and let us not lose our Choctaw language]. Let's not lose the language because you're here, I'm here, all these things are here because somebody fought to keep it alive.

KEEP TRYING BUT ENJOY THE RIDE

BRIAN BILLIE, B. 1973—RED WATER
TOLD ON JUNE 30, 2021

Y'all should be proud of yourselves. Y'all going to accomplish a lot of things because y'all are able to go out of your comfort zone and talk. Just keep on trying. The only time you fail is when you stop. When you stop, you quit on yourself.

But right now, y'all haven't reached twenty-one. Twenty-one, I'm going to do this, I'm going to do that. There's plenty of time. Don't be in a hurry to get to twenty-one. Y'all enjoy the ride. Enjoy the moment. Enjoy the trips.

LIVE A GOOD LIFE

HAROLD COMBY, B. 1955—PEARL RIVER
TOLD ON FEBRUARY 24, 2022

I think one of the things is that this will be good for everybody. This basically came from my dad. He used to say that "ihitchali̱ noktalha̱ hicha." There was a third thing that he used to say. *I̱hitchali̱* which means "vengeance" and *noktalha̱* is "jealousy." "Yakomikako̱ naksíka ish bohlicha ish a̱yak matoh achokma ish attana," which means that when you put these things aside, you will have a good life and live a good life.

NOTES TO STORIES

CHAPTER 1: THE LAND

SHARECROPPING

Fifty Cents a Day—Dolphus Henry. Compare to the interview with Annie Tubby titled " . . . A Dollar a Day" in the *Nanih Waiya* magazine (Wallace 1977).

Everybody Worked—Gordon Sam. Gordon continues to describe other chores on the farm, including killing chickens for Sunday dinner, as well as bailing and hauling hay, chores that fell to the boys rather than the girls. Chopping cotton was a common task in the field as the plants began to gain height. In order to avoid crowding the plants, excess plants were chopped up, and weeds were removed.

Friday Treats—Lorena Alex. Lorena also fondly remembers the rare occasions when they would all dress up and ride about ten miles in the back of her father's pickup truck to get a cheeseburger at the local cafeteria in the next town over.

Abusive Landowners—Linda Willis. Linda's story helps explain her Uncle Hubert's story that follows about why Cameron Wesley moved his family in the middle of the night to escape the violent and abusive sharecropper he worked for.

Moving in the Middle of the Night—Hubert Wesley. He added that the community in Mashulaville lasted until the 1950s, when families started moving to reservation land. He also shared this story in his interview for the Center for Oral History and Cultural Heritage at the University of Southern Mississippi (December 14, 1999). One of the reasons landowners might have been upset about Choctaw families leaving is that the system virtually ensured the sharecroppers would be in debt to the landowner at the end of the year, creating a form of indentured servitude. With little legal recourse, the only way out was to sneak away. Mississippi State Senator David Jordan grew up sharecropping and describes a similar situation among Black families: "We'd get $12 per bale, and we had to pick hard in order to have money to buy food during that season. If we had a rainy week where we couldn't pick at all, then we would have no money.

We would have to go get food and substances on credit. Some came out in the hole five or six times, and they never did get out of the hole. So what happened, they caught the midnight train or bus and headed to Chicago, and they never found them. Course that was the only way to get out of that miserable situation" ("Sharecropping in Mississippi" 2023).

Cheated into Debt—Barney Wesley. He sums up a bit later saying, "If they didn't have gardens, they sure will go hungry." When he mentions White landowners not wanting the Choctaw to come back, he may have been referring at least partially to the impact of New Deal subsidies that led many landowners to evict their sharecroppers in favor of mechanization, as well as minimum wage laws that encouraged large-scale plantation-style operations (Davis 2017).

Cheated—Melvin Henry. Staying in Mississippi or moving to Oklahoma was a difficult decision for many, with families moving back or splitting up between the two states. Although Melvin describes stories of regret in having moved, Esbie Gibson describes her grandfather as "one of them that hid and didn't get to go to Oklahoma," suggesting a change in views of the second removal in the first decade of the 1900s, where initial reluctance shifted for some to a missed opportunity.

Catching a Cheater—Bradley Alex. Bradley clarifies that the man cheating them was a White man.

Moved to the Delta for Work—Terry Ben. Terry ends by giving the example of a colleague whose parents moved from Pearl River to the Mississippi Delta area for work, only moving back to Pearl River when land and jobs became available.

Moving to Reservation Land—Frank Henry. The land allotment was part of a land purchase program that began in 1921, though a formal reservation was not established until 1944 (McKee and Murray 1986:123–24). This program should not be confused with the Reconstruction-era policy of forty acres and a mule promised to freed enslaved peoples.

A Brick House—Frank Bell Joe. Frank explains his family were sharecroppers in Kemper County until they had the chance to move back among other Choctaw to reservation land and into their own home.

Chicken Catching, Sharecropping, or the Army—Brian Billie. Brian explained that the dreams his father had were about the death he saw in Vietnam: "All he ever said was he didn't want us to go through seeing what he saw."

Limited Options—Harold Comby. By "distribution," Harold is referring to the distribution of profits from their casinos that each enrolled tribal member receives twice a year.

Remembering Our Past—Rae Nell Vaughn. Rae Nell, speaking to a class of Butler University students said, "And as the Indigenous people of North America, it's important that you know we are the first people here."

FARMING AND GARDENING

Predicting Rain—Jackson Isaac. Jackson Isaac mentioned that prophets got their knowledge from God.

Rainmakers—Mark Patrick. Mark asked the YOP students if they had heard about this belief. Lakylee Martin from Conehatta said she had. Taylor Ben added: "I know there's if you burn the biscuits, it'll rain, but I guess it was just from keeping it from burning." Meka Willis, responding to Mark's comment about hanging a snake on a fence to bring rain, recounted the time her uncle did this: "So it did rain after we did hang a snake because my uncle needed to water the plants, and he was too lazy to water it with the hose, so he's like, 'Put the dead snake on the fence.' And I'm like, 'You sure that's going to work?' It worked for him, and I was in disbelief because that happened." It is also useful to point out that it had been raining fairly consistently for the past week when Mark told this story, helping to explain his comment on Facebook as well as that he's hurting.

Maple Trees Signal Spring—Eddie Johnson. Eddie noted that the older lady was Zula Chitto. He attributes this information to her in a post on the Choctaw Cultural Legacy Facebook page from March 3, 2022.

The Work of an Elder—Melvin Henry. Melvin Henry was one of the best-known white-oak basket makers in the community, an art form that is no longer practiced among the Choctaw at this time.

Hog Killing—Terry Ben. A few days earlier, Terry and I were talking, and since we hadn't just had lunch, he did share the process for killing a hog, noting that the hog was shot with a rifle right between the eyes. The tasks were divvied up by gender, where the men hung the hog and gutted it, while the women cleaned the intestines and made chitlins (chitterlings). "Everyone would come to eat fresh hog meat for lunch when they would also make cracklings. They all helped each other" (June 4, 2021).

Sharing the Meat—Martha Ferguson. Gordon Sam mentions that people also had smokehouses in order to preserve the hog meat through the winter (July 6, 2021). See also Terry Ben's story "Hog Killing."

Raising Hogs—Mark Patrick. I ask Mark how he recaptured the hogs: "We'd just follow their tracks and find out where they went, and then we'll take a slop bucket, go over there, and we'd lure them back, like that!" [*laughter*]

Not Dead Yet—Martha Ferguson. Gordon Sam also describes killing chickens as a young boy's chore, distinguishing between the laying hens that provided eggs and the "yard chickens" that were for frying (July 6, 2021).

Resourceful—Lorena Alex. Lorena also described learning how to cook outside, even biscuits. "Do you know how I did my biscuits my first time? [*laugh*] I didn't know how to roll it. You make a dough first, and you roll it to make a biscuit. I did, but I didn't know I'm supposed to watch it after I put it in the oven. It burned the first time. Then the second time, I learned. But I know how to do it now and how to cook it outside." She concludes: "Anything that's cooked outside, it tastes better."

Keeping the Deer and Birds Out—Rae Nell Vaughn. Williamson Isaac remembers that even tall fences couldn't keep deer out: "I planted some peas, and then one morning there were two deer in there. They were not scared. They turn around and looked at me and just get into the woods. Jumped over the fence, almost as tall as this building here [Hope Baptist Church, a one-story building]. I don't know how they get in, but you could see how they get out!" [*laughter*] (June 27, 2021).

HUNTING AND FISHING, CAMPING AND COOKING

Blowguns and Slingshots—Henry Williams. Laymon Shumake describes the step-by-step process of making blowguns out of swamp cane in a 1974 article in the student-run magazine *Nanih Waiya* titled "Blowgun."

Night Hunting—Terry Ben. Compare to the many stories people tell about seeing lights in the woods and about *bohpoli* included in *Choctaw Tales* 2004.

Blowguns at the Fair—DeLaura Henry Saunders (see Henry 1974). DeLaura also notes they used a stuffed rabbit on a long pole as a target for rabbit stick throwing. Video of this and footage of blowgun competitions at the fair are included in the video *Choctaw Indian Fair* produced by the Department of Chahta Immi (2017). In 2021, Melford Farve mentioned a friend in Conehatta who still hunts small birds with a blowgun.

Rabbit Hunting—Martha Ferguson. Martha explains that she was raised where women were not supposed to hunt. Her uncle told her, "Well, you stay out of hunting because that's not yours to do."

Outsmarting Rabbits—Henry Williams. His comment is pointed: the livestock hasn't changed from the past, just the protectiveness of Whites who no longer want to open up their land to their neighbors. For other descriptions of rabbit hunting, see interviews with John Mingo Jr. (2017) and Roger Richardson Smith (2017), who explains, "We didn't have a place to hunt, so we would go hunting on a White person's land. One of us would go two or three days in advance and talk to the landowner. If they agreed, we would go hunting there."

Hunting Squirrel—Melford Farve. Eddie Johnson describes "tell-tale signs of activity of squirrels" that help a hunter locate them that include nibbled pinecones and little holes in the ground where the squirrels have dug up nuts (June 11, 2021). Gordon Sam describes "the old ones" teaching him about the behavior of animals, such as woodpeckers and ants, as well as of animals they hunted, such as raccoons (July 6, 2021).

Fishing Trips—Barbara Sam. Barbara recounts this in a conversation with Lane Denson and Ruth Williams. They discuss how they used to set up lines at night to catch fish and check them in the morning to see what they caught. Some families stayed through the night; others went home after fishing all day. Barbara and Lane end by remembering how scared they were and still are of snakes (see the introduction for discussion of recurring theme of snakes).

Fishing Weekends—Caroline Morris. Harley Vaughn is Caroline's son-in-law. Caroline is the daughter of Gladys Willis, who also describes fishing in the summer as well as hunting in the winter. "In the wintertime, they used to hunt rabbits, squirrels, birds, just anything. They used to have robin dumplings. They'd cook four or five robins—the birds—and clean it up and boil it and make dumplings" (May 23, 1996). Squirrel was one of Gladys Willis's favorites. When it comes to preparing squirrels, some people prefer to singe and scrape them; others, to skin them. When I asked Gladys about hunting and fishing again the following year, she described in more detail how she prepared the squirrel: "When there's a big fire, there's a lot of hot coal down there. They would put a squirrel in the fire, and they would give me a stick and kind of turn it around. When that fur singe off, they used to scrape it off. That's how I learned to clean a squirrel. After that, they cooked it. They had that squirrel and cornbread. Cornbread's all they make when they're out camping. But that was something to eat" (August 6, 1997). Melford Farve also describes singeing the squirrel to remove the fur until the skin glistened (June 1, 2021). Many people mention storytelling as a common evening activity on these overnight fishing and hunting expeditions (see for example interview with Terry Ben May 30, 1996, Travis Willis June 14, 2021, Harold Comby February 24, 2022, and the story "Camping and Hunting Squirrel" by Mark Patrick).

Pole That Don't Catch Fish—Gladys Willis. Earlier, Gladys described the fishing and hunting trips her family and neighbors would take. She laughed about how the kids and adults were often at cross purposes: "And if we happened to be near the river, we used to play in the water if it wasn't cold. Lots of times they'd go fishing, too, in the summer. We'd spend weekends in the woods. Lot of times, we just stayed in the woods. Then summertime, when they'd fish, we'd go out and play in the water. They don't fish near the camp. They go out somewhere else to fish. With the kids around, they know they ain't going to catch fish. [*laughter*] But they used to bring in lots of fish."

Trapping and Paralyzing Fish—Eddie Johnson. Eddie has never fished this way himself, but he heard about it from others and read a similar account in Swanton's book that describes pools of water being poisoned with buckeye, as well as processes of dragging the river with brush fastened with creeper vines (1931:55). Eddie's coworker Ty Isaac shared a story from his mother who remembers seine fishing near Beaver Dam as a young girl. Her whole family would participate. They would position themselves in a row in close proximity to each other and walk forward, guiding the fish toward other family members positioned opposite them who were holding a net. Sometimes they would use a gardening hoe to help drive the fish forward toward the net (personal communication November 13, 2023).

Kill to Eat—Louise Wilson. Travis Willis echoes this sentiment, saying that his grandfather always told him: "What you kill is what you eat" (June 14, 2021).

Cooking Possum—Martha Ferguson. Martha explains why they feed the possum before eating it: "You know what possum eats? Dead animal. And about anything they find, that's its food. Anything that's dead. Usually, they eat a lot of them. So it's clean up all the system out from that. Otherwise, the smell is there, they call it, in the skin, in the meat." Simpson Tubby reported a similar process to John Swanton, who summarizes, "It was a common Choctaw belief that people got diseases from the food they ate, and therefore before killing a chicken, it was shut up and fed by the owner until what it had foraged for itself was out of it" (1931:235).

Picking Huckleberries—Eddie Johnson. Terry Ben describes picking blackberries and huckleberries alongside the road and in pastures that his grandmother would then freeze or can for wintertime pies at Thanksgiving and Christmas (June 10, 2021). Compare to all the other stories about encountering snakes, as well as stories about the land no longer providing food (see all related prophecies in Mould 2004).

Fetching Water—Amanda Bell. Amanda told a version of this story on July 1, 2021. She chose to completely rewrite it for the book on March 11, 2024.

CHAPTER 2: RECREATION

STICKBALL

Three-Day Celebration—Harold Comby. Beamon Charlie also describes negotiating with the White landowner a person sharecropped for in order to get permission to host a stickball game and kill a cow to feed everyone (January 23, 1975). The idea of host teams providing food for the festivities is seen in people's stories of stickball games as well as more recently in baseball and softball games.

Little Brother of War—Richard McMillan. Richard was interviewed by Sean Gantt for the video *Stickball: Grandfather of All Sports, Little Brother of War* (2017).

Rough Games—Bobby Joe. There were two Choctaw moieties in the eighteenth century, the Imoklasha Choctaw of the Western Division, the red or war party, and the Inholata Choctaw of the Eastern Division, the white or peace party. In dealing with the British and French, the two Choctaw groups considered themselves separate nations (Galloway 1994; Swanton 1931:76–79).

Whipping Up the Players—Theron "Duke" Denson. Compare this custom to the description offered by George E. Starr at the turn of the twentieth century in Indian Territory: "In one hand they carry a cup of coffee and in the other a quirt [short-handled whip] with which they whip the players when they think they are not playing hard enough. At times a player will get a woman to give him a pin, with which he will scarify his leg, making from three to five scratches from near the ankle to the middle of the calf, until the blood comes. This, they say, prevents cramps" (Culin 1907:604). Grady John also describes the women whipping the men on the sidelines (February 22, 1998).

Strong Medicine—Harold Comby. Henry Halbert also describes the *hopaii*—prophets and medicine men—using mirrors as part of their medicine during games: "Before and during the play, the prophets on each side in the midst of the players, continue their usual performances. Each carries a small looking glass. He turns to the sun, holds his glass towards it with a gyratory motion then turns and throws the rays upon the bodies of the players of his side" (cited by Swanton 1931:149).

Horse Tail—John Mingo Jr. In addition to the famous 1834 portrait by George Catlin of Tul-lock-chísh-ko that depicts the stickball player wearing a horse tail (Catlin 1834), Stewart Culin includes a drawing and description: "A tail used in the ball game, consisting of a piece of a horse's tail attached to a strip of wood by a thong and loop at the top; length, 25 inches" (1907:603).

Smack Talking—Mark Patrick. Chucalissa refers to the Chucalissa Indian Mounds and C. H. Nash Museum at the Prehistoric Chucalissa Archaeological Site established by the University of Memphis.

Mississippi versus Oklahoma—Hillary Vaughn. The Oklahoma Choctaw use a different orthography from the Mississippi Choctaw, who would spell Tvshka Homma as Tashka Homma, both of which mean "Red Warriors."

PICNICS AND BALL GAMES

Play All Day, Dance All Night—Evaline Davis. DeLaura Saunders describes a similar event in Bogue Chitto where they played softball, and the host team provided the food for both teams. In order to help cover the cost, some of the hosts sold drinks. See also Lorena Alex (June 10, 2021), Melford Farve (July 10, 1997, and June 1, 2021), and Will Wallace (2016).

Picnic—Melford Farve. Many people describe ball games similarly, though depending on when the games started, they might play some games first, break for lunch, and then play again after lunch.

Celebrating the Beginning and End of School—Willis. Gladys clarifies that these celebrations were within communities, not the whole tribe. She also notes they killed a cow and had beef for dinner as well as hominy.

Surprise in the Well—Melford Farve. Igloo is a brand of cooler.

Job Well Done—Bradley Alex. Bradley Alex introduced this story by talking about some of the great Choctaw baseball players of the past, such as Herbert Alex, Gordon Willis, and Bush York, the last of whom met the great athlete Jim Thorpe.

Coming Together—Brian Billie. Brian's description follows my question about whether he ever participated in ball games and community picnics.

Medicine on the Mound—Harold Comby. Eddie Johnson shares a story of one team finding the other team's medicine pouch on the mound and stomping it angrily, shouting "This ain't right! This is not how we're supposed to play." For a similar account of using a pouch of medicine during a baseball game, see "The Baseball Game" in *Choctaw Tales*.

Help for a Home Run—Eddie Johnson. Eddie added later that his mother used to tell this story all the time.

Preparing for Games—Carmen Denson and Dan Isaac. Refraining from marital relations also appears to have been common before ball games in the nineteenth and early twentieth centuries, in addition to not eating hog meat or grease (Swanton 1931:155). The taboo about women touching a man's stickball sticks has evolved over the years. Travis Willis remembers that a wife could touch her husband's sticks, but no one else's.

GAMES AND PLAY

Rabbit Stick Throwing Game—Jackson Isaac. Bill Brescia asked how rabbit sticks are used; Jackson's answer shows that they were not just for hunting but for betting games as well. Although rabbit sticks are used, this game can be compared to one of the ways chunkey was played, where people tried to throw their sticks closest to the rolling stone. At one point, Jackson says "ball stick" rather than "rabbit stick." It is unclear whether he meant both were used or not.

Ring Toss—Evaline Davis. Evaline clarifies that each ring that you get in the hole is worth five points. This is the same game that others call "washers." The variation in name appears to have more to do with generation than with community, with older generations referring to ring toss (see Blanchard 1981:56–57) and younger generations calling it washers. In either case, the game would have typically been referred to as *tali pila washoha* in the Choctaw language. For an additional story involving washers apart from those in this section, see "Rabbits and Washers" in the "Getting Together" section.

Pitching Washers—Linda Williams. Linda follows with a description of playing softball growing up when she did in fact become a pitcher (see "From Pitching Washers to Pitching Softball" in this collection).

Rag Ball—Susie Comby Alex. These "stick balls" were rag balls for playing baseball with sticks, as opposed to stickballs or *towa* made for playing Choctaw stickball. Nellie Billie from Red Water describes making their rag ball from "old torn clothes" and then playing with it until the ball fell apart (see "The Games

We Played" 2017). Blanchard argues that "during the '40s and early '50s, ragball, a game common throughout the rural South in this period, was the principal mechanism whereby many Choctaw children were introduced to baseball and developed its fundamental skills" (1981:48).

"Stick" Ball, Corn Dolls, and Musical Leaves—DeLaura Saunders. Reviewing this story a few years later on June 5, 2023, DeLaura laughed that while she didn't know the name of the grass, she could probably go outside and find it. She said, "Rain and bad knees kept us from doing it, however." After reviewing the story, she added the description of tying it with an additional husk.

Tire Casing—John Mingo Jr. A tire casing is the main structure of the tire. Without the inner tube, there was room for a child to get inside it.

Homemade Games—Harold Comby. "Rings" was a broad term and was applied to different games. For many, "rings" and "washers" refer to the same game. Roy Smith said that the rings Harold describes here as *tali chanaha pila* referred to the hoop-and-stick game.

Bottle-Tops Game—DeLaura Saunders. In a conversation a few years later on June 5, 2023, DeLaura explained that you had to catch the bottle caps on the back of your hand, which was much more difficult than the palm and disadvantaged people with small hands. She also noted that sometimes they played with red and black checkers. Compare to the game Bernard Romans describes from the 1770s: "The women also have a game where they take a small stick, or something else off the ground after having thrown up a small ball which they are to catch again, having picked up the other" (1962 [1775]:81) as well as the corn game, where corn kernels blackened on one side were thrown like dice, with 1 point scored for each kernel that landed blackened side up, unless *all* the kernels were plain side up, for which you received a point for each kernel (see Swanton 1931:159). In reviewing the story, DeLaura made a few slight additions to clarity her original description.

Hide and Seek—Terry Ben. According to Bernard Romans, a game similar to jacks was played in the eighteenth century as well: "The women also have a game where they take a small stick, or something else off the ground after having thrown up a small ball which they are to catch again, having picked up the other; they are fond of it, but ashamed to be seen at it" (cited in Swanton 1931:159). Similar games have been played since at least 3000 BCE, when ancient Egyptian and later Greek and Roman children played knucklebones with the toe bones of sheep.

Kick the Can—Martha Ferguson. The uncle who played kick the can was Uncle Charles, a relative who figures prominently in Martha's stories of growing up, no doubt because "Uncle Charles, he's always in trouble. He's the one who's always okay about playing" (June 4, 2021).

Cowboys and Indians—Claude Yates Allen. He follows with a story of how he came to realize he was Indian and that this came with discrimination against him, in this case, in the form of not being allowed to swim in the pool with his classmates (for additional stories of racial discrimination, see Mould and Vaughn 2025).

Ant Pile—Mark Patrick. Many of the games that Mark and his brothers and cousins came up with were rough and competitive. When they went swimming in ponds, inevitably, someone would come back and say, "'They almost drowned me.' Stuff like that. And then we'd all get in trouble!" Such games echo David Bushnell Jr.'s description of games played among the Choctaw of Bayou Lacomb: "During the hot months of the year a favorite pastime of the boys and men consisted in trying to swim blindfolded a wide stream to a certain point on the opposite bank. The first to reach the goal was declared the winner. A somewhat similar amusement participated in by the boys and young men consisted in rolling down hills while wrapped and tied in blankets or skins, the first to reach a certain line being the winner" (Bushnell 1909:20).

Pranking the Neighbor—Mark Patrick. When Mark mentioned jumping from hay bale to hay bale, YOP interviewer Taylor Ben exclaimed, "We used to do that too!"

CHAPTER 3: COMMUNITY EVENTS

IYYIKOWA

Broken Foot—Harold Comby. For other accounts and descriptions of *iyyikowa* not included in this book, see Judy Billie (June 3, 1997); Gordon Sam (July 6, 2021); DeLaura Saunders (June 29, 2021); and Travis Willis (June 14, 2021).

Helping to Read and Helping Out—Eddie Johnson. Following Eddie's first story of helping an elder in the community with her mail, he shared a story of participating in an *iyyikowa* for someone who had gotten hurt and was laid up in bed. He noted that "back then social service wasn't really doing that type of work. It was later when social service would come and provide. Even the tribe didn't have free cutting wood for people. They didn't do that. So the family had to depend on one another or friends or the community." Related to quilting as a form of communal work, Terry Ben tells a story of being tasked as a young boy to go buy the snuff for the women quilting (see "Quilting and Dipping" in "Gatherings"). See also Laline Farve describing *iyyikowa*, including making "blankets," in "The Generous Spirit of the Choctaw" on the Choctaw Cultural Legacy website. Also, chopping firewood appears again and again in people's stories of *iyyikowa* (see Travis Willis in this collection). Speaking in 1979, John Hunter Thompson remembers having enough firewood was never a problem until Whites came along: "A long time ago there weren't that many Choctaw. They didn't live in good houses. They would cut down trees and make their houses with a fireplace and a hole so the smoke would go out. No matter how cold it was, nobody was stingy with wood. If there was wood, they cut it and use it for fire. But nowadays, the Whites own the land and are stingy with the trees now."

Fish for the Elders—Brian Billie. Jay Wesley describes a similar situation: "If we had a good day at fishing, we'd come back, and we'd give a lot of fish to a family in need." One woman in particular cared for her many grandchildren and always appreciated the extra food. "She used to have these grandkids always running around. And then we'd drop off a whole lot of fish for them, and we'd sit and talk with them, and they'd start cleaning the fish together. And then we'd go home and get ours done."

Community Service—Mahlih Bowden. This is not *iyyikowa* per se, but it captures the spirit of *iyyikowa* and suggests how the tradition is being reinterpreted by new generations, focusing on helping out the community as a whole rather than a single family. The "we" in the story is Mahlih and a half dozen of her close friends. These same friends have organized beauty pageants and other fundraisers as well. Far more often, however, people talk about how family have filled the gap that community used to fill. Lorena Alex, for example, says she hasn't participated in *iyyikowa* but adds, "I can depend on my brothers and sisters" (June 10, 2021).

CEREMONIES, HOLIDAYS, AND FESTIVALS

Honoring the Origin of Corn—Terry Ben. The story of the origin of corn was originally published in the first edition of *Choctaw Tales* (Mould 2004).

New Fires, New Year—Harold Comby. When I talked to Harold in 1999, he noted that much of his understanding of the Green Corn Ceremony came from John Swanton's book (1931).

Lowak Moshólichi—Jesse Ben. Jesse shared this with Sean Gantt as part of Gantt's dissertation research (2013:163). Swanton notes: "Since, however, a year of twelve strictly lunar months must be corrected at intervals to agree with the solar year, the editor suggests that luak mosholi, which means "fire extinguished," may have been applied to an intercalary month or period at the beginning of the new year when the fires may have been extinguished and relighted, although we do not know certainly that the Choctaw shared this custom with the Creeks" (1931:45). Speaking in the 1920s, Simpson Tubby describes the Green Corn Dance being held in the summer, probably August, during which "laws were made for the ensuing year" (Swanton 1931:225), aligning with the idea that *lowak moshólichi* and the Green Corn Dance or Ceremony were practiced as one.

Good Luck for the New Year—Martha Ferguson. Harley and Rae Nell Vaughn also talk about the foods eaten at the New Year: greens, pork, cornbread, and black-eyed peas. Rae says, "All of it is for luck. But it's luck in certain areas, to be wealthy and stuff like that. But everything was always around food: food and gathering together" (July 13, 2021). These foods are symbolically eaten for good luck, wealth, and health throughout the southeastern United States, though most of the symbols are tied specifically to wealth, with peas representing coins, greens representing paper money, pork representing prosperity, and cornbread representing gold.

Fall Festival—Lillie Gibson. She explains this was back in the 1920s when she was a little girl, just eight or nine years old. The story of the car was originally published in the first edition of *Choctaw Tales* (Mould 2004).

On Display—Melford Farve. Brother Mal was a non-Indian who was a Catholic priest at Holy Rosary Catholic Church in Tucker. The *Nanih Waiya* staff interviewed him for their spring 1979 edition ("Brother Mal").

School Festivals—Rae Nell Vaughn. Rae begins by noting: "Culturally, the coronavirus has really impacted a lot of the things that we do here culturally. This is April, we would have been done with our Spring Festival." The Green Corn Festival as it is constructed today is a school festival held for the youth.

Thanksgiving at Church—Terry Ben. In 1973, Charlie Denson also described how Thanksgiving was celebrated at his church, with the pastor asking his congregation to find a passage in the Bible that they think speaks to the spirit of Thanksgiving. Charlie chose the Old Testament story of Abraham almost sacrificing his son Isaac. He also described eating a big meal with turkey at home with his family (December 3, 1973).

Candies for the Stocking—Charlie Denson. He adds that they cut a Christmas tree and brought it into the house and decorated it with cloth and paper but no lights.

All Day, All Night—DeLaura Saunders. Consistently, people remember being scared of the costumed *shilop* as children. As DeLaura suggests, this was not accidental but served to remind the children they needed to be good all year if they were going to receive presents. For other accounts of the Christmas Tree celebration in addition to those presented here, see Bradley Alex (June 30, 2021), Lorena Alex (June 10, 2021), Evaline Davis (June 3, 2021), and Dora Nickey (2018). In reviewing the story, DeLaura made a few slight additions to clarify her original description.

A Christmas Story—Harley Vaughn and Caroline Morris. Caroline and Harley continue to discuss the tradition. Both agree the ghosts were supposed to be scary. Harley played the role of ghost as often as he could, and both he and his wife, Rae Nell, cross-dressed as the parents to all the ghost kids. Years later, in 2021, Harley used the term "goblins" to describe the ghosts and noted that Santa was a "dirty Santa"; that is, he was crass and said inappropriate things. He also had to try to retrieve an apple tied to the very top of the holly tree at the end of the night, a task that always elicited great laughter (July 13, 2021). The event starts at dark on Christmas Day in Bogue Chitto, but Caroline thinks it may be done on other days in other communities. Different families may share in hosting from year to year (in Bogue Chitto, Harley remembers it mostly being members of the Bell and Morris families), but the event is always open to the whole community.

Harley's sister, Lorena Alex, describes a similar scene, mentioning the tree, fruit in bags, how "the guys would wear women dresses and girls would wear men dresses or pants," and the house dancing they did afterwards (June 10, 2021).

So Different from Oklahoma—Sarah Jane Sampson McMillan. Sarah Jane McMillan was born in Ardmore, Oklahoma. Her sister married a man from Tucker, so she and her family visited Mississippi from time to time, such as in 1965 when she attended the Christmas celebration at the age of fourteen. She eventually met her sister's husband's cousin, who was also from Tucker, and they married in 1969 and moved to Tucker, at which point she participated in the Christmas Tree celebration more often. She attended a predominantly White school in Ardmore and found the transition to Mississippi a difficult one. During her description of Christmas in Mississippi as compared to Oklahoma, she points out that family members didn't buy gifts for each other beyond a piece of fruit, nor did they put up a tree in their homes or have nativity plays. Her description offers an outsider's view of the tradition, one in which the customs seem strange and foreign. She notes that the cedar is placed in the front yard in the ground. "Sometimes they only have lights, but then some just put icicles on theirs." The people who play Santa and his helpers are typically chosen by the person who hosts the Christmas Tree.

FUNDRAISERS

Box Supper—Carmen Denson. For additional accounts, see Doris Bell, who describes how people tried to find out what was in the box and then worked to outbid one another for bigger, more desirable meals like fried chicken (June 25, 2021), and Linda Williams, who specified that money was used to buy new bats, balls, and uniforms (June 15, 2021).

Running Up the Price—Bradley Alex. Linda is the woman he was dating at the time; they eventually married.

Uncomfortable Dinner—Linda Williams. I ask her how old she was when this happened. "I might have been like ten, twelve, somewhere around there." She concludes: "But I didn't like it. I told her I never want to do that again." This helps explain why some fathers bid on their daughter's boxes as described in the previous "Big Box Supper" by Brian Billie.

FUNdraisers—Jay Wesley. At the Cultural Center, there is a photo of the group Jay took to France as part of a cultural exchange.

DANCING

Social Dancing—Henderson Williams. Billy Amos also remembers these dances, including when they shifted onto reservation land: "I remember, on the ballfield on the reservation, they used to dance from sundown to daylight. They got different songs" (June 19, 1997). Bradley Alex describes watching social dancing on the football field, with particularly energetic snake dances, where the tail whipped around so quickly, "you'd see people flying!" (June 30, 2021).

Walk Dance—Eddie Gibson. Others recall similar uses of the walk dance. For example, when a member of Melford Farve's social-dance group passed away, they did a walk dance to honor her at the gravesite.

Clash with Christianity—DeLaura Saunders. In a conversation a few years later on June 5, 2023, DeLaura elaborated on the transition her mother went through from accepting the Christian missionaries' views that Choctaw traditions were bad to recognizing the value in both Christian and Choctaw traditions. Eventually, she began to incorporate Choctaw cultural traditions into her lesson plans as a teacher. In reviewing the story, DeLaura made a few slight additions to clarify her original description.

House Dancing—Martha Ferguson. Later, Martha explained the important fundraising aspect of house dances; selling candy, fruit, gum, and drinks was a good way to make money. Although it was Martha's older relatives who kept track of her treats, Susie Comby Alex remembers the roles could be reversed as well so that when she was too young to dance herself, she and her siblings kept up with their female relatives' treats (June 9, 2021). For additional information on the music of house dancing, particularly fiddling, see Goertzen 2019.

Public Performance—Melford Farve. Mrs. Minnie Hand was a well-known figure in the Choctaw Tribal School System, a White BIA music teacher who was committed to ensuring Choctaw youth learned their traditional music and dance. She was one of a handful of teachers and administrators who took a group of Choctaw youth to Washington, DC, to dance at the Department of the Interior on May 4, 1973, where she was quoted as saying: "I have seen the magic of music work for Choctaw children. I have seen them—freed of inhibition as they dance, sing, and play small melody instruments. I have seen them lost in the mood of music, but I haven't seen them lost in music that really reached them deep down until I learned the Choctaw music and taught it to them" ("Choctaw Indian Children Sing, Dance, in Washington, DC" 1973).

GETTING TOGETHER

Quilting and Dipping—Terry Ben. Terry was paid to run errands, but the women quilting were not paid for their labor. While they might make a quilt to raise money, they might also make it to give to a family who needed help in the tradition of *iyyikowa*. Also, when asked how long she had been chewing tobacco, Conehatta basket maker Esbie Gibson noted: "I don't know since I started eating snuff because my brother insisted I eat it, and he made me learn how to eat it, even though he is not going to buy me any" (February 1982).

Extra Food—DeLaura Saunders. "Uncle Bob" is Bob Henry, a well-known drummer and medicine man in Bogue Chitto.

Community Visiting—Eddie Gibson. Eddie added that he grew up loving Choctaw hymns. "I can't carry a tune in a bucket now, but I like to hear it." He noted that "most of these churches are not singing the hymns, Choctaw hymns, as much as they used to." For a video on Choctaw hymn singing, see *Traditional Choctaw Hymns*, produced by the Department of Chahta Immi.

Church Fellowship—Terry Ben. Woman's Missionary Union or WMU is an auxiliary of the Southern Baptist Convention involved in educating church members and supporting missionary work.

Visiting—Louise Wilson. Bobby Joe describes similar visiting, noting how much shorter visits are now that people can travel quickly by car (January 6, 2000).

Host to All—Harold Comby. In some Native American cultures, it is common to refer to all other living creatures as "brother" or "sister." This is not common among the Choctaw, as Harold's confusion highlights. Compare to Eddie Johnson's story of Esbie Gibson staying with his family while she hunted for huckleberries.

Road-Trip Reunion—Amanda Bell. Amanda told a version of this story on July 1, 2021. She chose to completely rewrite it for the book on March 11, 2024.

Wandering Storyteller—Eddie Johnson. Zula Chitto was a well-known basket maker in Standing Pine. Eddie explained that those wanderers were *chokka abayyat nówah*, which means "one who visits from house to house." For more on the prophecies shared among the tribe, see Mould 2003 and 2004.

CHAPTER 4: LIFE CYCLE

PREGNANCY AND BIRTH

Pregnancy Customs—Louise Wilson. In the middle of telling the story, she clarifies that both her brother and her husband have passed away; her husband actually died before her son was born. For another version of the story of laughing at a hog, see Vickers 1985.

Don't Make Fun—Harold Comby. Harold explains that this taboo extends to the husband as well.

Watch What You See—Linda Williams. Mark Patrick also notes, "Pregnant women couldn't be around a dead person, a dead corpse, a wake, or a visitation," though he adds, "I'm not sure why." He also notes that children shouldn't be around dead people either (see "Carried Away").

Stay Calm—Dan Isaac. Dan followed with some general advice about good water, good food, and good thoughts, all to help with the development of the baby.

No Turtles—Susie Comby Alex. Susie's brother, Harold, echoed his sister: "If a woman is pregnant, she should never go fishing or deal anything with like turtles or snakes or anything, or the baby will be deformed" (June 4, 1997). Both Harold and Susie heard this from their mother.

No Gardening, No Funerals—Travis Willis. See also his niece Rae Nell Vaughn's explanation that menstruating women also should not be gardening.

No Funerals, No Cutting Hair—Rae Nell Vaughn. While pregnant women should not cut their hair, family members in mourning should: "You can cut your hair when immediate family dies; it's part of the sacrifice you make to show you're in mourning" (Harold Comby, January 10, 2000).

Crossing Water—Linda Williams. In addition to Mark Patrick's story "Carried Away" that follows, see Terry Ben's explanation from his grandmother noted in the introduction to this section.

Going Home—Harold Comby. The smoke is intended to purify. Harold uses the terms "smoking" and "smudging" interchangeably.

NAMING

Sharecropping Naming—Eddie Gibson. Eddie explained that his parents chose the names of the sharecroppers willingly, as opposed to being forced to take on such names.

Bear and Thunderstruck—Hubert Wesley. When asked to spell his name, Hubert laughed: "Well, we never did spell that, so I'm not sure." It was a name spoken, not written.

English Name—Hayward Bell. In the new Choctaw orthography, "warrior" is *taskha* and "proud" is *ná yokpah*.

Choctaw Name—Dan Isaac. Dan's translation of Pushmataha is one of many, including Apushamatahahubi: "Messenger of death, literally one whose rifle, tomahawk, or bow alike fatal in war or hunting" (Cushman 1962 [1899]:234); Pushmatahaw, meaning "the warrior's seat is finished" (Lanman 1870:168); "Apushimataha," where "Apushi im alhtaha literally translated, is 'The sapling is ready, or finished for him'" (Halbert 1898:108).

New Name—Casey Bigpond. In a conversation a few years later, on June 1, 2023, Casey further explains: "Most names, as I understand it, was given based on a person's personality. On the day that they're born, they got a name. So if it was a rainy day, it would be associated with rainy day or something. Sunny day, cloudy day, whatever the day was. They would associate the name with that type of day. And then as they got older, their names will change to reflect their personalities."

Naming Ceremony—Casey Bigpond. Casey has described this event to me on a number of occasions, including three times when we were recording. He tells the story with different details each time, as most storytellers do, crafting the story to fit the audience and the storyteller's goals in that moment. In order to provide a more complete version of the story, I have included two of the versions. The first, recorded on June 28, 2021, runs from the beginning to "That's one of the ways that they did things." The rest is from June 1, 2023. He explains that he instructed the chief to say his son's name three times, with the audience repeating it afterward each time. He also described the food: "We had traditional cooking. We killed a pig early in the morning that morning and then cooked it all day. And then the ceremony we did was probably three o'clock in the afternoon, four o'clock, somewhere around there."

Nicknames—DeLaura Saunders. DeLaura elongates the world Píla when she quotes her Afo; the dash in *pí—la* is meant to convey this.

Doc—Susie Comby Alex. Thomas Saunders, one of the YOP students, asked Susie about *bohpoli*. This was the story she followed with. Bob Henry was a well-known medicine man. The "Doc" in her story is her brother, Harold Comby. Later, she offers another explanation for Harold's nickname, one mentioned by others in the community too: that he knows so much about Choctaw culture, that he's like a professor. Doc became a fitting nickname. "When all the visitors or relatives come to visit, Mom and Dad would tell us, 'Y'all can stay outside and play,' and here we all go. Doc would curl up and sit by Mom and Dad, and he was putting all what they're saying in his head. Later on, he would write it. He goes around talking to elderlies and listens to them talking. Whenever I want to know something, I call him." Doc himself offered yet a third story explaining his nickname, but he joked: "If a lady's present, I'll tell the PG version; if it's all men, I'll tell the X-rated version" (June 1, 2021). Once it was just a few men left, he shared the story but asked that it not be included in the Tribal Archives or the book. What is clear is that often nicknames stick when they mark an embarrassing incident. For other stories about people's nicknames, see interviews with Melford Farve (June 1, 2021), Eddie Gibson (July 1, 2021), Leonard Jimmie (July 11, 2021), and Harley Vaughn (May 31, 1996). For other stories about encounters with *bohpoli*, see *Choctaw Tales* (2004 and 2025) and the "Becoming a Doctor" section of this book.

No Names for the Deceased—Martha Ferguson. The process of not naming deceased children but marking their absence silently with a folded finger echoes the historical practice that Claiborne describes:

> The Choctaws will not speak of the dead. Our instructions required us to exact proof of the number of children each claimant under the 14th article, had at the date of the treaty, because each was entitled to a certain portion of land. Upon being interrogated the claimants uniformly omitted in the enumeration those that were dead, although well aware that by this omission they would lose a portion of land. Very old claimants would even deny that they ever had more children than they presented to the commissioners, and the facts had to be proved by kindred or neighbors. To arrive at the truth in these cases, we required them to arrange their families in a line according to their ages. They uniformly left a vacancy in the line to denote where the deceased would have stood; and this established, not only the number but

> the age. Thus, if the second child be dead an interval of some three feet was left between the first and the third child. Sometimes they planted stakes along the line to represent the dead but could not be induced to mention their names. (1964 [1880]:519–20; see also Cushman 1962 [1899]:225)

The ambiguity of the word "gone"—which could mean gone as in died, but also gone away—operates similarly in both English and Choctaw, which is why she wonders which it is. DeLaura Saunders notes, "It kind of used to be—I don't know if it's still—after the person dies, you're not supposed to say their names. You can say, 'So-and-so's father or so-and-so's brother,' and that" (June 29, 2021). Harold Comby explains, "During a death, it's disrespectful to name a person. But if you must do it, you say the name and say *iksho* which means 'not here.' And that's almost like saying the late so-and-so in English" (June 1, 2021). In 1996, he repeated this, noting, "There's also a lot of information like death. You're not supposed to mention their names when you speak after they're dead and been buried. You say something like '*afo iksho*' which means 'my father, my long-gone father' or something like that. But you're not supposed to mention their names. Just showing respect, respect to the deceased's spirit I guess" (June 4, 1997). On June 1, 2021, he repeats this, noting that it's "almost like saying the late so-and-so in English." Others have noted that the avoidance of using the name of the deceased, particularly soon after they passed, was to avoid calling their spirit back, part of the larger tradition that includes packing up the deceased person's belongings and putting them away and lighting a fire to show them the way to leave.

COMING OF AGE

Braves Ceremony—Hubert Wesley. The log house Hubert mentions is probably Cameron Wesley's home that Hubert previously mentioned. Hubert recorded this story again on December 14, 1999. An audio recording can be found on the Choctaw Cultural Legacy website (see "How We Passed the Braves Ceremony"): http://choctawculturallegacy.com/audio-resources/.

Circling Up with the Elders—Bradley Alex. Hayward Bell describes a similar mode of teaching that he calls "campfire talk." A handful of elders, typically no more than three, would stand up and speak to the community gathered around the fire as a way of guiding and educating (June 30, 2021). This custom aligns with historical accounts of "the council fire" (see Mould 2004:l–liii).

Don't Play after Dark—Martha Ferguson. Martha never offers an explanation for who or what was playing basketball, but many people say that toys left out at night will attract *bohpoli*, the little people, who may entice children to come play with them. For similar accounts, see interviews with Dan Isaac (June 23, 2021, published in Mould and Vaughn 2025); Berdie John, March

14, 1996; Mark Patrick, July 7, 2021; Rosalee Steve, February 21, 1998; Rae Nell Vaughn, March 14, 1996). In the next story, however, Harold Comby connects the abandoned toys to a child's spirit.

Clean Up the Toys—Harold Comby. A year earlier, Terry Ben explained that *bohpoli* might also get the children lost in the woods: "In terms of young children, my grandma always told me never let the young children go to the woods, simply because of these little people up in the woods. They would take them away and get them lost" (May 30, 1996).

Division of Labor—Harold Comby. These gender roles were rarely strictly held. A few minutes later in the interview, Harold describes how his mother taught him to make biscuits in a cast-iron skillet. His sister, Susie Comby Alex, also describes a household where all children pitched in with kitchen work: "It was just my two brothers and me. We all ended up cleaning after they eat and wash the dishes" (June 9, 2021).

Sharecrop and Survive or Go to School—Hayward Bell. In a conversation on June 6, 2023, Hayward noted, "I finished two years of college and still maintained my work in the field." He stressed that it is possible to do both: abide by one's parents to get the work needed at home done and still get an education. He stressed that Choctaw parents recognized the importance of education and wanted their children to get a good education but that they had to balance that value with very real economic pressures to feed their families and keep a roof over their heads. Hayward continued, adding that one of the main problems with the education offered at the time was that for some children, it made them think they were better than their parents, that they didn't need to listen to their parents or their elders, and that they might stop speaking the language and maintaining the traditions and culture. He knows this firsthand. After college, he came home, and his grandfather told him: "'You talk funny, you look funny, you smell funny. You're not Choctaw anymore.' I didn't understand what he was saying until about ten years later. I made a strong turn and got back into the culture."

Sent Away to Boarding School—Jasper Henry. Jasper responds, "That's right," to the interviewer's question if he had to go out of state because Choctaws were not admitted to White schools.

School like the Military—Russell James (R. J.) Willis. The boarding school R. J. went to was the Sequoyah School, also known as Sequoyah-Tahlequah. It was founded in 1871 by the Cherokee National Council, and although it was developed to educate Oklahoma Cherokee students, it accepted students from across the country and continues to do so. Although the Cherokee Nation ran the school for the first few decades after its founding, the tribe sold it to the BIA, who ran the school until they sold it back to the tribe in 1984. Like other Indian boarding schools at the time, tribal languages and customs were banned at the school during the time R. J. attended. Chief of the Cherokee Nation of Oklahoma Chad Smith describes how his father was punished for speaking Cherokee at

Sequoyah High School: "If you spoke the language, your mouth was washed out with soap. It was an effort to destroy the language and it was fairly successful" ("Young Rescuers of Cherokee Tongue" 2003).

Cutting Their Hair—Harold Comby. Men typically did not cut their hair when they were in mourning, but as Harold suggests here, women did. Both acts were signs of sacrifice.

No Other Option—Eddie Gibson. The reason Choctaw students couldn't go to public school where they lived in Mississippi was that schools were not integrated, and Choctaw Central High School wasn't built until 1964. Meridian High School did begin to accept a limited number of Choctaw students by the beginning of the 1960s and desegregated for Black students in 1965. Eddie's brother Calvin was the brother who went to Haskell. His story follows.

A Change in Plans—Calvin Gibson. When Calvin was asked how he felt about his boarding school experience, he says, "I believe it helped me. I believe it did. You learn to rely on yourself," noting that he washed and ironed his clothes and felt greater responsibility at school than at home.

Tribal School—Terry Ben. Terry was speaking directly to the YOP students, connecting his experiences to theirs. He also clarified later that the teachers who hit students for speaking Choctaw were White.

Tattletales—Harold Comby. The incident Harold's mom described took place in school.

Pranking the Teacher—Henry Williams. Henry was prompted to tell this story after one of the custodians in the school in Conehatta came to tell him that someone had flushed a roll of toilet paper in the boys' bathroom and clogged it up. He laughs, saying, "We used to do that kind of thing at Choctaw Central."

School Memories—Frank Bell Joe. Mrs. Carson and Mrs. Dubrowski are pseudonyms. All the stories took place while Frank was attending Choctaw Central.

COURTSHIP

Winning a Bride with Turkeys—Jim Gardner. The story can be heard on the Choctaw Cultural Legacy website (see "Choctaw Wedding Story"): http://choctawculturallegacy.com/audio-resources/. Also, compare to the story Henry Williams tells in *Choctaw Tales* about a young suitor who was similarly poor at hunting and carried the same turkey past the woman's house day after day to suggest a hunting prowess he did not possess (Mould 2004:184). The test of a groom's eligibility for marriage according to his hunting abilities is described by Olman Comby in Swanton 1931:134.

All in the Family—Louise Wilson. The tradition of marrying the wife of a deceased brother or "levirate marriage" can be found throughout the world. It is also mentioned by Swanton as a common practice among the Choctaw, at least in the twentieth century (1931:138).

WEDDINGS

Choctaw Wedding—Hubert Wesley. Hubert clarifies that the person who led the ceremony was a well-respected man in the community. He mentions Archie Mingo as often serving in this role in Bogue Chitto. He did not remember the groom chasing the bride. Compare the custom of the bride's male relatives having to find the groom among all the groom's family to customs of hiding the bride from the groom and the bride running away from the groom, described in other descriptions of the wedding that follow, including Travis Willis's description recorded in the notes for "Family Weddings" by Lorena Alex. The tradition of having the bride live with the groom's family for a few days is also mentioned by Simpson Tubby, though he notes it could happen in reverse as well, depending on which family the couple was going to live with once married (Swanton 1931:136).

Uniting Families—Susie Comby Alex. I asked Susie if she ever saw a case when the groom didn't catch the bride. She replied, "No because they were ready to marry." Susie mentions that the groom's family used the same unwashed plates used by the bride's family, as does Louise Wilson in her story "Wedding Food" later in this collection. Unwashed plates were also reused during the Cry funeral tradition (see, for example, "Communal Event" by Martha Ferguson).

Family Weddings—Lorena Alex. Lorena explained that Granny is her younger sister Pauline's nickname not because she's old, but because she's short. While Lorena was not able to follow all that the preacher said in Choctaw, she was nonetheless able to follow along with the others in the rituals and customs expected of the attendees. Travis Willis, who has presided over at least one Choctaw wedding where the traditional customs described here were combined with Christian traditions, notes that in the wedding he presided over, the groom's family started from about a half a mile away. "They came down the road just hollering and screaming. The groom was in the middle and had two relatives on the side. And when they got to a certain point, the woman's two family members, brothers or cousins, they would go meet them. And if they accepted him, they would take him by the hand, both sides, and then bring him the rest of the way. And when they did that, they have accepted him into the family already. They just had to go through the motions" (June 14, 2021).

Wedding Kinship—DeLaura Saunders. For kinship terms, see Swanton 1931:86–90. The motif of the false bride (or substituted bride) is categorized as ATU K1911 and appears in Europe, Asia, and the Americas.

Wedding Food—Louise Wilson. *Banaha* is a traditional Choctaw dish made with cornmeal and beans or peas, wrapped in a corn husk and cooked, also referred to as shuck bread since it is cooked in corn husks like a tamale. Claiborne also mentions noon as the time for weddings (1964 [1880]:516–17).

MARRIAGE AND PARENTING

Marriage-Night Fright—Bradley Alex. Bradley began this story after talking about his forty-two-and-a-half-year marriage to his high school girlfriend Linda, noting that at first living together was an adjustment.

Grandparenting—Casey Bigpond. Casey ends by returning to the idea of respect, noting that as they youth got older, "they would learn to respect the grandparents more. They would cherish them more because they're the ones that raised them." Today, many grandparents do still help raise their grandchildren, but not to the extent Casey and many others in the community describe from the past.

Wake-Up Call—Bradley Alex. "Aunt Esbie" is Esbie Gibson, who shared a number of stories in *Choctaw Tales* (Mould 2004). *Cannon* was a TV crime drama starring William Conrad.

A Promise of Fruit—Rae Nell Vaughn. Afo means grandfather. An apple or orange was a common and prized gift for Christmas during the first half of the twentieth century (see "Ceremonies, Holidays, and Festivals" section). By the time Rae heard this from her grandfather in the 1970s, Choctaw children would have increasingly expected toys or other store-bought items.

Disciplining Kids—Eddie Gibson. Corporal punishment was common just a few generations ago, as it was in many regions of the country. While it remains in use, shifts away from spanking and whipping create a tension between older and younger generations.

Corporal Punishment—Hayward Bell. In a conversation two years later on June 6, 2023, Hayward asked to clarify his story, adding the final paragraph and noting that he was sober when he disciplined his children. He was particularly frustrated at teachers blaming Choctaw parents for undisciplined children in class when he felt it was the school system that was undermining their discipline by banning corporal punishment.

DEATH, WAKES, AND FUNERALS

Harbingers of Death and Danger—Simpson Tubby. The owl is an ambiguous creature for the Choctaw. For most, its presence is a sign that death is coming to someone near you, but whether it operates as an omen or is connected to witchcraft as an active agent of harm varies in belief. Simpson Tubby clearly believes the latter, where the horned owl is capable of evil deeds. His information was published in Swanton 1931:198–99.

Burn It Out—Eddie Johnson. The literal translation for Nishkin abá chi̱ho michilih is "I'm doing it to kill their eyes," but the meaning is somewhat metaphorical in the same way we say that sunlight is killing your eyes. In 1996, one elder in the community explained that an *ofo̱lo*, or screech owl, can be a bad medicine man. It will sit in a tree outside and call out. If you hear this, you need to twist your middle finger with your other hand as hard as you can. Eventually, if you hear the owl make a different sound, it's because he's being strangled (the twisting finger), and he will fly off and either leave you alone forever or go away until he becomes stronger when he may return for you.

Warning of Death—Harold Comby. Harold Comby explains that the owl as a harbinger of bad news is common among many Native communities in the United States. "From traveling, working on the Coushatta and Chippewa reservations, some of the nature things are similar, like the owl. I think all tribes consider that as a bad omen. And nobody deals with them unless they're a medicine people. In fact, it was even worse up in Chippewa country: there was a real taboo. You don't even look at an owl." In the past, barking foxes were also interpreted as an omen of death, according to French interpreter for the Choctaw Joseph Christophe de Lusser: "At midnight [January 31] I was awakened by three or four gunshots that were fired near me. I asked what was the matter. The chief [of the Yowanis] replied that it was on account of the barking of foxes which was a bad omen; that that usually happened when one of the band was going to die, and that it was well to fire guns in order to drive them away" (quoted in Swanton 1931:217). The belief in owls as harbingers of death is widespread throughout the Mississippi Choctaw community.

Beware Part 1—Staff of the *Nanih Waiya* magazine. This final taboo relates to the many taboos surrounding pregnancy that can be found in the "Pregnancy and Birth" section.

Beware Part 2—Staff of the *Nanih Waiya* magazine. Many of these taboos do not relate to death. They are included here since some do, and they were published together as part of a recurring section in the *Nanih Waiya* magazine. For a more complete list of the taboos and "no you don'ts," see the index.

***Holisso Inchuwa* and Beliefs!**—Staff of the *Nanih Waiya* magazine. This is presented just as it was printed in the *Nanih Waiya* magazine. They translate *holisso inchuwa* (or *i̱chowa* in the current orthography) as "writings." For similar beliefs shared in the stories in this collection, see "Bad Dreams," "Rainmakers" (footnote), and "Pointing at Rainbows."

Owl Omen—Louise Wilson. Louise interrupts herself when she begins to explain what it means for an owl to come to your yard by telling me, "Now you may have heard this before." This speaks to the widespread nature of this belief. Compare to "Burn It Out," which describes how to get rid of an owl.

Squirrel Omen—Harold Comby. Harold adds that his mother told him that the person who dies will be somebody that you know.

Bone Pickers—Frank Henry. Most bone pickers are described as men in the historical record, though one of the earliest records from a French writer referred to as Anonymous Relation de la Louisiane (estimated to have been written around 1755) describes female bone pickers (Swanton 1931:171). Charlie Denson said his grandpa told him, "Before the White man came, they had scaffolds just outside the door. They put it [the deceased] up there to rot out" (December 3, 1973).

Putting to Rest—Hubert and Gara Wesley. Later, Hubert explained that people were often buried with items the person valued in life. For example, they buried some of Cameron Wesley's doctoring tools with him. Dan Isaac notes that the women always covered their faces during the Cry (June 23, 2021). Compare to Swanton's historical survey of the Cry, particularly in terms of the gap in time between burial and the Cry, the taboo against men cutting their hair and against both men and women adorning themselves during the mourning period, as well as the communal feast on the day of the big Cry. The crosses put up to mark the grave appear to serve as a Christian version of the poles that were once erected at the grave and then pulled down at the end of the Cry to signal its end.

Wailing—Eddie Johnson. The custom of women coming to wail during a Cry is a paralleled in some ways by the tradition today of churches sending members of their choir to the gravesite to lead Choctaw hymns, something I witnessed at all three funerals I attended during the summer of 2021. Jay Wesley explains that Phyllis McMillan, coordinator of the Cultural Affairs Program, has helped as well: "Even the singing. Phyllis puts a group together and say, 'Hey, Jay, they need singers and Choctaw hymns.' And maybe they have a group that sings from church, but then they want somebody and like, 'Okay, let's put a group together, and we'll go out there and still do it. Even now'" (July 28, 2022).

Big and Little Cry—Harold Comby. Harold was not sure why the uncle was selected for these special duties. I asked him if they have the Big Cry anymore. He responded, "No. Some elderlies are saying that maybe that's why we are having a hard time with death because we don't mourn like we need to." He added that while the Cry was common when his mother was young, it has faded away since then. Swanton's survey also distinguishes between the Little and Big Cry by name; most simply describe the two in the process of describing the mourning process. For an interview with Cameron Wesley where he describes the Big Cry, see Beckett 1949:26.

Cry Ceremony—Jackson Isaac. The pole-pulling ceremony seems to have been replaced with a log serving as a stand-in for the deceased's body, with its placement and removal marking the beginning and end of the mourning period. This custom is repeated in many other descriptions of the Cry, including Susie Comby Alex (June 9, 2021); Doris Bell (June 25, 2021); Judy Billie (June 3, 2007); and Travis Willis (June 14, 2021). This log should not be confused with logs used as seating.

Wakes in Transition—Travis Willis. The maintenance of a fire during the mourning period exemplifies the dynamic funerary traditions and the competing interpretations for what is old and what is new. Terry Ben remembers growing up in Standing Pine and watching men tend to the fire during the period from death to interment, usually three days. Martha Ferguson also grew up in Standing Pine and learned that the smoke from the fire allows the spirit of the deceased to "travel," visiting the places they saw in life one last time before leaving the earth for good upon burial.

Cleaning and Smoking—Linda Williams. See also Elizabeth Bell Allen describing how the spirit of *iyyikowa* extended to funerals: "After work he would come home. If he's going to chop firewood, he goes and does it. Then he visits the family of the deceased person. Or he goes to the store because he would say, 'People attending the wake all night will want coffee; they will also want things such as cookies.' He says, 'They're going to eat,' so he goes and gets biscuits, then takes it to the wake" (Choctaw Cultural Legacy 2017; "The Generous Spirit of the Choctaw"; Choctaw Tribal Elders Oral History Project; Department of Chahta Immi, http://choctawculturallegacy.com/cultural-features/). Smoking, or smudging the house with smoke, is used throughout Indian country to cleanse a space and has become part of mainstream US culture, with popular retailers selling sage bundles for smudging. Smudging has also expanded within Choctaw culture beyond funerary rites and formal rituals and ceremonies. Linda Williams, for example, describes her daughter smudging her car after working with cadavers as part of her job in a forensics lab (June 15, 2021). Travis Willis is one of many who also mentions how a medicine person or someone trained in medicine would smoke the house and yard after the funeral with cedar, adding, "But nowadays, what they say is when it rains during the wake or thereafter, they say it's to wash away their tracks." The belief was that the smoke or rain would keep the spirit of the deceased from returning (June 14, 2021).

Communal Event—Martha Ferguson. "Bob" is Bob Ferguson, her husband. Eddie Johnson also describes the style of communal feasting, where plates were not washed during the weeks-long Cry but covered and then reused for each meal. Some have suggested this was because the family was supposed to refrain from working during mourning. However, reusing plates was also part of traditional Choctaw weddings, as mentioned by Susie Comby Alex and Louise Wilson earlier in this collection. Although the Cry had mostly died out by the end of the nineteenth century, many describe it still being done in Bogue Chitto well into the twentieth century. The event Martha describes here was fairly unique where a family brought the Cry back in an intentional act of reclamation.

Taking Time to Mourn—Frank Henry. Judy Billie offers a similar description of the process, including the delay in dating again and complete switch from dressing down to dressing up: "Nowadays when there's a funeral, we all dress up. We even have lipstick. We all have earrings and jewelries and all of that. When they were in mourning, you don't wear all of that stuff. You're just as plain as you can be" (June 3, 1997).

Burying the Dead—Terry Ben. John Stephens is the funeral home the tribe has commissioned to handle most tribal members' funerals.

Highlighting the Good Life—Brian Billie. Eddie Gibson also notes that the "wake is another time that people tell stories, especially around the fire. And I've spent some time around the fire, years ago. I don't do that anymore. But I have spent some time during the fire, and they tell stories. Sometimes it's just a funny story; it might not have anything to do with tradition or anything like that. It's just something funny happened to somebody, or to them, and they'd tell. But people enjoyed it" (July 1, 2021).

Burial Ground—Harley Vaughn. Susie Comby Alex's brother, Harold Comby, explained the reason a deceased person's belongings are gathered together upon their death: "What was explained to me is that that gives the deceased his spirit to take what they want into the spirit world." Carmen Denson concurs: it is so "they can come back in spirit and get their belongings" (June 27, 2021). Their belongings then needed to be stored away for a period of time, often six months or a year, to ensure the spirit did not linger or come back for them (a number of stories that follow describe the consequences of not adhering to this custom).

Buried Possessions—Harold Comby. Harold has done extensive reading on Native American history and culture. Frequently, he references connections among the Choctaw and other tribes in his conversations. In an interview on July 23, 1999, Harold was talking about the war bonnet that Cameron Wesley was photographed in (a photo of which can be found in Mould 2004) when he noted: "Cameron Wesley's granddaughter and I were talking, and we were trying to find out where that bonnet was, but they told us that they had placed it in the coffin when he died. He was buried with it. They used to bury their favorite stuff with the deceased so that they would journey on to the next world in a good way or be happy when they got there."

Hubert Wesley, Cameron's son, confirms that his father was buried with some of his personal possessions: "They buried some equipment that he used as a herb doctor. They buried that stuff with him. I know they put it in a bag then they put some of the beadwork he always wore when he dressed up" (December 18, 1992). This custom is also mentioned in Swanton's survey of burial customs (1931:190).

Let the Dead Rest in Peace—Harold Comby. Many believe that the bones of their ancestors were buried in the Nanih Waiya Mound. Here, Harold suggests that they may have been buried in the Cave Mound as well.

Bad Omens—Harold Comby. Harold offers two possible explanations for why these children died—both rooted in Choctaw belief systems—one related to the taboo against afternoon funerals, the other about fighting over children. Travis Willis also noted the taboo against afternoon burials (June 14, 2021). David Bushnell Jr. notes that the time appointed for the death and burial of a convicted murderer was also noon (1909:25).

Unnatural Death—Grady John. Grady says that the type of death impacts whether or not a spirit is likely to remain. Unnatural and accidental deaths could lead to a spirit remaining; natural deaths from illness would not.

Burn It All—Susie Comby Alex. Many in the community explained that this tradition of burning all the wood was aligned with putting all the deceased's things away for a year. You did not want anything left that could attract the deceased to stay or return.

Healing a Haunting—Terry Ben. Terry elaborates on the three-day time span: "You go to church on Sunday, right? Christ died on Friday, and Sunday, supposedly three days later, he awoke, so everything kind of centered around that span, that important span."

Spirit at the Wake—Terry Ben. Terry names the woman whose father died; I have replaced that with "a woman" to ensure her privacy. A number of stories that follow involve the spirit of the deceased lingering before the mourning period is over. For historical descriptions of these spirits or *shilop*, see Wright 1828, cited in Swanton 1931:215–17.

Wait a Year—Linda Williams. Linda clarifies that putting the clothes up near the corner of the head of the casket is what you would do during the wake, but then you put the deceased's items in storage for a year.

Take It Back: The Cane—Susie Comby Alex. As Susie was telling her story, she interrupted briefly to explain, "At that time, when they were sharecroppers, some of them would cook lunch for you all. I was mostly babysitters. There were other Choctaw families that were there too, so I was a babysitter; I kept the little ones." As the story makes clear, cemeteries could be scary places. DeLaura Saunders tells a story of running past the cemetery in Bogue Chitto, afraid that spirits might be lurking nearby (June 29, 2021). Travis Willis tells a story of walking past a cemetery with his brother and hearing voices whispering, though now he thinks it may have been the sound of the river (June 14, 2021).

Take It Back: The Pot and the Ring—Susie Comby Alex. Susie added later that they did go back after six months and got the things they wanted and gave the things they didn't want to others who could use them.

Travel and Returns—Martha Ferguson. Martha's husband, Bob Ferguson, was White, which explains the conversation she has with her mother about where his spirit goes upon death. "Ferg" is short for Ferguson.

Guardian Angel—Susie Comby Alex. Susie's mother had her legs amputated; when Susie sees her spirit, however, she notes that her legs had been restored.

Death without Ceremonies—Rae Nell Vaughn. The family of Rae Nell's father, who was White, conducted a wake and funeral like many White families, with an abbreviated viewing and visitation followed quickly by a funeral. Not being able to adhere to her Choctaw customs and mourn more extensively was very difficult, a feeling she has seen many in her Choctaw community face because of the disruption of COVID-19. Susie Comby Alex is one of many who explain that the tribal government banned wakes for safety reasons, restricting gatherings to brief, masked visitations at the funeral home and then burial (June 9, 2021). Evaline Davis explains that normally, "They're still taking the body to the house, but on account of this virus, now they're not doing it. So we don't have anybody. We haven't been keeping anybody at the house on account of this messed-up thing" (June 3, 2021).

Wakes in the Time of COVID—Jay Wesley. When Jay mentions taking "leave" he's referring to the formal process of getting time off work. See the late Jesse Ben's explanation of *lowak moshólichi* in the "Ceremonies, Holidays, and Festivals" section. The ceremony at Lake Pushmataha was organized by Harold Comby and his family. His daughter, Nikki, posted information about it on Facebook with a flyer that advertised a "Sunrise Ceremony" at Lake Pushmataha on June 5, 6:30 a.m., with the caveat: "Bring your own chair. Covid-19 Safety Guidelines will be followed. Stay home if you are sick." In the post itself, she explained:

> Trying something a lil different beginning this week. Starting this Saturday at sunrise, we would like to offer a time for us to come together, pray and smudge as we begin a new month. Ceremony won't be too long . . . but it's a good time for us to recenter as we begin our life post Covid together. Please be respectful and honor this time. Harold 'Doc' Comby will start us off this Saturday, but all are welcome [hang ten emoji] Hope you can join us [hugging face emoji, peace sign emoji] PS- I will walk afterwards up towards Goat Ranch if anyone would like to join [hugging face emoji].

CHAPTER 5: HEALTH AND HEALING

BECOMING A DOCTOR

Ways of Becoming a Doctor—Terry Ben. The "little people" Terry references are the *bohpoli*. Terry describes the little people approaching youth in their teens to begin their training in medicine, though as others recount, *bohpoli* may first appear to children when they are much younger. Compare to his story "Little Helpers" later in this collection. In the 1970s, Choctaw Central High School students talked to Pete Dyer and published many of the stories he shared in the *Nanih Waiya* magazine. Some of those stories are included in this chapter. See also the interview with him in Marion Ben 1982. As Terry says, Pete did work at the hospital, tending to Choctaw patients with traditional Choctaw medicine.

Lost: A Personal Experience Story—Caroline Morris. Caroline Morris's son-in-law, Harley Vaughn, was also at the table when Caroline first referenced *bohpoli*. He turned to me and translated *bohpoli*: "What you would call leprechaun." I asked Caroline why her mother didn't want her to be a medicine woman, and she responded with the information about the good and bad doctors and how bad doctors could become jealous of your power and come after you. Many people have stories of children being approached by *bohpoli* to be trained as doctors, but families, wary of the responsibility, power, and danger of being a doctor, take the child to a doctor to stop the process (see stories told by Judy Billie [June 3,

1997]; Berdie John [March 14, 1996]; Rae Nell Vaughn [May 31, 1996]; and the story told by Susie Comby Alex in this collection titled "Doc").

Lost: A Mother's Story—Gladys Willis. Gladys Willis's granddaughter, Rae Nell Vaughn, initiated this story by asking, "Can you tell him a little bit about when Momma got lost in the woods when she was little?" Gladys replied, "Not in the woods; in the backyard." Nannie is Nannie Willis, Gladys's sister-in-law.

HEALING AND PROTECTION

Mule and a Rattlesnake—Hubert Wesley. Hubert's wife, Gara, points out that Sydney Wesley's photo is in the Smithsonian. Ken Carleton, one of the interviewers, adds that he was once an informant of both John Swanton and Frances Densmore. His photo and more information about him can be found in Densmore 1943.

Healing His Neighbors—Hubert Wesley. The interviewer asked him where his father learned this, and he replied, "He learned it from his dad."

A Hog for a Cure—Linda Willis. I asked Linda if she knew how to make that tea. She said, "Yes. That's the only thing I learned from him. But my kids won't touch it. [*laughter*] They don't believe in that stuff."

Back from the Dead—Jessica Miller. Jessica added that her grandmother lived a couple of months after this experience.

Process of Healing—Pete Davis Dyer. Pete says he can cure diabetes, high blood pressure, venereal disease, the common cold, headaches, and asthma, but he can only delay cancer.

Bartering for a Cure—Terry Ben. In addition to the stories here, Frank Henry describes the common practice of bartering with livestock or corn (July 23, 1997), as does DeLaura Saunders, mentioning a bag of flour or baked goods (June 29, 2021).

Bloodletting—Eddie Gibson. Eddie mentions the names of the doctors in Tucker when telling his story; since they may still be alive, we have omitted them because, as Eddie mentioned later, people typically don't name living doctors because it can call their attention to you, and that can be dangerous. For other descriptions of how doctors used cow horns for bloodletting, see Dolphus Henry (Weill, Williams, and Ferguson 1985), and Russell James (R. J.) Willis (November 4, 1973).

Herbal Cure—Frank Bell Joe. Frank also mentions that there were trees that were used to make medicine to treat burns and other herbal medicines to treat high blood pressure.

The Better Doctor—Pete Davis Dyer. About a two-and-a-half-hour drive south of Tucker is the town of Fair River. With no access to the original recording, I cannot confirm this, but I believe the wrong word may have been transcribed and that he said, "Pearl River Community."

Removing the Pain—Pete Davis Dyer. The student interviewers ask for examples of people he has helped. He names a series of patients; I have substituted pseudonyms since permission was never granted by those named individuals. "Sugar" or "sugars" is a colloquial expression for diabetes. TB is tuberculosis.

Little Helpers—Terry Ben. Compare to his story "Ways of Becoming a Doctor" earlier in this collection. For other descriptions of *bohpoli* throwing rocks, see Lorena Alex (June 10, 2021) as well as stories *in Choctaw Tales* about *bohpoli* and *kowi anukasha* Making herbal medicine in an old gallon milk jug was common. When I was visiting Rosalee Steve in Tucker in 1996, someone came by needing some herbal medicine; she went back into her kitchen and came out with an herbal remedy the color of tea in a one-gallon plastic jug.

Help—Susie Comby Alex. A number of people in the community have noted that white stones were signs of *bohpoli.*

Children's Doctor—Susie Comby Alex. Susie's brother, Harold Comby, also notes that his mother used to treat children for thrush, noting, "Mom was a doctor: she used to heal children only. She got to be a doctor in one of the ways you were supposed to be—as a child who has never met his or her father. There was another doctor, same way. She used herbs and such to heal" (December 12, 2018). Louise Wilson heard the same from both Choctaw and White people who would tell her, "'Your son has a special gift.' And I said, 'What is it?' you know? I didn't even know this. They said, 'Well, you say your husband died before he was born, and it was your son. They usually have this special gift, that he would have healing powers.' Well, I wasn't aware of that" (January 11, 2000).

Turned Ankle—Carmen Denson. Later that day, during lunch, Carmen told me that love medicine was very popular when he was growing up, but his mother told him not to use it because once it wears off, the person feels nothing for you.

Herbal Steam Cure—Lillie Gibson. Glenda Williamson said to Lillie, "Tell us about Indian doctors," to which Lillie replied, "Why? You need one?" and everyone burst into laughter. A number of people, including Harold Comby, Mark Tubby, Mack Jimmie, and Linda Williams, talked informally about using steam and smoke to help cure people of various ailments. A person would dig a hole, build a little fire in it, sometimes cover the fire partially with sticks or perforated tin, and put a chair or mattress springs over it. The sick person would sit or lie with a blanket over them to trap the steam and smoke under the blanket. "It was like a sweat lodge," Linda explained. "It would help get the bad spirits out" (June 5, 1997). Compare to the "Shared Vision in the Sweat Lodge" story later in this collection.

Jealousy—Harold Comby. For additional stories on witchcraft and remedies for avoiding harm, see the stories at the beginning of the section on death in this collection.

Protective Medicine—Harold Comby. At least some of the spirits Harold is referring to are the spirits of people who used to live in the home. Compare to the stories told in the "Death, Wakes, and Funerals" section about lingering spirits.

HOME REMEDIES

Natural Baths—Louise Wilson. Afterwards, Louise said she has tried to abide by these rules more and that she sees their benefit now that she's getting older.

Cold or Cough—Harold Comby. *Ashíla* is typically made with both cornmeal and chicken.

***Wák bila*—**Rae Nell Vaughn. Berdie John adds that in addition to fever, you could use it for seizures.

Smoke Healing—Rae Nell Vaughn. A typical hole for washers was about four inches across, but these vary. Note that this process parallels the remedy Lillie Gibson describes the medicine man using in her story "Herbal Steam Cure."

Mosquito Handler—Melford Farve. Melford begins by noting that nowadays everyone has their faces in their phones and ends by noting that TV and movies have replaced the storytelling that used to happen at night.

RITUALS, CUSTOMS, AND LAWS

Avoiding Tornados—Brian Billie. By "lost" Brian means they died. By "There are others coming forward to come stand before you all," Brian means "They'll take the place of the elder that passed on." This story is in response to Lakylee Martin's question, "Have you ever heard about how the tribe, all the communities are sacred? That's why the tornados or hurricanes haven't touched down, and it goes over." In the middle of the story, he turned to Lakylee and said, "A̱ atokósh miya ish makachih ma siyimmih, I mean ná ittokalhi kano kiyo aki̱ni. But ik yohmo ta̱kla kano achokmah. [So that meaning, what you say (that the Choctaw are sacred), I believe. I mean It's not all the time. But it's good that it hasn't happened.]

Answered Prayers—Henry Williams. Many people describe prayer as a fundamental part of their lives. Linda Williams, for example, tells a story of her aunt telling her the power of prayer to help her daughter in life. "She gave me the words of wisdom. She said, 'Anything you want this child to be, anything in the future, whatever you want her or would like to see her to be.' She said, 'Always pray to God. Every day, pray to God that you want her to be a nurse, you want her to be a teacher; whatever it is that you want her to be, always pray to God because our Creator is the one that made all of us, the people'" (June 15, 2021).

Shared Vision in the Sweat Lodge—Jake York. There has been some disagreement within the community about whether the sweat lodge is an old Choctaw tradition or a new adoption from other Native peoples. Those skeptical of its authenticity as Choctaw point to the fact that most who use it in Mississippi learned the practice from other tribes and then brought it back with them. However, as Harold Comby has pointed out, historical records from the eighteenth and nineteenth centuries describe sweat lodges among the Choctaw (Bossu 1768 and the "Anonymous French Relation" circa 1755, both cited in Swanton 1931:231;

Cushman 1962[1899]:200). For a sustained discussion of the arguments around sweat lodges, see chapter 6 in Gantt 2013.

Tobacco as Thanks—Dan Isaac. Carmen is Carmen Denson. His father is Charlie Denson, who shared some stories in *Choctaw Prophecy* (Mould 2003) and *Choctaw Tales* (Mould 2004).

Greetings—Jay Wesley. Jay adds, "I'm trying to keep this, and I try to teach my girls." Brian Billie not only introduced himself this way at the beginning of our conversation with him, but he returned to the custom to encourage the YOP students with whom he was speaking to do the same and named not only his community and parents but also his siblings and children (June 30, 2021).

Goodbyes—Brian Billie. The Choctaw phrases that Brian translates himself are included in the text as he spoke them. To avoid redundancy, they have not been translated in brackets.

Returning to Nanih Waiya—Dan Isaac. The Cherokee word for hello is spelled *osiyo* but is pronounced *siyo*. Dan pronounces it correctly. Chahta is the Choctaw spelling and pronunciation for Choctaw. Dan is not the only person who feels compelled to take visiting Native people to the Nanih Waiya Mound. On July 23, 1999, Harold Comby described how he had taken some of the Oklahoma Indians who performed intertribal powwow dancing at the Choctaw Indian Fair out to Nanih Waiya. When they were there, they told Harold that there was strong medicine here. Rae Nell Vaughn then added that she regularly takes Native visitors to the mound as well who say the same thing about the spiritual power of the place.

Ritualized Protection—Harold Comby. Compare to the prophecy Linda Willis shared about hanging a Choctaw shirt or dress outside one's door to be left alone during war (Mould 2004). The stories are similar; one is shared as historical custom, the other, as an unfulfilled prophecy (for more discussion of how prophecy and history can overlap, see Mould 2003).

Choctaw Justice—Carmen Denson. Similar to Carmen's description of Choctaw justice, David Bushnell Jr. recounts a story of a man who killed another man during a drunken fight but asks to be allowed to participate in the dances that were occurring for the next few weeks. When the dances were over, he presented himself to the deceased's family, dug his own grave, and was shot and buried according to custom (1909:25). See also Swanton 1931:104–10 for a compilation of historical documents describing customs related to crime and punishment. With respect to customs of digging graves, Cameron Wesley's granddaughter, Linda Willis, said, "They say back in those days, it was a custom where if a person kills somebody that they dig the grave. If they were found guilty, then they dig their own grave too" (January 7, 2000).

Self-Defense—Carmen Denson. Carmen tells the story again on June 27, 2021, during a group interview.

Murder Trial—Hubert Wesley. The trial was held in Noxubee County in 1940. There are numerous newspaper accounts that offer additional versions of the case, including how the county sheriffs arrested Wesley, details of the court proceedings, and a description of the Choctaw trial. For a summary, see McDavid 2005. The name of the man killed is listed in the newspaper as either Evans Tubbee or Evein Tubbee (the name Tubbee is today more often spelled Tubby). Cameron Wesley's granddaughter, Linda Willis, explains how this murder has continued to shape community relations: "My mom used to tell us that he had killed a man, but in self-defense. Our family just couldn't get along with this family, one particular family. So I questioned my mom: 'Why does this family hate us so much?' So she sat me down, 'Well, I'm going to tell you. Because your grandfather had killed their grandfather. So that's one of the reasons they hate us.' So she went on to detail about how it happened. She said she wasn't even born yet when it happened" (January 7, 2000).

Family Intervention—Bradley Alex. Swanton offers a compilation of eighteenth-century accounts from European writers who describe the punishment for a woman who commits adultery but not a man (1931:110–11).

Infidelity—Louise Wilson. On July 29, 1999, Louise returned to this topic, noting that her grandfather, John Hunter Thompson, who told her this, framed his conversation within a prediction that marriages were going to weaken: "Grandpa was seeing that back then. He said it's not going to be like a strong marriage, even though you didn't have a piece of paper at the courthouse saying that you're Mr. and Mrs. so-and-so. Back then, he said when you were married, you were married. 'Til death do you part. That's what it has in the Bible, I think is what he was talking about." She adds, "Divorce is a dime a dozen. He was more or less saying, that's the way it's going to be. And in my life, now I guess I see it like that, that nobody takes marriage seriously as they did back then." But then after noting the vengeance that the women took on the cheating husband, beating him with everything they had, "even those sticks to make the hominy," Louise concludes laughingly, "I wonder if this has anything to do with women's lib!"

CHAPTER 6: ADVICE FROM THE ELDERS

Be Friends—Pete Davis Dyer. Pete is talking directly to the Choctaw Central High School students who are interviewing him.

Respect Nature—Henderson Williams. Henderson added that this respect extends to all animals, including owls: "They'll tell about the owl, the wise old owl. The stories and instructions are you don't harm the owl because it doesn't hurt you; it won't do anything to you." Compare this advice to stories about owls and bad omens.

Respect Your Elders—Martha Ferguson. Brian Billie tells a story of ensuring that his children watched out for their grandparents:

> When my mom was older, I told my daughters, I said, "It doesn't matter if I'm there or not there," I said, "you never let her fall. My father is going to be proud and say he doesn't want help, but you always watch out for him because when we get older, sometimes we don't mean to, but we'll fall faster and we're slower to catch ourself." And my kids were good enough to be right beside their grandparents and hold him, find a chair. And it didn't matter where we were at. When they showed up, you showed respect to them because they're a center part of your life. (June 30, 2021)

Keep Your Language and Your Culture—Mark Patrick. When I spoke to Mark a year later, he returned to this point: "I've always told people, it's like, if you're bilingual, you're intelligent. You can do things that 80 percent of the world can't do, speak two different languages. That's why I try to encourage people to keep speaking your language and understand it, so you could understand. It's to your advantage" (July 27, 2022).

NOTES

FOREWORD

1. *Na losa chito* translates as "big black thing." It is a supernatural being that Choctaw continue to encounter and tell stories about. Over the past few decades, many tribal members equate the being with Bigfoot (see Mould and Vaughn 2025).

PREFACE

1. His son Hubert Wesley said he and his siblings always figured they got the date wrong on his father's tombstone and that he was actually born about twenty years later than it said (1992).

2. "' . . . our baby won . . . '—An Interview with Choctaw Princess Linda Willis" 1973.

3. For some of these origin stories, including this one, see the "Naming" section in the "Life Cycle" chapter of this book.

4. Writing in 2002, tribal archivist Deborah Boykin notes, "Today, the Mississippi Band of Choctaw Indians is one of the state's largest employers, operating 19 businesses and employing more than 7,800 people, not all of them tribal members" (2002).

5. Only recently, writers have begun using the term "five tribes" rather than "five civilized tribes" since the former is derogatory and patronizing, suggesting that the Choctaw, Creek, Cherokee, Chickasaw, and Seminole only became civilized when they began to adopt Anglo cultural traditions and traits. For many still today, however, reference to five Indigenous tribes will continue to evoke the much more widespread derogatory term.

6. Since my work on *Choctaw Tales*, the tribe has developed a rigorous vetting process for any research conducted on the reservation with tribal members. We presented a research proposal first to the Tribal Council Cultural Committee chaired by Kendall Wallace, then, with their approval, to the full Tribal Council. The proposal passed as Resolution CHO2–026, signed by Chief Cyrus Ben on January 14, 2020. Chief Ben was elected chief on July 9, 2019, and reelected chief on June 6, 2023.

7. Harold says his mom was not a fan of "paleskin people." "She says they always try to trick you. She always says that. In books, it states that *nahollo* means 'sacred object.' When they saw de Soto and them, with armor, riding horses, they gave them that name. But if you talk to some of these people, they'll say that's not true. The proper name is *nán i̲ hollo*, which means to be greedy" (2000). The current dictionary being developed by the tribal language program defines *nán i̲ hollo* as "to be stingy with things," and *nahollo* or *náhollo as* "a White person." In

1931, John Swanton defined the term (spelling it *nahullo*) as "something supernatural or sacred," noting, "Later the term was applied to the white people, probably on account of the lightness of their skins" (199). Byington's dictionary gives a similar provenance, defining the term first as a supernatural being, "one that creates fear and reverence," and then noting, "This name was thus anciently used, but when the whites first visited the Indians this name was given to them."

INTRODUCTION

1. Most of the stories in the book are narratives that situate Choctaw customary life in a single moment in time, bringing to life how these customs and traditions were actually enacted. However, they also include in *Choctaw Tales* generalized experience narratives and used-to stories as well. Generalized experience narratives maintain a narrative structure but describe a regular pattern of behavior. These are particularly powerful as they harness the concrete, dramatic details and structures of narrative that make stories so memorable while avoiding critiques that the described events are not generalizable (see Mould 2020:258–71). Many of the generalized experience narratives can further be classified as "used-to stories," a genre we described but did not include in *Choctaw Tales* that include some narrative structural elements but are typically linear with little or no rising action and climax (see Mould 2004 and Mould and Vaughn 2025). We include such stories here. Finally, people also describe what used to happen with no introduction, complication, rising action, climax, falling action, or coda—in other words, with little or no narrative structure. We have included some of these recollections because they offer important descriptions of customary life in the words of the people themselves.

2. Other than biographical works, Cunningham's book *American Indians' Kitchen-Table Stories* is one of the few books that moves beyond the myths, legends, and folktales of Native peoples to attend to personal experience narratives shared informally among families and friends. However, no one to my knowledge has followed suit.

3. For books on the history of the Mississippi Choctaw, see Carson 2003, DeRosier 1970, Galloway 1995, Kidwell 1997, O'Brien 2005 and 2008, McKee and Schlenker 1980, Osburne 2014, Pesantubbee 2005, and Wells and Tubby 1986.

4. For example, in the 1990s, as the tribe received more and more requests for social-dance performances, dance groups competing for these paid gigs occasionally accused others of not performing a particular dance correctly and pushing for the codification of a single, correct way to dance each dance. Yet culture is dynamic, and Choctaw dance has always evolved to meet the needs and interests of its dancers, and for the most part, such rigid rules for a single, unchanging mode have been ignored. Sticking with the genre of dance for a moment, there are also tribal members frustrated, even angered, by the fairly recent adoption of powwow style dancing by some members of the tribe. There is no doubt that such dancing is intertribal, borrowed from primarily Plains Indian groups, but whether it will ever be incorporated sufficiently to become known as Choctaw, like frybread has for many, is unclear. For additional discussion on the topic, see Gantt 2013, chapter 6.

5. For more on these process of contextualization—when storytellers embedding external contexts within the story—and intertextuality—the connections among other texts, in this case primarily stories that link different versions or similar accounts into dialogue with one another—see Bauman 1986 and 2004.

6. When people are quoted in these introductory essays, we have included dates to orient the reader in time with one exception: when the speaker was recorded in our most recent round of research between 2021 and 2023. Since those are the most numerous, and because their

interviews are easily identified in the sources at the end of the book, we have omitted dates for a more seamless reading experience,

7. For the linguist interested in all aspects of the verbal performance including the verbal pauses, false starts, and feedback cues, the transcripts for all of the interviews we conducted can be found in the Tribal Archives in the Chahta Immi Cultural Center, where audio recordings of most of the interviews are also stored.

8. In anthropological terms, we used a process of grounded theory that began with open coding to identify the main topics and then looked for connections among the topics to suggest categories that, while not mutually exclusive, could nonetheless encompass all the stories told with as little overlap as possible. The biggest challenge we faced was whether to put all the taboos or "no you don'ts" into a single section. We ultimately decided against it since their meaning was most tied to a distinct tradition or moment in life. However, this is not what the student staff at *Nanih Waiya* magazine did in the 1970s when they developed the recurring "Beware" section that included these taboos and warnings. As a compromise, all of the taboos are grouped in the index under "Taboos" and cross-indexed with "No you don'ts."

9. See *Choctaw Tales* for versions of the various creation stories. I discuss the work-relocation programs later in this book.

10. Tribal archaeologist Ken Carleton notes that there were smaller mounds nearby that may have been constructed to house the bones of the dead but that "all clues have been lost to the plow" (1996:33). As for the Nanih Waiya Mound itself, he writes, "The archaeological history of this site is little known, with no substantial professional excavations ever having been conducted there" (32).

11. See Emily Buhrow Rogers's doctoral dissertation "Choctaw Arts and the Meaning of Making" (2020), where she examines traditional material culture, including basket making, clothing, and beadwork, in particular, both as a useful study of these genres and for a bibliography of other works related to Choctaw material culture. For foodways, see Akers 2013:115–28, "Choctaw Cooking" n.d., and "History and Development of Choctaw Foods" n.d.

12. The list of cultural traditions currently identified on the tribal website are basketry, clothing, beadwork, dancing, music, stickball, cooking, language, and Nanih Waiya (https://www.choctaw.org/culture/). In 1997, the mission statement for the Cultural Affairs Committee lists basketry; traditional land use including farming, hunting, fishing, and gathering; the umbrella category of social dance, which includes social, animal, and war dances; and stickball. In 2013, Sean Gantt conducted open-ended brainstorming and free-listing exercises with twenty-seven tribal members to identify what people considered to be part of traditional Choctaw culture. They identified thirty-one categories, each named by at least two people. In order of most common to least, they are: Choctaw language (27), Social Dancing/House Dance (25), Stickball (23), Outdoor Cooking (21), Basket Making (19), Respect/Care for Elders (18), Traditional Clothing (18), Visiting/Sharing/Generosity/*Iyyikowa* (17), Spirituality (Medicine, Supernatural Beliefs, etc.) (17), Beadwork (16), Funerary Customs/Wakes (15), Hunting/Fishing/Gathering (14), Marriage Customs (12), Oral History/Storytelling (8), Sports (8), Songs/Chanting (6), Community Gatherings/Feasting (6), Church/Services in Choctaw/Christian Morals (5), Sweatlodge/Native American Church/Pipes (5), Kinship (Extended Family/Matrilineal) (5), Games (Washers/Chunkey) (5), Community Involvement/Fundraisers (4), Drum Making (4), Quilt Making (4), Rabbitstick Hunting (4), Choctaw Fair (3), Choctaw Names (3), Nanih Waiya as Sacred (2), Blowguns (2), Appearance (Long Hair) (2) (2013:91).

13. Jean Bernard Bossu frames women's play as a means of avenging the stickball loss of their husbands, with play every bit as brutal but with bent sticks (cited by Swanton 1931:139). Henry Halbert provides merely a single sentence of description to note that women only played two sports: stickball and a game resembling battledore (cited by Swanton

1931:149). It is unclear, for example, whether the taboos about women touching men's stick-ball sticks worked in reverse.

14. I wrote down this story while Carter Williams told it. However, it was not recorded, so some of the wording may not be exact.

15. For a discussion of the concept of tradition that recognizes this dual need for continuity and change, see Glassie 2003. For a snapshot of shifts in belief and participation in three traditional Choctaw customs—weddings, funerals, and dance—among Choctaw Central High School students in the 1980s, see Isaac 1984.

16. For example, to kick off the start of stickball practice in preparation for the 2021 World Series of Stickball at the Choctaw Indian Fair, Red Water hosted a community dinner with steak or burgers for the adults and hot dogs for the kids. There were prayers, speeches, a stickball shootout, and powwow-style drumming.

17. For example, the Department of Chahta Immi has recently started a cultural education program for at-risk youth. Similar workshops are available for tribal members who want to learn more about their heritage.

THE STORYTELLERS

1. The majority of the photos were taken by Tom Mould at the time of each interview. The photos of Billy Amos, Frank Henry, Grady John, and Estelline Tubby were taken by Allyson Whyte in 1997. The photos of Gus Comby, John Hunter Thompson, and Gladys Willis were taken by Sue Weill in 1984. The Choctaw Bible Translation Committee gave permission to use the photos of Jesse Ben, Calvin Gibson, and John Mingo Jr. The Department of Chahta Immi gave permission, or secured the permission from family members, to use the photos of Claude Yates Allen, Elizabeth Beth Allen, Cubert Bell, Pete Davis Dyer (taken by *Nanih Waiya* staff), Mary Lou Farmer, Laline Farve, Jim Gardner, Dolphus Henry, Jasper Henry, Melvin Henry, Jackson Isaac, Frank Bell Joe, Barcom King, Richard McMillan (taken by Shanine McMillan), Jessica Miller (taken by Eddie Johnson), Caroline Morris, Barbara Sam, Barney Wesley, Hubert Wesley, Jay Wesley, Russell James (R. J.) Willis, and Baxter York. The Cultural Affairs Committee gave permission to use the photos of Ruth Williams, Billy Chickaway (basketball team photo in the Choctaw Central High School yearbook), Peter Davis Dyer (taken by the *Nanih Waiya* magazine), Carrie Tubby (taken by Austin Tubby), Simpson Tubby (Smithsonian Institute; photographer unknown), Rae Nell Vaughn (professional photo courtesy of Rae Nell Vaughn).

THE LAND

1. For those who did receive land, the Dawes Act (known as the General Allotment Act of 1887) provided yet another easy avenue for non-Native peoples to take land: "Furthermore, allotments were tax-exempt for only 25 years, so many people lost their land in 1912 (and after) when heavy property taxes came due. Altogether, the Allotment Act cost Native Americans a total of 86 million acres of land in 47 years and many reservations were made into checkerboards of Indian/white ownership" (Coulombe 2011:27, citing Janke 1994:159–61). The Choctaw Reservation is often described today as a checkerboard.

2. In the story "Cheated into Debt" in this collection, Barney Wesley mentions White landowners not wanting the Choctaw to come back. He may have been referring to the impact of New Deal subsidies that led many landowners to evict their sharecroppers:

> Although sharecropping lasted until the middle of the twentieth century in Mississippi and elsewhere in the South, the Great Depression of the 1930s and the New Deal agriculture relief programs fundamentally undermined the system. New Deal subsidies to southern cotton planters designed to encourage crop reductions and achieve higher crop prices were seldom passed on to sharecroppers. Instead, landlords simply evicted croppers from the land, and the federal subsidy dollars were used to mechanize cotton picking and planting. In addition, minimum wage laws after World War II further motivated the owners of large-scale plantations to abandon what little sharecropping still existed and even to reduce the use of fixed-wage hands. By 1965, a century after the Civil War, few southern farmers or farmhands worked as sharecroppers or share tenants. (Davis 2017)

3. For a summary of this program, see McKee and Murray 1986:125–26.

4. For more on this period in Choctaw history, see Wells and Tubby 1986, as well as the section "Coming of Age" in this book.

5. One of the most commonly shared jokes describes a hapless old Choctaw man who rides in a car with air conditioning for the first time and immediately asks to be let out so he can race home to slaughter his hog (see Mould 2004 for a few versions).

6. For these prophecies and many others, see Mould 2003.

7. Snakes are so pervasive in the stories we recorded that we considered a separate section on the topic. It never quite fit, however, so a separate article is planned for the future.

8. For a video of the 2020 Annual Youth Rabbitstick Hunt, see https://www.youtube.com/watch?v=q-aaNob2G8U produced by the Department of Chahta Immi as part of the Choctaw Cultural Legacy program. See also their film *Owatta* (Traditional Hunting) for more information about hunting more generally.

RECREATION

1. Stickball does appear to be the oldest organized team field sport in North America, even if all other field sports cannot be traced back to it as the ancestry that "granddaddy" implies.

2. While one could argue that the drum represents the history of warfare—it is a military-style drum after all—it more obviously evokes stickball games where the drum is beat throughout the game, today by multiple drummers on each side.

3. Chief Phillip Martin offered an explanation of the tribal flag, which includes the tribal seal in its center, "with the drum considered to be the voice of the people and the hickory stickball sticks representing the strong will of the people to survive and prosper" (July 12, 1994, posted on the tribal website: choctaw.org; accessed on Wikimedia Commons May 25, 2023). Baxter York also explained the important role of the drum, particularly in keeping pace with the game (Blanchard 1981:35). See also Frances Densmore's description of the drum in its use by medicine men during stickball games (Densmore 1943:117).

4. All of these descriptions can be found in Swanton 1931:140–53.

5. All of the historical records surveyed by John Swanton describe two sticks being used, except the description by Jean Bernard Bossu, an outlier so out of keeping with the rest of the record that Swanton declares it a reporting error (1931:140–41). For a thorough study of the sport, including its history and importance within the tribe, see Blanchard 1981.

6. Bradley Alex shared this on June 30, 2021. Anthropologist Kendall Blanchard suggests that stickball once served an important training ground for young men, as the skills needed in the game transferred over to war. In this way, stickball served as a kind of rite of passage. That

function becomes even more explicit in the period that Bradley Alex describes. As Blanchard describes: "Despite the exclusion from the games of their fathers and older brothers, Choctaw boys would devise stickball games of their own, improvising equipment and using a front yard for a playing field. By the time they were old enough to compete with the men, they had become fairly proficient at catching and throwing the small ball with their rackets. In some ways, the first real match in which a Choctaw adolescent participated symbolized his movement into manhood. If a boy could play stickball, he was no longer a boy; he was a man" (1981:72).

7. Tul-lock-chísh-ko or "Drinks the Juice of the Stone" is immortalized in the oft-replicated 1834 portrait by George Catlin.

8. See Blanchard 1981:43–55 for a discussion of baseball, softball, and the picnic as it evolved between 1918 and 1963. See Gantt 2013:112–14 for a discussion of current community identity formation as well as historical community boundaries.

9. The State Games of Mississippi began in 1992 with twelve hundred athletes competing in twelve sports. This year, forty-one sports will again attract amateur athletes from across the state for top competition.

10. John Swanton offers a summary of the historical descriptions of the game, noting both the variation in play—in one version, a player aimed for the stone, while the other player aimed for his opponent's pole; in a second version, both players aimed to land their poles closest to the chunkey stone when it stopped rolling—and its virtual demise by the turn of the nineteenth century (1931:155–58; Blanchard 1981:26). Billy Chickaway describes playing chunkey or "chunkgee" at the Choctaw fair as a form of cultural demonstration until 1980, when the lack of interest led to its discontinuance (Tubby 1984:47–48). For a description of handball, see Swanton 151–54.

11. Requiring little equipment other than a set of large washers, the game was played anytime people found time for leisure, including weekends, after a day of hunting, and more organized celebrations (see Travis Willis June 14, 2021). Writing in the 1980s, Bill Brescia offers a description of the basics: "Several washers from hardware store (2–3" in diameter and decorated with magic marker to show Choctaw designs) A 8" hole in the ground (or a large, heavy can)" (1982). Most people today remember the holes being much smaller, around four inches in diameter, the size typically used today. For an additional description, see Blanchard 1981:56–57.

12. Claude Yates Allen describes playing cowboys and Indians in a story in this collection, noting that he always chose to play a cowboy because the Indians he saw on television were always portrayed as the bad guys. His experience mirrors that of many children of color in the United States who, when offered a choice of playing with a White or Black doll, consistently chose the White doll. The "Doll Test," as it became known, contributed directly to the landmark Brown v. Board of Education case that outlawed racial segregation in schools.

COMMUNITY EVENTS

1. TANF is Temporary Assistance for Needy Families, what many refer to as "welfare," which provides financial assistance to families. SNAP is the Supplemental Nutrition Assistance Program, what many refer to as "food stamps," which provides funds to buy food. Both are federal means-tested programs.

2. Such reciprocal obligation is at the center of rigorous definitions of "community" (see for example Glassie 1982:148–49, 483–86 and Glassie 2006:24–31).

3. *Shokhannǫpa* is the Choctaw language term for both animal stories and humorous stories (see Mould and Vaughn 2025). The term translates literally as "hog talk" or "hog tales," mirroring its double meaning: stories about animals, and "hogwash."

4. Both Amanda Bell and Jay Wesley describe the role of churches in continuing the practice of *iyyikowa*.

5. Writings from the end of the eighteenth century suggest that many of the Choctaw festivals and celebrations occurred when the corn was green and ripe near harvest time. However, Reverend Alfred Wright spoke to Choctaws in the 1820s who told him, "They have heard of what is termed the green corn dance among the Creeks but deny having any knowledge that such a practice ever existed among themselves" (1828:180), though it is possible that Choctaw were wary of admitting to participating in what might be deemed a heathen custom to the Reverend. A hundred years later, Simpson Tubby describes "green corn dances" that were still being held in Mississippi (see Swanton 1931:225–26 for a record of these writings). In 2006, Choctaw elder Richard Thompson narrated a short video about contemporary efforts to maintain the Green Corn Ceremony: "The Mississippi Band of Choctaw hosts the Green Corn Festival in a different community each year. The festival this year is organized by Lola Jackson from Bogue Chitto Childcare. . . . The festival binds us together spiritually and culturally as a tribal people. We are like one when we come together like this. We remember what is important to us as a community. To me a Choctaw is a way of life, a way of being in a relationship to Creator. We come to the fire to purify ourselves, forgive, and signify a new beginning" ("Teach Your Children" 2017).

6. For a brief history of the fair, see Gantt 2013:153–58.

7. The concept of dual signification was developed by art historian Ruth Phillips in her work on Native North American souvenir art (1998).

8. For descriptions of Choctaw dancing, see Akers 2013:131–34; "Choctaw Dancing" 1976; Howard and Levine 1990; and Swanton 1931:221–24.

9. While outside organizations often seek out the tribe to participate in their festival or parade, Jay Wesley also has to be proactive and seek out opportunities, as he did with the Mississippi State Fair, whose organizers had completely overlooked the tribe for any of its cultural programming and performances.

10. For a video on the topic, see "Choctaw Christmas Traditions," produced by the Department of Chahta Immi and posted online on the Choctaw Cultural Legacy website.

11. The Choctaw term for dressing up as ghosts or monsters and performing the humorous "play" is *shilop washówa* or "playing as spirits." In most descriptions, the *shilop* were played by men, though women also participated (see Martha Ferguson's story "Travel and Return"). Rae Nell and Harley Vaughn describe the year they both participated as *shilop* or "goblins," each cross-dressing alongside a "dirty Santa" who made lewd comments and gestures throughout (July 13, 2021). Compare this to other forms of rural mumming that could be found throughout the Southeast, versions of which were known as "riding fantastic" or "serenading" (see Burrison 2003). Christmas mumming has a deep tradition in Ireland, Scotland, England, and other parts of Western Europe as well (see for example Glassie 1975). Eddie Johnson also noted parallels between this tradition and Cherokee booger masks and booger dances.

12. While Columbus Day has been replaced by Indigenous Peoples' Day in many states, Mississippi is not one of them. As an official Choctaw tribal holiday, Nanih Waiya Day replaced Columbus Day as an observed holiday on the tribal calendar (*Choctaw Community News* July–Aug. 2022:5).

13. For example, Joann Williams, better known as "Big Mama"—a well-known figure in Pearl River who often sells popcorn balls and "plates"—a dinner plate of either traditional foods such as hominy and fry bread or fast foods such as burgers and hot dogs—lost the use of her kitchen just before the 2021 Choctaw Indian Fair due to an electrical fire, a devasting blow at a time when she would normally have raised a lot of money through food sales. To help, family and friends put out collection jars at their food stands to help raise money for her, an act that fits within the legacy of *iyyikowa*.

14. For more extensive surveys and analyses of Choctaw music and dance, see Densmore 1943 (survey of the first decades of the twentieth century) and Howard and Levine 1990 (survey of the mid to late twentieth century). See also Smith 1976.

15. Buffalo nickels, also called "Indian Head nickels," were minted in the United States from 1913 to 1938, so called because they had a Native American bust on the front and a bison on the back.

16. For example, in the summer of 2021, the YOP students participating in this oral history project were invited to dance at the Mississippi Economic Council's Seventy-First Annual Meeting in Jackson, Mississippi. Jay Wesley as the director of Chahta Immi and Phyllis McMillan as the coordinator of the Cultural Affairs Program regularly get requests by non-Indian groups to perform, most often to dance but also to tell stories. For more information on contemporary music and dance, including powwow dancing, see Goertzen 2015.

17. In 2023, the event was advertised on Facebook as an "opportunity to immerse yourself in the joy of traditional dances but also a chance to stay active." Many of those in attendance remarked on the workout they got from participating, as well as being reminded of just how much fun social dancing is.

LIFE CYCLE

1. Choctaw myths vary on whether creation occurred at the Nanih Waiya Mound or the Nanih Waiya Cave Mound about a mile away. Terry Ben is describing the cave mound. Often, people simply refer to "Nanih Waiya." Both are held as sacred. For other versions of the myth, see Mould 2004.

2. We have included relatively few stories about nicknames because many are embarrassing or too personal.

3. Henry Halbert's manuscript can be found in the Tribal Archives, "Choctaw Mississippi" (manuscript page 46). See also the interview with Estelline Tubby, July 22, 1999.

4. Chief Phillip Martin recalls, "In those days—the late 1940s and early 1950s—the eighth grade was about as far as one could get in any of the elementary schools operated by the BIA on the reservation. There was no high school, and most of the grade schools in the outlying Choctaw communities went only as far as the sixth grade." He goes on to describe how his wife, Bonnie, was sent by her parents to Chilocco Indian School to complete the ninth through twelfth grades (Martin 2009:77). By the early 1960s, however, there was one additional option: Meridian High School. Ray Thomas explained:

> I'm from one of the parts of the Reservation called Conehatta, I was raised and went to elementary school in Conehatta through eighth grade. From there I came to Pearl River School. It wasn't high school then. It went up to tenth grade and when we finished the tenth grade, we had a choice of going to either boarding school in Lawrence, Kansas or in Oklahoma or some of us had an opportunity to go to Meridian High School, public school. And I was fortunate enough to be one of the students from the tribe, when we completed tenth grade, to attend Meridian High School where I graduated in 1963. (Hickmon 2017:62–63)

Meridian High School would not be integrated for Black students until 1965, when five Black women enrolled and graduated.

5. See for example Davis 2001; Reyhner 2018; Trafzer, Keller, and Sisquoc 2016.

6. Choctaw Central High School also served as a boarding school, primarily for students who lived in one of the outlying Choctaw communities too far away to commute each day. Many lived in the dormitories on the high school's campus during the week and went home on weekends. A few stayed throughout the school year. The dorms continue to be used today.

7. Dan Isaac evokes Pratt and his legacy when describing the trauma his parents and grandparents went through just to get an education: "We didn't go through it. But our moms' moms did, or Mom did maybe, or Grandma did. And what it is, is whenever you spoke your language, you were hit. You were beat. If you didn't conform to what they think you should be, what they call 'Kill the Indian, save the man,' that was big. And only because we knew who we were, we didn't want to conform. We know we were okay the way we are. But they were trying to make us think we're not okay unless we do it their way."

8. These statistics were reported in the *Choctaw Community News* under the headline "Choctaw Language to Be Lost by 2005" (December 1999:5). Happily, this prediction has not come to fruition, with the language continuing to be spoken among adults, and some children, today.

9. Olman Comby told John Swanton that dances were the primary context for courting, while Simpson Tubby explained that families would occasionally host "a courtship dance" with the express purpose of providing the youth an opportunity to engage in social dancing in order to find a potential spouse (Swanton 1931:134, 136).

10. In 2016, for example, Dylan Dixon and Danielle Kolie married according to traditional wedding customs in Pearl River.

11. All of these key elements of traditional Choctaw weddings remembered and practiced in the twentieth century are described in historical documents, albeit with additions and variations: (1) the drumming march of the groom (Bushnell 1909, Halbert 1882, Simpson Tubby, cited by Swanton 1931); (2) bride race (Bushnell 1909, Claiborne 1964 [1880], Comby, cited by Swanton 1931, Cushman 1962 [1899], Halbert 1882, Simpson Tubby, cited by Swanton 1931); (3) speech by male leaders (Bushnell 1909, Comby, cited by Swanton 1931, Simpson Tubby, cited by Swanton 1931); (4) placing gifts on the couples' heads (Claiborne 1964 [1880], Comby, cited by Swanton 1931, Cushman 1962 [1899], Halbert 1882, Simpson Tubby, cited by Swanton 1931); (5) gendered food preparation and order of eating (Bushnell 1909, Comby, cited by Swanton 1931, Cushman 1962 [1899], Halbert 1882, Simpson Tubby, cited by Swanton 1931); and (6) social dancing (Bushnell 1909, Halbert 1882). For additional sources describing traditional Choctaw weddings, see Isaac 1984 and Thompson 1975.

12. For example, about Choctaw men, Bernard Romans writes, "They help their wives in the labour of the fields and many other works" (1962 [1775]:86).

13. *Hattak fullih nipi foni* translates literally as "man who scrapes flesh from the bone." The phrase was given by Cushman (1962 [1899]:225). In the modern Choctaw orthography, the phrase would be written as *hattak fohlih nipi foni*. Henry Halbert uses the term *na foni afowa*, which he points out would translate literally as "bone gatherers" (1900). For additional sources describing traditional Choctaw funerary practices, see Isaac 1984.

14. See Swanton 1931:170–94 for a survey of primary documents that offer provide descriptions of this practice.

15. This brief summary is informed by the stories that follow but derived most directly from Henry Halbert's "Funeral Customs of the Mississippi Choctaw" (1900) and John R. Swanton's *Source Material for the Social and Ceremonial Life of the Choctaw Indians* (1931), both of which survey the historical record for a longitudinal study of funerary customs.

16. See Ketcher 1985 for interviews with a number of tribal members who talk about witchcraft and owls.

HEALTH AND HEALING

1. The answer was 1928 when the BIA recognized how poor the care the Choctaw received at the city hospital was, if they could get care there at all.

2. For a summary of historical descriptions of Choctaw medicine, see Swanton 1931:226–41. For a description from the 1970s and '80s that includes a discussion of medicine, doctors, the supernatural, and witchcraft, see Blanchard 1981:144–66.

3. See Mould 2003:148–55 and interview with Frank Henry July 23, 1997.

4. This book strives to seek a balance between protection and preservation, erring on the side of conservatism and not including information if there is too great a risk in doing so but including information that elders felt was important to pass on to their children, knowledge they wanted to retain and share, even with a non-Choctaw audience.

5. The descriptions of the extent of such practices are hard to believe, however. Le Clerc Milfort writes that when the patient could no longer afford treatment, the doctor encouraged a patient's family to strangle their relative to death, convincing them that death was inevitable and that this was the humane option (Swanton 1931:213–14).

6. For more information on the training process, see the description by Emil John (Mould 2004:131–32).

7. For additional stories of medicine used in sports beyond the stories in this collection, see Blanchard 1981:155–63 and Mould 2004.

8. Anthropologist and folklorist James George Frazer developed the term *sympathetic magic* to describe common forms of ritual practice not proven by science, distinguishing two types of magic: imitative magic, which pairs like with like; and contagious magic, where the properties of an object can be transferred through contact, or things once in contact retain their ability to impact each other. Whipping a person with an eel to become stronger has elements of both.

9. For video interviews with members of the tribal court system explaining the peacemaker system, see "Mississippi Band of Choctaw Indians: Peacemaking Court" and Vaughn 2009). For older Choctaw customs of justice that are primarily restorative, consider the story Bradley Alex tells of how a man who beat his wife was initially shunned and then reincorporated into the family structure ("Family Intervention"), as compared to the story that Louise Wilson tells about more permanent shunning done to women that is primarily retributive ("Intervention"; both stories are in this collection).

INTERVIEWS

Alex, Bradley. 2021. Interview with Makaylin Alex and Tom Mould, with Taylor Ben, June 30.

Alex, Bradley, Liasha Alex, and Makaylin Alex. 2023. Interview with Tom Mould, June 6.

Alex, Lorena. 2021. Interview with Tom Mould, Taylor Ben, Lakylee Martin, and Jaeden Wesley, June 10.

Alex, Susie Comby. 2016. "Meet Our Elders: Susie Comby Alex." Choctaw Tribal Elders Oral History Project. Department of Chahta Immi. http://choctawculturallegacy.com/meet-our-elders/.

Alex, Susie Comby. 2021. Interview with Tom Mould, Taylor Ben, Thomas Saunders, and Jaeden Wesley, June 9.

Allen, Claude Yates. 1973. Interview with Samuel Proctor, December 2.

Allen, Elizabeth Bell. 2016. "Meet Our Elders: Elizabeth Allen." Choctaw Tribal Elders Oral History Project. Department of Chahta Immi. http://choctawculturallegacy.com/meet-our-elders/.

Allen, Sallie [with Judy Billie and Regina Shoemake]. 1997. Interview with Tom Mould and Curtis "Buck" Willis, June 3.

Allen, Sallie [with Regina Shoemake]. 2000. Interview with Tom Mould, January 10.

Amos, Billy. 1997. Interview with Tom Mould and Liasha Alex, June 19.

Bell, Amanda. 2021. Interview with Tom Mould, Makaylin Alex, Taylor Ben, Lexi Flint, and Lakylee Martin, July 1.

Bell, Cubert. 2016. "Meet Our Elders: Cubert Bell." Choctaw Tribal Elders Oral History Project. Department of Chahta Immi. http://choctawculturallegacy.com/meet-our-elders/.

Bell, Doris. 2021. Interview with Tom Mould and Lexi Flint, June 25.

Bell, Hayward. 2021. Interview with Tom Mould, Taylor Ben, and Lakylee Martin, June 30.

Ben, Jesse. 2009. Interviewed by Sean Gantt, April 8.

Ben, Terry. 1996. Interview with Tom Mould and Rae Nell Vaughn, May 30.

Ben, Terry. 1996. Interview with Tom Mould, June 3.

Ben, Terry. 2021. Interview with Tom Mould, June 4.

Ben, Terry. 2021. Interview with Tom Mould, Taylor Ben, Lakylee Martin, Thomas Saunders, and Meka Willis, June 10.

Bigpond, Casey. 2021. Interview with Tom Mould and Thomas Saunders, June 24.

Bigpond, Casey. 2021. Interview with Tom Mould and Thomas Saunders, June 28.

Bigpond, Casey. 2023. Interview with Tom Mould, June 1.

Billie, Brian. 2021. Interview with Lakylee Martin, Tom Mould, Makaylin Alex, Taylor Ben, Lexi Flint, and Jaeden Wesley, June 30.

Billie, Judy [with Sallie Allen and Regina Shoemake]. 1997. Interview with Tom Mould and Curtis "Buck" Willis, June 3.

Billie, Nellie. 2016. "Meet Our Elders: Nellie Billie." Choctaw Tribal Elders Oral History Project. Department of Chahta Immi. http://choctawculturallegacy.com/meet-our-elders/.

Bowden, Mahlih Vaughn. 2021. Interview with Tom Mould, July 14.

Charlie, Beamon. 1975. Interview with *Nanih Waiya* staff members Jimmy Ben, Daniel Tubby, Roger Wishark, Jerry Hikman, and magazine advisor Charles Plaisance, January 23.

Chickaway, Billy. 2016. "Meet Our Elders: Billy Chickaway." Choctaw Tribal Elders Oral History Project. Department of Chahta Immi. http://choctawculturallegacy.com/meet-our-elders/.

Chickaway, Billy. 2017. "The Games We Played." Choctaw Tribal Elders Oral History Project. Department of Chahta Immi. http://choctawculturallegacy.com/cultural-features/.

Choctaw Cultural Legacy. 2017. "Choctaw Indian Fair." Choctaw Tribal Elders Oral History Project. Department of Chahta Immi. http://choctawculturallegacy.com/cultural-features/.

Choctaw Cultural Legacy. 2017. "The Games We Played." Choctaw Tribal Elders Oral History Project. Department of Chahta Immi. http://choctawculturallegacy.com/cultural-features/.

Choctaw Cultural Legacy. 2017. "Owatta (Traditional Hunting)." Choctaw Tribal Elders Oral History Project. Department of Chahta Immi. http://choctawculturallegacy.com/cultural-features/.

Clemmons, Nancy. N.d. Oral History Interview with Samuel Proctor, Samuel Proctor Oral History Program Collection, P. K. Yonge Library of Florida History, University of Florida.

Comby, Harold. 1996. Interviewed by Melford Farve and Eddie Johnson, December 9.

Comby, Harold. 1997. Interview with Tom Mould and Liasha Alex, June 4.

Comby, Harold. 1999. Interview with Tom Mould, July 23.

Comby, Harold. 2000. Interview with Tom Mould, January 10.

Comby, Harold. 2016. "Meet Our Elders: Harold Comby." Choctaw Tribal Elders Oral History Project. Department of Chahta Immi. http://choctawculturallegacy.com/meet-our-elders/.

Comby, Harold. 2017. "The Games We Played." Choctaw Tribal Elders Oral History Project. Department of Chahta Immi. http://choctawculturallegacy.com/cultural-features/.

Comby, Harold. 2017. "The Generous Spirit of the Choctaw." Choctaw Tribal Elders Oral History Project. Department of Chahta Immi. http://choctawculturallegacy.com/cultural-features/.

Comby, Harold. 2018. Interview with Tom Mould, December 12.

Comby, Harold. 2021. Interview with Tom Mould, Lexi Flint, Jaeden Willis, Taylor Ben, and Eddie Johnson, June 1.

Comby, Harold. 2022. Interview with Josh Foreman, February 24. https://www.youtube.com/watch?v=FvX8NmVeF_E.

Cotton, Donald. 2021. Interview along with Carmen Denson, Dan Isaac, and Williamson Isaac with Tom Mould, June 27.

Davis, Evaline. 2021. Interview with Tom Mould, Makaylin Alex, Taylor Ben, and Lexi Flint, June 3.

Denson, Carmen [with Charlie Denson]. 1996. Interview with Tom Mould, May 25.

Denson, Carmen [with Charlie Denson]. 2000. Interview with Tom Mould, January 12.

Denson, Carmen [with Charlie Denson]. 2021. Interview along with Donald Cotton, Dan Isaac, and Williamson Isaac with Tom Mould, June 27.

Denson, Charlie [with Carmen Denson]. 1996. Interview with Tom Mould, May 25.

Denson, Charlie [with Carmen Denson]. 1973. Interview with Sam Proctor, December 3.

Denson, Theron "Duke." 2021. Interview with Tom Mould, June 15.

Denson, Theron "Duke." 2021. Interview with Tom Mould, June 17.

Dyer, Pete Davis. 1975. Interview with John Lee Chickaway and Baron Gardner, November 4.

Dyer, Pete Davis. 1976. Interview with John Lee Chickaway and Baron Gardner, June 23.

Farmer, Mary Lou. 1973. Oral History Interview with Samuel Proctor, December 3, Samuel Proctor Oral History Program Collection, P. K. Yonge Library of Florida History, University of Florida.

Farve, Laline. 2017. "Owatta (Traditional Hunting)." Choctaw Tribal Elders Oral History Project. Department of Chahta Immi. http://choctawculturallegacy.com/cultural-features/.

Farve, Laline. 2017. "The Generous Spirit of the Choctaw." Choctaw Tribal Elders Oral History Project. Department of Chahta Immi. http://choctawculturallegacy.com/cultural-features/.

Farve, Laline. 2017. "The Games We Played." Choctaw Tribal Elders Oral History Project. Department of Chahta Immi. http://choctawculturallegacy.com/cultural-features/.

Farve, Melford. 1997. Interview with Tom Mould, July 10.

Farve, Melford. 2018. Interview with Tom Mould, December 14.

Farve, Melford. 2021. Interview with Tom Mould, Makaylin Alex, and Thomas Saunders, June 1.

Ferguson, Martha. 2021. Interview with Tom Mould, Makaylin Alex, Taylor Ben, Lexi Flint, and Thomas Saunders, June 4.

Ferguson, Martha. 2021. Interview with Tom Mould and Jaeden Wesley, June 14.

Ferguson, Martha. 2022. Interview with Tom Mould, July 28.

Gardner, Jim. n.d. "Choctaw Wedding Story." Choctaw Cultural Legacy, 2017. Choctaw Tribal Elders Oral History Project. Department of Chahta Immi. https://choctawculturallegacy.com/audio-resources/.

Gibson, Calvin. 1973. Interview with John K. Mahon, December 4. Samuel Proctor Oral History Program Collection, P. K. Yonge Library of Florida History, University of Florida

Gibson, Eddie. 2021. Interview with Jaeden Wesley and Tom Mould, with Taylor Ben, Lexi Flint, Lakylee Martin, July 1.

Gibson, Esbie. 1982. Interview with Bill Brescia and Marian Isaac, February.

Gibson, Lillie. 1997. Interview with Tom Mould, Glenda Williamson, and Meriva Williamson, August 5.

Henry [Saunders], DeLaura. 1974. Oral History Interview with Patricia Martin and Linda Willis, January 31, Samuel Proctor Oral History Program Collection, P. K. Yonge Library of Florida History, University of Florida.

Henry, Dolphus. 1985. Interviewed by Susan Weill, Susan, Julia Williams, and Bob Ferguson. *Stories from the Red Clay Hills: Various Stories by Choctaw Elders*. Choctaw Video Production.

Henry, Frank. 1974. Interview with the staff of *Nanih Waiya* magazine, April 8.

Henry, Frank. 1997. Interview with Tom Mould, July 23.

Henry, Jasper. 1973. Interview with John K. Mahon, December 3.

Henry, Melvin. 1982. Interview with Bill Brescia, Marian Isaac, and Caroilyn Reeves, February.

Isaac, Dan. 2021. Interview with Tom Mould, Makaylin Alex, Taylor Ben, Lexi Flint, and Lakylee Martin, June 23.

Isaac, Dan [with Donald Cotton, Carmen Denson, and Williamson Isaac]. 2021. Interview with Tom Mould, June 27.

Isaac, Jackson. 1982. Interview with Bill Brescia and Carolyn Reeves, February.

Isaac, Jackson. n.d. "Choctaw Cry Ceremony." Choctaw Cultural Legacy, 2017. Choctaw Tribal Elders Oral History Project. Department of Chahta Immi.https://choctawculturallegacy.com/audio-resources/.

Isaac, Judie Lene. 2017. "Life of a Choctaw Sharecropper." Choctaw Tribal Elders Oral History Project. Department of Chahta Immi. http://choctawculturallegacy.com/cultural-features/.

Isaac, Williamson. 2016. "Meet Our Elders: Isaac Williamson." Choctaw Tribal Elders Oral History Project. Department of Chahta Immi. http://choctawculturallegacy.com/meet-our-elders/.

Isaac, Williamson [with Carmen Denson, Donald Cotton, and Dan Isaac]. 2021. Interview with Tom Mould, June 27.

Jimmie, Leonard. 2021. Interview with Tom Mould. July 11.

Jimmie, Leonard. 2022. Interview with Tom Mould, March 17.

Joe, Bobby. 1999. Interview with Tom Mould, July 30.

Joe, Bobby. 2000. Interview with Tom Mould, January 6.

Joe, Frank Bell. 1975. Oral History Interview with Lonus D. Hucks, April 16, Samuel Proctor Oral History Program Collection, P. K. Yonge Library of Florida History, University of Florida.

John, Berdie [with Rae Nell Vaughn]. 1996. Interview with Tom Mould, March 14.

John, Grady. 1998. Interview with Tom Mould, February 22.

John, Grady. 1999. Interview with Tom Mould, July 17.

John, Grady. 2000. Interview with Tom Mould, January 15.

Johnson, Eddie. 2021. Interview with Tom Mould, June 11.

Johnson, Eddie. 2021. Interview with Tom Mould, June 14.

King, Barcom. 1973. Interview with board of editors of *Nanih Waiya* magazine, June 21.

McMillan, Richard. 2011. Interview with Sean Gantt. *Stickball: Grandfather of all Sports, Little Brother of War*. Documentary film, Sean Gantt Productions. https://www.youtube.com/watch?v=WhMeilfgKZk.

McMillan, Sarah Jane Sampson. 1973. Oral History Interview with Samuel Proctor, December 2. Samuel Proctor Oral History Program Collection, P. K. Yonge Library of Florida History, University of Florida.

Miller, Jessica. 2024. Interview with Tom Mould and Eddie Johnson, April 11.

Mingo, John, Jr. 2016. "Meet Our Elders: John Mingo Jr." Choctaw Tribal Elders Oral History Project. Department of Chahta Immi. http://choctawculturallegacy.com/meet-our-elders/.

Morris, Caroline [with Greg Morris and Harley Vaughn]. 1996. Interview with Tom Mould, May 31.

Nickey, Dora. 2016. "Meet Our Elders: Dora Nickey." Choctaw Tribal Elders Oral History Project. Department of Chahta Immi. http://choctawculturallegacy.com/meet-our-elders/.

Nickey, Dora. 2018. "Choctaw Christmas Traditions." Choctaw Tribal Elders Oral History Project. Department of Chahta Immi. http://choctawculturallegacy.com/cultural-features/.

Patrick, Mark. 2021. Interview with Tom Mould, July 7.

Patrick, Mark. 2021. Interview with Tom Mould, Makaylin Alex, Taylor Ben, Lakylee Martin, Thomas Saunders, and Meka Willis, July 12.

Patrick, Mark. 2022. Interview with Tom Mould, July 27.

Sam, Barbara [with Ruth Williams]. 2017. "Standing Pine Residents Discuss Language and Culture." Interview by Lane Denson. Choctaw Cultural Legacy. Choctaw Tribal Elders Oral History Project. Department of Chahta Immi. https://choctawculturallegacy.com/cultural-features/.

Sam, Gordon. 2021. Interview with Tom Mould, Taylor Ben, Lexi Flint, and Lakylee Martin, July 6.

Saunders, DeLaura (Henry). 1974. Interviewed by Staff of *Nanin Waiya*, January 31.

Saunders, DeLaura. 2021. Interview with Tom Mould, Thomas Saunders, Makaylin Alex, Taylor Ben, Lakylee Martin, and Jaeden Wesley, June 29.

Smith, Melba Jean (Bell). 2016. "Meet Our Elders: Melba Jean (Bell) Smith." Choctaw Tribal Elders Oral History Project. Department of Chahta Immi. http://choctawculturallegacy.com/meet-our-elders/.

Smith, Roger Richardson. 2017. "Owatta (Traditional Hunting)." Choctaw Tribal Elders Oral History Project. Department of Chahta Immi. http://choctawculturallegacy.com/cultural-features/.

Solomon, Lela. 1982. Interview with Bill Brescia, Marian Isaac, and Carolyn Reeves, February.

Steve, Rosalee. 1998. Interview with Tom Mould, February 21.

Thompson, John Hunter. 1979. Oral History Interview, with Benjie Dixon and Nancy Vaughn, April 29. Samuel Proctor Oral History Program Collection, P. K. Yonge Library of Florida History, University of Florida.

Thompson, Peggy. 2016. "Meet Our Elders: Peggy Thompson." Choctaw Tribal Elders Oral History Project. Department of Chahta Immi. http://choctawculturallegacy.com/meet-our-elders/.

Thompson, Richard. 2016. "Meet Our Elders: Richard Thompson." Choctaw Tribal Elders Oral History Project. Department of Chahta Immi. http://choctawculturallegacy.com/meet-our-elders/.
Tubby, Carrie. 1973. Interview with *Nanih Waiya* magazine staff members, November 1.
Tubby, Doyle. 1996. Interview with Tom Mould and Rae Nell Vaughn, May 30.
Tubby, Doyle. 1997. Interview with Tom Mould, July 2.
Tubby, Estelline. 1976. Interview with Vernon Tubby. Published in *Nanih Waiya*, 4(1):114–18.
Tubby, Estelline. 1996. Interview with Tom Mould, May 31.
Tubby, Estelline. 1997. Interview with Tom Mould, August 5.
Tubby, Estelline. 1999. Interview with Tom Mould, July 19.
Tubby, Estelline. 1999. Interview with Tom Mould, July 22.
Vaughn, Harley [with Caroline Moris and Greg Morris]. 1996. Interview with Tom Mould, May 31.
Vaughn, Harley [with Rae Nell Vaughn]. 2021. Interview with Tom Mould, July 13.
Vaughn, Hillary. 2023. Interview with Tom Mould, June 7.
Vaughn, Rae Nell [with Berdie John]. 1996. Interview with Tom Mould, March 14.
Vaughn, Rae Nell [with Caroline Morris and Harley Vaughn]. 1996. Interview with Tom Mould, May 31.
Vaughn, Rae Nell. 2000. Interview with Tom Mould, January 7.
Vaughn, Rae Nell. 2000. Interview with Tom Mould, January 14.
Vaughn, Rae Nell. 2020. Interview with Tom Mould and members of Anthropology 338: Native American Cultures, April 22.
Vaughn, Rae Nell [with Harley Vaughn]. 2021. Interview with Tom Mould, July 13.
Wallace, Will. 2016. "Meet Our Elders: Will Wallace." Choctaw Tribal Elders Oral History Project. Department of Chahta Immi. http://choctawculturallegacy.com/meet-our-elders/.
Wesley, Barney [with Lena Wesley]. 1982. Interview with Bill Brescia and Marian Isaac, February.
Wesley, Hubert [with Gara Wesley]. 1992. Interview with Jack D. Elliott Jr. and Ken Carleton, December 18.
Wesley, Hubert. 1993. Interview with Jack D. Elliott Jr., May 22.
Wesley, Hubert. 1999. Oral History Interview, December 14. Center for Oral History and Cultural Heritage of the University of Southern Mississippi. Audio available online: http://choctawculturallegacy.com/audio-resources/.
Wesley, Jay. 2022. Interview with Tom Mould. July 27.
Wesley, Jay. 2022. Interview with Tom Mould, July 28.
Williams, Carter. 1997. Interview with Tom Mould. Not recorded.
Williams, Henderson. 1997. Interview with Tom Mould with Robert Ben and Rae Nell Vaughn, July 25.
Williams, Henry. 1997. Interview with Tom Mould and Lionel "J. J." Dan, June 24.
Williams, Henry. 2011. Interview with Sean Gantt. *Stickball: Grandfather of all Sports, Little Brother of War*. Documentary film, Sean Gantt Productions. https://www.youtube.com/watch?v=WhMeilfgKZk.
Williams, Linda. 1997. Interview with Tom Mould and Danielle Dan, June 5. Not recorded.
Williams, Linda. 2021. Interview with Tom Mould, June 15.
Williams, Ruth [with Barbara Sam]. 2017. "Standing Pine Residents Discuss Language and Culture." Interview by Lane Denson. Choctaw Cultural Legacy. Choctaw Tribal Elders Oral History Project. Department of Chahta Immi. https://choctawculturallegacy.com/cultural-features/
Willis, Gladys. 1996. Interview with Tom Mould and Rae Nell Vaughn, May 23.
Willis, Gladys. 1997. Interview with Tom Mould, May 19.
Willis, Gladys. 1997. Interview with Tom Mould, August 6.

Willis, Linda. 2000. Interview with Tom Mould, January 7.
Willis, Russell James (R. J.). 1973. Oral History Interview with Samuel Proctor, November 4, Samuel Proctor Oral History Program Collection, P. K. Yonge Library of Florida History, University of Florida.
Willis, Russell James (R. J.). 2016. "Meet Our Elders: R. J. Willis." Choctaw Tribal Elders Oral History Project. Department of Chahta Immi. http://choctawculturallegacy.com/meet-our-elders/.
Willis, Travis. 2021. Interview with Tom Mould, June 14.
[Wilson] Willis, Louise. 1973. Oral History Interview with Dr. John K. Mahon, December 4, Samuel Proctor Oral History Program Collection, P. K. Yonge Library of Florida History, University of Florida.
Wilson, Louise. 1997. Interview with Tom Mould and Danielle Dan, June 10.
Wilson, Louise. 1999. Interview with Tom Mould, July 29.
York, Baxter. 1974. Interview with the *Nanih Waiya* magazine staff, April 8.
York, Baxter. 1974. Interview with the *Nanih Waiya* magazine staff, June 21.
York, Jake. 1997. Interview with Tom Mould, July 29.

SOURCES CITED

Akers, Donna. 2013. *Culture and Customs of the Choctaw Indians.* Santa Barbara, CA: ABC-CLIO.

Alex, Bradley, and Annie Williams. 1973. "Choctaw Social Dance." *Nanih Waiya* 1 (1): 30–33.

Alex, Bradley, and Austin Tubby. 1974. "Making Hominy." *Nanih Waiya*, Summer: 19–24.

Bauman, Richard. 1986. *Story, Performance, and Event: Contextual Studies of Oral Narrative.* Cambridge: Cambridge University Press.

Bauman, Richard. 2004. *A World of Others' Words: Cross-Cultural Perspectives on Intertextuality.* Malden, MA: Blackwell. http://www.loc.gov/catdir/toc/ecip0413/2004001155.html.

Beckett, Charlie Mitchell. 1949. "Choctaw Indians in Mississippi Since 1830." MA Thesis Oklahoma Agricultural and Mechanical College.

Ben, Marion. 1982. "Choctaw Health and Medicine." In *A Choctaw Anthology II*, edited by Jane Anderson and Nina C. Zachery, pp. 75–83. Philadelphia, MS: Choctaw Heritage Press.

"Beware." 1974. *Nanih Waiya*, Winter 1 (2): 16

"Beware." 1974. *Nanih Waiya*, Spring 1 (3): 50

"Beware." 1975. *Nanih Waiya* 2 (1–2): 54.

Billie, Harold, Austin Tubby, and Annie Williams. 1974. "' . . . how I used to do': Austin Interviews Carrie Tubby." *Nanih Waiya* 1 (4): 2–4.

Blanchard, Kendall. 1981. *The Mississippi Choctaws at Play: The Serious Side of Leisure.* Urbana: University of Illinois Press.

"Blowgun." 1974. *Nanih Waiya* 1 (2): 24–27.

Bounds, Thelma V. 1961. *Meet Our Choctaw Friends: An Indian Tribe of Mississippi.* New York: Exposition.

Bounds, Thelma V. 1964. *Children of Nanih Waiya*. San Antonio: Naylor.

Boykin, Deborah. 2002. "Choctaw Indians in the 21st Century." *Mississippi History Now.* Accessed July 10, 2023. https://www.mshistorynow.mdah.ms.gov/issue/choctaw-indians-in-the-21st-century.

Brescia, Bill, ed. 1982. *Tribal Government: A New Era.* Philadelphia, MS: Choctaw Heritage Press.

Brescia, Bill, and Carolyn Reeves. 1982. *By the Work of Our Hands: Choctaw Material Culture.* Philadelphia, MS: Choctaw Heritage Press.

"Brother Mal." 1979. *Nanih Waiya*, Spring–Summer 6 (3–4): 52–61.

Bushnell, David I., Jr. 1909. *The Choctaw of Bayou Lacomb, St. Tammany Parish, Louisiana.* Bulletin 48, Bureau of American Ethnology. Washington, DC: Smithsonian Institution.

Byington, Cyrus. 1915. *A Dictionary of the Choctaw Language*, ed. John R. Swanton and Henry S. Halbert. Bulletin 46, Bureau of American Ethnology. Washington, DC: Smithsonian Institution.

Carleton, Ken. 1996 "Nanih Waiya: Mother Mound of the Choctaw." *Common Ground: Archaeology and Ethnography in the Public Interest* 1 (1): 32–34.

Carson, James Taylor. 2003. *Searching for the Bright Path: The Mississippi Choctaws from Prehistory to Removal.* Lincoln: University of Nebraska Press.

Catlin, George. 1834. "Tul-lock-chísh-ko, Drinks the Juice of the Stone, in Ball-player's Dress." Smithsonian American Art Museum. Accessed May 26, 2023. https://americanart.si.edu/artwork/tul-lock-chish-ko-drinks-juice-stone-ball-players-dress-4035.

"Choctaw Cooking." n.d. *Mississippi Band of Choctaw Indians.* Accessed March 25, 2025. https://www.choctaw.org/culture/.

"Choctaw Indian Children Sing, Dance, in Washington DC." 1973. Press release from the Office of Indian Affairs, May 4. Accessed June 15, 2023. https://www.bia.gov/as-ia/opa/online-press-release/choctaw-indian-children-sing-dance-washington-dc.

"Choctaw Indian Fair." 2017. Video produced by the Department of Chahta Immi. Accessed July 7, 2023. choctawculturallegacy.com/cultural-features/.

"Choctaw Indian Fair Program." 1964. Mississippi Band of Choctaw Indians. Accessed July 19, 2023. http://choctawculturallegacy.com/1964-choctaw-indian-fair-program/.

"Choctaw Living Legends: Henry Williams." 2012. Choctaw Indian Fair Program. Mississippi Band of Choctaw Indians, pp. 28–31. Accessed July 19, 2023. http://choctawculturallegacy.com/henry_williams/.

Claiborne, J. F. H. 1964 [1880]. *Mississippi, as a Province, Territory, and State; with Biographical Notices of Eminent Citizens. Vol. 1.* [Baton Rouge]: Reprinted by Louisiana State University Press.

"Choctaw Chanter." 2019. Choctaw Tribal Elders Oral History Project. Department of Chahta Immi. http://choctawculturallegacy.com/cultural-features/.

"Choctaw Dances." 1976. *Nanih Waiya*, 3 (4): 125–32.

"Choctaw Traditional Remedies." 1974. *Nanih Waiya* 1 (2): 14.

Coulombe, Joseph L. 2011. *Reading Native American Literature.* New York: Routledge.

Cruikshank, Julie. 1991. *Life Lived like a Story: Life Stories of Three Yukon Native Elders.* Lincoln: University of Nebraska Press.

Culin, Stewart. 1907. Games of the North American Indians. *Twenty-Fourth Annual Report of the Bureau of American Ethnology.* Washington, DC: Smithsonian Institute.

Cushman, Horatio B. 1962 [1899]. *History of the Choctaw, Chickasaw, and Natchez Indians.* Oklahoma: Redlands Press of Stillwater.

Davis, Julie. 2001. "American Indian Boarding School Experiences: Recent Studies from Native Perspectives." *OAH Magazine of History* 15 (2): 20–22.

Davis, Ronald L. F. 2017. "Sharecropping." In *Mississippi Encyclopedia*, Center for Study of Southern Culture, edited by Ted Ownby and Charles Reagan Wilson. Accessed July 6, 2023. http://mississippiencyclopedia.org/entries/sharecropping/.

Densmore, Frances. 1943. *Choctaw Music.* Bulletin 136, Bureau of American Ethnology. Washington DC: Government Printing Office.

DeRosier, Arthur H. 1970. *The Removal of the Choctaw Indians.* Knoxville: University of Tennessee Press.

Foreman, Josh, 2022. "Harold 'Doc' Comby." Storystate. Mississippi State University. https://www.youtube.com/watch?v=FvX8NmVeF_E.

Galloway, Patricia. 1994. "'So Many Little Republics': British Negotiations with the Choctaw Confederacy, 1765." *Ethnohistory* 41 (4): 513–37.

Galloway, Patricia. 1995. *Choctaw Genesis: 1500–1700.* Lincoln: University of Nebraska Press.

"The Games We Played." 2017. Choctaw Tribal Elders Oral History Project. Department of Chahta Immi. http://choctawculturallegacy.com/cultural-features/.

Gantt, Sean. 2011. *Stickball: Grandfather of All Sports, Little Brother of War.* Documentary film, Sean Gantt Productions. https://www.youtube.com/watch?v=WhMeilfgKZk.

"The Generous Spirit of the Choctaw." 2017. Choctaw Tribal Elders Oral History Project. Department of Chahta Immi. http://choctawculturallegacy.com/cultural-features/.

Glassie, Henry. 1975. *All Silver and No Brass: An Irish Christmas Mumming*. Bloomington: Indiana University Press.

Glassie, Henry. 1982. *Passing the Time in Ballymenone: Culture and History of an Ulster Community*. Bloomington: Indiana University Press.

Glassie, Henry. 2003. "Tradition." In *Eight Words for the Study of Expressive Culture*, edited by Burt Feintuch, pp. 176–97. Chicago: University of Illinois Press.

Glassie, Henry. 2006. *The Stars of Ballymenone*. Bloomington: Indiana University Press.

Goertzen, Chris. 2015. "The Mississippi Choctaw Fair and Veteran's Day Powwow: Music, Dance, and Layers of Identity." In *This Thing Called Music: Essays in Honor of Bruno Nettl*, edited by Victoria Lindsay Levine and Philip V. Bohlman, pp. 28–40. Lanham, MD: Roman & Littlefield.

Goertzen, Chris. 2019. "Archaic Fiddling among the Mississippi Choctaw: R. J. Willis and the House Dance." In *Ón gCos go Cluas: From Dancing to Listening*, edited by Liz Doherty and Fintan Vallely, pp. 92–103. Aberdeen: Aberdeen University Press.

Halbert, Henry Sale. 1896. "The Indians in Mississippi and Their Schools." *Biennial Report of the State Superintendent of Public Education to the Legislature of Mississippi for the Scholastic Years 1893–1894 and 1894–1895*, pp. 534–45. Jacksonville, FL: Lance Printing Company.

Halbert, Henry Sale. 1898. "Creek War Incidents." *Transactions of the Alabama Historical Society*, 2: 107–19.

Halbert, Henry Sale. 1899. "Nanih Waiya, the Sacred Mound of the Choctaws." *Publications of the Mississippi Historical Society*, 2: 223–34.

Halbert, Henry Sale. 1900. "Funeral Customs of the Mississippi Choctaw." *Publications of the Mississippi Historical Society*, 3: 353–66.

Halbert, Henry Sale. n.d. Domestic Government. Unpublished manuscript housed in the Choctaw Tribal Archives.

Hickmon, Frederick L. 2017. "The Creation of Choctaw Central High School and Its Transition to a Bureau of Indian Affairs Contract School: An Oral History." Oxford: University of Mississippi.

"History and Development of Choctaw Foods." n.d. *Chahta Anumpa Aiikhvna: School of Choctaw Language*. Accessed July 19, 2023. https://www.choctawnation.com/biskinik/iti-fabvssa/history-and-development-of-choctaw-foods/.

"*Hollisso Inchuwa* and Beliefs." 1975. *Nanih Waiya*, Summer 2 (4): 47–50.

Howard, James H., and Victoria Lindsay Levine. 1990. *Choctaw Music and Dance*. Norman: University of Oklahoma Press.

Isaac, Cira. 1984. "Choctaw Ceremonies." In *A Choctaw Anthology II*, edited by Jane Anderson and Nina C. Zachary, pp. 17–42. Philadelphia, MS: Choctaw Heritage Press.

Janke, Ronald A. 1994. "Population, Reservations, and Federal Indian Policy." *Dictionary of Native American Literature*, edited by Andrew Wiget, pp. 155–73. New York: Routledge.

Ketcher, Roy. 1985. "Choctaw Perceptions: Legends and Superstitions." In *A Choctaw Anthology III*, edited by Jane Anderson and Nina C. Zachary, pp. 96–112. Philadelphia, MS: Choctaw Heritage Press.

Kidwell, Clara Sue. 1997. *Choctaws and Missionaries in Mississippi, 1818–1918*. Norman: University of Oklahoma Press.

Lanman, Charles. 1870. "Pushamatahaw." *Appletons' Journal: A Magazine of General Literature* 4 (71): 166–68.

"Life of a Choctaw Sharecropper." 2017. Choctaw Tribal Elders Oral History Project. Department of Chahta Immi. http://choctawculturallegacy.com/cultural-features/.

Lincecum, Gideon. 2004. *Pushmataha: A Choctaw Leader and His People*. Tuscaloosa: University of Alabama Press.

Martin, Phillip, with Lynne Jeter and Kendall Blanchard. 2009. *Chief: The Autobiography of Chief Phillip Martin, Longtime Tribal Leader, Mississippi Band of Choctaw Indians*. Brandon, MS: Quail Ridge.

McKee, Jesse O. 1989. *The Choctaw*. New York: Chelsea House.

McKee, Jesse O., and Steve Murray. 1986. "Economic Progress and Development in the Mississippi Band of Choctaw Indians Since 1945." In *After Removal: The Choctaw in Mississippi*, edited by Samuel J. Wells and Roseanna Tubby, pp. 122–36. Jackson: University Press of Mississippi.

McKee, Jesse O., and Jon A. Schlenker. 1980. *The Choctaws: Cultural Evolution of a Native American Tribe*. Jackson: University Press of Mississippi.

"Mississippi Band of Choctaw Indians: Peacemaking Court." 2017. *National American Indian Court Judges Association*. Accessed June 28, 2023. https://www.naicja.org/2020/04/14/mississippi-band-of-choctaw-indians-peacemaking-court/.

Mitchell, Jerry, James Finn, and Samuel Boudreau. 2020. "More Choctaws Have Died of COVID Than Those Who Died of the Disease in Hawaii. Or Alaska. Or Wyoming." *Mississippi Center for Investigative Reporting*. September 9. Accessed on January 11, 2023. https://pulitzercenter.org/stories/more-choctaws-have-died-covid-those-who-died-disease-hawaii-or-alaska-or-wyoming.

Mould, Tom. 2003. *Choctaw Prophecy: A Legacy of the Future*. Contemporary American Indian Studies. Tuscaloosa: University of Alabama Press.

Mould, Tom. 2004. *Choctaw Tales: Stories from the Firekeepers*. Jackson: University Press of Mississippi.

Mould, Tom. 2011. "A Backdoor into Performance." In *The Individual in Tradition*, edited by Ray Cashman, Tom Mould, and Pravina Shukla, pp. 126–43. Bloomington: Indiana University Press.

Mould, Tom. 2020. *Overthrowing the Queen: Telling Stories of Welfare in America*. Bloomington: Indiana University Press.

O'Brien, Greg. 2005. *Choctaws in a Revolutionary Age, 1750–1830*. Lincoln: University of Nebraska Press.

O'Brien, Greg. 2008. *Pre-Removal Choctaw History: Exploring New Paths*, vol. 255. Norman: University of Oklahoma Press.

Osburn, Katherine M. B. 2014. *Choctaw Resurgence in Mississippi: Race, Class, and Nation Building in the Jim Crow South, 1830–1977*. Lincoln: University of Nebraska Press.

"' . . . our baby won . . . '—An Interview with Choctaw Princess Linda Willis." 1973. *Nanih Waiya*, Fall 1 (1): 4–9.

Pesantubbee, Michelene E. 2005. *Choctaw Women in a Chaotic World: The Clash of Cultures in the Colonial Southeast*. Albuquerque: University of New Mexico Press.

Peterson, John Holbrook, Jr. 1971. *The Mississippi Band of Choctaw Indians: Their Recent History and Current Social Relations*. Ph.D. dissertation. University of Georgia.

Phillips, Ruth Bliss. 1998. *Trading Identities: The Souvenir in Native North American Art from the Northeast, 1700–1900*. Seattle: University of Washington Press.

Reyhner, Jon. 2018. "American Indian Boarding Schools: What Went Wrong? What Is Going Right?" *Journal of American Indian Education* 57 (1): 58–78.

Rogers, Emily Buhrow. 2020. *Choctaw Arts and the Meaning of Making*. PhD dissertation. Indiana University, Bloomington.

Romans, Bernard. 1962 [1775]. *A Concise Natural History of East and West Florida*. Vol. 1. Gainsville: University of Florida Press.

Sam, Sandra. "Making Bows with Tom Ben." *Nanih Waiya*, Summer 3 (4): 148–50.

"Sharecropping in Mississippi." 2023. American Experience. Accessed July 6, 2023. https://www.pbs.org/wgbh/americanexperience/features/emmett-sharecropping-mississippi/.

"Shilop Washówa: Choctaw Christmas Traditions." 2018. Choctaw Tribal Elders Oral History Project. Department of Chahta Immi. http://choctawculturallegacy.com/cultural-features/.

Smith, Nann. 1976. "Three Categories of Choctaw Dance." *Nanih Waiya* 3 (4): 125–33.

Swanton, John R. 1931. *Source Material for the Social and Ceremonial Life of the Choctaw Indians.* Bulletin 103, Bureau of American Ethnology. Washington, DC: Smithsonian Institution.

Teach Your Children. 2017. Blue Magnolia Films. Accessed August 8, 2023. https://vimeo.com/240854222..

Thompson, Peggy. 1975. "Choctaw Wedding." *Nanih Waiya* 2 (1–2): 19–26.

"Traditional Choctaw Hymns." 2017. Choctaw Tribal Elders Oral History Project. Department of Chahta Immi. http://choctawculturallegacy.com/cultural-features/.

Trafzer, Clifford E., Jean A. Keller, and Lorene Sisquoc, eds. 2016. *Boarding School Blues: Revisiting American Indian Educational Experiences.* Lincoln: University of Nebraska Press.

Tubby, Sonny. 1984. "Choctaw Games and Competition." In *A Choctaw Anthology II*, edited by Jean Anderson and Nina C. Zachery, pp. 43–58. Philadelphia, MS: Choctaw Heritage Press.

Vaughn, Rae Nell. 2009. "Rae Nell Vaughn: Tribal Court Systems in the 21st Century: The Choctaw Tribal Court System." Indigenous Peoples' Law and Policy Program. Accessed June 28, 2023. https://nnigovernance.arizona.edu/rae-nell-vaughn-tribal-court-systems-21st-century-choctaw-tribal-court-system.

Vickers, Ovid. 1985. "The 'Medicine Man' Still Plays an Important Role in Indian Tribes." *Union Appeal*, Wednesday, December 18, p. 3.

Wallace, John G. 1977. ". . . A Dollar a Day" [interview with Annie Tubby]. *Nanih Waiya* 4 (3): 19–24.

Weill, Susan, Julia Williams, and Bob Ferguson. 1985. *Stories from the Red Clay Hills: Various Stories by Choctaw Elders.* Choctaw video production.

Wells, Samuel J., and Roseanna Tubby. 1986. *After Removal: The Choctaw in Mississippi.* Jackson: University Press of Mississippi.

Williamson, Betty, ed. 2001. "Drums of the Toli . . . Excerpts from a *Times Picayune* Article Dated November 16, 1958." Mississippi Band of Choctaw Indians, 39–40. Accessed July 19, 2023. http://choctawculturallegacy.com/drums-of-the-toli-2/.

Willis, Hulon, Bradley Alex, Jimmy Ben, Rick Billy, and Johnny Osceola. 1975. "Baxter York Again." *Nanih Waiya* 2 (1–2): 11–18.

Wright, Alfred. 1828. "Choctaws: Religious Opinions, Traditions, &c." *Missionary Herald* 24: 178–216.

York, Kennith H. 2012. *Choctaw Nationalism: Choctaw Culture, Language and History.* Parker, CO: Outskirts Press.

"Young Rescuers of Cherokee Tongue." 2003. *New York Times*, September 21. https://www.nytimes.com/2003/09/21/national/young-rescuers-of-cherokee-tongue.html.

INDEX

ABOUT THE AUTHORS

Photo courtesy of the author

Tom Mould is professor of anthropology and folklore at Butler University. He is author of *Choctaw Prophecy: A Legacy of the Future*; *Choctaw Tales: Stories from the Firekeepers*; *Still, the Small Voice: Narrative, Personal Revelation, and the Mormon Folk Tradition*; and *Overthrowing the Queen: Telling Stories of Welfare in America*, which won the Brian McConnell Book Award and the Chicago Folklore Prize.

Photo courtesy of the author

Eddie Johnson is a tribal member of the Mississippi Band of Choctaw Indians, has served as the Special Projects/Media Program coordinator in the Department of Chahta Immi, and is now the tribal archivist.

Photo courtesy of the author

Jay Wesley is a member of the Mississippi Band of Choctaw Indians, and he is director for the Department of Chahta Immi, which consists of the Choctaw Tribal Language Program, the Cultural Affairs Program, the Special Projects/Media Program, and the Chahta Immi Cultural Center.

www.ingramcontent.com/pod-product-compliance
Lightning Source LLC
Chambersburg PA
CBHW081937280825
31554CB00004B/7

* 9 7 8 1 4 9 6 8 5 7 2 0 0 *